Reading for Results

Reading for Results

Second Edition

Laraine E. Flemming
Pittsburgh Informal Studies Program

Dr. Sara C. Mansbach, Consultant
Greenville Technical College
South Carolina

Houghton Mifflin Company   Boston
Dallas   Geneva, Illinois   Hopewell, New Jersey
Palo Alto   London

Cover art: Ellsworth Kelly. Yellow-blue, 1963. Des Moines Art Center, Coffin Fine Arts Trust Fund, 1971.

Design and Production: Phil Carver & Friends, Inc.

Photograph Credits: Library of Congress, pages 274, 360, 433; Museum of Fine Arts, Boston, page 36; National Library of Medicine, page 208; Stock, Boston, page 195 (Ira Kirschenbaum); The Bettmann Archive, pages 107, 367; The Picture Cube, page 87 (Judith Sedwick), page 134 (Frank Siteman), page 157 (Frank Siteman), page 169 (Bobby Carry); United Nations, page 251; United Press International Photo, pages 66, 82, 99, 228, 290, 419; Yerkes Observatory, p. 239.

Copyright ©1983 by Houghton Mifflin Company.

All Rights Reserved. No part of this work may be reproduced or transmitted in any form or by any means, electronic or mechanical, including photocopying and recording, or by any information storage or retrieval system, except as may be expressly permitted by the 1976 Copyright Act or in writing by the Publisher. Requests for permission should be addressed in writing to Permissions, Houghton Mifflin Company, One Beacon Street, Boston, Massachusetts 02108.

Printed in the U.S.A.

Library of Congress Catalog Number: 82-83172

ISBN: 0-395-32605-2

Contents

	To the Teacher	**vii**
Chapter 1	**Building Your Vocabulary**	**1**
	Word Analysis and Context Clues	1
	Using the Dictionary	25
	The Story Behind the Word	32
	The Vocabulary in Your Textbooks	41
Chapter 2	**Defining the Terms General and Specific**	**57**
	General and Specific Words	57
	Levels of Specificity	60
	The Use of Modifiers	68
	General and Specific Sentences	73
	The Relationship Between General and Specific Sentences	79
Chapter 3	**Finding the Topic and Main Idea**	**97**
	Finding the Topic	97
	From Topic to Main Idea	106
	The Unstated Main Idea	124
	The Disappearance of the Main Idea	139
Chapter 4	**Understanding How Sentences Provide Support**	**151**
	Supporting Sentences Convince	151
	Supporting Sentences Illustrate	156
	Supporting Sentences Suggest the Main Idea	160
	Supporting Sentences Describe	166
	Major and Minor Supporting Sentences	171
Chapter 5	**Learning More About Sentence Functions**	**197**
	Sentences Can Make Transitions	197
	Sentences Provide Introductions	206
	Sentences Provide Emphasis	212
	Sentences Provide a Conclusion	216
	Taking Notes	221

Chapter 6	**Identifying Types of Paragraphs**	**245**
	Sequence of Dates and Events	245
	Sequence of Steps	255
	Lists of Characteristics	262
	Comparisons	268
	Causes and Effects	279
	Classifications	291
	Mixed Paragraphs	300
Chapter 7	**Reading an Essay**	**325**
	Sample Essay	325
	Introductory Paragraph	327
	Topic Paragraph	328
	Supporting Paragraphs	329
	Concluding Paragraph	332
	Analyzing an Essay	333
	Taking Notes on an Essay	334
Chapter 8	**Reading a Textbook**	**371**
	Surveying	371
	Reading	382
	Writing	386
	Taking Notes	390
	Reviewing	395
Chapter 9	**Critical Reading**	**413**
	Facts and Opinions	414
	Faulty Arguments or Fallacies	420
	Connotations of Words	425
	Tone and Mood	429
	Appendix	**443**
	Borrowed Words and Phrases	443
	Words That Confuse	447
	Recognizing the Unfamiliar Word	462
	Speech Sounds and Letters of the Alphabet	463
	Vowel and Consonant Sounds	464
	Words into Syllables	486
	Sounding the Vowels	492
	Index	**499**

To the Teacher

Because of an enthusiastic response from both teachers and students, much of the instruction in the second edition of *Reading for Results* remains the same. Written for college students who can read simple prose but who find their textbooks a source of frustration and confusion, the book presents reading skills in small, logical steps that move at a controlled pace from simple to more complex concepts. Each chapter builds upon the previous ones, and sufficient exercises are provided for both mastery and review.

Once again, nothing is assumed about the student's previous knowledge: all terms—from *general* and *specific* to *subjective* and *objective*—are defined and fully explained. As in the first edition, we include not only a number of textbook selections but also numerous paragraph-length passages that draw upon student interests and experiences. The many reading selections, chosen deliberately to appeal to and stimulate student readers, deal with such varied topics as the threat of killer bees, the popularity of video games, and the fascination of horror movies. We have replaced the dated reading paragraphs with more timely topics but have retained the contemporary flavor and variety of the first edition.

At the request of many reading instructors, we have not altered the basic format of the text: explanations, written in prose that students can understand, are followed by a series of exercises. We have, however, added extensive, free-standing review tests at the end of every chapter. These tests allow for a quick and efficient measurement of student comprehension.

To increase its usefulness, Chapter 8 has been revised and expanded to deal more comprehensively with the special conventions of textbook organization. Students are encouraged to see the similarities and differences between the organization of a typical prose essay and the organization of a textbook chapter, so that they can then adapt their reading to the material at hand.

Chapter 9, "Critical Reading," is completely new. It refers to skills already learned, but is also provides a basic introduction to the key terms and skills necessary for critical reading. From this chapter, students learn to sort *fact* from *opinion* and to distinguish between *mood* and *tone*. Moreover, there is a brief section devoted to three of the most important and most common logical fallacies, *direct attack on the person, appeal to the emotions,* and *hasty generalizations.* We consider these skills crucial for the practical tasks of reading advertisements, newspapers, political propaganda, and pamphlets. Too often textbooks on reading ignore the fact that students receive much of their information from sources that are presenting only one side of an issue and distorting the information for their own self-interest.

We have retained the original appendix, adding a list of common foreign words and phrases that often appear in college textbooks and scholarly works. Although, in general, this book is not intended for students who have difficulty decoding words, we have chosen to retain the section on sound and symbol relationships. Response to our text suggests that other teachers share our experience that reading classes are far from homogeneous: one or two students each year have difficulty with decoding. With the appendix—and supplementary material provided by the instructor—these students are free to work individually at their own pace.

Less specialized, the list of commonly confused words provides ideal material for group exercises. No matter what their level, students can always profit from a discussion of these recurrent problems of usage.

The first edition of *Reading for Results* has been successful; many instructors have agreed that the text lives up to its title and produces more skillful readers. We are confident that this second edition will do the same. After working with our text, students will find their textbooks are no longer sources of frustration and confusion. In short they will have learned the skill of reading for results.

We would like to thank the following reviewers for their contribution to the second edition: Hilda Attride, Riverside City College; June S. Belker, San Diego State University; Patricia Byrne, Camden County College; Barbara Culhane, Nassau Community College; Lois A. Dotson, Georgia Southern College; Judith Fischer, Nassau Community College; Russell D. Gregory, Linn-Benton Community College; Beatrice P. Tignor, Prince George's Community College; and Sister Karen Werra, Mercy College of Detroit.

Laraine Flemming
Sara C. Mansbach

Chapter 1

Building Your Vocabulary

This chapter is devoted to techniques that will help you develop your vocabulary. You will learn how to add new words to your vocabulary; how to use the dictionary; and how to define, without using the dictionary, words you have neither seen nor heard before.

WORD ANALYSIS AND CONTEXT CLUES

Probably the best way to find out what a word means is to look it up in the dictionary. The only problem is that sometimes when you're reading, you just don't have enough time to look up all the words you don't know. That's understandable, but lack of time does not mean that you should skip over unfamiliar words altogether. There are other ways to figure out what a word means. For example, you can use context clues and word analysis to arrive at a definition. In this section we will explain how to use both methods, but we'll begin first with word analysis.

When we use the term *word analysis,* **we mean that it is possible to take an unfamiliar word, figure out what a part or parts of the word mean, and come up with a definition.** For example, let's say you came across the following sentence: "He thought it might be a good idea to study dermatology." Suppose further that you didn't have the slightest idea what the word *dermatology* means. It would undoubtedly help if we told you that *derma* means "skin" and *logy* means "study of." Then you would be able to figure out that dermatology is the study of skin.

At this point you may be asking yourself how word analysis can save time since you have to go to a dictionary to find out what parts of a word mean. But that's where you're wrong. Instead of having to look up every word in the dictionary, you can memorize some of the most important prefixes and roots, as well as a few of the most important suffixes. That way you will have these useful clues with you at all times. Whenever you see an unfamiliar word, you can look and see if it contains a *prefix*, *root*, or *suffix* you know. If it does, you may be able to work out a definition without looking the word up.

If the words *prefixes*, *suffixes*, and *roots* are at all confusing to you, keep in mind the following:

1. **Prefixes** can consist of one letter, two letters, or a group of letters. Prefixes are word parts that appear at the beginning of many different words (*re*turn, *re*peat, *ex*cept, and *ex*clude).

2. **Suffixes,** like prefixes, can consist of one letter, two letters, or a group of letters. But unlike prefixes, they do not appear at the beginning of words; instead, they always appear at the end (farm*er*, law*yer*, hypnot*ist*, and scient*ist*).

3. **A root** is that word or part of a word to which prefixes and suffixes are attached in order to form new words (re*spec*t, *spec*ulate, and intro*spec*tion).

You will probably notice in the following pages that we spend more time working with prefixes and roots than with suffixes. We do that because suffixes tell you more about the function of a word (they can help you figure out what part of speech the word is) than they do about the meaning. Also, the meaning of many suffixes is very vague. Therefore, they are not always useful clues to the definition of unfamiliar words. Usually, recognizing the root of a word will provide you with the best clue.

Similarly, you may wonder why we include so many Greek and Latin prefixes and roots. We do so because the English language has borrowed heavily from both these languages, and much of the vocabulary we use in formal writing and speaking comes from Greek and Latin.

Before introducing the exercises, which contain some of the most important prefixes, roots, and suffixes, we'd like to stress an important point on the use of word analysis: although word analysis is extremely useful, remember that simply combining the meanings of the parts of a word will not always give you the most useful definition. For example, take the following sentence: "I can't imagine a more credulous person; he actually believed that I was attacked by men from Mars on my way home from the party."

If you don't know what the word *credulous* means, we can help by explaining that *cred* means "belief" and *ous* usually means "full of."* You can then take "full of belief" for a first definition of the word *credulous*. But what exactly does that mean? You can imagine a bottle full of milk, but what is a person full of belief?

If you read the sentence again with the first definition in mind, you'll understand what *credulous* means. The person who is described as credulous obviously believes a story that most people would laugh at. A person who is credulous then is ready to believe something most people would not. As a matter of fact, he or she is ready to believe almost anything. This second definition explains the first one, which was derived from word analysis. Someone who is full of belief is ready to believe anything.

In the preceding example you could use information in the sentence to figure out the definition of the word *credulous*. As you may have already guessed, that method of figuring out a definition is what we meant when we talked about using context clues. The *context* of a word is the sentence, paragraph, or selection in which the word appears. Whenever you use the sentence, paragraph, or selection in which a word appears in order to discover the meaning of a word, you are using context clues. Here are three examples of important types of context clues. They will help you in the following exercises.

Example Clue

The context of the word will often contain an example of behavior associated with the word; for example, "His feelings for his cousin were *ambivalent;* sometimes he delighted in her company and sometimes he couldn't stand the sight of her." From this sentence it is clear that someone with ambivalent feelings tends to have mixed emotions. Certainly, the sentence gives you an example of someone who is in conflict: ". . . sometimes he delighted in her company; sometimes he couldn't stand the sight of her." Since that's an example of what it's like to be ambivalent, we can say that *ambivalent* in this sentence means "conflicting."

Before we go on to the next kind of clue, we'll give you one more example: "George was one of my most *diligent* students; he was willing to spend hours working on mastering a new subject." If someone is diligent, then he or she doesn't mind

---

*ous can also mean "in possession of" or "having"

spending hours working toward some goal. Since that's an example of diligent behavior, we can say that *diligent* in this sentence means "hard working."

Contrast Clue

The context may also tell you what the word does *not* mean; for example, "She wanted to give me the impression of being *erudite*, but instead she gave me the impression that she knew absolutely nothing." It is clear from this sentence that if someone is erudite, he or she is the opposite of someone who knows nothing. It wouldn't be very sensible to claim that a person who is erudite knows everything, but we can say that someone who is erudite knows a great deal.

We can use the following sentence to give you another example of a contrast clue: "They had come claiming that they would *ameliorate* the problems in the ghetto, but they had only succeeded in making them worse." Clearly from this sentence we know that to ameliorate a problem is the opposite of making it worse. Therefore, we can say that *ameliorate* in this sentence means "to improve."

Restatement Clue

The context may actually contain a definition of the word; for example, "His *redundancy* was not one of the things that pleased me about his style. As a matter of fact, the way he repeated himself drove me almost insane." There are two sentences in this example. From the first one we learn that redundancy is irritating; from the second, we learn that redundancy means "repetition."

The following sentences also contains an example of a restatement clue: "They said she was *penurious*, and I didn't need a dictionary to know that meant 'cheap.'" This is an obvious example of a restatement clue. The second half of the sentence makes it clear that *cheap* is another word for *penurious*.

These three preceding context clues are very important. Nevertheless, you should keep in mind that most context clues are not so obvious. Often you will have to combine ideas in a paragraph or selection with your own knowledge and experience to figure out the meaning of a word, as in the following selection:

> For months he had dreamed of being able to *redeem* his medals. He had been unable to think of anything else. Now with the vision of the medals shimmering before him, he hurried to the pawnshop.

In this short selection none of the context clues previously presented appear. However, it is still possible to figure out that the word *redeem* in this context means "reclaim" or "recover." Most people go to a pawnshop to buy or to sell, and it is doubtful that the man described as hurrying to the pawnshop would be in such a rush to sell something he had dreamed of for months. Clearly, he is going to buy back what he has already sold.

Remember, too, that the use of context clues, like word analysis, has its limitations. Take, for example, the following sentence: "She was an *articulate* student, ready and willing to speak on every subject." Here the word *articulate* means "capable of speaking clearly and expressively." However, given the description of the student's behavior—she was "ready and willing to speak on every subject"—it would be just as easy to assume that *articulate* means "talkative."

Sometimes context clues alone are simply not good enough to lead you to the correct definition of a word. Therefore, you should rely on them only when you have no choice, for example, if you are taking a test and cannot look up a word. Whenever you can, use word analysis and context clues together. Combining these two methods will usually lead you to the correct definition of a word.

The following exercices have been designed to give you practice in using word analysis and context clues. Do the exercises carefully, *and, above all, memorize each list of prefixes and suffixes.*

EXERCISE 1   **Practice Exercise:** Read through the following list, and then look at the sentences that follow. Each sentence contains an italicized word that may not be familiar to you. Make use of context and word analysis to figure out the meaning of the italicized word in the sentence.

Place a *C* next to the sentence if you were able to use context clues. Don't mark the sentence at all if there were no context clues.

1. circum   (Latin prefix)   around
2. inter   (Latin prefix)   between
3. loqu, locut   (Latin root)   speak, talk

4. spec   (Latin root)   see, look
5. scrib, script (Latin root)   write
6. ven   (Latin root)   come
7. ous, ious   (suffix)   full of, in possession of, having

C 1. He had been silent and withdrawn in his youth, but old age had made him *loquacious*.

The word *loquacious* in this sentence means <u>talkative</u>.

Explanation: In this example you can use word analysis and context clues. You know that *loqu* means "talk" and the suffix *ous* means "full of." Thus someone who is *loquacious* is "full of talk."

The context of the word also contains a clue. It tells you that someone who is loquacious is the opposite of someone who is silent and withdrawn. Someone who is not silent is willing to talk; in fact, not only willing, but, as you learned from word analysis, he or she is full of talk, or talkative.

Do the rest of the exercises in the same manner.

1. American colonies did not like British *intervention* in their affairs.

   The word *intervention* in this sentence means:

   _____

2. After his accident he was decidedly more *circumspect* when driving in heavy traffic.

   The word *circumspect* in this sentence means:

   _____

3. What formula do you use to figure out the *circumference* of a circle?

   The word *circumference* in this sentence means:

   _____

Word Analysis and Context Clues 7

4. Her actions were rigidly *circumscribed* by the club's rules and regulations; she could not make any decisions for herself.

   The word *circumscribed* in this sentence means:

   _____

5. The scientists were unable to read the strange *script*.

   The word *script* in this sentence means:

   _____

6. Unfortunately, the speaker was guilty of *circumlocution;* he just couldn't seem to come to the point.

   The word *circumlocution* in this sentence means:

   _____

7. Because she was dressed as the devil, her entrance was the most *spectacular* event of the season.

   The word *spectacular* in this sentence means:

   _____

8. He tried to *circumvent* the attack, but he failed and died in battle.

   The word *circumvent* in this sentence means:

   _____

9. That was written *circa* A.D. 1500.

   The word *circa* in this sentence means:

   _____

10. Danton, one of the leaders of the French Revolution, was famous for his *eloquence;* crowds listened to him in fascination and went home convinced that he was telling the truth.

    The word *eloquence* in this sentence means:

    _____

11. In the Middle Ages, people did not believe it was possible to *circumnavigate* the globe.

    The word *circumnavigate* in this sentence means:

    _____

12. He decided to take *elocution* lessons because he knew his new job required a lot of public speaking.

    The word *elocution* in this sentence means:

    _____

13. After much *speculation,* she decided to enter the religious order.

    The word *speculation* in this sentence means:

    _____

14. There was an *inscription* on the back of the locket, but it was written in a foreign language.

    The word *inscription* in this sentence means:

    _____

15. Because they stopped talking as soon as she arrived, she felt like an *interloper* in their conversation.

    The word *interloper* in this sentence means:

    _____

Before we go on to the rest of the exercises, we need to make an important point concerning word definitions. When we ask you to give a definition, you'll notice that we always ask what a word means within a particular sentence (for example, "The word *speculation* in this sentence means . . ."). We never ask you to define a word outside of a particular context.

We do this for a very good reason: The meaning of a word depends on its context. In the exercise you just completed, the word *speculation* meant "thinking." But *speculation* in the following sentence has a different definition: "Her *speculation* in stocks had cost her a great deal of money." Here the word *speculation* refers to business dealings involving a certain amount of risk; the word does not refer to the consideration of an object or idea. Clearly the meaning of a word can change when its context changes.

You should never assume that a word has only one meaning; such an assumption will lead to confusion. Most words have several meanings, and all word definitions are dependent on context.

If you think you know the definition of a word but find that your definition just doesn't make sense in relation to the rest of the sentence, use context clues and word analysis to work out another meaning. If that's not possible, then look the word up and try to find a definition that fits the particular context of the word that is puzzling you.

EXERCISE 2

Directions: Read through the following list, and then look at the sentences that follow. Each sentence contains an italicized word that may not be familiar to you. Use context and word analysis to figure out the meaning of the italicized word in the sentence.

Put a *C* next to the sentence if you were able to use context clues. Don't mark the sentence at all if there were no context clues.

Note that whenever possible, we have included prefixes, suffixes, or roots you have already learned.

1. in, im, il   (Latin prefix)   into, not
2. super   (Latin prefix)   over, above
3. vid, vis   (Latin root)   see
4. brev   (Latin root)   short
5. clar   (Latin root)   clear
6. cred   (Latin root)   believe
7. er, ar, or   (suffix)   one who has something to do with the idea expressed in the root

1. The *brevity* of his letter convinced her that she could no longer consider him a good friend.

   The word *brevity* in this sentence means:

   _____

2. His story about being attacked on the way home was hardly *credible;* he didn't have a mark on him.

   The word *credible* in this sentence means:

   _____

3. I just can't give any *credence* to what he says; it's impossible to believe him after all the lies he's told.

   The word *credence* in this sentence means:

   _____

4. His *supercilious* attitude offended them; he acted as if they were not good enough to talk to him.

   The word *supercilious* in this sentence means:

   _____

5. It was *evident* that she was uncomfortable because she kept on picking imaginary threads off her coat and fixing her scarf.

   The word *evident* in this sentence means:

   _____

6. After hearing the story about the UFOs, he had an *incredulous* look on his face.

   The word *incredulous* in this sentence means:

   _____

7. You'll have to *abbreviate* that phrase.

   The word *abbreviate* in this sentence means:

   _____

8. Because she had been able to foresee the storm, they believed her to be a *visionary*.

   The word *visionary* in this sentence means:

   _____

9. The Christian *creed* spread rapidly to the rest of the world.

   The word *creed* in this sentence means:

   _____

10. The press asked the president to *clarify* his last statement.

    The word *clarify* in this sentence means:

    _____

11. His *credulity* never failed to surprise his friends; there was nothing he was not ready to believe.

    The word *credulity* in this sentence means:

    _____

12. The *spectators* were not pleased with her performance.

    The word *spectators* in this sentence means:

    _____

13. Unfortunately, his speech lacked *clarity* and didn't do much to straighten out the confusion.

    The word *clarity* in this sentence means:

    _____

14. Because of the strange things that happened when she was present, they believed she had *supernatural* powers.

    The word *supernatural* in this sentence means:

    _____

15. The *video* portion of this telecast will undergo a short interruption.

The word *video* in this sentence means:

_____

EXERCISE 3

Directions: Read through the following list, and then look at the sentences that follow. Each sentence contains an italicized word that may not be familiar to you. Use context and word analysis to figure out the meaning of the italicized word in the sentence.

Place a *C* next to the sentence if you were able to use context clues. Don't mark the sentence at all if there were no context clues.

Note that whenever possible, we have included prefixes, suffixes, or roots that you have already learned.

1. syn, sym   (Greek prefix)   together, alike
2. pre   (Latin prefix)   before
3. de   (Latin prefix)   removal, down from, reduce, away
4. dic, dict   (Latin root)   speak
5. capit   (Latin root)   head
6. popul   (Latin root)   people
7. plen, plet   (Latin root)   full

1. It had once been a *populous* city, but over the years it had turned into a ghost town.

The word *populous* in this sentence means:

_____

2. Smallpox had managed to *depopulate* the village.

The word *depopulate* in this sentence means:

_____

3. The *capital* of the column is beautifully carved.

The word *capital* in this sentence means:

_____

Word Analysis and Context Clues

4. Many people believe in *predestination;* they believe there is nothing they can do to change their fate.

   The word *predestination* in this sentence means:

   _____

5. The word *holler* is a *synonym* for the word *shout*.

   The word *synonym* in this sentence means:

   _____

6. To become an actor, he was forced to improve his *diction*.

   The word *diction* in this sentence means:

   _____

7. The citizens threatened to *decapitate* the king.

   The word *decapitate* in this sentence means:

   _____

8. She was sure that everything in her life had been *predetermined* before she was born.

   The word *predetermined* in this sentence means:

   _____

9. His savings had been sadly *depleted* by the depression.

   The word *depleted* in this sentence means:

   _____

10. The *populace* suffered terribly under the rule of the cruel king.

    The word *populace* in this sentence means:

    _____

11. She tried to *synthesize* everything she had read about the nineteenth century, but she still felt that she didn't have the complete picture.

    The word *synthesize* in this sentence means:

    _____

12. The *per capita* income in the village was only two hundred dollars a year.

    The word *per capita* in this sentence means:

    _____

13. Can you *dictate* that sentence once more?

    The word *dictate* in this sentence means:

    _____

14. The meal was *replete* with every possible kind of delicacy; there was nothing more he could have asked for.

    The word *replete* in this sentence means:

    _____

15. One could hardly accuse her of having a *plentitude* of ideas; one a year was her average.

    The word *plentitude* in this sentence means:

    _____

EXERCISE 4

Directions: Read through the following list, and then look at the sentences that follow. Each sentence contains an italicized word that may not be familiar to you. Use context and word analysis to figure out the meaning of the italicized word in the sentence.

Place a *C* next to the sentence if you were able to use context clues. Don't mark the sentence at all if there were no context clues.

Note that whenever possible, we have included prefixes, suffixes, or roots that you have already learned.

1. pseudo   (Greek root)   false
2. homo   (Greek root)   same
3. psych   (Greek root)   spirit, life
4. crypt   (Greek root)   secret
5. onynm   (Greek root)   name, word
6. log, logy   (Greek root)   word, study of
7. ambi   (Latin root)   both

1. Many men and women write mysteries under *pseudonyms* because they do not consider mystery stories to be completely respectable.

   The word *pseudonyms* in this sentence means:

   _____

2. The group was clearly *homogeneous;* every member came from the same age group and income bracket.

   The word *homogeneous* in this sentence means:

   _____

3. The war had damaged his *psyche;* he was no longer able to think clearly.

   The word *psyche* in this sentence means:

   _____

4. Her smile was somewhat *ambiguous.* She could have been happy or sad; I couldn't tell which.

   The word *ambiguous* in this sentence means:

   _____

5. In the army he had learned to read *cryptic* messages.

   The word *cryptic* in this sentence means:

   _____

6. Unfriendly is an *antonym* for the word *friendly*.

   The word *antonym* in this sentence means:

   _____

7. Astrology is a *pseudoscience;* the stars have no influence on our lives.

   The word *pseudoscience* in this sentence means:

   _____

8. She decided to study *zoology* because animals had always interested her.

   The word *zoology* in this sentence means:

   _____

9. She refused to deliver the *eulogy* for the dead man because she had never liked him and could not praise him.

   The word *eulogy* in this sentence means:

   _____

10. They thought he had *psychic* powers because he claimed to know about the future.

    The word *psychic* in this sentence means:

    _____

11. The cook was clearly *ambidextrous;* he could cut carrots with one hand and flip eggs with the other.

    The word *ambidextrous* in this sentence means:

    _____

12. *See* and *sea* are *homonyms*.

    The word *homonyms* in this sentence means:

    _____

13. The words *Wac* and *radar* are both *acronyms;* the word *Wac* came from *W*omen's *A*rmy *C*orps and *radar* came from *ra*dio *d*etecting *a*nd *r*anging.

    The word *acronyms* in this sentence means:

    _____

14. If the author of the poem is unknown, write the word *anonymous* after it.

    The word *anonymous* in this sentence means:

    _____

15. "Pigeon" was the *cryptonym* for the head of the spy ring.

    The word *cryptonym* in this sentence means:

    _____

EXERCISE 5   **Directions:** Read through the following list, and then look at the sentences that follow. Each sentence contains an italicized word that may not be familiar to you. Use context and word analysis to figure out the meaning of the italicized word in the sentence.

Place a *C* next to the sentence if you were able to use context clues. Don't mark the sentence at all if there were no context clues.

Note that whenever possible, we have included prefixes, suffixes, or roots that you have already learned.

1. contra	(Latin prefix)	against
2. ante	(Latin prefix)	before
3. mort	(Latin root)	death
4. phil	(Greek root)	love
5. anthrop	(Greek root)	man
6. chron	(Greek root)	time
7. ist	(suffix)	person who does what is described in the rest of the word

1. He insisted on *contradicting* everything she said.

   The word *contradicting* in this sentence means:

   _____

2. Most of us dream of being *immortal,* but in reality no one would like to live forever.

   The word *immortal* in this sentence means:

   _____

3. If you say yes, she says no. She just likes to be *contrary.*

   The word *contrary* in this sentence means:

   _____

4. The *mortuary* was burned to the ground.

   The word *mortuary* in this sentence means:

   _____

5. *Anthropology* was his favorite subject.

   The word *anthropology* in this sentence means:

   _____

6. The *anterior* of the church was poorly lit.

   The word *anterior* in this sentence means:

   _____

7. We'll have to *synchronize* our watches if we want to do this correctly.

   The word *synchronize* in this sentence means:

   _____

8. He had spent his entire life making money from the labor of others, but as he grew older, he wanted to be known as a *philanthropist.*

   The word *philanthropist* in this sentence means:

   _____

Word Analysis and Context Clues

9. After living in France for more than a decade, he had become a devoted *Francophile*.

   The word *Francophile* in this sentence means:

   _____

10. Unfortunately, her son was a *chronic* liar. Even though she wanted to believe him, she couldn't bring herself to do so; he had lied once too often.

    The word *chronic* in this sentence means:

    _____

11. The *mortality* rate for those under thirty is extremely high in the poorer countries of the world.

    The word *mortality* in this sentence means:

    _____

12. He tried to give the events in *chronological* order; he began with the first thing that happened after he awoke.

    The word *chronological* in this sentence means:

    _____

13. The *anteroom* of the private eye's office was filled with old beer cans, dirty ashtrays, and tattered magazines.

    The word *anteroom* in this sentence means:

    _____

14. The death of someone who is near to us forces us to accept the fact that we are all *mortal*.

    The word *mortal* in this sentence means:

    _____

15. All her life she had dreamed of being an *anthropologist*, and her dream was finally going to come true.

The word *anthropologist* in this sentence means:

_____

EXERCISE 6

Directions: Read through the following list, and then look at the sentences that follow. Each sentence contains an italicized word that may not be familiar to you. Use context and word analysis to figure out the meaning of the italicized word in the sentence.

Place a *C* next to the sentence if you were able to use context clues. Don't mark the sentence at all if there were no context clues.

Note that whenever possible, we have included prefixes, suffixes, or roots that you have already learned.

1. bi   (Latin prefix)   two
2. mono   (Greek prefix)   one, alone
3. pro   (Latin prefix)   forward, forth
4. reg, rec   (Latin root)   straighten, rule
5. gam   (Greek root)   marriage
6. voc   (Latin root)   call
7. mo, mot, mob, mov   (Latin root) move

1. He spoke in a *monotone* and managed to bore everyone during his lectures.

The word *monotone* in this sentence means:

_____

2. She tried to *rectify* her mistake, but she soon discovered that she could not.

The word *rectify* in this sentence means:

_____

3. He *invoked* the Fifth Amendment to save himself.

The word *invoked* in this sentence means:

_____

Word Analysis and Context Clues

4. He felt terrible when he found out that she was a *bigamist;* she had never divorced her first husband.

   The word *bigamist* in this sentence means:

   _____

5. She tried to *provoke* a quarrel with her rival.

   The word *provoke* in this sentence means:

   _____

6. With a few exceptions most societies in the world practice *monogamy.*

   The word *monogamy* in this sentence means:

   _____

7. He was very *vocal* in his objections to the new law.

   The word *vocal* in this sentence means:

   _____

8. After studying abroad, she had become *bilingual;* she spoke perfect French as well as English.

   The word *bilingual* in this sentence means:

   _____

9. Do you have any idea what could have *motivated* him to do a thing like that?

   The word *motivated* in this sentence means:

   _____

10. The soldier stood *erect* when the colonel passed by.

    The word *erect* in this sentence means:

    _____

11. When the president died, an *interregnum* was formed to take control until a new president could be elected.

    The word *interregnum* in this sentence means:

    _____

12. The actor's *monologue* was not well received.

    The word *monologue* in this sentence means:

    _____

13. The people suffered horribly under the new *regime* that came into power after the president's death.

    The word *regime* in this sentence means:

    _____

14. The sight of the mountains *evoked* memories of her childhood.

    The word *evoked* in this sentence means:

    _____

15. Since early childhood, she had viewed preaching as her life's *vocation*.

    The word *vocation* in this sentence means:

    _____

EXERCISE 7

Directions: Read through the following list, and then look at the sentences that follow. Each sentence contains an italicized word that may not be familiar to you. Use context and word analysis to figure out the meaning of the italicized word in the sentence.

Place a *C* next to the sentence if you were able to use context clues. Don't mark the sentence at all if there were no context clues.

Note that whenever possible, we have included prefixes, suffixes, or roots that you have already learned.

Word Analysis and Context Clues

1. re   (Latin prefix)   back, again
2. com, con, col   (Latin prefix)   together, with, jointly
3. bene   (Latin adverb used as prefix)   good, well
4. mal   (Latin prefix)   bad, badly
5. sub   (Latin prefix)   under
6. string, strict   (Latin root)   draw or bind
7. ver   (Latin root)   true

1. Shortly after he was in an accident, they *revoked* his license.

   The word *revoked* in this sentence means:

   _____

2. The young woman thanked her *benefactor* for helping her get the job.

   The word *benefactor* in this sentence means:

   _____

3. Can you *verify* the man's statement that he was not at the scene of the crime?

   The word *verify* in this sentence means:

   _____

4. As they filed out of the church, the priest gave the assembled villagers his *benediction*.

   The word *benediction* in this sentence means:

   _____

5. There is no question about it; she is a *veritable* genius.

   The word *veritable* in this sentence means:

   _____

6. The doctor gave him the news that the tumor was *benign*.

   The word *benign* in this sentence means:

   _____

7. She left the office in tears after being told that the tumor was *malignant*.

   The word *malignant* in this sentence means:

   _____

8. Not all that long ago *malefactors* were punished according to their crime. Pickpockets, for example, were punished by having their hands cut off.

   The word *malefactors* in this sentence means:

   _____

9. The lieutenant treated his *subordinates* with contempt; he gave them orders without even looking into their faces.

   The word *subordinates* in this sentence means:

   _____

10. The police *restricted* her movements until the case was solved.

    The word *restricted* in this sentence means:

    _____

11. The *confluence* of streams formed a large body of water.

    The word *confidence* in this sentence means:

    _____

12. The lion tamer *subdued* the animals in only a matter of minutes.

    The word *subdued* in this sentence means:

    _____

13. His *malicious* laughter echoed in her ears, and she knew that he hated her.

    The word *malicious* in this sentence means:

    _____

14. His throat *constricted* with fear when he had to face the audience.

    The word *constricted* in this sentence means:

    _____

15. She tried to *compress* the information into one short paragraph, but it was simply impossible.

    The word *compress* in this sentence means:

    _____

USING THE DICTIONARY

YOUNGER BROTHER	I just found the word *paltry* in the newspaper. You told me if I learned all those Greek and Latin prefixes and roots, I'd be able to figure out words I didn't know. Well, it doesn't work with *paltry*.
OLDER BROTHER	It doesn't work because that word doesn't have anything to do with either Greek or Latin. I told you that you couldn't always use word analysis. This time you'll just have to look up the word. That's the only way you'll learn.
YOUNGER BROTHER	Well, I'm not looking it up. It won't do me any good anyway. I never understand all that stuff in the dictionary. They give you about ten different definitions and throw in a lot of extra signs and symbols that don't make any sense.
OLDER BROTHER	You can learn how to use the dictionary. You just have to learn how the entries are organized.
YOUNGER BROTHER	That's a lot of help. I don't even know what an *entry* is.

Unfortunately, a great many people share the younger brother's point of view in the preceding dialogue: they don't want to use the dictionary. They view it as a source of trouble and confusion, not as a source of information.

Actually this attitude is understandable because a dictionary does contain a large amount of information. And sometimes it is difficult to sift through all of it, especially if you don't know what all the different symbols mean or are not sure how the definitions of the word are organized.

With these problems in mind, we have outlined the different kinds of information contained in a dictionary. After reading this section, you should no longer be unwilling to turn to the dictionary; you may even start reading it for pleasure.

Selecting a Dictionary

Probably the first thing you should learn about dictionaries is that they are not all the same. That means you should look at several different college dictionaries before you choose the one you like the best. A good way to decide on your favorite is to look up the same word in several dictionaries. By doing so, you will discover that some dictionaries contain more information than others, and you may find that one of the dictionaries is printed in a format that is easier for you to read.

It is important to buy a current dictionary. After about ten years on the market, dictionaries become outdated. New uses for old words are accepted or found, and completely new words enter our language. For example, the word *Xerox* is frequently used today, but it didn't exist fifty years ago. We urge you to acquire a dictionary that has been published recently and discard the family treasure that has been gathering dust on the shelf for twenty-five years.

The following dictionaries are commonly recommended for student use:

- *The Random House Dictionary.* New York: Random House, 1981.
- *The American Heritage Dictionary of the English Language.* Boston: Houghton Mifflin, 1980.
- *Funk and Wagnalls Standard College Dictionary.* New York: Funk and Wagnalls, 1980.
- *Webster's New Collegiate Dictionary.* Springfield, Mass.: Merriam, 1981.

- *Webster's New World Dictionary of the American Language,* Second College Edition. Cleveland, Ohio: Collins-World, 1979.

We suggest that you purchase not only a hardbound college dictionary but also a paperback edition. You can use the hardbound edition for working at your desk and carry the paperback edition to class.

Reading the Entry

Normally the *entry* in a dictionary is defined as the word or phrase that is set out slightly from the margin and printed in boldface type. However, to make our explanation easier to follow, we are going to use the terms *entry* and *entry word*. When we talk about the "entry word," we mean the word printed in boldface type; when we talk about the "entry," we mean the text that follows the entry word.

As we mentioned before, a dictionary entry contains a great deal of information. Even very short entries contain a lot of information; you just have to know how to look for it. Look at the following example:

> **bed·roll** (bĕd′rōl′) *n.* A portable roll of bedding used especially by campers and others who sleep outdoors.[1]

The first thing we learn from the entry is that *bedroll* is written as one word, not two. The dictionary we are using divides words into syllables with dots. If there were no dot but instead a space between *bed* and *roll*, that would mean that *bedroll* was spelled as two words. We also know that there is only one acceptable spelling for the word. If there were other acceptable ways of spelling *bedroll*, they would follow the entry word.

Following the entry word are parentheses containing letters and symbols. The symbols over the letters are called *diacritical* marks, and they tell us how the word is pronounced. For example, if you did not know how to pronounce the ĕ and the ō in the word *bedroll*, you would look down at the bottom of the dictionary page and find the following key:

[1] © 1980 Houghton Mifflin Company. Reprinted by permission from *The American Heritage Dictionary of the English Language.*

ă pat/ā pay/âr care/ä father/b bib/ch church/d deed/ĕ pet/ē be/f fife/g gag/h hat/hw which/ĭ pit/ī pie/îr pier/j judge/k kick/l lid, needle/m mum/n no, sudden/ng thing/ŏ pot/ō toe/ô paw, for/oi noise/ou out/ŏŏ took/ōō boot/p pop/r roar/s sauce/sh ship, dish/ . . .[2]

The key tells us that *e* is pronounced like the *e* in *bed*, while the *o* is pronounced like the *o* in *toe*.

After seeing the word respelled in the parentheses, we also know for sure which syllable is stressed or spoken louder. We stress *bed*, not *roll*, when we pronounce the word *bedroll*. We learn which syllable to stress from the heavy black mark that follows the first syllable. The lighter mark following the second syllable tells us that this syllable is not stressed as much as the first.

The letter *n.* that follows the parenthesis tells us that the entry word is used as a noun. If it could also be used as a verb or an adjective, that information would appear in the entry.

Finally, a definition of the word is given. We learn that a bedroll is some kind of bedding that can be carried.

The entry for *bedroll* was a fairly simple one to read, especially since there was only one definition for the word and no history given. Some entries are more complicated; but with a little practice, they won't give you any trouble either. The following is a good example of a longer, more complicated entry:

bra·zen (brā′ zən)* *adj.* **1.** Made of brass. **2.** Resembling brass in color, quality, or hardness. **3.** Having a loud, resonant sound like that of a brass trumpet. **4.** Impudent; bold. —See Synonyms at **shameless**. —*tr. v.* **brazened, -zening, -zens.** To face or undergo with bold or brash self-assurance. Usually used with *out*. [Middle English *brasen*, Old English *bræsen*, from *bræs*, BRASS.] —**bra′ zen · ly** *adv.* —**bra′ zen · ness** *n.* [3]

Here again, we learn how many syllables there are in the word and how it is pronounced. It is the definitions of the word

---

[2] ©1980 Houghton Mifflin Company. Reprinted by permission from *The American Heritage Dictionary of the English Language.*

*The symbol ə *is called a schwa,* and it represents a sound much like the one given to the a in the word *above.*

[3] ©1980 Houghton Mifflin Company. Reprinted by permission from *The American Heritage Dictionary of the English Language.*

that make this entry different from the first entry example. Instead of one definition, we find four.

Actually, the number of definitions should not be too surprising since it is clear that words can have different meanings depending on how we use them. A good dictionary takes this fact into account and presents several definitions.

However, keep in mind that not all dictionaries organize the different definitions of a word in the same way. Some give the oldest meaning of the word first; others, like *The American Heritage Dictionary,* give the most common meaning of the word first. Therefore, you should always check the opening pages of your dictionary to see what method has been used.

Looking again at the entry, we see that after the fourth definition there is a note to "See Synonyms at **shameless**." *Synonyms* are words with similar meanings. Therefore, if we wanted to find a synonym for *brazen* when it means "bold" or "impudent," we would look under the entry word *shameless*.

Following the note on synonyms, we see the abbreviation *tr. v.* That notation means the entry will now give the meaning of *brazen* when it is used as a transitive verb. (A *transitive verb* is one that takes an object.) The entry also provides the different forms of the word *brazen*. We need to know the various forms if, for example, we want to use the word *brazen* as a verb.

According to the entry, there is only one meaning for the word *brazen* when it is used as a verb: to "brazen something out" means "to face it boldly and with assurance." Note that we also learn that *brazen* is used with the word *out*.

At the end of the entry is a brief history of the word. This is the information contained in brackets. Here we learn that the modern word *brazen* can be traced back to the period when Middle English was spoken (1100–1500) and even further back to when Old English was spoken (800–1100). The entry also gives earlier forms of the same word that we now use in modern English.

Finally, the entry gives two additional parts of speech formed from the word *brazen: brazenly,* which is an adverb, and *brazenness,* which is a noun.

Clearly, the second example of an entry was longer than the first example, and some entries contain even more information. Some contain labels that tell you more about how and when a word may be used. We aren't going to give you seven more entries, each containing a different label, but we will introduce you to some of the important ones, and you should learn what all of them mean.

1. *Nonstandard* or *Substandard*. If either one of these labels follows a word, you know that the use of that particular word is not considered correct by most speakers of the English language. Words like *ain't* and *nowheres* are examples of nonstandard English.

2. *Informal* or *Colloquial*. If either one of these labels follows a word, you can use the word freely in conversation. However, you should not use the word when you make a speech, nor should you use it when you write an essay or a term paper. For example, the word *bugs* is often used to mean "defects"; for example, "The stereo system still had a few bugs in it." The use of the word *bugs* to mean "defects" is perfectly appropriate for normal conversation, but it is not appropriate for use in an essay or a term paper.

3. *Archaic*. If this label follows a word, it means that the word is rarely seen and belongs to a style of language no longer in use. The word *thou*, for example, appears in Shakespeare's plays, but it is almost never seen in anything written today.

4. *Vulgar*. If this label appears next to a word or expression, it means that you should be very cautious about using the word since many people are shocked or insulted when they hear it. The word *snot*, for example, is usually labeled "vulgar."

5. *Usage*. Following this label there is an explanation of any usage problems involving the entry word. For example, the entry for the word *between* usually contains a usage label because, for many speakers of English, there is some confusion about when it is correct to use the word *between* rather than the word *among*.

6. *Music, Logic, Technology*. Labels like these indicate that a given definition applies only when the word is used in connection with a particular field of study. The meaning of the word *base*, for example, differs depending on whether it is used in connection with the study of architecture or chemistry.

7. *Obsolete*. When this label follows a definition, it indicates that this meaning of the word is no longer in use. The word *ward*, for example, when it means "to imprison" is usually labeled "obsolete."

The information we have provided should enable you to understand an entry fairly easily, but if you need more information, check the table of contents in your dictionary and see if there is a section titled "Guide to the Dictionary" or "Explanatory Notes." Most good dictionaries include explanatory sections that help identify all terms and symbols contained in the entries.

The following exercise will give you some practice working with a dictionary.

EXERCISE 8   **Directions:** When you answer the question below, you will need to use a hardbound dictionary; a paperback edition will not contain all the information asked for in the exercises.

1. What did the word *bicker* originally mean?

2. According to the dictionary, should the word *semipro* be used when writing a formal composition?

3. Write the diacritical marks for the word *harangue*.

4. The phrase *sub rosa* means "in secret." What is the history of the word; how did it come into the English language?

5. How many syllables are there in the word *sidereal?*

6. According to the dictionary, which is the correct spelling of the following word: *crankcase* or *crank case?*

7. What part of speech is the word *crag?*

8. Is the word *submiss* still in use today?

9. Which syllable receives the accent in the word *cranny?*

10. What are some other forms of the word *lessen?*

THE STORY BEHIND THE WORD

Many words in the English language have come from the names of people, events, or places. These words usually have an interesting story behind them, and learning these stories is one of the easiest ways to add new words to your vocabulary. We call this learning the *etymology*.

On the following pages we have made several lists of words that have an interesting background. Learn both the definitions of the words and the stories that go with them.

The first two lists are comprised of words that come from the myths of the Greeks and Romans.

List 1

1. *Chaos.* Acccording to an ancient myth, before earth, sea, and heaven were created, all things were in confusion. Earth, sea, and air were all mixed up together in a shapeless mass called *chaos*. Today when we talk about *chaos*, we are referring to a situation in which disorder rules.

Sample sentence	After the jail break the prison was in *chaos*.
Definition	disorder, complete confusion
Other forms of the word	chaotic

2. *Tantalize.* Tantalus was a king who was cruelly punished by the gods. He was forced to stand in a pool of water that dried up whenever he tried to drink. Over his head was a luscious fruit tree that always rose higher than he could reach. Today when we say that we are *tantalized* by something, we mean that we are attracted to something that is just out of reach. To tantalize is to torment by keeping out of reach.

Sample sentence	The half-starved prisoners were driven mad by the *tantalizing* smell of fried potatoes.
Definition	to tease, torment by holding out of reach
Other forms of the word	tantalizing, tantalized, tantalizes

3. *Nemesis.* Nemesis was a goddess who punished those who had misbehaved, especially those who were overly proud and challenged the gods. Today when we say that someone or something is our *nemesis*, we mean that we are faced with someone or something that will bring about our downfall.

Sample sentence	Oral tests are my *nemesis*; I always fail them.
Definition	source of failure, cause of destruction, an unbeatable rival
Other forms of the word	nemeses

4. *Odyssey.* The book called *Odyssey* was about Odysseus, a Greek king who was forced to wander far from home for ten years. During that time he had many adventures. Today we use the word *odyssey* to describe someone's long and adventurous trip through strange territory. The trip, or *odyssey*, may be real or only imagined.

Sample sentence	After his long *odyssey* abroad, he no longer felt he could go home.

Definition	an extended trip or adventure
Other forms of the word	odysseys

5. *Titanic* and *Titan*. According to the myths of the Greeks, the Titans were members of a gigantic family of gods who inhabited the earth before people did. The Titans were huge and powerful. Today when we describe something as *titanic*, we mean that it is huge or enormous. When we say that someone is a *titan*, we mean that he or she has a great deal of power or is outstanding in some field.

Sample sentence	She made a *titanic* effort to move the huge rock.
Definition	powerful, huge, great
Sample sentence	Mozart is a *titan* in the world of music.
Definition	a person of great achievement or note

EXERCISE 9

Directions: Using the five words you have just learned, fill in the blanks in the following sentences. Be careful to use the correct form of the word.

1. The _____ smell of fried chicken from my neighbor's kitchen made my mouth water.

2. After my long _____ abroad, I don't feel like the same person.

3. Two small children in a house on a rainy day can turn the house into complete _____ .

4. I know that course will be my _____ ; I have never been good in languages.

5. Beethoven is considered a _____ in the world of music.

List 2

1. *Mentor*. Mentor was the trusted friend and teacher of Odysseus. While Odysseus was away, a goddess came down to earth to protect the family of Odysseus. To do so, she disguised herself as Mentor, a friend of the family, and took over his role as teacher and counselor. Today we use the word *mentor* to mean someone we consider a teacher and counselor.

Sample sentence	My older brother has always been my *mentor* in life.
Definition	teacher, counselor, guide

2. *Atlas*. Atlas was a Titan who, according to Greek mythology, held up the earth on his shoulders. The image of Atlas with the earth on his shoulders was used historically on map collections. Today when we talk about an *atlas*, we are usually referring to a bound collection of maps.

Sample sentence	She studied the *atlas* with much fascination.
Definition	book of maps, book of tables and charts
Other forms of the word	atlases

3. *Herculean*. Hercules was a Greek hero who possessed extraordinary strength. It was said that he could perform fantastic feats. Today when we use the word *herculean*, we are talking about something that demands a great deal of effort or strength.

Sample sentence	Before he became vice president, he had to complete the *herculean* task of reorganizing the entire office system.
Definition	difficult, demanding in mental or physical strength

4. *Flora* and *fauna*. Flora was the Roman goddess of flowers, and Faunus was the Roman god of nature and fertility. Today we use the expression *flora and fauna* to mean the plants and animals of a particular region.

Sample sentence	We spent three whole days studying the *flora* and *fauna* of New Zealand.

Definition	plants and animals of a particular region
Other forms of the word	florae *or* floras, faunae *or* faunas

5. **Narcissism.** Narcissus was a beautiful young man who loved no one until the day he saw his own reflection in a pool of water. From then on he was in love with himself. Today when we talk about *narcissism,* we are talking about excessive love or admiration for oneself.

Sample sentence	Only his incredible *narcissism* allowed him to ignore all the insulting remarks directed his way.
Definition	self-love, admiration for oneself
Other forms of the word	narcissist, narcissistic

Hercules was a Greek hero who possessed extraordinary strength.

EXERCISE 10   **Directions:**   Fill in the blanks with one of the words from List 2.

1. Most geography books have a section on the _____

   of different regions.

2. Practically every library has several _____ as a part of the reference section.

3. He was more than a friend; he was my _____.

4. His excessive _____ endangered their marriage.

5. The champion weightlifter's _____ strength impressed the crowd.

The following lists do not have anything to do with mythological figures. The words have come from the names of people, places, and customs. Once again, you should learn the meanings of the words and the stories that go with them.

List 3

1. *Bedlam.* The St. Mary of Bethlehem hospital was in London. It was used to house the mentally ill. Everyone knew of the hospital, and stories about it were repeated again and again. The name of the hospital was often pronounced "Bedlam" or "Bethlem." Today when we use the word *bedlam*, we are talking about a place or situation that is filled with noise and confusion.

   Sample sentence   When the children were home from school, the house was *bedlam*.

   Definition   place filled with noise and confusion

2. *Martinet.* Jean Martinet was a seventeenth-century French general who was famous for the way he disciplined his army. Today when we say that someone is a *martinet*, we mean that he or she follows the rules to the letter and expects everyone else to do the same.

   Sample sentence   The new sergeant was a *martinet*.

   Definition   person who demands strict discipline

3. *Quixotic.* Don Quixote was a famous hero of a Spanish novel that dealt with Quixote's attempt to do the impossible. Today when we say that someone is *quixotic*, we mean that

he or she is not very practical. He or she tends to have a romantic view of life and pursues impossible goals.

Sample sentence	His *quixotic* nature would not allow him to admit that he might fail.
Definition	romantic, impractical, unrealistic
Other forms of the word	quixotically, quixotical

4. *Tawdry.* St. Audrey was a queen who died of a throat tumor. After her death cheap lace neckties were sold in her honor at country fairs. The name of the necktie was shortened from St. Audrey's lace to *tawdry lace.* Today when we say that something is "tawdry," we mean that it looks cheap and gaudy.

Sample sentence	The *tawdry* wallpaper added to the ugliness of the apartment.
Definition	cheap, vulgar, gaudy
Other forms of the word	tawdrier, tawdriest, tawdrily, tawdriness

5. *Chauvinist.* Nicholas Chauvin was a legendary French soldier who was said to be extremely devoted to Napoleon and France. Today when we say that someone is a *chauvinist*, we mean that he or she is prejudiced in favor of his or her country or particular group.

Sample sentence	She is an impossible *chauvinist*; as she sees it, American policies are the only right ones.
Definition	a person who believes that his or her country or group is better than any other
Other forms of the word	chauvinism, chauvinistic, chauvinistically

EXERCISE 11

Directions: Fill in the blanks with one of the words from the preceding list.

1. The _____ room was extremely depressing.

2. Most _____ don't consider any other nation to

   to be of importance.

3. The boss was a _____ with her employees.

4. He was too _____ ; he just wasn't suited for the world of big business.

5. The class was complete _____ because the regular teacher was absent.

List 4

1. *Ostracize.* The word *ostrakon* is Greek for "shell." When in times of crisis or conflict the Athenians of Greece wanted to send someone out of the city for a period of years, everyone would write a name on a piece of shell. The person receiving the most votes would have to leave the city. Today when we say that we *ostracize* someone, we mean that we are excluding or shutting out that person from our group. (No vote is necessary to ostracize someone.)

Sample sentence	They *ostracized* him because of his political views.
Definition	exclude, banish, shun
Other forms of the word	ostracism, ostracizing, ostracizes, ostracized

2. *Utopian and utopia.* Utopia was an imaginary island that served as the subject and title of a book. The island was the perfect place to live because the people of the island used reason to guide their lives. Today when we talk about a *utopia,* we are talking about a condition, situation, or place that is socially and politically perfect. When we say that an idea is *utopian,* we mean that it is excellent but too impractical to be put into actual use.

Sample sentence	Anita's a fool; she thinks if she works hard enough she can make this society into a *utopia.*
Definition	place of perfection
Sample sentence	When will he stop trying to put those *utopian* schemes into practice?
Definition	unrealistic, excellent but impractical

3. *Jingoist.* In the eighteenth century, there was a music hall song sung by those who were ready to go to war. The song contained the words *by jingo.* Today when we say that someone is a *jingoist,* we are talking about a person who is always ready to go to war. A jingoist is almost eager to begin a war.

Sample sentence	Long before he was called into action, he was a proud *jingoist* who was ready to pick up a gun.
Definition	person who is eager for war
Other forms of the word	jingoistic, jingoism, jingo

4. *Mesmerize.* In the eighteenth century, a man named Franz Anton Mesmer used a form of hypnosis to put people into a strange, sleep-like state. People were fascinated by his skills and gathered to watch him. Today we still use the word *mesmerize* to indicate that someone is being put under hypnosis. However, frequently we use it to mean that we are fascinated by what we see.

Sample sentence	The audience seemed *mesmerized* by the sheer beauty of the ballet.
Definition	fascinate, hypnotize
Other forms of the word	mesmerism, mesmerizing, mesmerizes

5. *Laconic.* The Laconians were a Greek tribe who were known for their simple ways and briefness of speech. The legend goes that a Laconian general was once threatened by a rival. The rival claimed that if his army came to Laconia, his men would reduce it to ashes. The Laconian general is said to have answered with one word, *if.* Today when we say that someone is *laconic,* we mean that he or she doesn't use a great many words; someone who is laconic comes straight to the point.

Sample sentence	The heroes of old Westerns were nothing if not *laconic;* they hardly ever said more than "yep" or "nope."
Definition	brief and to the point
Other forms of the word	laconically

The Vocabulary in Your Textbooks 41

EXERCISE 12   **Directions:** Fill in the blanks with one of the words from the preceding list.

1. It took her a while to become accustomed to his _____ way of speaking.

2. He was _____ because of his rude behavior at the party.

3. The children seem to be _____ by the brilliant colors of the fireworks.

4. She is a _____ of the worst sort; for her, war is the only answer when two nations disagree.

5. You can't spend the rest of your life looking for a _____ ; you'll never find it.

THE VOCABULARY IN YOUR TEXTBOOKS

TEACHER   Today, to continue with the background for our study of energy in ecosystems, we'll look at the structure of the leaf of a plant. The leaves act as organs in which both photosynthesis and transpiration take place. In these processes the leaf's stomata play a central role. The stomata take up carbon dioxide from the air and release oxygen and water vapor.

STUDENT   Please, can you hold a minute. That explanation sounded like a foreign language. I know I've heard the word *photosynthesis* before, but I'm not sure what it means. I've never even heard of the word *stomata*, if that's what it was. Can you go back and define those words? Otherwise I'll never understand this stuff.

At one time or another, you too have probably been in the position of the student in the dialogue; that is, you have attempted to master a subject, for example, computer science or biology, and have found that the textbooks explaining those subjects made use of a vocabulary almost completely unknown to you.

Actually, many fields of study make use of what we are calling a *specialized vocabulary*. The words and terms of this vocabulary are used by students and scholars involved in a particular field. Such words are in general not widely used in everyday conversation, and their definitions are, to most people, vague or completely unknown.

There is no denying that textbooks which use a specialized vocabulary are difficult to read. But you can overcome that difficulty; you simply have to make a systematic attempt to learn the words necessary to master both the text and the subject.

We suggest that, first of all, you buy a loose-leaf notebook, one that you will use only for the study of what we are calling your *textbook vocabulary*. The notebook should be divided into sections of about thirty pages each, and each section should be labeled according to your courses, for example, Algebra, Bookkeeping, and Composition.

Beginning with your very first reading assignment, you should start listing and defining those words you think will be important to your understanding of the text. Look, for example, for those words printed in *italics* since italics are almost always used to emphasize important terms. Similarly, the inclusion of a definition next to a word signals that the word is important in understanding the subject.

Words printed in a color different from the surrounding type, underlined, or in any way set off from the text should also be added to your notebook. An author does not set words off from the rest of the text without reason. The author is drawing your attention to these words because they are important.

Once you have found a word you think is necessary to your understanding of the subject, turn to the correct section of your notebook and write down both the word and definition. For review purposes, we suggest that the word and the textbook page number on which it appears be written on the left-hand side of your notebook page; the definition should be put on the right. For example, if we wanted to record two important terms from the computer sciences, *hardware* and *software*, we would organize our notes like this:

hardware, p. 100   computer and machinery attached to it, for example, plotters and printers

software, p. 100   information processed by computer

If you think a word is important but you can't find a definition within the text, try to use context clues to work out an approximate definition. You can put this definition into your notes, circle it, and check it later with the dictionary or your instructor.

If the context doesn't help, turn to the back of the text and see if it contains a list of words and definitions under the heading *Glossary.* Usually words important to understanding the subject will appear in the glossary.

If neither context nor glossary provides a definition, write the word down anyway and continue reading. Once you are through with the reading, you can look in the dictionary or ask your teacher.

Should you have to use the dictionary, be sure to pay attention to the labels indicating the field of study to which a definition applies. Say, for example, the word *flat* was used in a music text, and you didn't know what it meant. If you looked up the word, you would find several definitions, but only the one following the label "Music" would interest you. Obviously, the definition following the label "Painting" would be of little use.

You should add to your notebook every time you have to complete a reading assignment containing a specialized vocabulary. However, making the list is only the first step. The next step is to constantly review the words so that they become part of your vocabulary. You can do this by simply covering the definitions and quizzing yourself. Once you are sure you know a word, mark it with a check and concentrate on the new words that you have added to your list.

The following exercise will give you practice picking out words that are part of the specialized vocabulary used in the study of geology.

EXERCISE 13   **Directions:**   The following pages (Figures 1–1 to 1–3) are taken from a geology text. Read through them and circle the words you think belong to the specialized vocabulary of geology.

When you are finished reading, complete the list we have begun for you below.

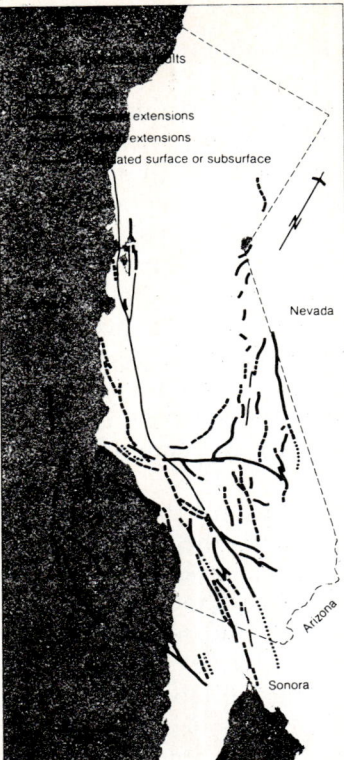

Figure 9-1
Active faults in California.

B"X" become the new position of the original survey line. But the final resting place is not achieved until AX has reached A"Y' and snapped back to A"X', and BX has reached B"Y" and snapped back to B"X".

Describing Earthquakes

The magnitude of an earthquake is the total amount of energy released. The magnitude is not measured directly, but is expressed on an arbitrary scale independent of the place of observation. At the present time the magnitude of an earthquake is most often expressed in terms of the Richter scale (Table 9-1). In contrast, the intensity of an earthquake is the amount of shaking of the earth's surface at any given locality, and may vary with the degree of consolidation of the geological materials at that locality.

Though faulting from an earthquake may extend for tens of miles, the first waves recorded by a seismograph, an instrument for measuring the different parameters of earthquakes, behave as though they originated at a point beneath the surface of the ground. This point, called the focus, may be located from a few kilometers to 600 kilometers below the surface. The epicenter is the point on the surface directly above the focus.

Movement on faults can be lateral (horizontal), vertical, or both. In an earthquake the ground motion is the back-and-forth and/or up-and-down movement of any given spot of ground. Like an ocean wave, a seismic wave moves laterally, but a house on the ground bobs up and down like a cork on rippled water, and is twisted as the groundswell passes beneath it. Acceler-

FIGURE 1–1 From *Geology: The Paradox of Earth and Man,* by Keith Young ©1975 by Houghton Mifflin Company. Used by permission.

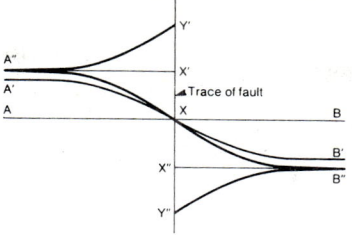

Figure 9–2
Elastic rebound theory of earthquakes. AB is the original line of survey.

Death and Destruction

Between 50,000 and 70,000 people died in the Peruvian earthquake of 1970. The great earthquake at Ardabil, Iran, in 893 or 894 A.D. is thought to have killed at least 100,000 people. To the earthquake specialist, or seismologist, there are not only too many people on earth, but too many in the wrong places. As population continues to expand and urbanization to accelerate, it becomes possible that a single earthquake could be responsible for a million deaths! This figure was nearly reached by the Shensi, China, earthquake of 1556, responsible for an estimated 830,000 deaths.

The relatively large number of deaths in earthquakes of magnitude 7 in the Iranian Plateau is attributable to the design of buildings and villages there. The buildings are constructed of cobbles or adobe, and the mortar is weak and crumbles under the rolling motion of the groundswell. Consequently, houses collapse on their occupants, and many who escape are killed in

ation, the change in the rate of movement of any one spot on the ground per unit of time (Figure 9-3), is usually measured in centimeters or inches per second; with earthquakes of great magnitude, it is expressed in meters or feet per second. Acceleration is described as vertical and horizontal, since the structural design of buildings is different for these two components.

Table 9–1 Energy equivalents of earthquakes compared to the Richter scale of earthquake magnitude. From *California Geology* 22:72, 1969.

Earthquake magnitude	TNT equivalent	Example	Earthquake magnitude	TNT equivalent	Example
1.0	6 ounces		6.0	6,270 tons	
1.5	2 pounds		6.3	15,800 tons	Long Beach, 1933
2.0	13 pounds		6.5	31,550 tons	
2.5	63 pounds		7.0	199,000 tons	
3.0	397 pounds		7.1	250,000 tons	El Centro, California, 1940
3.5	1,000 pounds		7.5	1,000,000 tons	
4.0	6 tons		7.7	1,990,000 tons	Kern County, California, 1952
4.5	32 tons		8.0	6,270,000 tons	
5.0	199 tons		8.2	12,550,000 tons	San Francisco, 1906
5.3	500 tons	San Francisco, 1957	8.5	31,550,000 tons	Anchorage, Alaska, 1964
5.5	1,000 tons		9.0	199,999,000 tons	

FIGURE 1–2 From *Geology: The Paradox of Earth and Man,* by Keith Young ©1975 by Houghton Mifflin Company. Used by permission. Table 9–1 from California Division of Mines and Geology.

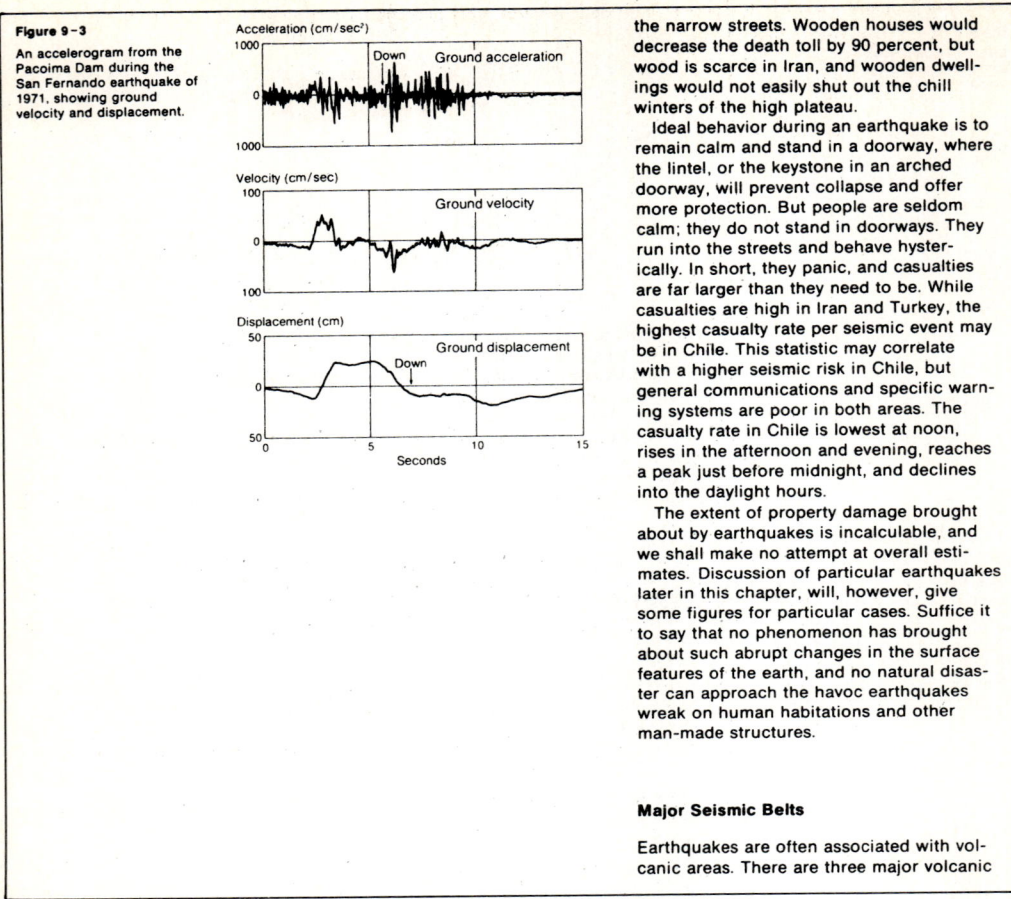

Figure 9-3
An accelerogram from the Pacoima Dam during the San Fernando earthquake of 1971, showing ground velocity and displacement.

the narrow streets. Wooden houses would decrease the death toll by 90 percent, but wood is scarce in Iran, and wooden dwellings would not easily shut out the chill winters of the high plateau.

Ideal behavior during an earthquake is to remain calm and stand in a doorway, where the lintel, or the keystone in an arched doorway, will prevent collapse and offer more protection. But people are seldom calm; they do not stand in doorways. They run into the streets and behave hysterically. In short, they panic, and casualties are far larger than they need to be. While casualties are high in Iran and Turkey, the highest casualty rate per seismic event may be in Chile. This statistic may correlate with a higher seismic risk in Chile, but general communications and specific warning systems are poor in both areas. The casualty rate in Chile is lowest at noon, rises in the afternoon and evening, reaches a peak just before midnight, and declines into the daylight hours.

The extent of property damage brought about by earthquakes is incalculable, and we shall make no attempt at overall estimates. Discussion of particular earthquakes later in this chapter, will, however, give some figures for particular cases. Suffice it to say that no phenomenon has brought about such abrupt changes in the surface features of the earth, and no natural disaster can approach the havoc earthquakes wreak on human habitations and other man-made structures.

Major Seismic Belts

Earthquakes are often associated with volcanic areas. There are three major volcanic

FIGURE 1–3 From *Geology: The Paradox of Earth and Man,* by Keith Young ©1975 by Houghton Mifflin Company. Used by permission.

(1) magnitude - total amount of energy released

Building Your Vocabulary

REVIEW TEST: CHAPTER 1

PART A

The following pages will test your mastery of the words and skills introduced in Chapter 1.

Directions: Read over the following list of words. Then read through the following sentences and fill in the blanks with the correct words.

Some sentences may require you to change the endings of words. For example, you may want the word *malignancy* rather than the word *malignant*. Be sure to change the ending whenever necessary.

Please note that not all the words appear exactly as they did in the chapter. In some cases you may not have seen the word before, but you will have learned the meaning of the prefix, suffix, or root contained in that word. Use this knowledge to select the correct answer. Some of the sentences contain context clues. Make use of them whenever possible.

loquacious	dictum	regicide
eloquence	conflate	invocations
circumvent	pseudonym	malignant
video	ambivalence	spectre
creed	homogeneous	rectitude
synonym	antecedent	scripture
preludes	chronic	ambiguous
clarity	autonomy	
philanthropist	monotheism	

1. This sentence is far too _____. I'm not sure if you mean to agree or disagree.

2. She used a male _____ because she was afraid her public would reject the idea that a woman could create such a cruel and vicious character.

3. If the population is truly _____, members of the community will agree on almost every subject.

4. The old _____ "Neither a borrow nor a lender be" is still good advice.

Review Test: Chapter 1

5. Chopin's _____ serve as a beautiful introduction.

6. My boss is so _____ ; our party line is always busy.

7. He definitely has important ideas but he lacks _____ . As a result no one pays any attention.

8. They have no official _____ . They simply believe that everyone in the world belongs to one universal family.

9. If they attempt to _____ those laws in any way, they will be severely punished. We don't break the law in this town.

10. Every time I turn on the television, I see a sign that says: We are having difficulty with the _____ portion of this program. We may as well get a radio.

11. Whisper is not a _____ for "shout." It's an antonym.

12. Somehow you have managed to _____ two very distinct ideas that should have been kept separate from one another.

13. His _____ was obvious. He didn't know whether to laugh or cry.

14. Although she could have been a well-known _____, she did not like to advertise her generosity.

15. His _____ bouts with bursitis made it difficult for him to join a team. He never knew when he might not be able to play.

16. In this sentence, "John" is a noun, and "he" is a pronoun. Because the word "John" comes before the word "he," it is called the _____.

17. The ancient priests carried out ceremonies that were _____ to the gods. If the gods were pleased, they answered the call.

18. Originally the Egyptians were polytheistic, believing in many different gods, but eventually they also turned to _____.

19. Guilty of _____, the three judges fled to America. They knew their countrymen would never accept the murder of a king.

20. The audience was so moved by the speaker's _____ they did not truly realize what he was saying.

21. She considered herself a perfect example of moral _____; she never for a moment considered the

possibility that her behavior might be improper or incorrect.

22. Clutched in the mummy's hand were the ancient _____, which told the story of his life and death.

23. Whatever it was, real or imaginary, _____ or human, he only knew one thing: he had to get out of there.

24. I pray that the tumor is not _____.

25. The rebels demanded _____ for their country. They refused to have a ruler over them any longer.

PART B

Directions: The following test covers all the words in the section titled "The Story Behind the Word." Read through the description of the word; then fill in the blank with one of the words from the list.

Unlike the preceding exercises, you will not have to change the form of the word.

Use one of the following words to fill in the blanks.

chaos	herculean	chauvinist
tantalize	flora and fauna	ostracize
nemesis	narcissism	utopia
odyssey	bedlam	jingoist
titan	martinet	mesmerized
mentor	quixotic	laconic
atlas	tawdry	

1. This word originally referred to the shapeless mass existing before earth, sea, and air were divided. Today we use it to refer to a situation where disorder rules.

   The word is _____.

2. A goddess who hoped to aid a famous Greek hero disguised herself as a trusted friend. In this way she was able to guide and protect his family without causing suspicion. From the name of that friend, we derived a word that refers to a trusted friend or teacher.

   The word is _____.

3. According to the myth, there was once a king who was cruelly punished by the gods. He was forced to look at fruit and drink placed just out of reach. Today we use his name to say we desire something just out of reach.

   The word is _____.

4. According to Greek mythology, there was a giant who held the earth upon his shoulders. Pictures of the giant frequently appear on maps. Today we use the word taken from his name to describe collections of maps.

   The word is _____.

5. There was a Greek king forced to wander for many years. During that time he had countless adventures. Today we use the word taken from his name to refer to a strange trip or journey.

   The word is _____.

6. There was a hospital in London used to house the mentally ill. The name of the hospital was difficult to pronounce, and there were at least two mispronunciations. From these mispronunciations, we derive a word which describes a place or situation filled with noise or confusion.

   The word is _____.

7. According to mythology, there was a beautiful young man who fell in love with his own reflection. We use the word taken from his name to describe excessive admiration or love for one's own abilities.

   The word is _____.

8. The word originally referred to an imaginary island. Because the people of the island used reason to guide their

lives, the island was the perfect place to live. Today we use the name of that island to refer to a condition, situation, or place that is socially and politically perfect.

The word is _____.

9. The hero of a famous Spanish novel spent his days looking for dragons to slay and lovely ladies to save. He never found them because they didn't exist. Today when we want to talk about a person or idea that is romantic and unrealistic, we use the word taken from his name.

The word is _____.

10. A form of this word originally appeared in a popular eighteenth-century song. The lyrics stressed the need to take up arms. We now use a word taken from the song to describe someone ready and willing to go to war.

The word is _____.

11. Hypnosis became popular in the eighteenth century. All of France came to watch one man in particular because he was able to put people into a strange, sleeplike state. Today we use the word taken from his name to indicate that someone is fascinated almost to the point of being hypnotized.

The word is _____.

12. The Greeks had a goddess ready to punish all who misbehaved, especially those who were overly proud and challenged the authority of the gods. We use the word taken from the name of the goddess to describe someone or something that signals the coming of failure.

The word is _____.

13. The Romans had a goddess of flowers and a god of nature. Today their names are used together to refer to the plants and animals of a particular region or area.

The word is _____.

14. It is said that the Greeks had a hero of extraordinary strength. In order to prove his strength, he performed

several feats that seemed impossible to ordinary men. Today we use the word derived from his name to describe a task demanding a great deal of effort and strength.

The word is _____.

15. Army rule books still recall a seventeenth-century French general who insisted on the strictest possible discipline for his men. The word derived from his name refers to someone who insists on following rules to the letter.

The word is _____.

16. The Greeks used a special method to expel someone from the city of Athens. The name of the person was written on a shell. The person receiving the most votes was forced to leave. We use a word derived from the name of that shell to talk about excluding or shutting someone out from a larger group.

The word is _____.

17. St. Audrey's lace was sold in country fairs. Over time the name for these pieces of lace was mispronounced. From that mispronunciation, we derived a word that means cheap or gawdy.

The word is _____.

18. This word comes from a Greek tribe known for their briefness of speech. We use it to describe someone who doesn't use many words.

The word is _____.

19. Legend has it that Napoleon was worshipped by a soldier who thought his leader could do no wrong. Today we use the word derived from his name to describe someone prejudiced in favor of one country or group.

The word is _____.

20. According to Greek mythology this word originally referred to giants who inhabited the earth before people did. Today we use it to describe a man or woman who is outstanding in a particular field.

   The word is _____ .

Chapter 2

Defining the Terms General *and* Specific

Throughout the following chapters, we will repeatedly use the terms *general* and *specific*. We will use them to help you identify the different kinds of words, phrases, and sentences appearing in your reading. Because we do use the terms so frequently, we are devoting the following chapter to an explanation of what we mean when we say that a word, phrase, or sentence is either **general** or **specific.**

GENERAL AND SPECIFIC WORDS

At the end of this chapter, you'll learn about the difference between general and specific sentences, and we'll explain their relationship to one another. But at this point it is easier to begin with general and specific words. Once you understand the difference between them, it will be easier to distinguish between general and specific sentences.

To discover the difference between general and specific words, think about the two words *apples* and *fruits*. We say that the word *fruits* is more general than the word *apples*. The question now is why do we say that the word *fruits* is more general than the word *apples?*

To answer that question, write the two words on a piece of paper, and using the two words as headings, list all the items that can be included underneath each word. Your lists should look something like this:

apples	**fruits**	
Macintosh	apples	cherries
Golden Delicious	pears	blueberries
Granny	bananas	strawberries
Crab apple	grapes	blackberries
Gravenstein	apricots	raspberries
Jonathan	plums	
Winesap	oranges	

We called *apples* the more specific word because the items to which this word refers are all varieties of the same fruit; they are all about the same size and shape although they do vary in color and taste. We called *fruits* the more general word because the items to which this word refers are all different kinds of fruits; they can have very different sizes, shapes, colors, and tastes.

With this example in mind, we can answer the question we raised before: *General words* **refer to a greater number of things, and the things referred to are more dissimilar than similar;** *specific words* **refer to a lesser number of things, and the things referred to are more similar than dissimilar.**

Using what you just learned about general and specific words, look at the two words *vegetables* and *lettuce*. Decide which word you would call more general and which one you would call more specific. If you have any trouble deciding, make two lists, like the ones we made before. Your lists should look like the following:

vegetables		**lettuce**
tomatoes	lettuce	Romaine
carrots	cabbage	Iceberg
potatoes	spinach	Boston
eggplants	beans	Endive
squash	corn	Chinese

Notice that the list of items appearing under the heading "vegetables" is a great deal longer than the one following the heading "lettuce." The items under "vegetables" are very different from one another; they have different sizes, shapes, and tastes. The items under "lettuce" tend to resemble one another in size, shape, and color. Clearly, we can say that *vegetables* is the more general word.

At this point you are ready to test your understanding of general and specific words.

General and Specific Words   59

EXERCISE 1   **Practice Exercise:** In the following word parts, underline the word that is more general.

1. <u>tool</u>, saw
2. ring, <u>jewelry</u>

Explanation: The word *tool* is more general than the word *saw*. It refers to a greater number of things, and the things to which it refers are quite different from one another. The word *jewelry* is more general than the word *ring*. It refers to a greater number of things, and the things to which it refers are all quite different from one another.

Do the rest of the exercises in the same manner.

1. instruments, violin
2. cigarettes, Marlboro
3. cancer, illness
4. clothing, belt
5. rock, music
6. pine, tree
7. language, Spanish
8. love, emotion
9. carrot, vegetable
10. music, song

EXERCISE 2   **Practice Excercise:** In the following word pairs, underline the word that is more specific.

1. animal, <u>rabbit</u>
2. <u>violet</u>, flower

Explanation: The word *rabbit* is more specific than the word *animal*. It refers to a lesser number of things, and the things to which it refers are more alike than unlike. The word *violet* is more specific than the word *flower*. It refers to a lesser number of things, and the things to which it refers are more alike than unlike.

Do the rest of the exercises in the same manner.

1. building, church
2. tennis, sport

3. literature, newspaper
4. Catholicism, religion
5. food, meat
6. creature, person
7. lake, water
8. game, chess
9. woman, policewoman
10. pollution, smog

LEVELS OF SPECIFICITY

In the previous exercises we compared only two words at a time, but we can expand our comparison to include three words or more. For example, take the words *movie*, *Western*, and *Shane* (title of a famous Western). To illustrate the relationships among these three words, we can draw a ladder and put each word on a rung of the ladder to indicate how general or specific each word is when compared to the other two. Each word will be located on what we call a *different level of specificity*. The word on the top level, or rung, will be the most specific, and the word on the lowest level will be the most general:

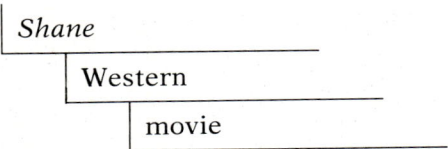

From our illustration, it is clear that *Shane* is the most specific word of the three. It refers to one particular movie. The word *Western* is more general than the word *Shane* because it refers to many different movies, but it is more specific than the word *movie*. The word *movie* refers to all kinds of movies, not just Westerns.

We can also include more than three words on our ladder. For example, we can use a ladder with five rungs, as shown in Diagram 2-1, to illustrate the relationships among the following five words: *animals, four-legged animals, dogs, collies,* and *Lassie.*

Lassie	The word *Lassie* refers only to a dog bearing the name Lassie. All other dogs are excluded from this level.
collies	The word *collies* refers to one particular group of dogs. The members of this group look alike. At this level all other breeds are excluded.
dogs	The word *dogs* refers to one particular group of animals. Members of the group called *dogs* are more similar to one another than are members of the group called *four-legged animals*.
four-legged animals	The term *four-legged animals* refers only to those animals having four legs; all other animals are excluded. Members of the group are more dissimilar than similar.
animals	The word *animals* refers to all kinds of living things. Members of the group called *animals* are very different from one another; they are more dissimilar than similar.

DIAGRAM 2–1

Whenever we speak, think, or write, we use words that if diagrammed would fall on different levels of specificity. We use general words when we want to refer to a great number of things, and we use specific words when we want to put limits around the number of things we want to discuss. When we use general words, we include more things; when we use specific words, we exclude more.

Before we go on to the exercises, we want to emphasize an important point: Words can be more or less specific only in relationship to other words. For example, taken by itself, the word *dogs* seems to be fairly general, but when the word is compared to the word *animals*, it is more specific than general.

EXERCISE 3

Practice Exercise: Three words are given. Arrange them according to specificity. The most specific word goes on the top level, and the most general on the bottom level. You need not write the words. Simply fill in the blanks with the letter standing next to the word.

Defining the Terms General and Specific

1. a. musician
   b. artist
   c. violinist

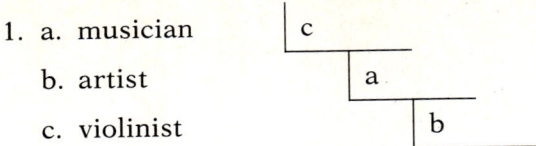

Explanation: The word *artist* can refer to many different kinds of people, for example, painters, sculptors, writers. It is the most general word and therefore appears on the bottom level. *Musician* is somewhat more specific than the word *artist* because it excludes all people not concerned with music. It appears on the middle rung. *Violinist* is the most specific word because it refers to only those people who play the violin.

Do the rest of the exercises in the same manner.

1. a. literature
   b. book
   c. *Uncle Tom's Cabin*

2. a. politician
   b. person
   c. Kennedy

3. a. army
   b. military
   c. United States Army

4. a. drugs
   b. penicillin
   c. antibiotics

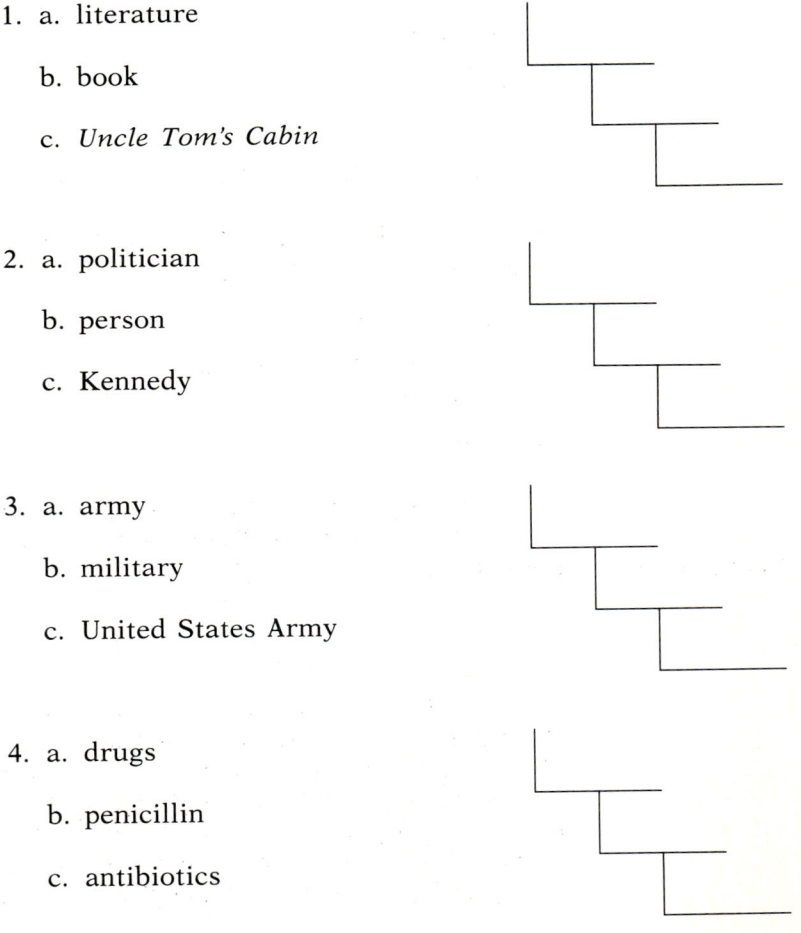

Levels of Specificity 63

5. a. entertainer

   b. Bruce Springsteen

   c. singer

6. a. gin

   b. liquor

   c. liquids

7. a. flu

   b. diseases

   c. Hong Kong flu

8. a. clothing

   b. coat

   c. raincoat

9. a. detergent

   b. products

   c. Tide

10. a. continent

    b. Venezuela

    c. South America

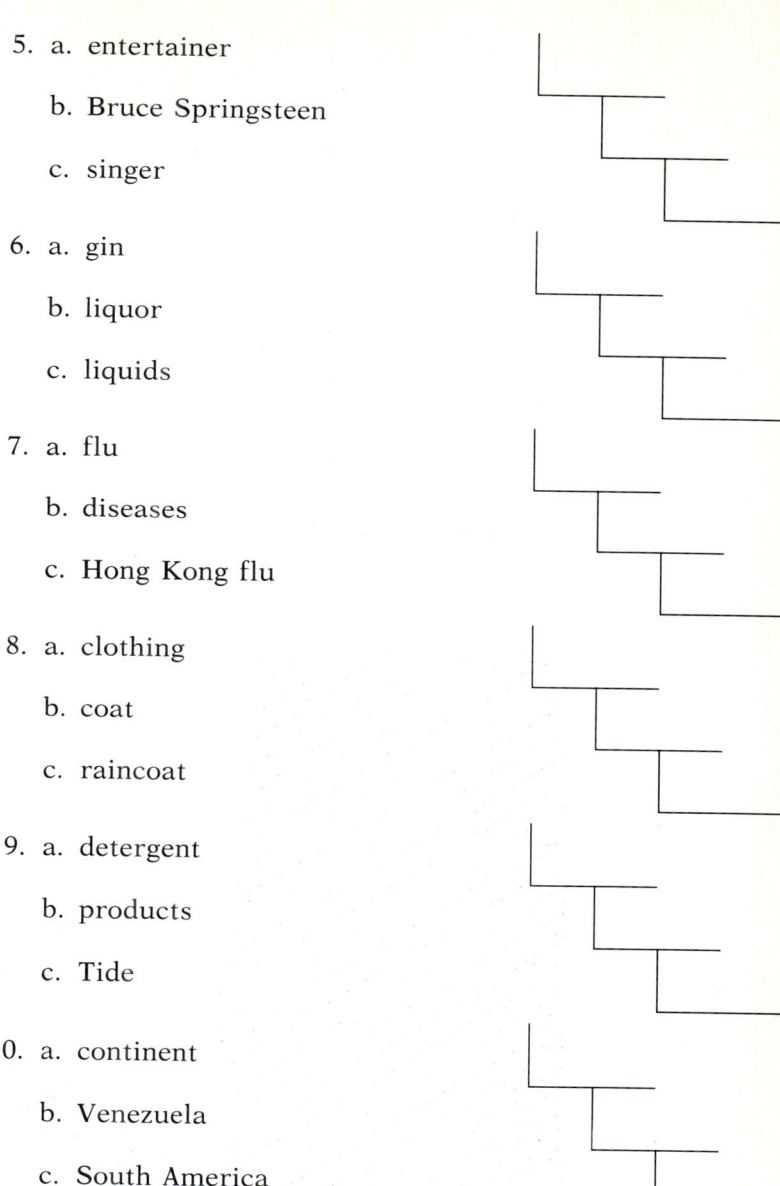

EXERCISE 4   **Practice Exercise:** In this exercise you are to put words on the blank rungs. The words you add should be more specific than the words on the lower rungs and more general than the words on the higher rungs.

Be sure that the sequence of words is logical. For example, if the words on the first two levels are *living things* and *human beings,* you cannot fill in the third level with the word *cats* because the term *human beings* has already excluded all other animals.

1.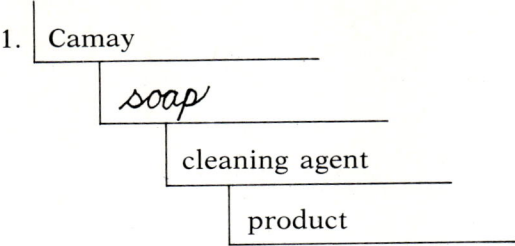

Explanation: We have written in the word *soap* because it is more general than the word *Camay* and more specific than the word *cleaning agent.*

Do the rest of the exercises in the same manner.

1.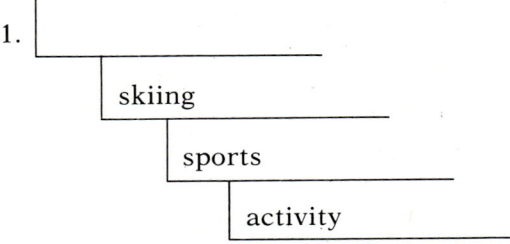

2.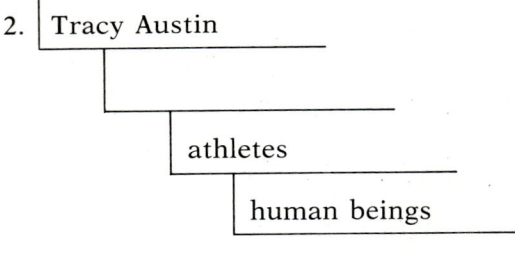

3.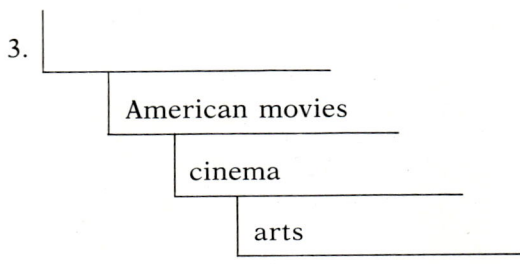

Levels of Specificity

4.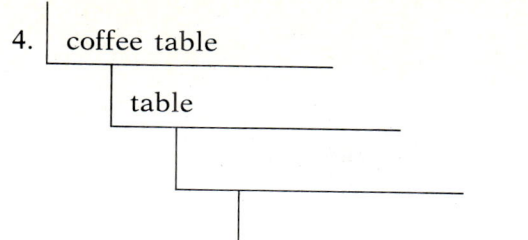

5.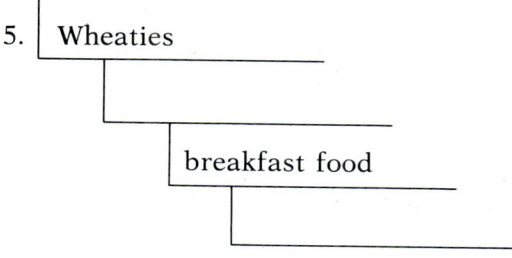

6.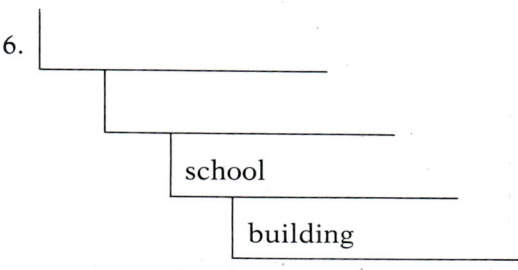

7.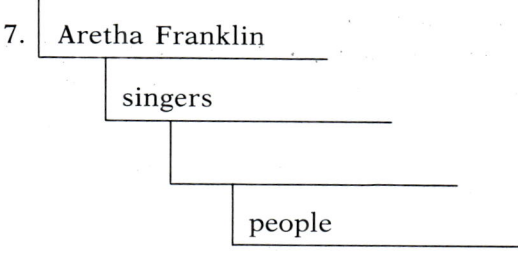

8.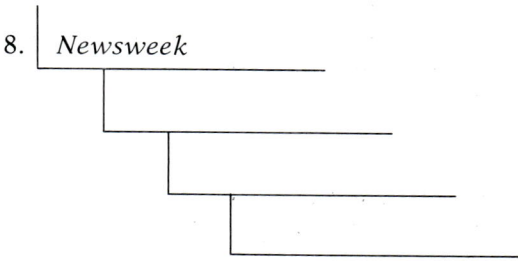

Defining the Terms General and Specific

Aretha Franklin, the queen of soul.

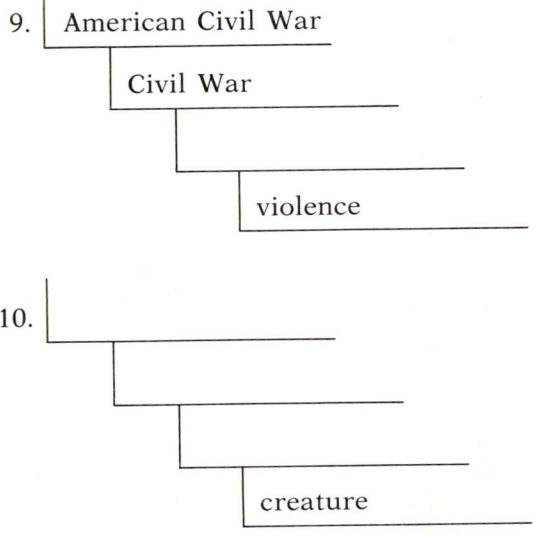

9. American Civil War / Civil War / violence

10. _____ / _____ / creature

Levels of Specificity

Throughout the preceding pages, we've talked about words that are more general and more specific, but now think for a moment about the words *fruit, apple,* and *peach.* Obviously, *fruit* is the more general word of the three, but what about the other two words? We cannot say that the word *apple* is more specific than the word *peach,* or vice versa. In such a case, we would have to say that the words are equally specific or on the same level of specificity.

EXERCISE 5

Practice Exercise: In the following exercise write an *S* after the two words that are on the same level of specificity. Note: There may not always be two words on the same level of specificity.

1. church
   building
   St. Peter's in Rome   <u>S</u>
   St. Mark's in Venice   <u>S</u>

Explanation: *Building* is obviously more general than *church,* and the two names of churches are equally specific.

Do the rest of the exercises in the same manner.

1. object
   knife
   weapon
   gun
2. clothing
   dress
   coat
   wedding dress
3. food
   meat
   hot dogs
   hamburgers
4. machine
   automobile
   Ford
   motorcycle

5. creature
   rabbit
   animal
   deer

6. entertainment
   television
   soap opera
   General Hospital

7. communication
   French
   English
   language

8. liquid
   Scotch
   drink
   gin

9. gambling
   gin rummy
   cards
   poker

10. machine
    Ford
    car
    Ford Mustang

THE USE OF MODIFIERS

FIRST MAN
(to his shy friend)
That woman over there smiled at you.

SECOND MAN
Are you sure she was really looking at me? Maybe she'd dance with me. I'll go over there and ask her. Which woman was it?

FIRST MAN
The one over there.

SECOND MAN
There are five women over there; which one was it?

FIRST MAN
The one over there.

Had this conversation taken place in real life, the first man would have been more exact in his description once he realized that his friend wanted to dance. He would have said that the woman who smiled wore black slacks or a purple scarf. He would have selected some physical detail that separated her from the other women with whom she stood.

However, we did not include the above dialogue to illustrate how difficult it is to find a dance partner. Instead, the dialogue shows that single words or groups of words, called *phrases*, are frequently needed to help increase specificity. These words or phrases are called *modifiers*, and they help make words more specific.

Take, for example, the word *war*. Alone, the word can refer to many different kinds of conflicts. But if we add the word *civil*, we are talking about a particular kind of war, one where the people of the same country fight one another. If we further add the word *American* to make the phrase "American Civil War," we have made it clear that we are talking about one particular war in America's history.

As the preceding example illustrates, modifiers help increase specificity by eliminating all those things not under discussion. You'll understand what we mean by that statement if you imagine the following situation. Suppose that you were registering for spring semester and saw that a course called "Drawing" was offered. You would probably not be sure if you wanted or needed the course because the word *drawing* can refer to the drawing of people or objects. Similarly, a course in drawing could be introductory or advanced. However, if the word *drawing* were changed to the phrase "Advanced Mechanical Drawing," you would have a much better idea of what the course offered, and you would know whether or not you wanted to take it.

Phrases, like words, can also be more or less specific, as you can see from the following example:

1. students in school
2. students in college

Phrase 1 is more general than phrase 2. It refers to all the students in school, and the students could be five years old or fifty. The second phrase is more specific because it eliminates all those students who are not attending college.

EXERCISE 6   Practice Exercise: Underline the more specific phrase.

1. a. an American male wearing clothes
   b. <u>an American male wearing Bermuda shorts</u>

Explanation: Phrase *a* is more general than phrase *b*. Phrase *a* can refer to an American male wearing any kind of clothing. Phrase *b* refers only to those American males wearing Bermuda shorts; all other males are excluded.

Do the rest of the exercises in the same manner.

1. a. musicians playing music
   b. musicians playing rock

2. a. the woman carrying traveler's checks
   b. the woman carrying American Express checks

3. a. the terrible weather
   b. the stormy weather

4. a. underneath the table
   b. near the table

5. a. the visitor from the South
   b. the visitor from Atlanta, Georgia

6. a. the tall man
   b. the six-foot-tall man

7. a. the swerving traffic
   b. the dangerous traffic

8. a. the unhappy man
   b. the weeping man

9. a. the European woman
   b. the Italian woman

10. a. the female walking from the room
    b. the girl walking from the room

EXERCISE 7

Practice Exercise: Put the most specific phrase on the top rung of the ladder and the most general on the bottom rung. You need not write out the phrase; instead, fill in the blanks with the letters next to the phrases.

The Use of Modifiers

1. a. students in school today
   b. black students on scholarship today
   c. students on scholarship today

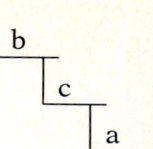

Explanation: Phrase *a* is the most general. It can refer to all students in school at the present time. Phrase *c* appears on the middle rung because it is more specific. It refers only to those students on scholarship; all others are excluded. Phrase *b* is the most specific. It further limits possible interpretations. The phrase refers only to those black students on scholarship; all others are excluded.

Do the rest of the exercises in the same manner.

1. a. young women today
   b. American women today
   c. today's young American college women

2. a. popular American music
   b. rock-and-roll
   c. the songs of Elvis Presley

3. a. problems in going to college
   b. difficulties of a freshman year in college
   c. adjusting to a roommate during the freshman year

4. a. modern American movies about social problems
   b. modern American movies about divorce
   c. modern American movies about family problems

5. a. the problems of the young
   b. suffering from adolescent acne
   c. the problems of adolescence

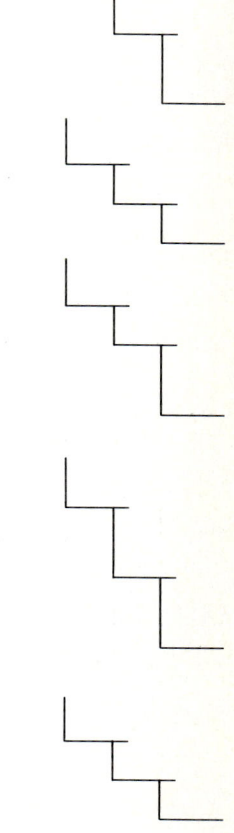

6. a. the beagle
   b. the old beagle
   c. the dog

7. a. problems of a modern society
   b. pollution in a modern industrialized society
   c. problems of a modern industrialized society

8. a. the young soldier
   b. the young man
   c. the young corporal

9. a. popular sports
   b. soccer and tennis in Europe
   c. popular sports in Europe

10. a. trends in films
    b. trends in current films
    c. trends in current American films

In the following exercise we ask you to make the phrases more specific. There are two ways to do this. First of all you can add words. For example, the phrase *the old man* becomes more specific if we add just three words: *... with a limp.* This phrase is more specific because it excludes all those elderly men who do not limp.

Specificity can also be increased by simply changing a single word. The phrase *terrible weather,* for example, can refer to several different kinds of weather. But if we change the word *terrible* to *snowy,* it is clear that very hot or rainy weather has been excluded.

EXERCISE 8

Practice Exercise: In the following exercise, we provide a general phrase. Use your imagination and make the phrase more specific. You can add words or merely change a word or two.

1. a. the old house   (general)
   b. <u>The old house with a hole in the roof</u>   (more specific)

Explanation: Phrase *b* is more specific because it further limits or restricts the first phrase. There may be several old houses before us, but we are concerned with only the one that has a hole in the roof.

Do the rest of the exercises in the same manner.

1. the young singer

_____

2. the terrible food

_____

3. the tall man

_____

4. the awful weather

_____

5. the old clothes

_____

GENERAL AND SPECIFIC SENTENCES

Up to this point, Chapter 2 has dealt with individual words and phrases, but that was only preparation for work with complete sentences. Sentences, like individual words or phrases, can be more general or more specific. Take, for example, the following two sentences:

1. The woman left the room.
2. The woman stormed angrily from the room.

Both sentences describe an event, but sentence 1 is more general than sentence 2 because sentence 1 is open to a variety of interpretations. We know that a woman left the room, but she might have walked out slowly or left quickly; she might have been happy or sad. However, when we say "the woman stormed angrily from the room," we know immediately that she left quickly and was not happy. Sentence 2 is the more specific because it allows us to eliminate possible interpretations.

The following exercises will give you more practice seeing the difference between general and specific sentences.

EXERCISE 9

Practice Exercise: In this exercise a general sentence is given. Change only a word or two to make a more specific version of the same sentence.

1. She *drank* a glass of gin.   (general)

   She *sipped* a glass of gin.   (more specific)

Explanation: The addition of the word *sipped* makes the sentence more specific. We know exactly how she drank.

In this case we had to change only one word to make the sentence describe her actions more specifically. In the following exercises concentrate on changing the italicized word or words, although you may have to change one or two other words to write a correct sentence.

Do the rest of the exercises in the same manner.

1. He was *pleased* with his gift.

___

2. Her father was a *bad man*.

___

3. The way she *eats* her food makes me sick.

___

4. The ex-soldier *walked* to the platform.

___

5. The movie was *good*.

___

General and Specific Sentences 75

EXERCISE 10 **Practice Exercise:** In this exercise description of an action or attitude is given. Change only a word or two to write a more general version of the same sentence.

1. He *stared* at the strangely dressed man.   (more specific)
   He *looked* at the strangely dressed man.   (general)

Explanation: Changing the word *stared* to *looked* makes the sentence more general. It can now be interpreted in several different ways. We do not know if he just glanced at the strangely dressed man or if he looked him over quite thoroughly.

Do the rest of the exercises in the same manner.

1. She *whispered* to the man next to her.

___

2. He was *miserable* over the loss of his wife.

___

3. The slaves were constantly *overworked and hungry*.

___

4. Her parents were *furious* about her behavior.

___

5. The elderly man was dressed *in a worn-out overcoat*.

___

EXERCISE 11 **Practice Exercise:** Circle the letter of the sentence that is more specific.

1. (a) The house was quite old.
   (b) The house was built in the seventeenth century. *[b circled]*
2. (a) Smoking endangers your health.
   (b) Smoking causes lung cancer. *[b circled]*

3. (a) The book is very good.
   (ⓑ) The plot of the book is excellent.

Explanation: The sentences following the letter *b* are all more specific; for example, sentence *b* in the first item tells us exactly how old the house is. Sentence *b* in item 2 tells us exactly how smoking can endanger health. Sentence *b* in item 3 describes exactly what about the book was good. All the sentences following the letter *a* are more general; they are open to several interpretations.

Do the rest of the exercises in the same manner.

1. (a) Thomas Jefferson was born in Virginia.
   (b) Thomas Jefferson was a Southerner.

2. (a) To learn a foreign language quickly requires at least four hours' study a day.
   (b) To learn a foreign language quickly requires hard work.

3. (a) A good teacher must have several very special characteristics.
   (b) A good teacher must be patient and good humored.

4. (a) The sight of a uniform has strange effects on many people.
   (b) Many people are frightened by the sight of a uniform, and they behave like children in front of a stern parent.

5. (a) Computers can store and locate huge amounts of information.
   (b) Computers are extremely useful.

6. (a) Overeating can indicate that a person feels nervous and insecure.
   (b) Excessive eating can be a symptom of more than hunger.

7. (a) Large automobiles have several disadvantages.
   (b) Large automobiles are difficult to park, require too much gas, and are expensive to maintain.

8. (a) The works of Aristotle range over a wide variety of subjects.

   (b) Aristotle wrote about psychology, biology, physics, astronomy, politics, and poetry.

9. (a) Charles VII, king of France, would not have become king without the help of Joan of Arc, but still he did not lift a hand to help save her from the stake.

   (b) Charles VII, king of France, would not have become king without the help of Joan of Arc, but still he betrayed her.

10. (a) The role women played during World War II contributed to the change in their status after the war.

    (b) The widespread employment of women during World War II helped many people realize that women's place did not have to be in the home.

EXERCISE 12   **Practice Exercise:** One general sentence is provided. In the blank that follows the general sentence, write a more specific version of the same sentence.

1. The man liked bright clothing.
   <u>The man favored red, yellow, and orange sports shirts.</u>

Explanation: The second sentence is more specific than the first. It tells us exactly what kind of clothing (sport shirts) and what bright colors (red, yellow, and orange) he preferred.

Do the rest of the exercises in the same manner.

1. The Mafia chief wore jewelry.

2. The man talked a lot.

3. The woman smoked a lot.

4. The president of the United States is a powerful person.

_____

5. The ballplayer's uniform was dirty.

_____

EXERCISE 13

Practice Exercise: One specific sentence is provided. In the blank that follows the specific sentence, write a more general version of the same sentence.

1. Too much exposure to the sun may be one cause of skin cancer.
   <u>Too much exposure to the sun is not good for anyone.</u>

Explanation: The first sentence is more specific. It tells us exactly what problem too much exposure to the sun may cause. The second sentence is more general. Although we know that too much exposure to the sun is not good, we do not know why it is not good. The second sentence is open to several different interpretations.

Do the rest of the exercises in the same manner.

1. Many people have found that playing tennis helps decrease general anxiety.

_____

2. Gossip can ruin a person's reputation.

_____

3. Reading is one way to learn how other people think and feel.

_____

4. During the winter months, more than a few enthusiastic skiers return home with twisted ankles and badly bruised knees.

_____

5. Modern movies stress rape, robbery, and murder.

THE RELATIONSHIP BETWEEN GENERAL AND SPECIFIC SENTENCES

Almost every textbook you read will consist of general and specific sentences. They work together to explain an author's ideas. **General sentences make a statement about a number of different but in some way related events, ideas, people, or things. Specific sentences help limit the number of ways in which the more general sentence can be interpreted; they also help develop and support the statement made in the general sentence.** We can use the following excerpt from a paragraph as illustration:

> Deep in debt, working land they didn't own, the Southern farmers were completely flattened by the postwar agricultural depression. Prices plunged across the board; the price of cotton dropped in half from 1873 to 1877, until in some instances it sold for less than it cost to raise.[1]

In the sample paragraph the author cannot possibly list individually all the farmers affected by the Civil War; nor is it possible to explain exactly what happened to each and every farmer in the South. Instead, the author uses a general sentence that sums up the different experiences of those many farmers who suffered from the war, and we learn that they "were completely flattened."

But there are several ways to interpret the phrase "were completely flattened," and the addition of the second sentence in the paragraph puts limits on those interpretations. When the author says that the farmers "were completely flattened," he means that they were barely able to make a living because the price of their most important crop had fallen.

The second sentence in the paragraph also helps make the first sentence more convincing. Once we know that the price of cotton had plunged and that growing cotton was, in some cases, no longer profitable, we are ready to believe that the farmers "were completely flattened."

---

[1] From *History of the United States* by Harvey Wasserman. Copyright ©1972 by Harper, Colophon Books. Reprinted by permission.

For decades, alligator weed had been surely, and not so slowly, taking over the lakes and rivers of much of the South. It fouled the boat propellers and knocked water skiers off their balance; it grew so thick in some lakes that a person could walk on the water. For twenty years, the Army Corps of Engineers had spent $4 million annually on herbicides to control the weed — and failed.[2]

This sample paragraph begins with a general sentence. This sentence tells us that alligator weed has been taking over the lakes and rivers in the South. Sentences 2 and 3 in the paragraph are more specific, and they tell us exactly what the author means by claiming that the weed has been taking over the lakes and rivers. At the same time these sentences make the first statement more convincing because they provide evidence that the weed is all over.

The following exercises will give you more practice analyzing the relationship between general and specific sentences.

EXERCISE 14

Practice Exercise: We have provided one general sentence. Read it and decide which of the specific sentences that follow help clarify and support that statement.

1. The production of the movie *The Exorcist* was haunted by difficulties.
   (a) During the filming, director William Friedkin was forced to increase the original budget by six million dollars.
   (b) The set of the film was the scene of countless little accidents.
   (c) The book *The Exorcist* is said to have been based on an incident taken from real life.
   (d) Many parents refused to allow their children to see the film.
   (e) William Peter Blatty, the author of *The Exorcist*, and director Friedkin did not part on friendly terms: At one point Blatty wanted Friedkin fired.
   (f) Many people who viewed the film were overcome with nausea and dizziness.

Explanation: The initial general sentence says that the production of *The Exorcist* was haunted by difficulties. Since that

[2]"Chew, Beetle, Chew," *Newsweek*, September 2, 1974, p. 76. Copyright 1974 by Newsweek, Inc. All rights reserved. Reprinted by permission.

sentence could mean a great many things, we have to look for specific sentences that would clarify it. Sentences *a, b,* and *e* provide that clarification. Sentence *c* was not selected because it deals with the book, not the movie. Sentences *d* and *f* were not selected because they do not deal with the production of the film.

Do the rest of the exercises in the same manner.

1. In 1981, the appointment of the first woman justice of the Supreme Court of the United States was an event of extraordinary importance.
   (a) For 191 years, women had been excluded from the Supreme Court.
   (b) Judge Sandra Day O'Connor from Arizona was appointed to the Supreme Court.
   (c) *First Monday in October* was a hit play about the conflict between two Supreme Court justices, one a male liberal, the other a female conservative.
   (d) Arizona is the only state without Medicaid.
   (e) Prior to Judge O'Connor's appointment to the bench, women's issues like sex discrimination and affirmative action* were decided by an all male court.
   (f) Judge O'Connor is the mother of three sons.

2. The 1981 eruption of the Mount St. Helens volcano was one of the largest volcanic eruptions the world has ever seen.
   (a) The Mount St. Helens eruption was more powerful than any nuclear device ever exploded.
   (b) Mount St. Helens has erupted at least twenty times over the past four thousand years.
   (c) Mount St. Helens is one of the most active volcanoes in the world.
   (d) Only two eruptions have ever surpassed that of Mount St. Helens, the eruption of Krakatoa in Indonesia and Katmai in Alaska.
   (e) The power of the Mount St. Helens eruption was more than the total output of all the electric power stations in the United States.
   (f) Experts predict that the volcano may erupt again before the end of the century.

*affirmative action: policies employers must follow in order to encourage the hiring of women and minorities and to discourage discrimination.

Sandra Day O'Connor, the first woman justice appointed to the Supreme Court in 1981.

3. The fear of rabies is well founded.
   (a) Rabies is found in a wide variety of animals, but dogs are the most frequent carriers.
   (b) Few people recover from the disease once the symptoms have appeared.
   (c) Rabies has an ancient history, and there are references to it as early as 700 B.C.
   (d) Once the disease takes hold the victim can neither stand nor lie down comfortably.

The Relationship between General and Specific Sentences

- (e) Recently scientists have begun to improve upon the painful treatment for rabies, and the new vaccine requires only six doses rather than the standard twenty-one.
- (f) In the early stages of rabies, a dog is likely to appear tired and nervous. It will try to hide, even from its master.

4. Many people believe that mystery stories are a product of modern times, but the mystery story actually has a long history.
   - (a). Historians of the detective story claim to have found elements of mystery fiction in the Bible.
   - (b). Dorothy Sayers was for some years an enormously popular mystery writer.
   - (c) Poe's "The Murders in the Rue Morgue," published in 1841, presented the classic mystery problem of a dead body found in a room that was completely sealed.
   - (d). Mystery historians are continuously haggling over what books may or may not be classified as mystery stories.
   - (e). In the nineteenth century, Charles Dickens created a highly amusing character, Inspector Bucket, who, in a general way, resembles many modern-day detectives.
   - (f) Many mystery writers do not use their own names.

5. Mohammed, spiritual leader of the Moslems,* had an enormous infuence on the world's history.
   - (a) Mohammed was born somewhere around the year A.D. 570.
   - (b) Mohammed founded a religion, Islam, which was to become Christianity's greatest rival.
   - (c) Until his fortieth year, Mohammed lived the ordinary life of a well-to-do merchant.
   - (d). Mohammed was the source of the Koran, the sacred text of the Moslems, which is still accepted by the Moslems as the final authority on all spiritual matters.
   - (e) Mohammed founded an empire that included lands in Syria, northern Africa, and Spain.
   - (f) Mohammed was born in Mecca.

*Moslems: believers in Islam, a religion based on the teachings of Mohammed. Moslems believe in one God (Allah). They also believe in paradise and hell

EXERCISE 15 Practice Exercise: We have provided three specific sentences. After reading them, decide which general sentence they could support.

1. a. Teeth in the front of the mouth are called *incisors;* they cut large pieces of food into smaller ones.
   b. The molars crush and grind food.
   c. We use our canine teeth when we eat the meat off of bones.

General Sentences

(1) Teeth are subject to decay.
(2) With the correct dental care, human beings can retain their teeth on into old age.
(3) The teeth are important because they prepare food for digestion.

Explanation: The correct answer is 3. Sentence 1 is not a possible answer because none of the sentences mention decay. Sentence 2 is not a possible answer because none of the sentences even mentions dental care.

Do the rest of the exercises in the same manner.

1. a. Often when students go to register, all the classes they have chosen are closed out.
   b. Lines are often a mile long during registration.
   c. The unlucky student often ends up with a schedule that features classes beginning at eight and ending at five.

General Sentences

(1) Eight o'clock classes are a disaster.
(2) College life is extremely difficult.
(3) Registration is not always a pleasant process.

2. a. When Sly of "Sly and the Family Stone," a famous rock group, got married, the ceremony was performed on the stage of Madison Square Garden.
   b. Twenty-three thousand fans attended.
   c. The six-tiered wedding cake was topped by a gold record.

The Relationship between General and Specific Sentences

General Sentences

(1) Everyone had a terrific time at Sly's wedding.

(2) The wedding was not a success.

(3) Sly Stone, whose real name is Sylvester Stewart, did not have a traditional wedding.

3. a. The citizens of Sparta, a city-state of ancient Greece, were not allowed to become farmers; they were made to train as warriors and nothing else.
   b. Family life in Sparta was severely limited because both boys and girls spent long hours in physical training.
   c. From the ages of seven to thirty, boys received instruction in the art of waging war.

General Sentences

(1) The Spartans were obedient to the laws of their land.

(2) The Spartan life was hard and devoted to war.

(3) Spartan men and women were known for their heroism in war.

4. a. During World War II German invaders devastated some of Russia's richest agricultural regions.
   b. According to official reports, more than seven million Russians were killed while defending their country against German attacks.
   c. Many Russians lost their lives in concentration camps.

General Sentences

(1) The Russians suffered heavy losses in World War II.

(2) The Russians suffered more losses than any of the other great powers.

(3) Russia was not prepared for the Germans' attack.

5. a. John Keats, one of England's most romantic poets, died at the age of twenty-six.
   b. Percy Bysshe Shelley, admirer of Keats and poet in his own right, died when he was thirty.
   c. George Gordon, Lord Byron, one of the most well known of the romantic poets, died when he was only thirty-six.

General Sentences

(1) Many of the romantic poets died when they were very young.

(2) The romantic poets lived short, exciting lives.

(3) Keats, Shelley, and Byron were all good friends.

The following exercises will give you some practice writing both general and specific sentences.

EXERCISE 16

Practice Exercise: We have provided three specific sentences. In the blank that follows, write one general sentence that these specific sentences could support and clarify.

1. a. Men and women who wish to become successful professional athletes must be ready to spend long hours in rigorous training.
   b. Professional athletes have to watch their diets constantly; they cannot afford to be either too fat or too thin.
   c. Many professional athletes find that they have little time for a personal life because their profession demands too much time and energy.

General Sentence

Most professional athletes lead difficult and demanding lives.

Explanation: The sentence written in the blank is quite general as the two words *difficult* and *demanding* can be interpreted in a variety of ways. The three specific sentences, however, make it clear just what is difficult and demanding about an athlete's life.

Do the rest of the exercises in the same manner.

1. a. Automobile accidents occur quite frequently in rainy weather.
   b. Snow- and ice-covered streets make it easy for automobiles to skid.
   c. A thick fog can make safe driving almost impossible.

General Sentence

The Relationship between General and Specific Sentences 87

Most professional athletes lead difficult and demanding lives.

2. a. Many articles have been written about the poor treatment some elderly people receive when they are forced to live in nursing homes.
   b. Frequently elderly people find it difficult to find work because after a certain age they are considered unemployable.
   c. Because so many people fear death and aging, they try to avoid the elderly, who are living reminders that everyone must grow old and die.

General Sentence

3. a. There is a great deal of evidence that smoking causes cancer.
   b. There is more and more evidence that smoking contributes to heart disease.
   c. Anyone with emphysema should not smoke because smoking only aggravates the disease.

General Sentence

_____

_____

4. a. Just like human beings, dogs can become mentally ill.
   b. Lung cancer has increased not only in humans but also in dogs.
   c. Dogs have been known to suffer from epilepsy, hysteria, and depression.

General Sentence

_____

_____

5. a. Refined sugar is a well-known cause of tooth decay.
   b. Many investigators believe that eating large quantities of refined sugar increases the chance of cholesterol deposits.
   c. Refined sugar is a source of calories, but it is not a source of vitamins and minerals.

General Sentence

_____

_____

EXERCISE 17 Practice Exercise: We have provided one general sentence. You are to write out three specific sentences that clarify and support the general sentence.

The Relationship between General and Specific Sentences

1. The freshman year in college is almost always a frustrating one.

Specific Sentences

a. Many freshmen have to get used to living with a roommate; they may even have to get used to living with a roommate they don't like.
b. The workload, for many freshmen, seems to be impossibly heavy.
c. Adjusting to being away from family and friends for long periods of time is, for many, very difficult.

Explanation: The general sentence can be interpreted in many ways, but the specific sentences that follow explain exactly what the author means by maintaining that freshman year is frustrating. The specific sentences also help convince us that the first year is frustrating.

Do the rest of the exercises in the same manner.

1. Many movies seem to specialize in murder and violence.

a. _____

b. _____

c. _____

2. It is good for children to have pets.

a. _____

b. _____

c. _____

_____

3. People are destroying the environment.

a. _____

_____

b. _____

_____

c. _____

_____

4. Many people claim it is a good idea to keep a daily journal or diary of experiences.

a. _____

_____

b. _____

_____

c. _____

_____

5. Parents and children sometimes have difficulty communicating with one another.

a. _____

_____

b. _____

_____

c. _____

    The following pages will test your mastery of Chapter 2. If you complete the test without difficulty, go on to Chapter 3. If you miss more than three of the questions, you may want to review earlier parts of this chapter.

REVIEW TEST: CHAPTER 2

PART A

1. The word *cat* is more specific than the word *animal*. How would you describe the difference between the two words?

2. Here are three words: *exercise, aerobic dancing, dancing*. Arrange them according to specificity. Place the most specific word on the top level, and the most general on the bottom level.

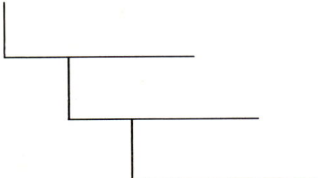

3. What is the function of a *modifier?*

4. Which of the following sentences is more specific, *a, b,* or *c*?
   (a) The war had hurt the young soldier's health.
   (b) After the war, he had difficulty sleeping, and he was troubled by bad dreams.
   (c) The young man had suffered a great deal.

5. An author uses *general* sentences to talk about a number of different but in some way related events, ideas, people, or things. What is the purpose of *specific* sentences?

PART B

Directions: In each group of sentences, there is one sentence that is more general than all the others. The rest of the sentences explain or support the idea contained in the more general sentence. Select the general sentence.

1. (a) There are at least two hundred separate bones in the human body.
   (b) The bones of the head are separated at the time of birth, but they slowly grow together to protect the brain.

(c) The skeleton of the human body is an enormously complex structure.

(d) The bones of the skeleton are of two distinct types.

(e) The bones of the skeleton also manufacture blood.

(f). The exact number of bones in the skeleton differs with each person.

2. (a) Users of amphetamines mistakenly believe that all their problems have been solved.

(b) People who use large doses of amphetamines have trouble sleeping.

(c) Those who use amphetamines often find that they are unable to stop talking.

(d) Under the influence of amphetamines, people usually feel they are working more efficiently; unfortunately this impression is seldom accurate.

(e) Amphetamines, also known as *speed*, are dangerous drugs, but not enough people are aware of their effects.

(f) Loss of appetite is another common side effect.

3. (a) In the African country of Dahomey, musical historians were carefully trained to preserve important records.

(b) African music tells a very special story; it literally* sings the history of the African people.

(c) Men followed soldiers to war and recorded great actions in song.

(d) In the not so distant past, many African countries trained men and women to be living books who recorded important events in song.

(e) If the songs contained important information, the musicians had to learn them in secret.

(f) During Sudanese festivals, singers recited the history of the nation.

4. (a) The human nervous system is highly developed and extremely complex.

(b) The central nervous system includes the brain and spinal cord.

(c) There are three parts to the human nervous system.

(d) The autonomic nervous system includes nerves that serve the internal organs.

*literally: really, actually, in reality

(e) The peripheral nervous system includes the spinal and cranial nerves.

(f) The brain is the control center of the human nervous system.

5. (a) John Merrick could not go into the street without being mobbed.

(b) Before he came under a doctor's care, John Merrick was exhibited in the circus.

(c) Merrick could not sleep like other people; he had to sit up with his heavy head resting on his knees.

(d) The head of the Elephant Man was enormous and misshapen.

(e) John Merrick, also known as "the Elephant Man," had a short and terribly difficult life.

(f) Although the last years of his life were spent in pleasant surroundings, Merrick never forgot the brutal beatings and terrible humiliation of his life in the circus.

6. (a) Cirrus clouds are the highest clouds in the sky; they are thin and feathery.

(b) Stratus clouds resemble fog, but they are not so close to the ground.

(c) When cumulus clouds darken, there is a storm ahead.

(d) Cumulus clouds are perhaps the most beautiful; they are very white, light, and fluffy clouds.

(e) Scientists actually classify clouds into ten major groups, but the three most familiar are: (1) cirrus, (2) stratus, and (3) cumulus.

(f) There is much to learn about clouds.

7. (a) The oldest extant* poem by a black American is "Bars Flight" by Lucy Terry.

(b) Because Terry's poem said little about the black experience, most critics cite Jupiter Harmon as the first American black to have a poem printed.

(c) Jupiter Harmon's first poem, "An Evening Thought," is dated December 25, 1760.

*extant: in existence, not destroyed

(d) As a written form, black poetry began somewhere around the middle of the eighteenth century.

(e) Black poet Phillis Wheatley used her poems to praise liberty and damn slavery.

(f) Early poets, like Moses Horton, frequently employed the rhythms of hymns.

8. (a) Tornadoes are clouds that take the shape of funnels; they reach all the way to the ground, doing enormous damage.

   (b) Although all storms have fearful aspects, tornadoes are the most frightening.

   (c) Winds within the funnel of the tornado can reach speeds of more than several hundred miles per hour.

   (d) Luckily tornadoes are short-lived, if they were not damage could be even greater.

   (e) Sometimes buildings actually blow up as the funnel of the tornado passes over them.

   (f) The heavy rain and hail that accompany a tornado also do much damage.

9. (a) *The Female Man* by Joanna Russ tells the story of Whileaway, a world where men have been dead for thousands of years.

   (b) In the *Left Hand of Darkness* Ursula Le Guin has created a world where men and women can be "in kemmer," that is, both can become pregnant.

   (c) For years science fiction was thought to be the province* of men, but in the last twenty years women have become important figures in the field.

   (d) *New Women of Wonder* concentrates almost entirely on what women will be like in the year 2000.

   (e) In Dorothy Bryant's *The Kin of Ata Are Waiting for You* only dreams are important; reality doesn't exist.

   (f) On Anarres, the setting for Ursula Le Guin's *The Dispossessed,* there is no such thing as money.

---

*province: territory, field

10. (a) The brain is the enlarged end of the spinal cord.
    (b) Although many animals have larger brains, the brain of a human has more surface area.
    (c) It has been said that a computer, built to be as complex as the brain, would require the Pentagon to hold it.
    (d) The part of the brain furthest away from the spinal cord is in charge of the more complicated activities.
    (e) Probably no other part of the body is as complex as the brain.
    (f) The cerebrum is the part of the brain that controls thinking.

Chapter 3

Finding the Topic and the Main Idea

Many of the paragraphs you encounter in your reading will not be too difficult to understand. Some, however, may prove to be confusing. When you run across such paragraphs, you will usually have to analyze them step by step.

In this chapter we'll explain how to carry out such step-by-step analyses. You will learn how to find the topic and main idea in three different kinds of paragraphs: (1) **paragraphs containing a topic sentence,** (2) **paragraphs suggesting a main idea,** and (3) **paragraphs containing a topic but no main idea.**

As this chapter illustrates, all paragraphs are not the same; however, they do all have one thing in common: all paragraphs have a topic. Since this is the one thing in a paragraph you can always count on, we will begin our explanation with a discussion of the topic.

FINDING THE TOPIC

Whenever you are trying to understand a difficult paragraph, you should begin by finding the topic. **The topic is the person, place, or thing mentioned or referred to most frequently in the paragraph.**

You can usually find the topic by asking a simple question: Who or what is repeatedly mentioned or referred to in this paragraph?

We can use the following paragraph to illustrate how this question leads us to the topic.

> The doctrine* of the Jehovah's Witnesses, a religious sect founded by Charles Taze Russell, is based on the belief that there will be a second coming of Christ. According to Witness doctrine, the coming of Christ is not far off, and his arrival is to be eagerly awaited because only he can conquer the devil. Once the devil is conquered, an era of peace and harmony can begin, and people will no longer be plagued by evil. The Witnesses are anxious to explain their beliefs, and for this reason they publish and sell two magazines, *Watchtower* and *Awake*.

Every sentence in the preceding paragraph refers to the doctrine of the Jehovah's Witnesses; this then is the topic of the paragraph. The topic is not Charles Taze Russell or *Watchtower*. The man and the magazine are mentioned only once; the topic of a paragraph will be repeatedly mentioned or referred to, not mentioned and forgotten.

You will notice that the topic of the sample paragraph was expressed in five words ("doctrine of the Jehovah's Witnesses"), not one. This is important because two or more words are frequently necessary to express the topic of a paragraph. We can use the following example:

> True to character, Charles Lindbergh planned his own burial just a few days before his death from cancer. The decision to plan his own burial was typical of Lindbergh's personality; he was a man who knew what he wanted and insisted on living according to his beliefs. In 1927 he decided to fly nonstop over the Atlantic. Nobody believed he could do it, but he did, and news of his flight went around the world. When popular sentiment demanded that Lindbergh return a medal given him by the Nazis, he refused. Considering his past, it's not surprising that Lindbergh wanted to end his life as he had lived it, on his own terms.

If we asked you to give the topic of the previous paragraph, you might answer with the name Charles Lindbergh. But if you look again, you'll see that topic is too general. The paragraph does not deal with the many things that might fall under the heading "Charles Lindbergh," such as his family, hobbies, or illness. Instead, the paragraph is limited to a discussion of Charles Lindbergh's personality; this is the precise topic of the paragraph. It is neither too general, nor too specific. It is precise because it includes everything discussed in the paragraph and excludes everything not discussed.

*doctrine: principles of belief presented for acceptance by a religious or political group

In 1927 Lindbergh flew nonstop over the Atlantic in the *Spirit of St. Louis*.

Read the following paragraph and see if you can find the precise topic. Remember, it should be neither too general nor too specific. Look for a topic general enough to include points discussed in the paragraph yet specific enough to exclude what is not discussed or only casually mentioned.

Alexander Graham Bell probably never realized how many uses modern society would find for his invention. Today's telephone fills a number of important and different functions, probably more than Bell ever dreamed. For example, the telephone can help save lives. Many cities have a permanent crisis number listed, and anyone feeling frightened or depressed can call and ask for help or advice. At the same time the telephone helps fulfill a less important, but still necessary, function: It helps in the search for entertainment. In many cities a person need call only a single number to find out what's featured at several movie theatres. Occasionally the telephone even helps to entertain. Not too long ago New York City instituted a "Dial-a-Joke" number, and anyone feeling a little blue could call and hear sixty seconds of jokes.

At first it might seem that telephones is the topic of the above paragraph. But if you look again, you'll see that the word *telephones* is too general. The author does not deal with everything that could fall under that heading such as the history, mechanics, and varieties. Instead, the author limits the topic to the functions or uses of the telephone. This is the precise topic of the paragraph.

Since we have already given you an example of topics that are too general, we should also give you an example of a topic that is too specific. "Dial-a-Joke" is a perfect example. The paragraph does not focus on this one particular function of the telephone; it mentions several different functions. The topic "Dial-a-Joke" would be too specific to include all the things discussed in the sample paragraph.

Before we go on to the exercises, we want to introduce another sample paragraph. This paragraph is important because it illustrates that the word or phrase needed to express the topic may not appear in the paragraph:

> A bicycle consists of two wheels and a simple steel frame equipped with handles, pedals, cranks, and a saddle. The rider sits on the saddle, grasping the handlebars. The pressure of the rider's foot on the pedals turns the cranks. This action drives a chain over the front and rear sprockets, causing the rear wheel to revolve and setting the bike in motion.

The preceding paragraph talks about riding a bicycle; this is the subject to which the author repeatedly refers. We can say then that "riding a bicycle" is the precise topic of the paragraph. Notice, however, that this phrase does not appear anywhere in the paragraph. To express the precise topic, we had to provide the phrase ourselves.

Frequently you will encounter paragraphs resembling our sample paragraph; the topic will be suggested but not stated anywhere in the paragraph. When this happens, you will have to provide a word or phrase that expresses the precise topic.

While doing the following exercises, keep in mind that the topic is always the person, place, or thing frequently mentioned or referred to in the paragraph.

EXERCISE 1 **Practice Exercise:** Following each paragraph is a list of possible topics. After reading through the paragraph, decide which word or phrase best expresses the topic. If none of the choices fits, use the empty blank to write in the appropriate word or phrase.

1. Over the years many different systems of physical exercise designed to improve the health and appearance of the body have emerged. One of the best ever to come forth was Hatha Yoga, a form of Yoga consisting of various postures that exercise the whole body. Facial muscles, for example, can be toned by daily performance of "The Lion," a posture that imitates the face of a roaring lion. Back muscles can become more flexible by regular practice of "The Cobra," a posture that imitates the arching head of that poisonous snake. "The Crow," which resembles the headstand, is said to improve circulation and relieve tension.

   (a) systems of physical exercise

   (b) the Cobra

   ((c)) Hatha Yoga postures

   (d) _____

Explanation: Topic *a* is too general. The paragraph does not deal with the many different systems of exercise that exist. Topic *b* is too specific. The paragraph does not focus on any one particular posture. "Hatha Yoga postures" is the precise topic because it is the subject to which the author repeatedly refers.

Do the rest of the exercises in the same manner.

1. Outwardly, the arrival of British baby Louise Brown, in 1978, seemed to be like any other ordinary birth. But in fact, it was far from an ordinary event, for Louise Brown was living proof that a scientific procedure known as *in vitro** fertilization could produce normal, healthy babies, even though the actual process of fertilization in this controversial method takes place outside the human body. For countless couples who had expected to remain childless because of problems with the initial stages of pregnancy,

---

**in vitro:* Latin for "in a glass" since fertilization takes place in a glass container

Louise's birth was a scientific miracle that gave them new hope, and since 1978 there have been many more such babies born in England, Australia, and the United States with the result that the nonscientific term "test-tube babies" has become part of the English language. In America, an entire clinic has been set up in Virginia to devote time, money, and research to the study of *in vitro* fertilization.

(a) Louise Brown

(b) *in vitro* fertilization

(c) pregnancy

(d) _____

2. Anxiety frequently expresses itself in two types of behavior known as *obsessions* and *compulsions*. Obsessions are recurring thoughts that a person cannot seem to get out of mind. For example, a young man who thinks continuously about the possible death of his parents is suffering from an obsession. Compulsions, on the other hand, are recurring activities that a person must perform to avoid anxiety. A woman who insists on washing her hands every few minutes even though her hands are not dirty is showing compulsive behavior.

(a) compulsions

(b) anxiety

(c) obsessions

(d) _____

3. Few reasonable men and women would praise Benito Mussolini for being a good man who helped his country. But even those who have nothing but contempt for him would admit that Mussolini's treatment of the Mafia did benefit Italy and the Italians. A proud and ruthless dictator, Mussolini was obsessed with the idea that the Mafia was a direct challenge to his power. Determined to rid himself of any organization he could not control, Mussolini organized a campaign to stamp out the Mafia. With the aid of police officials who were themselves familiar with violence, Mussolini managed to bring the dreaded organization under control, at least temporarily.

(a) Benito Mussolini

(b) the Mafia

(c) Mussolini's treatment of the Mafia

(d) _____

4. Joseph Boulogne, the eighteenth-century black composer, led a life so active and so exciting, it is surprising that he still found the time to write music. Son of an African slave and a French official, Boulogne was born in Guadeloupe* but was educated in Paris, where he acquired all the graces of an accomplished gentleman. By the age of eighteen, he could skate, dance, fence, and ride with any man in Paris. When the French Revolution bloodied the streets of Paris, Boulogne commanded an all-black regiment, proving himself a brilliant military man. However, none of these activities interfered with the composer's love of music, and he wrote and performed throughout most of his life, stopping only when he was imprisoned for a brief period after the Revolution.

(a) Boulogne's active life

(b) Boulogne's life in prison

(c) Boulogne's love of music

(d) _____

5. Well-known dog lovers for years, Americans seem to be undergoing a change: cats are taking over the country. Currently there are as many as 250 cat books being offered by publishers. However, it is the cartoon feline Garfield who has won America's heart. Initially rejected by two newspaper syndicates, Garfield has, since his debut in 1978, earned over $20 million, and books devoted to his daily doings have routinely climbed to the top of the bestseller list. Paws, Inc., a corporation founded by creator Jim Davis to control and market Garfield products, now boasts a variety of items, including underwear, tablecloths, diaries, luggage and T-shirts. CBS even plans a Garfield special in which the opinionated cat falls hopelessly in love with a lasagne.

(a) dog lovers

(b) cats

*Guadeloupe: islands in the West Indies

(c) Garfield, the cat

(d) _____

6. *Casablanca* is a movie classic. Starring Humphrey Bogart and Ingrid Bergman, the film, made in 1942, has delighted audiences for almost half a century. Yet despite its phenomenal success, both critically and financially, the movie was created under the worst possible circumstances, and no one involved in the film thought it would be finished, let alone become a success. When shooting began, the script was incomplete. While filming continued, no one knew how the movie would end as five different writers worked feverishly on five different scripts. Annoyed by the confusion, the stars of the film quarrelled with one another, and Humphrey Bogart threatened to quit every other day. But in the end he stayed, and movie audiences can still hear his famous line, not "Play it again, Sam," but "You played it for her; you can play it for me."

(a) Humphrey Bogart

(b) the making of *Casablanca*

(c) the ending of *Casablanca*

(d) _____

7. In World War II the Nazis surrounded the Russian city of Leningrad and cut off the Russians' access to all supplies. During that time the men and women of Leningrad suffered a tragedy that few who were not there could comprehend. Countless numbers of people starved to death, and corpses piled up in the streets. Families were forced to eat once-beloved pets, and stories of cannibalism were whispered and believed. It took the men and women who lived through the siege months and, in some cases, even years to regain their former health.

(a) Leningrad

(b) stories of cannibalism in the siege of Leningrad

(c) the siege of Leningrad

(d) _____

8. When Americans think of the Wild West, they usually do not imagine it inhabited by black cowboys. This image of the West — without the presence of black people — is completely inaccurate and was fostered by Hollywood rather than reality. In fact, thousands of black cowboys were involved in the settling of the West, even though few commercial films have acknowledged their existence until quite recently. In the forties, for example, a movie called *Tomahawk* was made, featuring a character named James Beckworth. In reality, Beckworth was a black cowboy who was famous during the California gold rush. But in the movie, he is played by white actor Jack Oakie. Similarly, Oklahoma, the location for many Westerns, was also the site of several all-black communities, none of which ever appeared on film. Fortunately, due to the continued and growing interest in black history, Hollywood's white cowboys have begun to ride the range with their black brothers, as Western films have begun to acknowledge Western reality.

   (a) *Tomahawk*

   (b) cowboys in the forties

   (c) blacks in the West

   (d) _____

9. Frances Wright was a brilliant woman who believed that men and women could work together to improve the society in which they lived. Guided by her beliefs, Wright founded Nashoba, a colony where black men and women could work until they paid for their freedom. The experiment began in 1826, but hopes for its success died quickly. Bad weather and sickness plagued the community, and the members seemed able to produce nothing but debts. By 1830 the colony had been forgotten by almost everyone.

   (a) the failure of Nashoba

   (b) slavery

   (c) Frances Wright

   (d) _____

10. Napoleon Bonaparte plunged France into war and took away her political liberty; but at the same time he gave her a government that was both generous and efficient.

Through Napoleon's insistence a committee of lawyers worked constantly until the laws of France were codified. At the same time he appointed new and more competent judges and instituted special courts that helped bring order to the widespread confusion that had reigned in France. Following the Revolution, the leaders had begun to plan for a system of national education. But it was Napoleon who, with his customary efficiency, carried the plans through to completion. And perhaps most important to the poor of France, under the rule of Bonaparte, taxes were decreased.

(a) Napoleon Bonaparte

(b) the poor of France

(c) French government under Napoleon

(d) _____

FROM TOPIC TO MAIN IDEA

ALEX	What were you and Ann just whispering about?
JACK	You.
ALEX	Well, what exactly were you saying about me? I don't like to pry, but after all, it was me you were talking about. I have a right to know what you said about me.
JACK *(heading for the door)*	Oh, nothing much.
ALEX *(following)*	Hey, wait a minute!

As you can see from the preceding dialogue, discovering the topic under discussion is just not enough. Like Jack, you need to know what was said about the topic. Having found the topic of a paragraph, you want to know what the author had to say about that topic.

In most of the paragraphs you read, you'll discover that the author had one idea in mind when writing the paragraph, one idea he or she hoped to communicate. We call this one idea *the main idea* of the paragraph.

Usually, after having found the topic, you can discover the main idea by asking yourself another question: what does the author want to say about the topic? We can use the following paragraph as an example:

From Topic to Main Idea 107

Bela Lugosi plays Count Dracula.

In some mysterious way the old movie monsters always managed to arouse the sympathy of the audience. Watching the old mummy films, starring Boris Karloff, a person actually feels sorry for the centuries-old corpse who must drag himself across the desert in search of his long-lost princess. And anybody who watches the old King Kong movies usually roots for the ape. Even Frankenstein's monster calls forth a certain amount of sympathy. After all, he never asked to be born, or perhaps "put together" is a better phrase.

Here the author repeatedly refers to movie monsters; this is the topic of the paragraph. Now that we have the topic, the next question follows quite naturally: what does the author say about movie monsters?

The first sentence in the paragraph tells us that the old movie monsters could arouse the audience's sympathy. Sentences 2, 3, and 4 provide particular examples of movie monsters who were somehow, in spite of their horrible appearance, able to draw forth sympathy. The author returns to the idea that movie monsters could arouse people's emotions. Since this is the one idea to which the author repeatedly returns, we call it the main idea of the entire paragraph.

Read through the next sample paragraph and see if you can discover the main idea:

For a period of about seventy-five years (1765-1840), the Gothic novel, an early relative of the modern horror story, was popular throughout Europe. Many of the most popular novels, those written by Horace Walpole, Ann Radcliffe, and Monk Lewis, were sold by the thousands, quickly translated, and frequently plagiarized.* The stories were the object of fascination because they described a world where mysterious happenings were a matter of course, and ghostly, hooded figures flitted through the night. Gothic novels were read and discussed by men and women of the upper classes, and publishers, ever alert to a ready market, made sure that copies of the books were available at bargain prices. Even the poorest members of the working class could afford to pay a penny to enter the Gothic world of terror, and they paid their pennies in astonishing numbers.

The topic of the preceding paragraph is the Gothic novel; this is the subject to which the author repeatedly refers. Now we have to discover what the author had to say about that topic.

The first sentence tells us that the Gothic novel was very popular in Europe in the years between 1765 and 1840. The second, third, fourth, and fifth sentences provide specific examples of the books' popularity; we learn that books from popular authors sold in the thousands and were widely discussed and purchased by rich and poor alike. The author returns repeatedly to the idea that the Gothic novels were very popular; this, then, is the main idea of the paragraph.

We would like to point out now that the first sentence in each sample paragraph is more general than the other sentences in the paragraph. As we already pointed out in the last chapter, general sentences almost never appear alone; they are usually accompanied by specific sentences that develop and support the idea contained in the general sentence. Our paragraphs are no exception. The first sentence in both paragraphs is further explained in the more specific sentences that follow.

We point out the first sentence in both paragraphs to you because they are good examples of what we call *topic sentences*. **According to our definition, a topic sentence is a general sentence that contains the main idea developed throughout the paragaph.** If a paragraph contains a topic sentence, almost every sentence in the paragraph will refer to the idea contained in that sentence.

*plagiarize: to steal someone else's ideas or writings and use them as one's own

From Topic to Main Idea

To find the topic sentence of a paragraph, you should ask yourself the following questions:

1. What general sentence contains an idea that is developed throughout the paragraph?
2. What general sentence ties together the other sentences in the paragraph?

We can use the following paragraph to illustrate how these questions can lead you to the topic sentence:

> All the early horror movies that have become classics had strange and mysterious settings. *King Kong,* for example, took place somewhere in the dark jungles of Africa, and Dracula was usually found in the woods of Transylvania. When he wasn't there, he was in London. The Mummy, star of *The Mummy's Hand,* dragged himself across half of Egypt.

The precise topic of the sample paragraph is the "settings of the early horror movies"; this is the subject to which the author repeatedly refers. The first sentence of the paragraph tells us that the early horror films used mysterious settings, and the remaining sentences give specific examples. Only one idea is developed throughout the paragraph: The old horror movies emphasized exotic settings.

If we ask what general sentence contains an idea that is developed throughout the paragraph, there is only one answer: the first sentence because it is the most general sentence in the paragraph. It is also the only sentence containing an idea that is further explained. The author does not return repeatedly to the idea that the movie *Dracula* made use of foreign locations; indeed, *Dracula, The Mummy's Hand,* and *King Kong* are cited only because they help make the statement contained in the first sentence more convincing.

To check and see if we have really found the topic sentence, we can ask the second question: does the first sentence tie all the other sentences in the paragraph together? The answer to that question is yes since the paragraph does not make much sense if we take the first sentence away:

> *King Kong,* for example, took place somewhere in the dark jungles of Africa, and Dracula was usually found in the woods of Transylvania. When he wasn't there, he was in London. The Mummy, star of *The Mummy's Hand,* dragged himself across half of Egypt.

When the first sentence is left out, we have no idea why the author has decided to mention all these old horror films. The first sentence is necessary because it provides the other more specific sentences with a purpose. They are there to prove that old horror movies really did emphasize foreign and mysterious locations.

On the previous pages we presented three basic steps for understanding a paragraph:

1. To find the **topic,** ask who or what is repeatedly mentioned in the paragraph.

2. To find the **main idea**, ask what the author wanted to say about the topic.

3. To find the **topic sentence,** look for the general sentence that contains the main idea and ties together all the other sentences in the paragraph.

In the next exercise we ask you to follow the three steps just described. However, occasionally you may find it difficult to get past step 1; that is, you'll find the topic but have trouble figuring out the main idea. When that happens, you can try reversing steps 2 and 3. That means you should find the topic and then look for all general sentences that describe that topic. Put the ideas contained in those sentences into your own words and see which one of those ideas is developed throughout the paragraph. The sentence containing an idea developed throughout the paragraph is the topic sentence.

We'll use the following paragraph to illustrate this method of arriving at the main idea and topic sentence:

> Over the years Bram Stoker's novel *Dracula* has been filmed many times, but perhaps the most famous version is the one made in 1931 by Tod Browning. The film still turns up regularly on television and in movie theaters. Certainly one reason for the film's success is the presence of actor Bela Lugosi, who plays the count; no one before or after Lugosi has played the count so well. Even though the film is almost half a century old, audiences still fidget when Lugosi bends over a soft, white throat. With his pale face and thick accent, Lugosi was just charming enough and just horrible enough to be truly terrifying.

In the preceding paragraph the author repeatedly returns to Lugosi's performance as Count Dracula. We can say then that Lugosi's performance is the topic of the paragraph. Now that we know that, we can look for the general sentences that describe or explain that topic.

As you can see, only the third sentence in the paragraph makes a general statement about Lugosi's performance as Dracula. The first two sentences are general ones, but they do not deal with Lugosi's performance. Sentences 4 and 5 are specific descriptions of his performance; they are too specific to function as a topic sentence.

If we put the idea contained in sentence 3 into our own words, it would read something like this: "Bela Lugosi's performance as Count Dracula helped make Tod Browning's film a great success." Since the remaining sentences in the sample paragraph develop this idea in more detail, we know that we have found the topic sentence containing the main idea.

This sample paragraph illustrates another important point: **the topic sentence is not always the first sentence.** It can, in fact, appear anywhere within the paragraph. Many times the very last sentence will be the topic sentence. This is one reason why some speed-reading techniques suggest you look at the first and last sentence if you are trying to obtain the most information in the least amount of time. Keep this point in mind while completing the following exercises.

EXERCISE 2

Practice Exercise: Find the precise topic and main idea for each paragraph. Once you have discovered both topic and main idea, begin filling in the blanks.

Place a word or phrase expressing the topic in the first blank. Put the number of the topic sentence in the second blank and use the last blank to put the main idea of the paragraph into your own words.

1. [1] As a young man, Bela Lugosi was rich and famous, but as he grew older, his fame and his wealth disappeared. [2] Audiences had come to associate him so strongly with the role of Count Dracula that producers were hesitant to star him in any other films. [3] Once the Dracula films were no longer popular, Lugosi was unable to find work, and his debts began to increase. [4] Forgotten by Hollywood and his fans, Lugosi became addicted to drugs, and the last few years of his life were filled with poverty and bitterness.

Topic: Lugosi's later years

Topic sentence: 1

Main Idea: As Lugosi grew older, his life seemed to fall apart.

Explanation: The paragraph refers repeatedly to the later years of Lugosi's life; this is the precise topic. Note again that this phrase does not appear anywhere in the paragraph. We had to provide it.

Only one idea about Lugosi's later years is developed throughout the paragraph. The author repeatedly emphasizes that the actor's last years were miserable ones. This is the main idea of the paragraph. Only one sentence, the first sentence in the paragraph, contains a general statement of this idea. Therefore, the first sentence is the topic sentence.

Do the rest of the exercises in the same manner.

1. [1] Fans of the Dracula films are usually shocked to hear that centuries ago there did exist a Prince Vlad who is said to be the source of the Dracula legends. [2] Prince Vlad, however, did not spend his time seeking out fresh young victims; instead, he had disobedient members of the villages he ruled brought to his castle where he decided on their punishment, which was usually death. [3] It is said that on one occasion, Vlad became furious because some visiting Turkish diplomats failed to remove their turbans. [4] They meant no disobedience; it was simply not their custom to do so. [5] As punishment for this supposed insult, Vlad had the turbans nailed to their heads.

Topic: _____

Topic sentence: _____

Main idea: _____

_____

_____

2. [1] In the film *An American Werewolf in London,* movie audiences watch breathlessly as the charming, young hero turns into a grizzly werewolf, bent on the destruction of the human population. [2] Similarly, a high point in the film *Cat People* is the moment when the exquisitely beautiful Nastasia Kinski, slowly and horribly, changes into a monstrous and bloodthirsty leopard. [3] If older horror films, like the 1940 original version of *Cat People,* lack such gruesome scenes, it is because their creators did not have the technical sophistication to produce them. [4] How-

ever, to the best of their ability, even the makers of early horror films tried to put the mysterious moment of metamorphosis* on film, as movies like *Dr. Jekyll and Mr. Hyde* readily attest. [5] Clearly there is something strangely compelling about the idea of human metamorphosis that makes such scenes a crucial ingredient in horror films.

Topic: _____

Topic sentence: _____

Main idea: _____

_____

_____

3. [1] The old horror movies attempted to create an atmosphere of terror; modern movies ignore atmosphere and specialize in blood and gore. [2] In the early films starring Boris Karloff and Bela Lugosi the right atmosphere was created by the sound of wild screams in the background. [3] Open windows revealed a pair of shadowed eyes or the weird smile of a madman. [4] Modern films concentrate on filling the screen with buckets of blood, and the audience doesn't hear screams anymore; instead, it witnesses brutal murders. [5] The old shots of wild eyes and crazy smiles are gone. [6] Now there are long close-ups of someone being stabbed to death.

Topic: _____

Topic sentence: _____

Main idea: _____

_____

_____

4. [1] Daphne du Maurier's story "Don't Look Now" is a masterpiece of suspense; it is unfortunate that the film made from the short story was not nearly as good. [2] Du Maurier's story is suspenseful and mysterious, but it is

*metamorphosis: a marked change in appearance

also logical. [3] The reader understands, for example, why the woman in the cape murders the architect. [4] The movie, however, seems determined to avoid any logical explanation of the architect's death. [5] The audience never understands why the woman in red chooses to attack a man she had never seen before. [6] It is regrettable that the film chose to ignore du Maurier's logical explanation of the mystery.

Topic: _____

Topic sentence: _____

Main idea: _____

_____

_____

5. [1] There is no denying that a large segment of the population enjoys watching horror movies. [2] Lines at the box office lengthen whenever theater owners run films with titles like *Return of the Grave Snatchers* or *Night of the Living Lunatics*. [3] Similarly, ratings go up when late-night movie programs present old standards: *Dracula*, *Frankenstein*, and *The Mummy*. [4] Movie producers, who are always ready to fulfill the public's desires, churn out several thrillers a year because they know the films are guaranteed to turn a profit.

Topic: _____

Topic sentence: _____

Main idea: _____

_____

_____

6. [1] Bette Davis, a superstar of the forties and fifties, was once again a hit in a horror movie about a forgotten child star, *Whatever Happened To Baby Jane?* [2] Davis's co-star in that film was her sometime screen rival Joan Crawford, who made her own comeback through horror movies such

as *Strait Jacket.* [3] Olivia de Havilland, who is still remembered for her role in the 1939 classic *Gone with the Wind,* returned to the screen in a horror movie called *Lady in a Cage.* [4] Most recently, Betsy Palmer, a comic actress of the fifties, was again seen on film in the notoriously gruesome *Friday the 13th.* [5] It seems that many female film stars of the past have used horror films to make their screen comeback.

Topic: _____

Topic sentence: _____

Main idea: _____

_____

_____

7. [1] Bram Stoker's classic horror story *Dracula* was first printed in 1897, and since that time, it has had extraordinary success. [2] Undoubtedly, one reason for the story's popularity is the figure of the count, a strange mixture of the real and the supernatural. [3] When Dracula first appears in the novel, he is a polite and almost charming host. [4] But it is not long before he emerges as the inhuman fiend who can hypnotize victims with his glowing red eyes and turn himself into a bat or a puff of smoke.

Topic: _____

Topic sentence: _____

Main idea: _____

_____

_____

8. [1] Edgar Allen Poe is usually praised for having written some of the very first detective stories. [2] However, another aspect of Poe's work is frequently ignored: his understanding of abnormal psychology.* [3] Although to-

*abnormal psychology: study of mental illness

day it is known that human beings may be motivated by dark and irrational* desires that are contrary to normal morality, Poe was writing in the nineteenth century, not the twentieth. [4] Yet in "The Tell-Tale Heart" and "The Black Cat," he managed to realistically describe two characters who were well aware that they have no reason to desire the death of their victims. [5] As Poe makes clear, reason has nothing to do with their decisions; they are driven by cruel desires beyond their control.

Topic: _____

Topic sentence: _____

Main idea: _____

_____

_____

9. [1] *Wieland*, one of the first novels written in America (published 1789), clearly shows the influence of the Gothic novel.* [2] Based on a real case, the book, written by Charles Brockden Brown, describes the mental collapse of Theodore Wieland. [3] Wieland, a resident of Philadelphia, leads a normal life until the day a ventriloquist* comes to town and decides to make Wieland hear voices. [4] The ventriloquist succeeds in his game although he soon tires of it; his victim, however, does not. [5] He starts to hear his own voices, heavenly ones, who command him to slay his family. [6] Obedient to his voices, Wieland murders his family and is ready to murder his sister when the ventriloquist, appalled by what he has caused, tells him to "hold." [7] Once Wieland comes to his senses and realizes what he has done, there is nothing left for him but death.

Topic: _____

Topic sentence: _____

*irrational: contrary to reason
*Gothic novel: a novel that emphasizes the ghostly and mysterious
*ventriloquist: one who can produce sounds that seem to come from another source

From Topic to Main Idea   *117*

Main idea: _____

_____

_____

10. [1] As early as 1908, Thomas Alva Edison shot a picture of Frankenstein, and a film about a man-made monster *(The Golem)* appeared prior to World War I. [2] Throughout the twenties a number of German directors produced some classic horror films, among them *Nosferatu,* a brilliant interpretation of Bram Stoker's *Dracula.* [3] By 1930 the German horror film was in decline, and Hollywood producers discovered that the public would pay to be frightened. [4] 1930 was the year that Tod Browning directed *Dracula,* a box-office blockbuster. [5] The history of horror films is almost as long as the history of film itself.

Topic: _____

Topic sentence: _____

Main idea: _____

_____

_____

    The next set of exercises will give you more practice finding the main idea and the topic sentence in paragraphs. It will also give you more practice putting the main idea into your own words.

    Whenever you read, you should always try to put the author's thoughts into your own words. If you can do that, you have really understood what you have read. It is easy, when you are reading and have the book in front of you, to think that the author's ideas are absolutely clear. However, later when you try to review what you've read, you may discover that those ideas were not all that clear. To avoid this problem and find out immediately if you have really understood what you've read, try translating the author's thoughts into your own words.

EXERCISE 3

Practice Exercise: Read through the following paragraphs and find the topic sentence. Place the number of the topic sentence in the first blank. Then translate the main idea into your own words.

1. [1] Three days before Christmas in 1894, Captain Alfred Dreyfus, a Jewish officer in the French army, was found guilty of treason and sentenced to life imprisonment on Devil's Island. [2] In 1906 Dreyfus was completely exonerated,* but in those twelve years before Dreyfus was proved innocent, every possible attempt was made to prove him guilty. [3] Key officers in the military gave the newspapers material that supposedly proved Dreyfus's guilt. [4] The newspapers, for their part, printed the stories without questioning their authenticity.* [5] Evidence proving Dreyfus innocent was ignored, and attempts to open the case were blocked because an examination of the Dreyfus case was considered dangerous to the prestige of both the army and the government.

Topic sentence: ___2___

Main idea: In 1906 Dreyfus was proved innocent, but not before many attempts were made to prove him guilty.

Explanation: Since the second sentence is the topic sentence, we have put 2 in the first blank and put the main idea contained in that sentence into the second blank.

Do the rest of the exercises in the same manner.

1. [1] Possessed by the desire to modernize his country and his subjects, Peter the Great, Tzar of Russia,* literally tried to whip his subjects into living in the style of the modern world. [2] The nobles of his court were told to clip their beards and shorten their robes while their wives were summoned to court. [3] The ladies, who had previously been told to stay at home, were terrified and tended to huddle in a corner; still, they were forbidden to go home. [4] To import new ideas from the West, Peter demanded that young Russians go abroad to study, and he invited Europeans to come and visit Russia. [5] The Europeans he

*exonerate: to prove innocent of any crime

*authenticity: accuracy

*Tzar of Russia: king or emperor of Russia

invited could have refused if they chose, but his subjects had no such freedom of choice. [6] If they refused to become modernized, they were beaten and in some cases executed.

Topic sentence: _____

Main idea: _____

_____

_____

2. [1] Initially America was not overly receptive to the idea that two unknown young men, Wilbur and Orville Wright, had actually succeeded in building a machine that could fly. [2] Following their first successful flight in 1903, the brothers notified as many people as possible, but little attention was paid to their talk of flying machines. [3] The army, to whom the invention had been offered, showed little or no interest and refused to see a demonstration until 1908. [4] Long after the Wright brothers had become well known in Europe, the American papers still chose to play down the brothers' achievements and devoted only a few paragraphs to their demonstrations.[1]

Topic sentence: _____

Main idea: _____

_____

_____

3. [1] The moon, like the sun, has always been a source of wonder and fascination; and, like the sun, many myths surround it. [2] Very young children, for example, still talk of the man in the moon and cling to the idea that the moon is made of green cheese. [3] Furthermore, many adults are convinced, although science has yet to prove them correct, that the moon affects their temperament and it is claimed that emotional outbreaks are more frequent during the time when the moon is full. [4] According to the beliefs

[1]George Canning, *100 Great Modern Lives* (London: Souvenir Press, 1972), p. 317

120   Finding the Topic and the Main Idea

of some primitive tribes, the moon is the source of life and women can only bear children when they have been touched by its rays.[2]

Topic sentence: _____

Main idea: _____

_____

_____

4. [1] For years, parents of autistic* children have blamed themselves for producing children who cannot escape the world of fantasy. [2] But new research suggests that the disease may have less to do with parental error and far more to do with genetic inheritance.* [3] The chromosomes that determine sex are called X and Y. [4] In some cases, the X chromosome may be abnormal or "fragile," and there appears to be a link between a fragile X chromosome and the appearance of autism. [5] Although scientists are not yet convinced that a genetic defect is the crucial element in all cases of the disease, they are almost positive it plays a significant role in many cases.

Topic sentence: _____

Main idea: _____

_____

_____

5. [1] In the seventeenth century the emotionally disturbed suffered more from their treatment than they did from their illness. [2] Since the devil was thought to be the cause of mental illness, brutal attempts were made to drive him out. [3] Patients were whipped and beaten, and scalding liquids were poured over them. [4] If the treatments failed, and they usually did, the patients were simply locked away

[2]Esther Harding, *Woman's Mysteries* (New York: Bantam Books, 1973), p. 24

*autism: a form of childhood mental illness characterized by extreme withdrawal and the rejection of reality

*genetic inheritance: the passing on of traits from parents to children

in hospitals that were little more than jails. [5] There they were left to the mercy of attendants who were underpaid and not much more emotionally stable than the patients.

Topic sentence: _____

Main idea: _____

_____

_____

6. [1] Robert Falcon Scott (1868–1912) hoped to be the first to explore the South Pole, but he failed in his attempt, and the Norwegian explorer Roald Amundsen reached the Pole before him. [2] Scott and his party set out from Cape Evans, a site about nine hundred miles away from the Pole, and although the ponies on which they were relying did not take well to the Antarctic conditions, the group thought they were ahead of Amundsen. [3] They did not realize that the Norwegian was four hundred miles beyond them. [4] As the ponies grew weaker and blizzards slowed down their progress, Scott and his companions grew steadily more discouraged. [5] Their depression increased when they found traces of Amundsen's party. [6] When they finally reached the Pole, they discovered that their fears had been well founded; Amundsen had camped at the Pole and was already returning home. [7] Scott's party had no other choice but to turn around and try to make its way back home; the return journey was a nightmare filled with cold weather and hunger. [8] None of the men survived.

Topic sentence: _____

Main idea: _____

_____

_____

7. [1] How much do you reveal about yourself when you speak? [2] According to a book called *Verbal Behavior*, probably more than you care to. [3] The book's author, Dr. Walter Weintraub, maintains that much can be said about personality just by paying close attention to speech

habits. [4] According to Dr. Weintraub, the impulsive person who reverses decisions as soon as they are made is fond of words like *but, although,* and *nevertheless* whereas people who are unsure of themselves tend to employ phrases such as *kind of, sort of* and *maybe.* [5] In the same vein, he suggests that young children use the word *I* more than *we* because they are still not familiar with group experiences. [6] Adolescents, however, who care a great deal about group membership, employ *we* far more than *I.*

Topic sentence: _____

Main idea: _____

_____

_____

8. [1] For centuries earthquakes were considered warnings from the gods; both the suddenness of the quakes and the amount of damage they left behind was enough to convince even the unbelieving that such things must be the work of supernatural beings. [2] It is only fairly recently that a comprehensive* theory of the cause of earthquakes has been developed. [3] According to this theory, called *plate tectonics,* the earth's surface consists of about a dozen huge seventy-mile-thick rock plates. [4] Propelled by unknown forces, the plates are constantly in motion. [5] Sometimes the plates meet and become temporarily locked together. [6] The locking together of the plates causes stress to build up on the edges of the rocks. [7] Eventually the rocks fracture, and the plates resume their motion, but the sudden release of energy causes the quakes.

Topic sentence: _____

Main idea: _____

_____

_____

*comprehensive: complete, thorough

9. [1] To us the earth appears to be a solid mass, but scientists know it is composed of several distinct layers. [2] Called the *outer crust,* the layer closest to the surface consists of lightweight rock that extends for about twenty miles beneath the earth's surface. [3] Just underneath the crust is a second layer, about two thousand miles thick, known as the *mantle;* portions of the mantle are extremely hot. [4] Beneath the mantle lies the *core* of the earth. [5] Made up of nickel and cobalt, this core layer also undergoes extremely high temperatures, hot enough to melt both metals, but the sixty pounds of pressure borne by each square inch keeps them solid.

Topic sentence: _____

Main idea: _____

_____

_____

10. [1] The early Americans led hard lives that left little time for the pleasures of the table; at least that is the modern view. [2] Certainly, Europeans who journeyed to America reinforced the idea that the American diet was both limited and tasteless. [3] Journals, letters, and notes from Americans, however, belie this depressing picture of American cooking (or "cookery," as it was then called); on the contrary, Americans seem to have enjoyed a variety of delicious foods. [4] Game, for example, was one of the staples of the American diet since wild turkeys, passenger pigeons, and canvas-backed ducks were all plentiful. [5] Food from the sea was also available, and oysters, terrapin, and turtles are mentioned in letters describing American fare. [6] Most families raised vegetables, and broccoli, asparagus, and cauliflower were enjoyed in season.

Topic sentence: _____

Main idea: _____

_____

_____

THE UNSTATED MAIN IDEA

ANN   Mr. Allen is really worrying himself sick about his wife's illness.

SAM   How do you know that? I talked to him on the phone yesterday, and he didn't say anything to me about it.

ANN   I saw him coming out of the store yesterday. He looked terrible. His clothes were all rumpled, and he looked like he hadn't slept in a week.

TOM   You don't wait for me after class anymore; you don't call me, and you never eat lunch with me.

JOAN   I told you. I'm really busy lately.

TOM   Don't kid me. I know you're just not interested in going out with me anymore.

FATHER   Come out of there at once!

SUE   What's the matter?

FATHER   You know as well as I do what the matter is! The hall smells of smoke; you've been in the bathroom for fifteen minutes, and you just had a coughing fit. You're smoking in there.

In the preceding dialogues, three different people—Ann, Tom, and Sue's father—are all drawing **inferences; that is, they are drawing conclusions about something they have not observed on the basis of what they have observed.** Ann doesn't know for sure that Mr. Allen is worrying himself sick, but given the facts she does know to be true, this seems to be the best inference. Similarly, Sue's father cannot be sure that Sue is smoking in the bathroom—after all, he cannot see her—but he can draw almost no other conclusion or inference from his observations.

Obviously, you too are no stranger to drawing inferences. You have observed someone's way of dressing, laughing, or talking and come to some conclusion about his or her personality or background. In your relationships with people you draw inferences all the time; and whether you are conscious of it or not, you draw inferences when you read.

Frequently authors will not put their main ideas in sentences. Instead, they provide a number of sentences that all combine to suggest a main idea. After reading the sentences, the reader has to infer the suggested main idea in much the same way the people in the dialogues had to draw conclusions on the basis of the evidence they had.

It is important, however, to be careful when you try to find the suggested main idea of a paragraph. You cannot let your imagination run away with you and infer any main idea simply because there is no topic sentence in the paragraph to prove you wrong.

We'll use the following paragraph to illustrate what we mean when we talk about careful and careless inferences:

> My son used to be an articulate,* friendly young man of whom I was very proud. That was before he started going to movies on a regular basis. Since that time he seems to have learned that real men don't talk very much. After all, Chuck Norris hardly says a word in his movies. When my son does get around to talking, his conversation is composed of one-syllable words like "yeah," "no," and "oh, yeah." Actually his conversation very strongly resembles the kind of snappy dialogue that made Clint Eastwood famous. Before he became a movie freak, my son had female as well as male friends. Now he refers to girls as "chicks" and "broads" and starts doing a poor imitation of Burt Reynolds every time a "chick" comes into view.

Since the paragraph returns again and again to the behavior of the author's son, we can say that "my son's behavior" is the topic of the paragraph.

Now that we have the topic, it is not hard to figure out what the author wants to say about it. The sentences in the paragraph combine to suggest a main idea that would, if put into a sentence, read something like this: "Movies have had a terrible effect on my son's behavior."

Now the question is: how did we arrive at this particular main idea? To answer that question, we'll try to retrace our steps so that you can see how we came to our conclusion. We'll also explain why we would consider our inference to be careful, not careless.

We claim, first of all, that the author is not pleased with the change in the boy although this statement does not appear anywhere in the paragraph. We made that inference on the basis of the first sentence that tells us the author used to be proud because the boy was friendly and well spoken.

If those were the qualities that made the parent proud, he or she cannot possibly be pleased with the change in the boy

---

*articulate: well spoken

since he is no longer friendly and well spoken; he is quite the opposite.

Nowhere in the paragraph does the author state that the movies caused the changes in the boy, but the specific sentences combine to suggest that idea. The boy imitates his favorite movie heroes, and they are not friendly and articulate; therefore, neither is he. Moreover, the author stresses throughout the paragraph that the behavior described began only after the boy started going to the movies. We cannot avoid inferring that the movies brought about the changes in the boy's behavior.

What we have gone to some length to point out is that our inference is based on the information given in the paragraph. For this reason, we can call it a careful inference. We could have come up with another main idea, for example, one that could be expressed in the following sentence: "My son behaves badly because he hates me." However, we would not be on such solid ground. Indeed, that would be an example of a careless inference. There is nothing in the paragraph to support this idea.

When you read and draw inferences, be sure to base your inferences on the facts given in the paragraph. Do not assume that you can read anything you choose into the paragraph. Make sure that the information given supports your inferred idea.

Read through the following paragraph and see if you can infer the main idea:

> As a young man, British soldier and writer T. E. Lawrence took part in an archaeological* expedition in the Middle East. The work fascinated him, as did the land, and he became possessed by a dream: The Arabs would overthrow the Turks and rule their own country. During World War I, Lawrence saw a chance to make his dream become reality when the British showed an interest in helping the Arabs revolt. Lawrence quickly seized on the idea and brought about a meeting between British and Arab leaders. Supplied by British arms and aided by Lawrence's military strategy, the Arabs rose and captured several major Turkish strongholds. By 1919 the war was over, and the Turks had been defeated. Thrilled by the Arab victory, Lawrence was called to the Paris Peace Conference, where he learned for the first time that the British did not intend to give up their control in the Middle East.

The preceding paragraph repeatedly returns to Lawrence's dream for Arab freedom; we learn what the dream was, how

*archaeology: study of ancient culture

he became possessed by it, and how he hoped to realize it. We can say then that "Lawrence's dream for Arab freedom" is the topic of the paragraph.

If we ask what the author wanted to say about the topic, the answer is clear: Lawrence's dream of Arab freedom was only partially realized. This main idea is not contained in a sentence, but it is clearly implied. The second sentence in the paragraph tells us that Lawrence dreamed of the Arabs revolting against the Turks and ruling their own land. The remainder of the paragraph makes it clear that the Arabs did throw off Turkish rule, but the last sentence in the paragraph tells us that the Arabs still did not rule their country. Thus our inferred main idea is based solidly on the facts given in the paragraph.

The following exercises will give you practice in the drawing of careful inferences.

EXERCISE 4 **Practice Exercise:** We provide three specific sentences; each one describes the behavior or appearance of a different person. Read through the three sentences and then choose the inference that best fits the information given in the specific sentences.

1. a. Although the man's clothes were old and dirty, it was easy to see that they were well cut and expensive.
   b. The walls of his run-down shack were papered with autographed pictures; many of the inscriptions on the photos contained his name.
   c. Articulate and well read, he liked to talk of the places he had been and the famous people he had known.

Inferences

(1) The man was an alcoholic.
(2) The man was unhappy with his life.
((3)) The man had not always been so poor.

Explanation: We did not choose sentence 1 because the specific sentences tell us nothing about his drinking habits. There is no evidence to support such a statement. Sentence 2 was not chosen because there is no information about the man's state of mind. We know that he likes to talk about his past, but that does not necessarily mean that he is unhappy with his life. Sentence 3 is the correct inference because every sentence tells us that the man had lived another kind of life, one not associated with poverty.

Do the rest of the exercises in the same manner.

1. a. The student squinted when she sat at the back of the room and looked at the blackboard.
    b. She left out words when she copied anything from the blackboard.
    c. After she read for an hour, she got a headache.

Inferences

(1) The student gets excellent grades.
(2) The student needs glasses.
(3) The student wants to get out of doing any work.

2. a. Whenever he felt anxious, he went to the refrigerator to find something to munch on.
    b. When he got promoted, he was so happy he managed to lose twenty pounds, and his friends said that he was almost too thin.
    c. When he lost his job, he put on thirty pounds.

Inferences

(1) He couldn't get the kind of job he wanted because he was too heavy.
(2) He was always disgusted with himself after he had eaten too much.
(3) His weight fluctuated with his state of mind: when he was happy, he was slender; when he was unhappy, he was overweight.

3. a. Her hands remained clamped to the lectern while she gave her speech.
    b. Her voice trembled slightly when she spoke.
    c. She didn't look at her audience once.

Inferences

(1) She was used to giving speeches.
(2) The audience did not like her speech.
(3) She was not used to giving speeches.

4. a. Sue stood on the edge of the group and smiled timidly at the other children; intent on their game, they did not smile back.

   b. When the game broke up, everyone else walked home in pairs; Sue walked home alone.

   c. When Sue's mother asked if she had enjoyed the play group after school, the child burst into tears.

Inferences

(1) The child is unhappy because she feels left out and lonely.

(2) The child cried because the mother asked too many questions.

(3) The other children did not like Sue.

5. a. Many cat and dog owners buy their pets clothing, special food, and toys.

   b. A great many men and women talk to their pets.

   c. It is not uncommon for a dog or cat who has died to receive a headstone with a poetic inscription.

Inferences

(1) Many cat and dog owners treat their pets as if they were human beings.

(2) Most people who like dogs and cats don't like other human beings.

(3) It is unnatural for human beings to treat their pets like humans.

The following exercise contains paragraphs rather than single sentences. Read the paragraphs and then decide what main idea the author wishes to express.

To check your inference, ask the following questions:

1. Could the sentence function as the topic sentence of the paragraph?

2. Do the specific sentences in the paragraph support the sentence you've chosen?

If the answer to both questions is yes, then you can be fairly sure that you have drawn a correct inference.

Normally when you read, the final test of an inference comes after you have completed the entire essay or chapter. It is then that you know if your inference fits the author's other statements on the subject discussed.

EXERCISE 5

Practice Exercise: The following paragraphs all suggest one main idea. Read them through and then select the sentence that expresses that main idea. If none of the sentences seem to fit, fill in the blank with a sentence you think expresses the main idea.

1. When Annie Sullivan first arrived to teach her young pupil Helen Keller, she found a little girl who could not see or hear or speak. Cut off from the rest of the world around her, the child behaved like a little savage, biting and kicking whenever anyone approached her. In less than a month, however, Sullivan had taught her wild little charge that things had a name and that human beings could use those names to communicate with one another. In the years that followed, with Sullivan as a teacher and friend, Helen Keller learned to read Braille* in English, Latin, Greek, French, and German. She learned to use sign language, and above all, she learned to speak.

   ((a)) Annie Sullivan was an enormously important influence on Helen Keller's life.

   (b) Annie Sullivan was an amazing woman.

   (c) Helen Keller was an amazing woman.

   (d) _____

   _____

Explanation: Sentence a is the correct choice. The entire paragraph deals with the progress Helen Keller made under Sullivan's guidance. Sentence b is incorrect because it deals only with Sullivan, and the paragraph obviously emphasizes the relationship between the two women. Sentence c is incorrect for the same reason; only this time it is Sullivan's role that is ignored.

Do the rest of the exercises in the same manner.

*Braille: system of writing and printing for the blind in which raised dots represent letters

1. Left on his own at a very young age, Charles Chaplin quickly learned to survive on London's city streets. He learned how to charm friends and strangers into giving him food or money, and he learned how to avoid the police, who were none too fond of a young boy who had no home and no steady job. When Chaplin finally managed to get a steady job as an actor in silent films, it did not take him long to discover a character that was completely his own: the little tramp. Dressed in shabby clothes, cadging food and money wherever he could, the little tramp spent most of his twenty-five years on the screen trying to avoid the police who pursued him in one hilarious scene after another.

   (a) As a young man, Chaplin was a juvenile delinquent.
   (b) Chaplin used his experiences from his youth to mold the character he made famous on the screen.
   (c) Chaplin had a hard time surviving on London's city streets.

   (d) _____

   _____

2. Russia's Siberia extends from the Ural Mountains to the Pacific Ocean, embracing over five million square miles, yet the population of the region is quite small and does not appear to be growing. Historically a place of exile for those who offended the Russian government, the region is still used to punish political dissenters.* Although some native inhabitants deny their country is cold, morning temperatures are as low as sixty degrees below zero, and layers upon layers of clothing are needed to survive the brutal temperatures. For those Russians who volunteer to live and work in Siberia, there is a definite monetary reward: they can make from 30 to 40 percent more than their counterparts* in other areas of the Soviet Union. In addition, foods in short supply in urban Moscow—fruit, fish, and game—are plentiful in Siberia. Still, there are few volunteers.

*dissenters: people who refuse to accept established political or religious doctrine

*counterparts: someone or something that is similar in function or relationship

(a) Siberia is a beautiful, untouched landscape with clean air and abundant natural resources.

(b) Political dissent in Russia is punished by exile to Siberia.

(c) Because of its extreme cold, Siberia is vastly underpopulated.

(d) _____

_____

3. In World War II while America was at war with Japan, more than 100,000 Japanese people living on the Pacific Coast were rounded up and put into special camps. During this same period many Japanese were forced to give up their jobs because fellow employees were convinced that anyone who was Japanese must be on the side of the Axis powers.* Families were forced out of their homes because constant threats made life unbearable. For some Japanese men and women, it was not even safe to be seen on the street because the color of their skin was liable to arouse hostile feelings.

(a) Many Japanese in America were mistreated because of the hostile feelings aroused by World War II.

(b) Many Japanese were imprisoned during World War II.

(c) Japanese who sympathized with the enemy were treated badly by the Americans.

(d) _____

_____

4. The philosopher Schopenhauer lived most of his life completely alone; separated from his family and distrustful of women, he had neither wife nor children. Irrationally afraid of thieves, he kept his belongings carefully locked away and was said to keep loaded pistols near him while he slept. His frequent companion was a poodle called *Atma* (a word that means "world soul"), but even Atma occasionally disturbed his peace of mind. Whenever she was

*Axis powers: the name given Germany, Italy, and Japan during World War II

bothersome or barked too much, her master would grow irritated and call her *Mensch,* the German word for "human being."

(a) Schopenhauer had an unhappy childhood.

(b) Schopenhauer did not care for his fellow human beings.

(c) Schopenhauer was fond of dogs.

(d) _____

_____

5. It is commonplace to hear outrage expressed at the callousness* with which some Americans can view violence. We are, it seems, shocked to hear that five people can walk by while an old woman is beaten senseless because she refused to give up her handbag. It is similarly unbelievable that crowds can gather and wait in fascinated expectation for a young man or woman to jump from the top of a high building. Years ago when a young woman called Kitty Genovese was murdered in New York City, the American public could not believe that more than twenty people had heard her screams and seen her attacked without trying to help her. Yet after the countless hours of blood and gore that have filled our television screens and the numerous movies that have presented violence in glorious Technicolor, how can we claim to be shocked or even surprised?

(a) Due to the massive increase in violent crime, fewer and fewer people are shocked when someone gets hurt.

(b) Violence is not a problem in European cities.

(c) The violence in television and movies has made it easier to accept violence in reality.

(d) _____

_____

6. As more and more citizens have become aware of the destruction of forests and wildlife, signs demanding the preservation of natural resources have begun to spring up

*callousness: lack of feeling

Destruction of wildlife along polluted rivers.

all across the country. Attempts are being made to clear polluted rivers because in recent years the rivers in America have become filled with waste and chemicals. Concerned citizens have begun to demand that animals such as the beaver not be allowed to go the way of the passenger pigeons, which were hunted out of existence.

(a) Many animals have been saved by efforts of conservationists.

(b) All over America people are becoming concerned about the environment.

(c) The rivers are polluted.

(d) _____

_____

7. As some have discovered to their great misfortune, poison hemlock, said to have killed the philosopher Socrates, looks much like parsley, and its roots resemble wild carrots. A close relation, water hemlock resembles the wild parsnips, but is far more deadly. The bulb of the lovely autumn crocus is sometimes taken for a wild onion. When consumed, it causes heart failure. The jimson weed, also known as *thorn apple*, got its name from soldiers in Jamestown, Virginia, who made a meal of the leaves and became horribly ill. In more recent times, drug enthusiasts

have swallowed the leaves in hopes of a fantastic high and have ended up suffering from cramps, nausea, and delirium.

(a) Socrates is said to have been killed by hemlock.
(b) Wild mushrooms are dangerous delicacies.
(c) The consumption of wild plants can be dangerous, even fatal.

(d) _____

_____

8. In the eighteenth century, the English economist Thomas Malthus predicted that future populations would increase faster than food supplies — with disastrous results. But in the past two hundred years, technological advances* have profoundly influenced food production methods. In the developed countries, the same amount of food can be produced in less time that it took half a century ago. Similarly, increased knowledge of agriculture has helped grow more food on less land. By the same token, land once considered unfit for food production has become arable. With time, as we learn more about the ocean, we may be able to produce food not just from land but from the sea as well.

(a) In time we may be able to use the ocean for food production.
(b) Increased knowledge of agricultural methods has helped produce greater amounts of food.
(c) The theory that population increases faster than food supplies has not proved true for the more developed countries.

(d) _____

_____

9. Unfortunately, adoption practices have not changed since the early 1940s. Once an adoption takes place, the records are sealed, and it is extremely difficult for anyone, especially the person who has been adopted, to discover

*technological advances: progress in applying scientific knowledge to industry or commerce

anything about his or her history. In general, it is assumed that the adopted child and adoptive family will fare better if contact with the natural parents is not possible. Recently, however, several newspaper and magazine articles concerning adopted children's search for their past have appeared, and groups have been formed to help adopted children find out more about their past. Similarly, many social workers involved with adoption cases have begun to question the practice of denying the adopted children information about their past since, in many cases, it has resulted in needless misery.

(a) Social workers are beginning to question the need to deny adopted children access to their files.
(b) Adoption practices should not be changed.
(c) Many adopted children desire to know more about their real parents.

(d) _____

10. In the last twenty years, countless numbers of men and women have paid large sums of money for a treatment known as *cell therapy*. Their reason was simple: they believed that the injection of cells taken from baby sheep could help them maintain their youth. They either did not know or did not choose to believe what any doctor would tell them. Animal cells when injected into the body of a human being are treated like any other foreign substance. The body gathers its defenses to eject the cells, and within three or four days they are destroyed.

(a) Cell therapy is a fraud.
(b) The body treats the cells of animals like any other foreign substance.
(c) Doctors should not charge such high prices for cell therapy.

(d) _____

EXERCISE 6   **Practice Exercise:** None of the following paragraphs contain a topic sentence; however, the paragraphs do suggest one main idea. Read over the paragraphs and decide on a main idea you think could be inferred from the paragraph. Put the main idea into a sentence, and then write the sentence in the blank following the paragraph.

1. Not too long ago, there was a diet rage called *staple puncture,* and many people claimed that putting a staple in their ears had helped reduce excess poundage. Then there was the low-carbohydrate diet, which also came in for its share of praise. Men and women following this diet ate lots of bacon and eggs and avoided bread and sugar. Prior to the arrival of the low-carbohydrate diet, everyone concerned with keeping his or her weight down seemed to be swallowing eight glasses of water a day and gobbling cottage cheese.

Fad diets are constantly changing._____

_____

Explanation: We chose our main idea because all of the sentences given deal with diets which have had only brief success.

Do the rest of the exercises in the same manner.

1. British actor Bob Hoskins first became widely known to American audiences with his portrayal of a gangland leader in the movie *The Long Good Friday.* Fans of educational television, however, had already learned to recognize Hoskins' name when he played the malevolent and crafty Iago in a production of Shakespeare's *Othello;* in addition, they had seen another side of his varied talents in the comedy *Flickers,* produced by "Masterpiece Theatre." At the same time that filmed versions of the actor's performances were delighting Americans, the man himself was ensuring the successful revival of the musical *Guys and Dolls* in London. Singing and dancing, Hoskins charmed a packed house night after night.

_____

_____

2. Cosmetic counters are stocked with creams that remove wrinkles although every sensible person knows that wrinkles, once they appear, cannot be removed with creams. Next to the creams stand lotions and packs that are guaranteed to firm the skin. The problem is that firm skin has almost nothing to do with substances contained in jars and bottles. Firm skin depends on age and proper nutrition. Probably the largest display at the cosmetic counter is the collection of lipsticks and eyeshadows, all of which are guaranteed to make the customers look just like the models in the advertisements. Unfortunately, after applying both lipstick and eyeshadow, most of the hopeful customers bear little resemblance to those shining creatures in the magazines.

_____

_____

3. Almost every automobile advertisement has a gorgeous model somewhere in the background. Usually she doesn't drive the car; she simply stands by it and looks beautiful. Similarly, liquor advertisements are fond of showing breathtaking women hanging on the arms of men smart enough to buy brand X whiskey. Men aren't even allowed to advertise shaving lotion by themselves. Most commercials for shaving creams and lotions include some lovely young woman who appears to be swept off her feet by just one whiff of brand Y.

_____

_____

4. Before she was kidnapped on February 4, 1974, by members of a radical group known as the Symbionese Liberation Army (SLA), Patty Hearst, heir to one of America's greatest fortunes, was a nineteen-year-old college student, who majored in art history. Engaged at the time to Steve Weed, a former teacher, she was happily preparing for her wedding collecting silver and china for her new home. After being taken prisoner by the SLA, she spent fifty-seven days in capitivity,* during which time she was frequently bound

*captivity: state or period of being a prisoner

and gagged. To save her life, the young woman eventually became a member of the SLA, and she participated in several robberies with the group. Finally, caught by the police, she spent two years in jail before her sentence was commuted by President Jimmy Carter.

_____

_____

5. In the not too distant past, the unmarried American woman was an "old maid," while the unmarried man was a swinging bachelor. The forty-year-old man with a family and a career was thought to be an admirable success, while a woman in the same position was often accused of not tending to the needs of her family. The hostess planning a dinner party was happy to accommodate the unattached male; the unattached woman, however, was considered a worry and a bother. Over the years, the English language has acquired more than a few words to criticize a woman's sexual behavior, among them "tart" and "floozy," but there are very few such words to criticize a man whose morals are suspect.

_____

_____

THE DISAPPEARANCE OF THE MAIN IDEA

Most paragraphs have a main idea that is either contained in a general sentence or else suggested by several specific sentences. But, as we'll stress in the following pages, some paragraphs do not contain a main idea. The following paragraph, for example, does not contain a topic sentence, nor do the specific sentences combine to suggest one main idea:

> Following his graduation from Harvard in 1755, John Adams entered into Massachusetts politics, and in 1774 he became a delegate to the First Continental Congress. Two years later Adams added his signature to the Declaration of Independence. At the end of the Revolutionary War (1783), he helped to work out a peace settlement with Great Britain, and six years later he became the country's first vice president. Following his term as vice president, Adams became America's second president.

Again, the first thing to look for is the precise topic. Since the author refers again and again to the different events in Adams's career, we can say that "events in Adams's career" is the topic of the paragraph. This phrase does not appear anywhere in the paragraph, but it is the phrase that best expresses the topic.

Having discovered the topic, we can ask the questions we used to analyze the previous paragraphs.

1. What does the author want to say about the topic?

2. What idea about the topic does the author develop throughout the paragraph?

Previously, asking those questions led us to the main idea of the entire paragraph. This time, however, no main idea emerges. The author describes several special events in Adams's career but doesn't make any general statement about those events. The paragraph does not have a topic sentence containing the main idea, nor do the sentences in the paragraph combine to suggest a main idea.

We could, if we chose, force a main idea out of the paragraph, one that could be expressed in the following sentence: "There were several important events in John Adams's career." However, such an attempt would be useless since the sentence provides us with almost no information; anyone's career contains several important events.

The paragraph is not meant to convey a main idea. Its purpose is simply to present a list of dates and events, all of which deal with one particular topic. The paragraph does not present any one main idea about Adams; it simply outlines the man's career.

Before we go on to the exercises, we'll give you one more example of a paragraph without a main idea:

> The Jehovah's Witnesses, a religious group formerly known as the Russellites, was founded by Charles Taze Russell in the late nineteenth century. Members of the group believe that there will be a second coming of Christ, at which time Satan will be defeated, and God's rule on earth established; they are firmly opposed to war and government authority. The Witnesses publish and distribute *Watchtower* and *Awake*, two pamphlets that outline their religious beliefs.

The preceding sample paragraph resembles the paragraph at the beginning of this chapter. The paragraphs, however, do differ. If you compare them, you'll see that the opening paragraph has a main idea while the paragraph just presented has none. The preceding sample paragraph does not contain one sentence that is more general than the others; all the sentences are equally specific. None of the sentences in the sample paragraph contain an idea that is developed throughout the paragraph. Instead, each sentence introduces a new fact concerning the Witnesses, and the sentences do not combine to suggest a main idea.

In the following exercises, you will be asked to recognize paragraphs without a main idea. You will have little difficulty if you keep the following points in mind:

1. Paragraphs without a main idea will not have a topic sentence.

2. The sentences in the paragraph will not combine to suggest a main idea.

3. The sentences in the paragraph will all be almost equally specific. The paragraph will not contain one sentence far more general than the others.

EXERCISE 7

Practice Exercise: After reading through each paragraph, decide if the paragraph contains a topic sentence. If it does, write the number of the topic sentence in the first blank. If the paragraph contains only a topic, find a word or phrase to express the precise topic and fill in the second blank. *Note:* The following exercise does not contain any paragraphs with an implied main idea.

1. [1] Although their ancestors swam in the ocean millions of years ago, sea snakes are still in existence today. [2] There are more than fifty different kinds living in the waters of the Pacific and Indian Oceans. [3] Unlike sea turtles who must crawl from the water to give birth on land, sea snakes give birth below the surface of the ocean. [4] The only time a sea snake surfaces is when it needs to fill its single lung with air. [5] Once the lung is filled, the sea snake can stay underwater for hours. [6] Some of the snakes are quite beautiful, but all of them are quite dangerous, possessed of a lethal venom.

Topic sentence: _____

Topic: *sea snakes* _____

Explanation: The paragraph does not develop any one main idea; each sentence provides a new fact about the topic of sea snakes.

Do the rest of the exercises in the same manner.

1. [1] In 1900 Chinese hatred of European control reached its peak, and China erupted in the Boxer Rebellion. [2] Supported by the Empress Tzu Hsi, the Boxers were members of a secret society (*i-he-chüan*, or "righteous united band") who were determined to force the Europeans out of China. [3] Driven by the hatred of the foreign devils who had exploited China and the Chinese, the Boxers rebelled and murdered several hundred Europeans.

Topic sentence: _____

Topic: _____

_____

2. [1] The mandrake is a poisonous plant found in regions near the Mediterranean; it has a short stem and purple or white flowers. [2] The thick and frequently forked root of the Mandrake is said to have special healing powers, among them the ability to induce sleep and revive sexual desire. [3] The root's resemblance to the shape of man is often so distinct that some have claimed to be able to distinguish sex differences. [4] Thus there are said to be "mandrakes" and "womandrakes."

Topic sentence: _____

Topic: _____

_____

3. [1] With a huge white horn planted firmly in the middle of its head, the rhinoceros is a very comical-looking animal, but there is nothing comical about what presently appears to be its unhappy fate. [2] Pursued by poachers* who sell rhino horns for profit, the animals are rapidly being

*poacher: person who hunts or fishes illegally

destroyed in what is a senseless slaughter for profit. [3] Laws to stop the poaching have been enacted in parts of Africa where the animals are found, but so far they have not been very successful. [4] In fact, only a few small-scale poachers have been arrested. [5] Large-scale poaching rings, responsible for much of the slaughter, remain intact. [6] Free of significant interference, they continue to kill the animals in order to make their horns into fancy daggers or useless aphrodisiacs.*

Topic sentence: _____

Topic: _____

_____

4. [1] The word *cereal* refers to edible seeds or grains like wheat, oats, or corn. [2] It also refers to the grasses that produce the seeds and grains. [3] The word originated with the "Cerealia," Roman festivals in honor of Ceres, the goddess of agriculture. [4] At present different types of cereal are used all over the world, and for many countries cereals like rice make up the majority of the daily diet. [5] Americans are perhaps most familiar with breakfast cereals, the prepared grains sold in boxes. [6] This form of cereal did not appear until the end of the nineteenth century.

Topic sentence: _____

Topic: _____

_____

5. [1] The layer of air closest to the earth is known as the *troposphere;* it is the part of the atmosphere inhabited by human life. [2] Although the troposphere varies in height, it is lowest over the North and South Poles and highest over the equator. [3] Just above the troposphere is a layer of air called the *tropopause*. [4] In this region, the high-speed winds called *jet streams* can sometimes exceed 250 miles per hour. [5] The existence of jet streams was unknown until

*aphrodisiacs: drug or food said to intensify sexual desire

World War II pilots encountered them during their flights over Japan.

Topic sentence: _____

Topic: _____

_____

EXERCISE 8

Practice Exercise: The paragraphs in the following exercise may have a topic sentence containing the main idea; they may have a main idea that is suggested by specific sentences, or they may have no main idea at all.

Read through every paragraph. If the paragraph has a topic sentence, underline it; put the main idea into your own words and fill in the blank following the paragraph. If the paragraph has a main idea suggested by the specific sentences, put the main idea into a sentence and fill in the blank. If the paragraph does not have a main idea, find a word or phrase that expresses the topic and fill in the blank.

1. The topaz, a yellow gemstone, is the birthstone of those born in November, and it is said to be under the influence of Saturn and Mars. In the twelfth century, the stone was used as a charm against evil spirits, and a person had only to tie the stone to a thread made out of donkey's hair and hang it over the left arm to drive off the evil powers. According to the Hindus the stone is bitter and cold, and it can, if worn above the heart, keep away thirst. Christian tradition viewed the topaz as a symbol of honor, and the fifteenth-century Romans used the stone to calm the winds and break evil spirits.

   There are many superstitions associated with the topaz.

Explanation: In the preceding paragraph, all the specific sentences describe different superstitions associated with the topaz, and the sentences combine together to suggest that there are many different superstitions about the yellow stone. This is the main idea of the paragraph although it does not appear in a topic sentence. After putting the main idea into a sentence, we filled in the blank.

Do the rest of the exercises in the same manner.

The Disappearance of the Main Idea   145

1. The Yanomano, an Indian tribe in South America, call themselves "fierce people," and they live up to their name. This is particularly true of male members of the tribe. To be officially considered a man, a boy must compile a record of successful battles, and if he is to be taken seriously, by the time he reaches puberty his body must be covered with scars. Older men, hardened to injury, duel with each other constantly in an effort to prove which man has the greater capacity to bear pain. Even women do not escape tribal savagery since men will frequently prove just how fierce they are by beating, mutilating, or wounding their wives. A wife cannot even escape to her family because to the family the husband's behavior is simply part of a long tradition.

_____

_____

2. A flaming ball of hot gases, the sun measures about 860,000 miles in diameter. Flames shoot out of the sun from all directions, making it impossible for the sun to remain in a solid state. Thus its temperatures are high enough to melt any metal on earth. Even though it seems still and quiet, there are always storms, called *sunspots,* taking place on its surface. They become active every ten years. The star closest to the earth, the sun is only ninety-three million miles away, a fact that makes it appear larger than it really is. Although the sun seems enormous to us, it is really only an average size star.

_____

_____

3. The affair that was to be known as the "Teapot Dome Scandal" began in 1921 when the Department of Interior was allowed to dispose of rich oil reserves. In 1922 Secretary of the Interior Albert B. Fall leased the Teapot Dome Reserve to the Mammoth Oil Company and the Elk Hills Reserve to the Pan American Petroleum Company. There was no competitive bidding involved in the leasing of the reserves, and Fall was generously rewarded for his help. Seven years later he was sentenced to a year in prison after being convicted of taking a bribe, and the Supreme Court ruled that the leases were no longer legal.

4. The twenties were the years when drinking was against the law, and the law was a bad joke because everyone knew of a local bar where liquor could be had. They were the years when organized crime ruled the cities, and the police seemed powerless to do anything about it. Classical music was forgotten while jazz spread throughout the land, and men like Bix Beiderbecke, Louis Armstrong, and Count Basie became the heroes of the young. The flapper was born in the twenties, and with her bobbed hair and short skirts, she symbolized, perhaps more than anyone or anything else, America's break with the past.

5. Avalanches are one of the world's most treacherous natural disasters. Rocketing down mountainous slopes, masses of ice, snow, rocks and mud can suddenly cover an entire village. Fortunately, most avalances occur in remote mountain areas where they threaten neither human life nor property. Occasionally, however, a sudden avalanche can catch an unsuspecting group of hikers or skiers by surprise. This is precisely what happened more than a century ago when a small group of mountain climbers tried to scale the huge alpine peak, Mont Blanc. Without warning they were overtaken by an avalanche that left only a few survivors. Three members of the party were buried in the snow. When, after almost half a century, the bodies surfaced in the snow, they were perfectly preserved. They were so well preserved that a member of the original party, by then an old man, was able to recognize them.

The following pages will test your mastery of Chapter 3.

REVIEW TEST: CHAPTER 3

PART A

1. If you are trying to understand a difficult paragraph, what is the first thing you should do?

_____

2. What is the definition given for a topic sentence?

_____

3. How did we define the word "inference"?

_____

4. What is the difference between a careful and a careless inference?

_____

5. Does every paragraph have a main idea?

_____

PART B

Directions: The paragraphs in the test that follows (1) may have a topic sentence containing the main idea, (2) may have a main idea that is suggested by the specific sentence, or (3) may have no main idea at all.

   Read through each paragraph. If the paragraph has a topic sentence, underline it; then put the main idea into your own words and fill in the blank following the paragraph. If the paragraph has a main idea suggested by the specific sentences, put the main idea into a sentence and fill in the blank. If the paragraph does not have a main idea, find a word or phrase that expresses the topic and fill in the blank.

1. *Bulimia,* the Greek word for hunger, is also the name of an eating disorder that afflicts thousands. Victims, frequently young women, respond to stress or anxiety by binge eating; that is, they continue to eat long after their hunger has been satisfied. Having devoured a mountain of food, they then force themselves to vomit or swallow laxatives. Most suffers

of *Bulimia* recognize that they are ill, but they are too embarrassed to seek help. They fear laughter or ridicule for what may be perceived as a silly habit. Although this has been a problem in the past, many physicians have begun to acknowledge the seriousness of *Bulimia* and they are now prescribing a program that includes a combination of nutrition counseling, family therapy, and individual psychotherapy.

Topic: _____

Topic sentence: _____

Main idea: _____

_____

_____

2. Every week literally millions of women perform difficult dance routines to tape-recorded music. Although less enthusiastic, men have now also begun to kick up their heels in aerobic dancing classes. However, that is not to say that running is a forgotten fad. Each week thousands of men and women who have never played a sport in their lives buy track shoes and start running, while marathons for the more experienced runners are growing bigger all the time. Those who don't fancy either speed or pain have quietly begun to sign up for yoga classes. Weights, formerly the province of men, have now become popular with women, too. Like their masculine counterparts, women have begun to build firm muscles. Increasingly, corporations are including fitness centers in their office buildings. Before starting the day, executives work out and prepare themselves for the grueling office routines. Twenty years ago, Americans had to be badgered into keeping fit; today it's a national pastime.

Topic: _____

Topic sentence: _____

Main idea: _____

Review Test: Chapter 3

3. Some scientific discoveries happen through pure accident. For example, in the seventeenth century, sailors aboard ship for long periods of time frequently suffered from muscle weakness and unexplained bleeding. Occasionally the mysterious disease proved fatal until it was discovered that those sailors who ate lemons or limes did not get the disease—or else suffered from a milder form of it. As a result, British navy officials passed a law requiring that every ship provide lemons and limes for the crew to add to its diet. Eventually scientists discovered that the vitamin C contained in the fruit prevented the disease we now know as *scurvy*.

Topic: _____

Topic sentence: _____

Main idea: _____

4. Vitamin A helps prevent colds and other infections. A deficiency in vitamin A can produce eye diseases. Eggs, butter, and yellow vegetables all contain vitamin A. Vitamin C also helps prevent infections, and it is essential to healthy teeth. Oranges, lemons, tomatoes, and strawberries all contain this important vitamin. Vitamin D, the sunshine vitamin, helps keep bones and teeth strong. The lack of vitamin D can contribute to arthritis suffering. Liver and eggs are the best sources of this vitamin. The Vitamin B Complex is also extremely important. It helps keep the skin healthy and affects muscle tone. Vitamin B may even help reduce stress and tension. Green, leafy vegetables, milk and grains help supply this important group of vitamins.

Topic: _____

Topic sentence: _____

Main idea: _____

_____

_____

5. Less than twenty years ago, cancer victims might hope to live normal lives but few actually survived. Today most patients with Hodgkin's disease, a rare but devastating form of cancer, survive. Before chemotherapy was invented, children with leukemia were condemned to death. Today more than 50 percent are completely cured by the use of drugs. Recently chemotherapy has been used to fight lung cancer, and sometimes it succeeds. Interferon, a relatively new weapon against cancer, has managed to help slow the growth of tumors in patients whose illness is already in the advanced stages.

Topic: _____

Topic sentence: _____

Main idea: _____

_____

_____

Chapter 4

Understanding How Sentences Provide Support

We have already introduced three different types of paragraphs: (1) paragraphs that have a main idea contained in a topic sentence, (2) paragraphs that suggest a main idea but contain no topic sentence, and (3) paragraphs that describe a topic without developing any main idea. Clearly, the emphasis in the last chapter was on your ability to identify the topic and main idea in a paragraph.

In this chapter we will again stress the need to find the topic and main idea, but we will also describe the role supporting sentences play in a paragraph, and you will learn about three kinds of supporting sentences: (1) **supporting sentences that illustrate the topic sentence and help make it convincing**, (2) **supporting sentences that suggest the main idea**, and (3) **supporting sentences that describe a topic.**

SUPPORTING SENTENCES CONVINCE

ALAN   I'm gonna buy a tiger-skin rug as soon as I move into my apartment. I know that sounds strange, but I've always wanted one.

ANN   It doesn't just sound strange. It sounds irresponsible, thoughtless, and, in my opinion, completely disgusting.

ALAN   You must be kidding! I know a tiger-skin rug is not exactly an example of gracious living, but why are you getting so excited?

ANN Did it ever occur to you that thirty years ago there were thousands, do you hear, *thousands* of tigers, and now there are just about two thousand left? You know why? Because jerks like you had to have tiger-skin rugs. That's why I think your idea is disgusting.

We're not going to find out how this discussion ended, although we do know that Ann had some convincing reasons to back up her opinion. We introduced the dialogue to give you an example of how people give reasons to back up or support what they believe.

Having read the dialogue, it may have occurred to you that people don't just give reasons when they speak; they also give reasons when they write. Frequently, an author will make a statement that will be opposed by at least some members of the reading audience. To meet that opposition, he or she will give reasons for that particular opinion. We can use the following paragraph as illustration:

> There should be a course in women's history taught in every high school. Such a course is necessary because it would eliminate the idea that women had nothing to do with shaping history. A women's history course would also provide young girls with female models whom they could admire and imitate.

The topic sentence of the preceding paragraph tells us that women's history should be taught in every high school. After reading the topic sentence, you may be nodding in agreement, but the author cannot take your agreement for granted. He or she has to support that opinion in order to win your agreement. Therefore, the sample paragraph contains two reasons that are meant to make the topic sentence convincing:

1. The course would eliminate the idea that women had nothing to with shaping history.

2. The course could provide young girls with models to admire and imitate.

We call the sentences containing these reasons supporting sentences. **According to our definition, supporting sentences used to convince are usually more specific than the topic sentence, and they provide reasons that back up the idea contained in the topic sentence.**

The following paragraph is another example of how supporting sentences help make a debatable idea convincing:

> Soap operas, the dramatic serials shown on afternoon television, are extremely popular, and every day millions of viewers tune into their favorite serial to discover the fate of a beloved hero or a hated villain. Soap operas, however, although they lay claim to realism, cannot be considered realistic; they do not show what really happens in the world outside the television studio. In soap operas people who commit vicious crimes are quickly punished, or else they die an untimely death. Even when suicide or murder enters the story, there's usually a happy ending. Problems, which in real life may have no solution, are always solved on television.

The second sentence of the preceding paragraph is the topic sentence; it tells us that soap operas are not realistic. Since not everyone may agree with that opinion, the author includes supporting sentences containing three reasons:

1. People who commit crimes in soap operas are punished or die young.
2. There's always a happy ending, even when suicide or murder is involved.
3. Problems are always solved.

Frequently authors will not present their own ideas; they will present the ideas of others. Nevertheless, it is still necessary to include supporting sentences to make those ideas more convincing. The following paragraph is an example:

> A growing number of scientists are worried about the destruction of wildlife. The most outspoken among them seem to be the zoologists* who warn that continued hunting and slaughtering of wildlife will endanger humanity. Zoologists claim that people can learn much about their own lives by studying other species and that useful knowledge is lost when animals are carelessly destroyed. Perhaps even more dangerous, according to the scientists, is the way the careless destruction of wildlife disturbs the balance of nature.

In the sample paragraph the topic sentence tells us how zoologists view the killing of wildlife: they consider it dangerous. Following the topic sentence are two supporting sentences containing the specific reasons zoologists use to support their claim:

---

*zoologists: men and women who study animals

1. People could learn much from the animals they are killing.
2. People are upsetting the balance of nature.

Whether or not you examine supporting sentences in a paragraph to find the reasons that make the main idea convincing will depend on your purpose in reading. If you are reading simply for your own enjoyment, you may be satisfied knowing just the main idea. But if you are reading to write a paper, take a test, or answer questions in class, you cannot limit yourself to finding the main idea. Test questions will ask you to give reasons; your teachers will ask you to explain what support the author offered, and any paper you write will require that you explain how an author arrived at his or her opinions.

Actually, even if you are reading for your own enjoyment, we hope you will look for the reasons given in the supporting sentences; these reasons can help you decide if an author's ideas should really be taken seriously. **No one should accept another person's ideas without knowing if there is evidence to back them up.**

On the following pages, we have prepared a series of exercises that will help sharpen your ability to see the relationship between topic sentences and the supporting sentences that make them convincing.

EXERCISE 1

Practice Exercise: In the following exercise one topic sentence is given, followed by four supporting sentences used to convince the reader. Circle the sentence that does not help convince.

1. Smoking should not be allowed in places where nonsmokers are present.

   (a) Inhaling the smoke of other people's cigarettes may be as dangerous as smoking.
   (b) Nonsmokers resent having to bear with reddened eyes and scratchy throats simply because someone else enjoys smoking.
   ((c)) Most smokers bitterly resent having to put out their cigarettes when nonsmokers are present.
   (d) Many nonsmokers find the smell of tobacco unpleasant.

Explanation: The author claims that smokers should not be allowed to smoke when nonsmokers are present. Sentences *a*, *b*, and *d* all give reasons for this statement. Sentence *c*, however, does not tell us why smoking should be forbidden; instead, it tells us how smokers would react to being told they should not smoke.

Do the rest of the exercises in the same manner.

1. We all should read more than we do.
   (a) Television has, unfortunately, caused people to read less.
   (b) Books can teach us how other people think and help us understand one another better.
   (c) Books help us understand not only other people but also ourselves.
   (d) It is in books that we can find out about our past mistakes and triumphs so that we may learn from them.

2. Every man and woman who drives a car should know how to change a tire.
   (a) There should be more courses that teach the basic skills necessary to maintaining an auto, for example, how to change oil and fix a flat tire.
   (b) Learning to change a tire is easy, and knowing how to change one can help a man or woman avoid being stranded far from help.
   (c) Having to call a garage simply to fix a flat is a waste of money.
   (d) Anyone who has to call a garage just for a flat is wasting time unnecessarily.

3. In the sixties and seventies many Americans, believing that they were on the verge of discovering a new life style, began experimenting with communal living; they did not realize such experiments actually had a long history.
   (a) Communal living can never replace the family.
   (b) Between 1790 and 1850 thousands of Americans joined religious communities.
   (c) In 1825 Robert Owen founded New Harmony, a communal experiment that did not end successfully.
   (d) Brook Farm, a communal experiment founded in 1841 by George Ripley, was supported by several leading American writers.

4. Growing numbers of critics are demanding that research in nuclear power come to a halt.

   (a) The critics maintain that nuclear power plants have not developed sufficient safeguards against mechanical failures.
   (b) Those opposed to continued research insist that the Nuclear Regulatory Commission (NRC), which was formed to supervise research in nuclear power, is actually biased in favor of the production of nuclear power.
   (c) NRC safety requirements are quite stringent.*
   (d) Those opposed to the use of nuclear power maintain that research will cost billions of dollars and that results are not guaranteed.

5. Although they are frequently forgotten, many women made important contributions to American literature.

   (a) Dorothy Parker used her famous sense of humor to write some very good short stories and poems.
   (b) Lillian Hellman wrote plays dealing with social problems other people were afraid to mention.
   (c) *Madame Bovary* was a famous novel about a woman's desire for excitement and romance.
   (d) Willa Cather wrote beautiful short stories and novels about what it felt like to be an outsider in America.

SUPPORTING SENTENCES ILLUSTRATE

JOHN	Honestly, raising a child is difficult.
DAVID	I know exactly what you mean. You can't do what you want anymore; you're tied down all the time. Once you have a child, your life is all over.
JOHN	I didn't mean that at all. I just mean that I find it difficult to make decisions for another human being. I'm always so afraid of making the wrong one.

*stringent: strict, rigid

Note the communication problem between these two people. John makes a statement about raising children. David immediately assumes that he has understood what John means, but actually he hasn't understood at all. To make David see what he means, John has to illustrate his idea; he has to offer a specific example to show how raising a child can be difficult.

Naturally, this kind of confusion does not occur only when we talk to one another; it may also occur when we read what somebody else has written. An author makes a statement that can be understood in more than one way, and we mistakenly choose a meaning that was never intended. The result is a complete breakdown in communication.

Fortunately, good writers are aware of this problem and take pains to illustrate their ideas so that the reader will not be confused. We'll use the following example to explain what we mean:

> Old age can be a very painful time of life. Loneliness becomes more and more a part of life as children grow up and leave home and friends grow old and die. Society, unfortunately, does not take much interest in the old, and it becomes harder and harder to form new friendships to replace old ones. The young, forgetting that one day they too will grow old, treat the elderly like relics of a bygone age, too old and worthless to be of any use.

Old age is filled with memories.

The topic sentence of the sample paragraph tells us that old age is a painful time of life; but from just this sentence it is not clear if the author is talking about physical or mental pain. However, the additional sentences make it clear that the author is talking about mental pain. The specific sentences that follow the topic sentence are supporting sentences that provide illustration and help eliminate possible confusion.

At this point you should notice that the supporting sentences in the preceding paragraph can also be used to make the main idea convincing. Likewise, the supporting sentences in the sample paragraphs in the previous section did not just make the main idea convincing; they also provided illustration for those readers who did not immediately understand what the author had in mind.

Supporting sentences can illustrate and convince at the same time. But in most cases one of these functions is more important than the other. In the last section the ideas contained in the topic sentence were fairly easy to understand but somewhat hard to accept. The supporting sentences, therefore, were primarily used to convince.

On the other hand, in this section the main ideas are easier to accept once they are properly understood, and the supporting sentences exist mainly to clear up possible confusion. The following paragraph provides another example of supporting sentences used mainly to illustrate:

> Most people who have survived auto accidents have certain characteristics in common. They are afraid of driving even a mile over the speed limit and absolutely refuse to go any faster than the law allows. When they are not at the wheel, their terror increases, and they keep an eye on the driver, offering advice about taking curves and stopping for lights.

The first sentence in the preceding paragraph is a topic sentence, and it tells us that people who have been in auto accidents have certain characteristics in common. Few people would disagree with that statement, but most would want to know exactly what characteristics the author had in mind; therefore, the author provides illustration.

The following exercises will give you practice working with supporting sentences that function mainly to illustrate the topic sentence.

EXERCISE 2

Practice Exercise: The first sentence is a topic sentence. It is followed by four supporting sentences used as illustration. Circle the one that does not help to illustrate the topic sentence.

1. Students who graduate from college and go to work for the first time are in for the surprise of their lives.
   (a) Gone are those wonderful ten-to-two classes, and many ex-students have to adjust to a nine-to-five schedule.
   (b) Graduation might not produce so much anxiety if students would only prepare themselves better for the job market.
   (c) In college everyone talks about getting an interesting job, but many students end up doing work they don't like.
   (d) Many students find it difficult to wear respectable suits and dresses every day of the week after being used to blue jeans and T-shirts.

Explanation: Most of us probably have a fairly good idea of what kind of surprise the author has in mind, but we cannot be sure until we look at the supporting sentences. The surprise could be pleasant or unpleasant. Sentences *a, c,* and *d* force us to only one conclusion: the surprise is not pleasant. Sentence *b* tells us nothing whatsoever about the surprise; therefore, it does not help illustrate the topic sentence.

Do the rest of the exercises in the same manner.

1. Freshman year is a difficult one for many students.
   (a) Although parents may have been a nuisance at home, they tend to be sorely missed at school.
   (b) The loss of old friends from home is difficult even though new ones can be found.
   (c) The change in landscape and scenery can help increase the feeling of homesickness.
   (d) Fraternities and sororities are not as popular with freshmen as they once were.

2. The first year of marriage is bound to be a difficult one.
   (a) Suddenly two people discover that they are no longer responsible only to themselves; instead, they have to consider the feelings and needs of another.
   (b) No one should make the mistake of rushing into marriage.

(c) In the first year of marriage, both partners have to learn to accept the annoying little habits that both are bound to possess.

(d) It is in the first year that a married couple must learn how to deal with their in-laws.

3. Students who joined a fraternity twenty years ago had to go through a painful process called *hazing*.

   (a) New members were often subjected to beatings with thick, wooden paddles.

   (b) They were asked to do chores and run errands until they were physically exhausted.

   (c) Today's fraternities are increasingly interested in social causes.

   (d) During hazing, stringent rules were set out for the pledges, and the slightest disobedience resulted in severe punishment.

4. Falling in love for the first time is an extraordinary experience.

   (a) Suddenly it's almost impossible to sleep at night.

   (b) Nobody should avoid falling in love even if it is painful.

   (c) Hours are spent daydreaming about the last conversation, date, or embrace.

   (d) Quite often, the first love affair is accompanied by a complete loss of appetite.

5. There are many difficulties involved in driving a taxicab.

   (a) There is always one customer who feels that the fare is too high.

   (b) Driving in heavy traffic is nerve-racking.

   (c) No cab driver is ever completely free from the fear of robbery.

   (d) More and more women are beginning to drive cabs.

SUPPORTING SENTENCES SUGGEST THE MAIN IDEA

In the last sections we dealt with the relationship between supporting sentences and the topic sentence. But as you learned in Chapter 3, there are paragraphs that do not contain a topic sentence. Such paragraphs, however, may contain a main idea, one that is suggested by the other sentences in the paragraphs. As our heading indicates, we also call those sentences that combine to suggest a main idea supporting sentences.

In Chapter 3 we gave a fairly detailed explanation of the role supporting sentences play in paragraphs where the main idea is suggested. However, in this chapter we would like to introduce further examples of paragraphs containing a suggested main idea. Further examples are necessary because inferring the correct main idea requires a great deal of practice.

The following paragraph contains supporting sentences that suggest a main idea:

> Less than fifty years ago families used to place a great deal of importance on the evening meal; it was a time to get together and talk over the news of the day. Today this idea is considered old-fashioned. The same families who considered the family meal important also made it a habit to sit around the radio together and listen to the broadcasts. Today the kids have a stereo in their room. Gone too is the family outing on Sunday. Most working mothers and fathers are too tired from a long workweek to go on family trips, and no child over the age of ten would be caught dead spending the day with the family.

The sample paragraph consists of six supporting sentences containing the following information:

1. Families used to eat together and discuss the news of the day.

2. Today it is considered old-fashioned to eat together.

3. Families used to listen to the radio together.

4. Today kids have a stereo in their room.

5. Family outings have disappeared.

6. Parents are too tired, and children don't want to go anyway.

If we combine the information given in the supporting sentences, we can draw the following inference: families of today spend far less time together than those of yesterday. This is the inferred main idea of the paragraph, and the sentences that helped us draw this inference are all supporting sentences.

The following exercise will give you more practice working with supporting sentences that suggest the main idea.

EXERCISE 3 Practice Exercise: Each exercise contains four sentences which if combined in a paragraph would suggest one main idea. Read the sentences and decide what main idea they suggest. Put the main idea into a sentence and fill in the blank.

After you fill in the blank, read through the four sentences that follow it. Two of the four could be used to support the main idea. Circle the appropriate two.

1. a. During the nineteenth century, factory owners hired young orphans whom they could force to work fifteen hours a day.
   b. Many factory owners preferred to hire women, who could move lightly among the machinery and were easily frightened if threatened with dismissal.
   c. Whenever possible, the employers increased their profits by reducing the workers' wages.
   d. Workers who complained about the hours or poor working conditions were promptly fired; and whenever possible, employers saw to it that rebellious workers were thrown into jail.

Main idea: Factory owners in the nineteenth century cruelly exploited the men, women, and children who worked for them.

(1) In the nineteenth century groups of workers known as the "Luddites" attempted to destroy the machinery they believed was ruining their lives.

(2) Employers resented government attempts to interfere in their affairs.

((3)) Children who worked in nineteenth-century factories were often clothed and fed by their employers; as a result the children were usually cold and hungry.

((4)) Some children working in factories were chained to their machines because their employers feared they would not devote themselves to their work if they were allowed too much freedom of movement.

Explanation: The first four sentences give examples of the way nineteenth-century employers misused and abused their employees. The sentences combine to suggest one main idea: Factory owners of the nineteenth century cruelly exploited the men, women, and children who worked for them.

Supporting Sentences Suggest the Main Idea   163

Of the four sentences that follow, only two, sentences 3 and 4, support the main idea. These two sentences illustrate the way in which factory workers were exploited. Sentences 1 and 2 do not describe how workers suffered at the hands of the factory owners.

Do the rest of the exercises in the same manner.

1. a. Rumors of traffic with the devil were widespread in seventeenth-century New England.
   b. In the seventeenth century if crops were destroyed or a child died suddenly, New Englanders were quick to cry "witchcraft."
   c. In 1692 two young girls in Salem, Massachusetts, accused several townspeople of practicing witchcraft.
   d. The girls' accusations triggered a series of witchcraft trials.

Main idea: _____

_____

_____

(1) William Penn, the founder of Pennsylvania, made fun of witchcraft trials, claiming that broomstick riding was not against the law.

(2) The Puritans of New England were known for their stern self-discipline.

(3) During the Salem witchcraft trials, nineteen people were hanged and hundreds were imprisoned for "having made pacts with the devil."

(4) In 1693 Cotton Mather, a New England clergyman, wrote a book defending several of the witchcraft trials.

2. a. During the six years that World War II raged, an estimated fifteen million men died in battle.
   b. Ferocious air attacks reduced many European cities to little more than rubble.
   c. Six million Jews were murdered by the Nazis.

d. Millions of men and women lost their lives in German concentration camps.

Main idea: _____

_____

_____

(1) During World War II families throughout Europe were separated, never to be united again.

(2) Rather than face defeat, Adolf Hitler committed suicide.

(3) In World War II millions of men and women were forced to flee their homes and immigrate to foreign countries.

(4) American aid helped to rebuild Western Europe once the war was over.

3. a. The Greek Historian Herodotus reports that it was the custom of the ancient Persians to bury alive those who had been convicted of crimes.
   b. The Greeks preferred to banish their guilty citizens.
   c. In Persia the innocent children of guilty parents were executed along with their mother and father.
   d. The Greeks rejected the custom of killing the children of their parents.

Main idea: _____

_____

_____

(1) A Persian who had been condemned to death would usually be tortured before being executed.

(2) The Persians sought to conquer the Greeks and failed.

(3) In the battle of Thermopylae, the Greeks refused to surrender although they knew there was no chance of victory.

(4) A Greek citizen who had been condemned to death would die quickly; torture was not used to increase his suffering.

4. a. Most of the men and women living during the Middle Ages found it almost impossible to travel because roving bands of robbers attacked all but the large and heavily armed traveling parties.
   b. If illness swept the land, the rich could close their doors or journey to another country, but the men and women who were not rich, and that was the majority of the population, could only suffer and die.
   c. Since there was no knowledge of flood control, floods were more frequent in the Middle Ages, and entire villages were simply swept away.
   d. Villages were constantly prey to starvation because too much or too little rain would wipe out crops that were needed to survive.

Main idea: _____

_____

_____

(1) In the perpetual* wars waged among the nobles, it was the poor who were most deeply affected because their villages were destroyed and their lands ruined.

(2) In the Middle Ages the nobles worried that the poor, if given too much freedom, might spent their time drinking and gambling.

(3) The average man and woman who lived during the Middle Ages seldom had meat to eat, and wine was a rare treat.

(4) On religious holidays the men and women of the villages rejoiced at the chance to take a day off from work.

5. a. Before the French Revolution, the nobility made up about one percent of the population, but received income from one-fifth of the land.
   b. Peasants, who had trouble feeding their families, were forced to give a percentage of their crops to nobles living nearby.
   c. Anyone not of the nobility could be imprisoned indefinitely.

*perpetual: constant, continual

d. To pay for the king's pleasures, high taxes were levied on the middle class and peasants.

Main idea: _____

_____

_____

(1) Nobles who were loyal to the king had little to fear from the law, but the peasants and members of the middle class knew that they could be tortured and executed for minor offenses.

(2) France, before the revolution, was divided into three classes: the clergy, the nobility, and the third estate (peasants and middle class).

(3) Before the revolution, a few members of the nobility had urged social reform.

(4) If the houses of the nobles needed repairs, the peasants were ordered to make them, even if their own crops rotted while they were working on the repairs.

SUPPORTING SENTENCES DESCRIBE

All the paragraphs we've dealt with in this chapter contained a topic sentence or suggested a main idea. But as you know from Chapter 3, there are paragraphs that neither contain nor suggest a main idea. We can use the following paragraph as an example:

> The famous Lindbergh kidnapping case began on March 1, 1932, when the Lindbergh baby was taken from his home in Hopewell, New Jersey. The family paid the fifty-thousand-dollar ransom demanded by the kidnappers, but the baby was not returned, and his body was discovered on March 12. Two years later Bruno Hauptmann, a carpenter, was arrested after attempting to pass a twenty-dollar bill from the ransom money. Hauptmann was tried and later executed, but doubts about his guilt persist.

The Lindbergh case is the topic of the paragraph, but no main idea is stated or suggested. The reader simply learns about a sequence of events that, taken together, make up the Lindbergh kidnapping case. All the sentences describing these events are on the same level of specificity, and each sentence adds a new event to the sequence.

Paragraphs like the preceding one are concerned with providing information about a topic; they are not concerned with developing a main idea. Nevertheless, we call the sentences that provide this information supporting sentences. They do not illustrate or suggest a main idea; instead they describe a topic that might not be familiar to all readers.

Before we introduce the exercises, we want to present one more sample paragraph:

> In 1921 Golda Meir settled in Palestine and helped found Mapai, the Zionist Socialist Party. She was also active in the General Federation of Labor, becoming in 1929 a member of the executive committee and in 1936 head of the political department. In 1948 just before the outbreak of the Arab-Israeli war, Meir was sent to Transjordan to discuss a compromise settlement, but she was unsuccessful. Following the war she became minister of labor and remained in that position until 1956 when she became foreign minister. Meir left the government in 1966 to become general secretary of Mapai, but three years later she returned when she was chosen to succeed Levi Eshkol and become prime minister.

Here the topic of the paragraph is the "events in Golda Meir's career between 1921 and 1969." Once again the topic is not developed into a main idea. The supporting sentences in the paragraph simply describe a sequence of events so that the reader has a clear picture of Meir's career between 1921 and 1969.

Now that we have explained all three types of supporting sentences, we can introduce the following exercise, which will give you practice recognizing the different functions of supporting sentences.

EXERCISE 4 **Practice Exercise:** The supporting sentences within the following paragraphs serve different functions.

After you have read each paragraph, fill in the blank that follows with a sentence that expresses the main idea. If there is no main idea, fill in the blank with a word or phrase that expresses the topic. Then circle the letter of the sentence that best describes the role of the supporting sentences.

1. The Creeks were a tribe of southern Indians who inhabited parts of Georgia, Florida, and Alabama. They made their living by farming and were organized into a confederacy* of

*confederacy: a union of persons, parties, villages, or states

small villages. In the War of 1812 the Creeks chose to fight against the United States, and they were defeated by Andrew Jackson. As punishment for making war, they were forced to give up a major portion of their land. By the 1830s the Creeks had been forced off their land altogether and were settled on a reservation.

The Creeks _____

_____

(a) The supporting sentences illustrate the topic sentence and make it convincing.
(b) The supporting sentences suggest the main idea.
((c)) The supporting sentences describe the topic.

Explanation: The paragraph develops no main idea. The supporting sentences simply describe the topic, "The Creeks." Therefore, we have circled sentence *c*.

Do the rest of the exercises in the same manner.

1. Learning karate requires a great deal of time, energy, and concentration. For example, the *katas*, a series of movements practiced against an imaginary opponent, must be repeated in training until the movements can be done smoothly and effortlessly. To protect themselves against attack, karate students must carefully study the nerves and vital areas of the body and must be ready to spend years, not months, in training. Above all, they must learn to cultivate the appropriate state of mind. A calm and serene consciousness is crucial for learning karate.

_____

_____

(a) The supporting sentences illustrate the topic sentence and make it convincing.
(b) The supporting sentences suggest the main idea.
(c) The supporting sentences describe the topic.

2. The religious sect known as the Shakers originated in France and was founded in America in 1787. The leader of

Learning karate requires a great deal of time, energy, and concentration.

the Shakers was Ann Lee, the unschooled daughter of a blacksmith. She established the doctrine that God had a dual nature, masculine and feminine; and she predicted that God, in the second coming, would be female. The name *Shakers* was derived from the dance that formed part of the group's religious rituals. Initially called the "shaking Quakers," members eventually came to be known as "Shakers." At their peak, the Shakers were estimated to have at least six thousand members, but today there are only a handful left.

_____

_____

    (a) The supporting sentences illustrate the topic sentence and make it convincing.
    (b) The supporting sentences suggest the main idea.
    (c) The supporting sentences describe the topic.

3. For some people it is driving; for others, elevators; for still others, flying. The objects differ but the reaction is the same—an intense, persistent, and irrational fear called a *phobia*. The name comes from the Greek word *phobos* meaning fear or flight, and it describes an anxiety disorder that affects millions of Americans in many different forms. Those suffering, for example, from *agoraphobia* are afraid of open spaces; they venture unwillingly from their homes, carefully avoiding all large and crowded places. In contrast, there are those who suffer from *claustrophobia*, a fear of narrow, enclosed spaces. Closets, elevators, and even small rooms can create severe and painful stress. For men and women who suffer from *hydrophobia*, water is the enemy, and water sports are the occasion for terror rather than fun.

_____

_____

    (a) The supporting sentences illustrate the topic sentence and make it convincing.
    (b) The supporting sentences suggest the main idea.
    (c) The supporting sentences describe the topic.

4. When Howard Hughes, the millionaire inventor, died in 1976, almost no one knew what he looked like; he had not allowed himself to be photographed since 1957. Determined to avoid being seen, he moved from hotel to hotel, always surrounded by a collection of secretaries and bodyguards who followed his orders without question. Fearful about his health, Hughes is said to have spent the last years of his life covering everything he touched with Kleenex, lest he become infected by dangerous germs. Anxious to avoid per-

sonal contact, he spent long hours on the telephone, initially to give directions to the people who worked for him and later to complain that he was being watched. As Hughes's health grew worse, doctors and aides pleaded with him to seek treatment in a hospital, but he refused, trusting instead to his own diet of health foods.

_____

_____

(a) The supporting sentences illustrate the topic sentence and make it convincing.

(b) The supporting sentences suggest the main idea.

(c) The supporting sentences describe the topic.

5. Hornets are a type of stinging wasp whose venom is usually more toxic* than that of bees. They are not closely related to the slightly larger orange-and-black honey bee and are more aggressive than bees. The most common type is the yellow-and-black striped yellow jacket, which will prey on the food and liquids on picnic tables in the summer. They make nests of a paperlike material, either underground or in low bushes. The colony, except for the queen, who hibernates, will die in the winter; but the queen will lay eggs in the spring and produce a new brood.[1]

_____

_____

(a) The supporting sentences illustrate the topic sentence and make it convincing.

(b) The supporting sentences suggest the main idea.

(c) The supporting sentences describe the topic.

MAJOR AND MINOR SUPPORTING SENTENCES

All the paragraphs we have dealt with up to this point have consisted almost entirely of major supporting sentences, but it is

*toxic: poisonous

[1]From the *New York Times*, October 27, 1981, p. C3. ©1981 by the New York Times Company. Reprinted by permission.

time to point out that paragraphs can also contain minor supporting sentences. Minor supporting sentences follow major ones, and they provide specific details about the person, place, event, or idea described in the major supporting sentence.

Since we realize that the difference between the two kinds of sentences may not be immediately clear, we offer some sample paragraphs. The first one contains only major supporting sentences:

> At the present there are a number of people who believe that the famous Loch Ness monster really exists. They maintain that the monster must exist because several witnesses claim to have seen it emerge from the lake in which it is said to live. Furthermore, their belief has been strengthened by the appearance of what seem to be actual photographs of the creature.

The topic sentence tells us that some people really do believe in the Loch Ness monster. The supporting sentences supply reasons why some people believe in the monster's existence:

1. There are witnesses.

2. There are photographs.

Both reasons help explain why men and women living in the twentieth century could believe in the Loch Ness monster. They are of equal importance; that is, both are necessary to make the topic sentence more convincing (see Diagram 4–1):

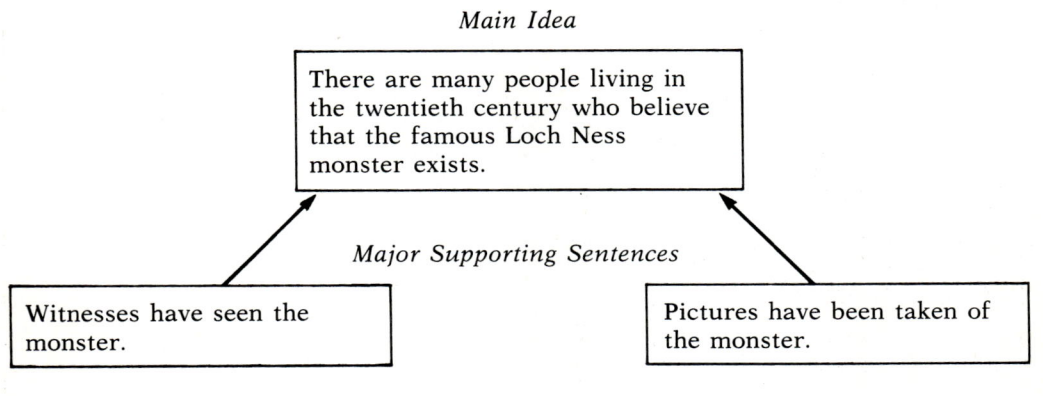

DIAGRAM 4–1

Major and Minor Supporting Sentences

Now let's expand the paragraph to include minor supporting sentences.

At the present there are a number of people who believe that the Loch Ness monster exists. They believe it because several witnesses claim to have the seen the monster emerge from the lake in which it is said to live. *Believers in the monster's existence emphasize that eyewitness reports are strikingly similar in their description of the monster.* Furthermore, their belief has been strengthened by the appearance of what seem to be actual photographs of the creature. *The photographs show a large creature which resembles an ancient sea serpent.*

The italicized sentences in the sample paragraph are minor supporting sentences that expand on what was said in the major supporting sentences. Diagram 4–2 illustrates what we mean:

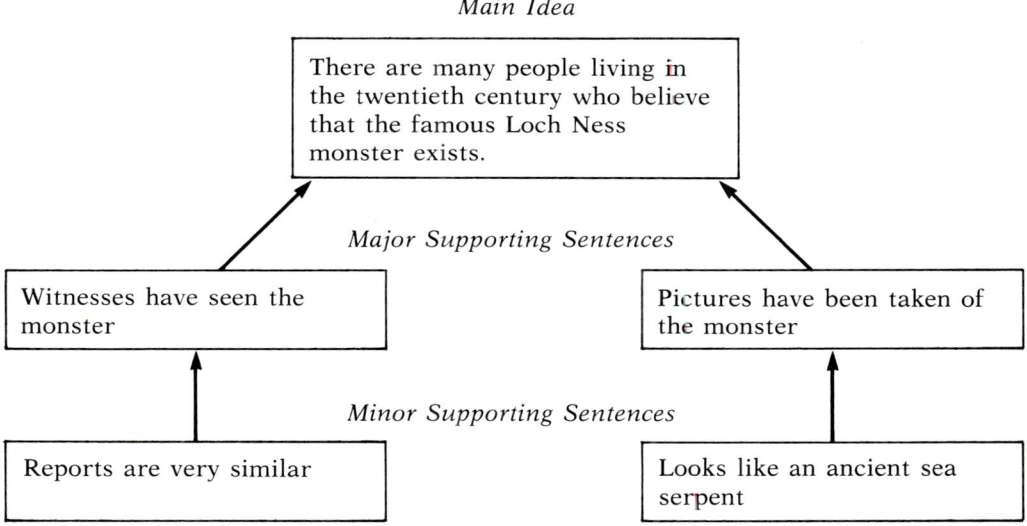

DIAGRAM 4–2

At this point you may be wondering if minor supporting sentences contain important information. Is it possible, perhaps, to read these sentences once and forget them?

There is no one answer to that question. If you are reading purely for your own enjoyment, it is possible to forget the information contained in the minor supporting sentences. Usually they do not add information that is absolutely necessary to your understanding of the paragraph.

If the reading you are doing is for school, you must take into account the nature of your assignment. If you are reading only to answer questions in class, you will usually not be responsible for all the details mentioned in a paragraph. However, if you are reading to write a paper, you will usually need to be quite detailed in your explanation, and minor supporting sentences will become important.

In any case, to remember or forget at will the information contained in minor supporting sentences, you need to be able to recognize them. Therefore, we offer one more example (see Diagram 4–3).

On July 3, 1947, a United States C-54 Superfortress bomber vanished while flying near the region known as the Bermuda Triangle. The plane was never heard from again. On January 30, 1948, a British airliner, the *Star Tiger*, disappeared while flying over the same region. Nothing was ever heard from either crew or passengers. In 1968 the *Scorpion*, a nuclear submarine, disappeared, and months went by without a trace of the craft. After a lengthy search it was found in waters located on the fringes of the Triangle.

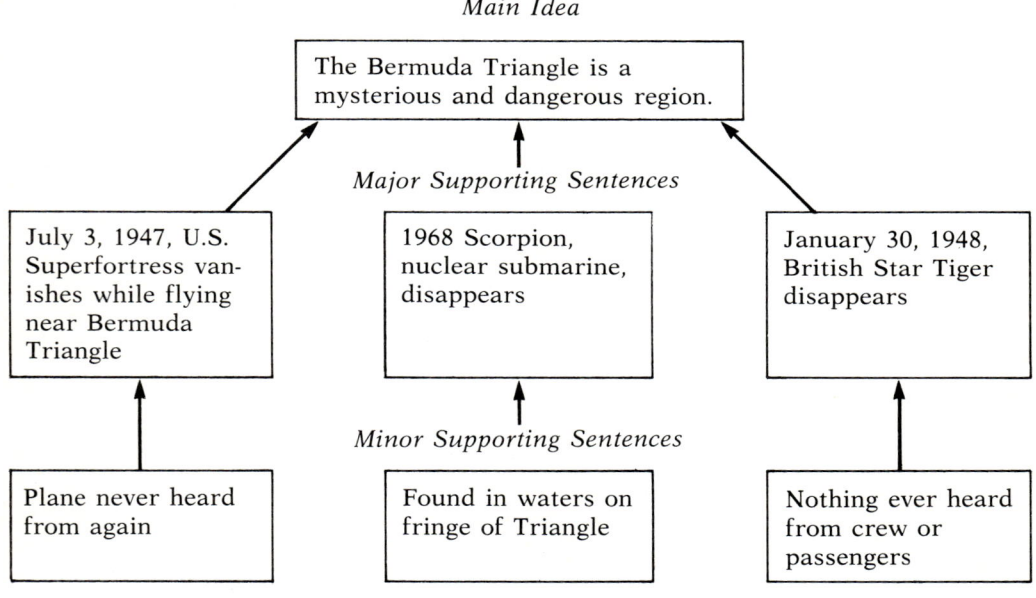

DIAGRAM 4–3

The supporting sentences in the sample paragraph suggest a main idea: The Bermuda Triangle is a mysterious and dangerous place. Since the major supporting sentences can con-

Major and Minor Supporting Sentences

tain only a limited amount of information, the author follows each major sentence with a minor one. The minor supporting sentences add specific details.

The minor supporting sentences are not as important as the major ones. Indeed, if you separated the minor sentences from the major ones, the minor sentences would not make much sense. However, they do help further explain what was said in major sentences.

As you may have already guessed, minor supporting sentences can also be followed by other minor sentences. Take, for example, this version of the previous paragraph (see Diagram 4–4):

On July 3, 1947, a United States C-54 Superfortress bomber vanished while flying near the region known as the Bermuda Triangle. The plane was never heard from again. On January 30, 1948, a British airliner, the *Star Tiger,* disappeared while flying over the same region. Nothing was ever heard from either crew or passengers. In 1968 the *Scorpion,* a nuclear submarine, disap-

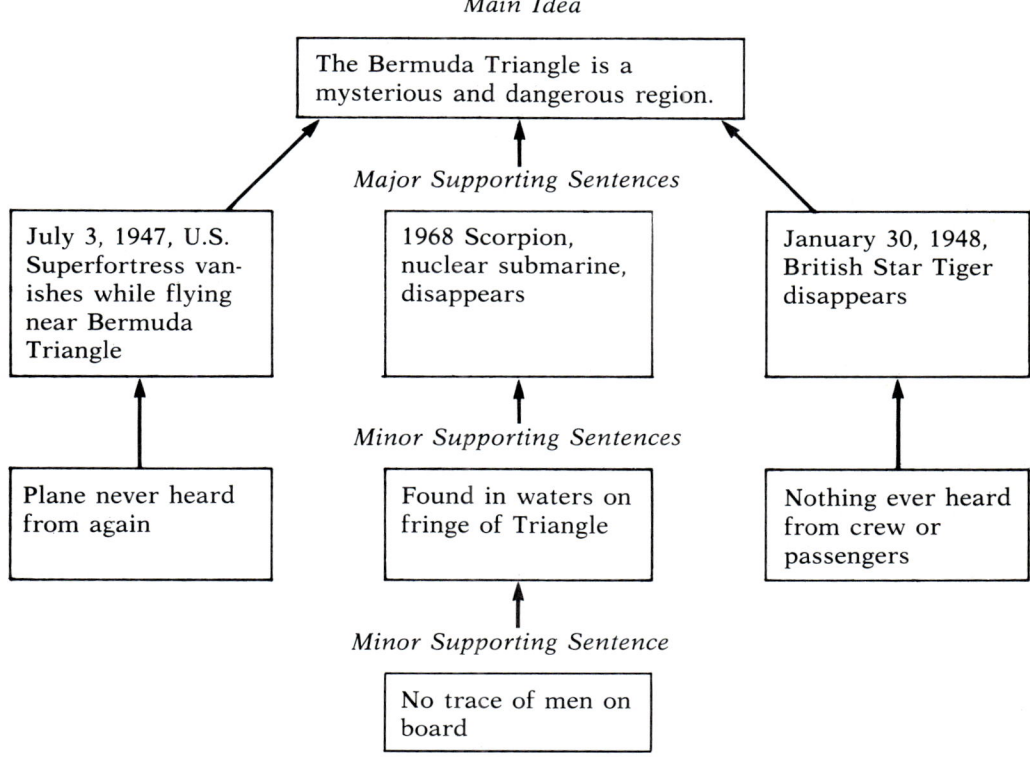

DIAGRAM 4–4

peared, and months went by without a trace of the craft. After a lengthy search it was found in the waters located on the fringes of the Triangle. There was no trace of the one hundred men who had been on board.

Those minor sentences that follow other minor supporting sentences are usually not essential to understanding a paragraph, but they do offer specific details that may be important if you are reading to take a test or to write a detailed paper.

The following exercises will give you some practice seeing the relationship between major and minor supporting sentences.

EXERCISE 5 **Practice Exercise:** Read over the paragraphs and then fill in the boxes that follow. You do not have to use complete sentences; you can rephrase or else give a shortened version of the sentences.

Note: Every paragraph will not contain exactly the same number of major and minor supporting sentences. For example, one paragraph may have one major supporting sentence and two minor ones; another might have two major supporting sentences and no minor ones. Therefore, you will not always be able to fill in all the boxes in the diagram.

1. It is impossible that large prehistoric* creatures could have remained on land to this day without being discovered. On the other hand, there is a possibility that huge creatures from the dinosaur age still exist beneath the sea. After all, as fossil remains show, dinosaurs had relatives who lived in the sea. They were huge, had long necks and snake-like heads. Those who maintain that monsters from the time of the dinosaurs still live, point out that accounts of strange creatures seen in the sea fit the description of ancient sea monsters. According to reports, the modern-day sea creatures have long necks and snake-like heads.[2]

*prehistoric: of or belonging to an age before history was written

[2]DeWitt Miller, *Impossible Yet It Happened* (New York: Ace Books, 1947), p. 30

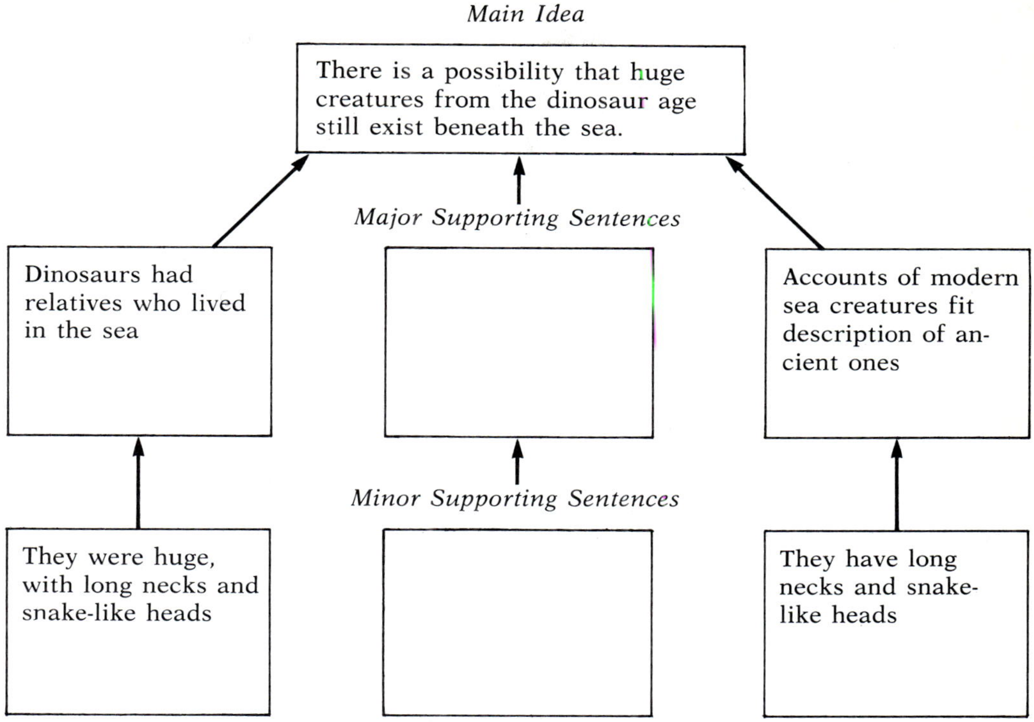

Major and Minor Supporting Sentences

Main Idea

There is a possibility that huge creatures from the dinosaur age still exist beneath the sea.

Major Supporting Sentences

Dinosaurs had relatives who lived in the sea

Accounts of modern sea creatures fit description of ancient ones

Minor Supporting Sentences

They were huge, with long necks and snake-like heads

They have long necks and snake-like heads

DIAGRAM 4–5

Explanation: The topic sentence makes the claim that huge creatures from the dinosaur age might still exist beneath the sea. Two major supporting sentences help make the topic sentence more convincing. Each major supporting sentence is followed by a minor one that adds some more information.

Do the rest of the exercises in the same manner.

1. The word *Poltergeist* is German, and it means "noisy ghost." To many people the word is a joke, but to others poltergeists are no laughing matter. They exist! In 1935 Dr. Hereward Carrington collected 318 cases of poltergeist phenomena to prove their existence.[3] His cases included reports of nails, pieces of tile, stones, and walnuts being mysteriously thrown into the air.

[3]Ibid., p. 57

Major and Minor Supporting Sentences

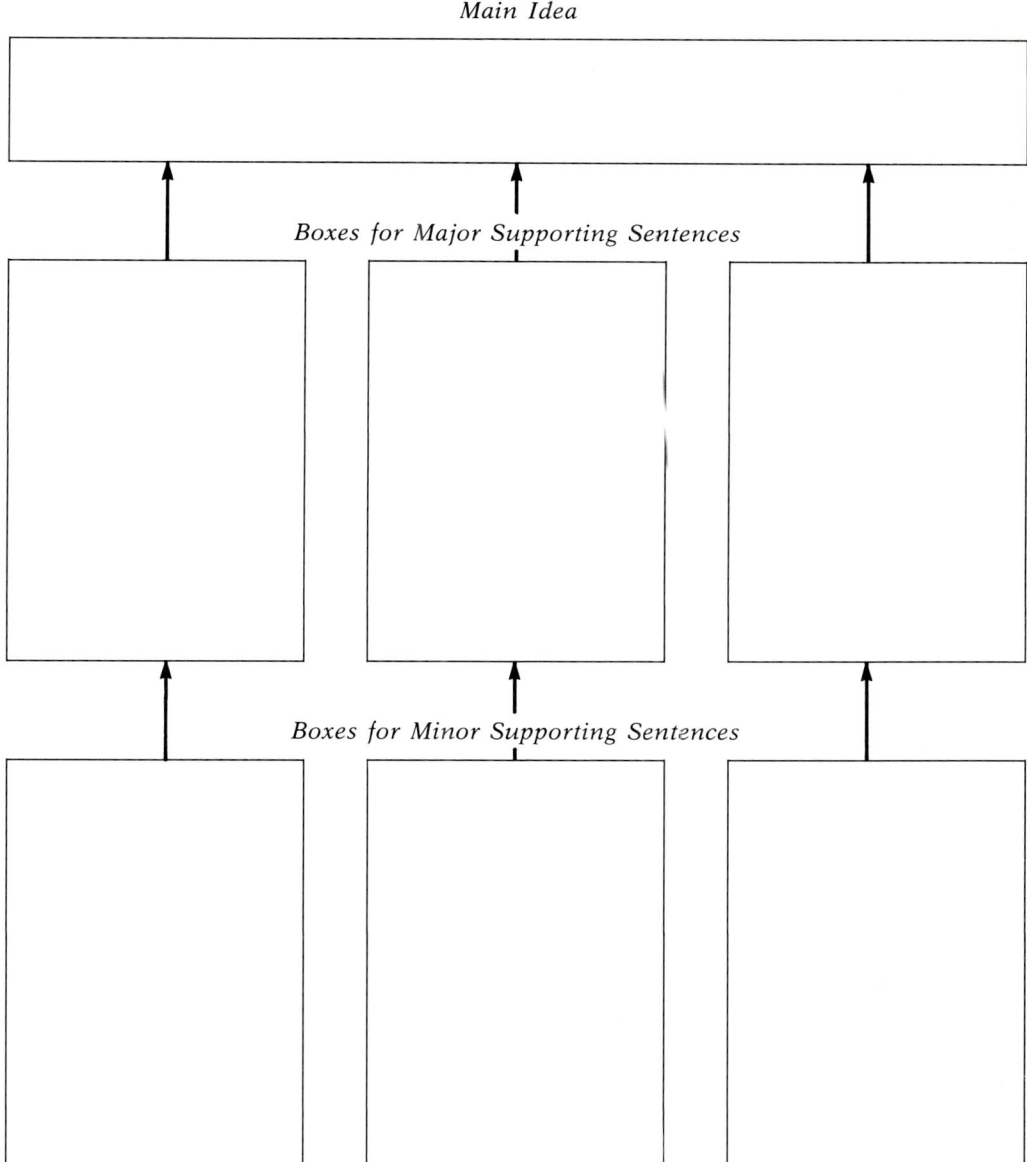

DIAGRAM 4–6

2. For years anyone interested in extrasensory perception*
was considered either a fraud or a fool, but that attitude has
been slowly changing. Serious books and essays have been
published on the subject. For example, Arthur Koestler's
book *Roots of Coincidence* gives a clear and well-supported
account of the research that has been done in extrasensory
perception. Even members of the scientific world are beginning to show a very real interest. At California's Stanford
Research Institute, two physicists have tested the psychic*
powers of Israeli magician Uri Geller.[4]

*extrasensory perception: the ability to know things without the normal use of the five senses—touch, smell, hearing, taste, and sight

*psychic: in this case one who knows things without the normal use of the five senses

[4] "Probing New Worlds," *Newsweek,* January 6, 1975, p. 47

Major and Minor Supporting Sentences 181

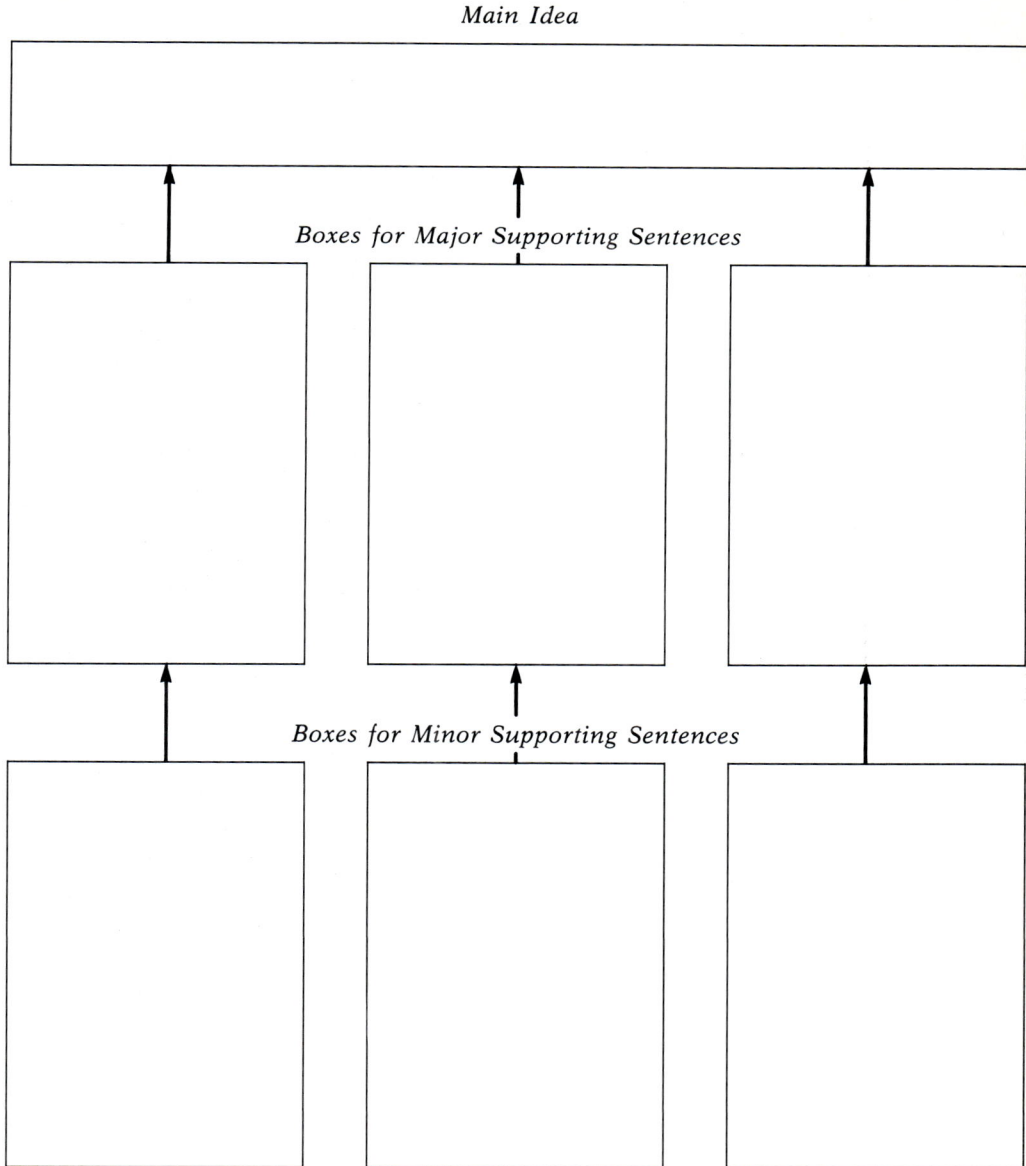

DIAGRAM 4-7

3. Respected psychologist* Carl Jung was very interested in extrasensory perception. In his autobiography, *Memories, Dreams, Reflections,* he describes several instances where he was able to predict something that was about to happen. On one occasion he predicted that a loud noise would come from a very innocent-looking bookcase; no sooner had he spoken, then the bookcase exploded with a loud bang.

*psychologist: one who studies the mind and behavior

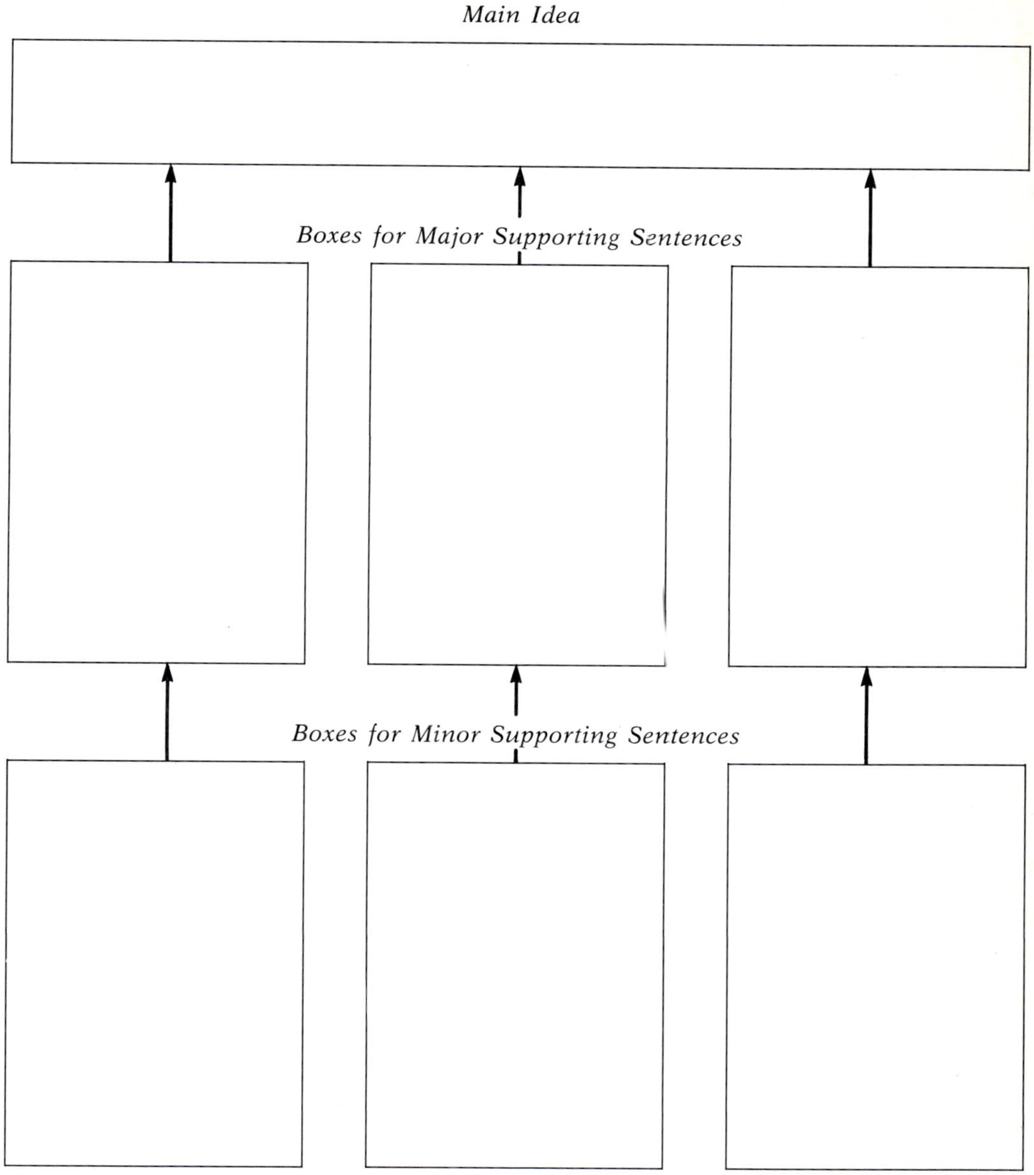

Main Idea

Boxes for Major Supporting Sentences

Boxes for Minor Supporting Sentences

DIAGRAM 4–8

4. Although Harry Houdini, the world famous magician, could have benefited from the public's belief in the supernatural, he spent much of his time trying to expose the fraud and trickery behind supposed supernatural happenings. Over the years, Houdini collected a huge file of all the frauds and hoaxes he had managed to expose. On his death the file was turned over to the famous magician Joseph Dunninger, who was to make sure the evidence would not be lost.[5] Houdini is also reported to have spent much time and energy trying to convince Arthur Conan Doyle, creator of Sherlock Holmes, that most of the miracles Doyle believed in were simply tricks. Unfortunately, Doyle remained unconvinced and was made a fool of on at least one well-known occasion: He assumed that pictures of fairies perched upon leaves were actually authentic, unretouched photographs.

---

[5]Miller, *Impossible*, p. 87

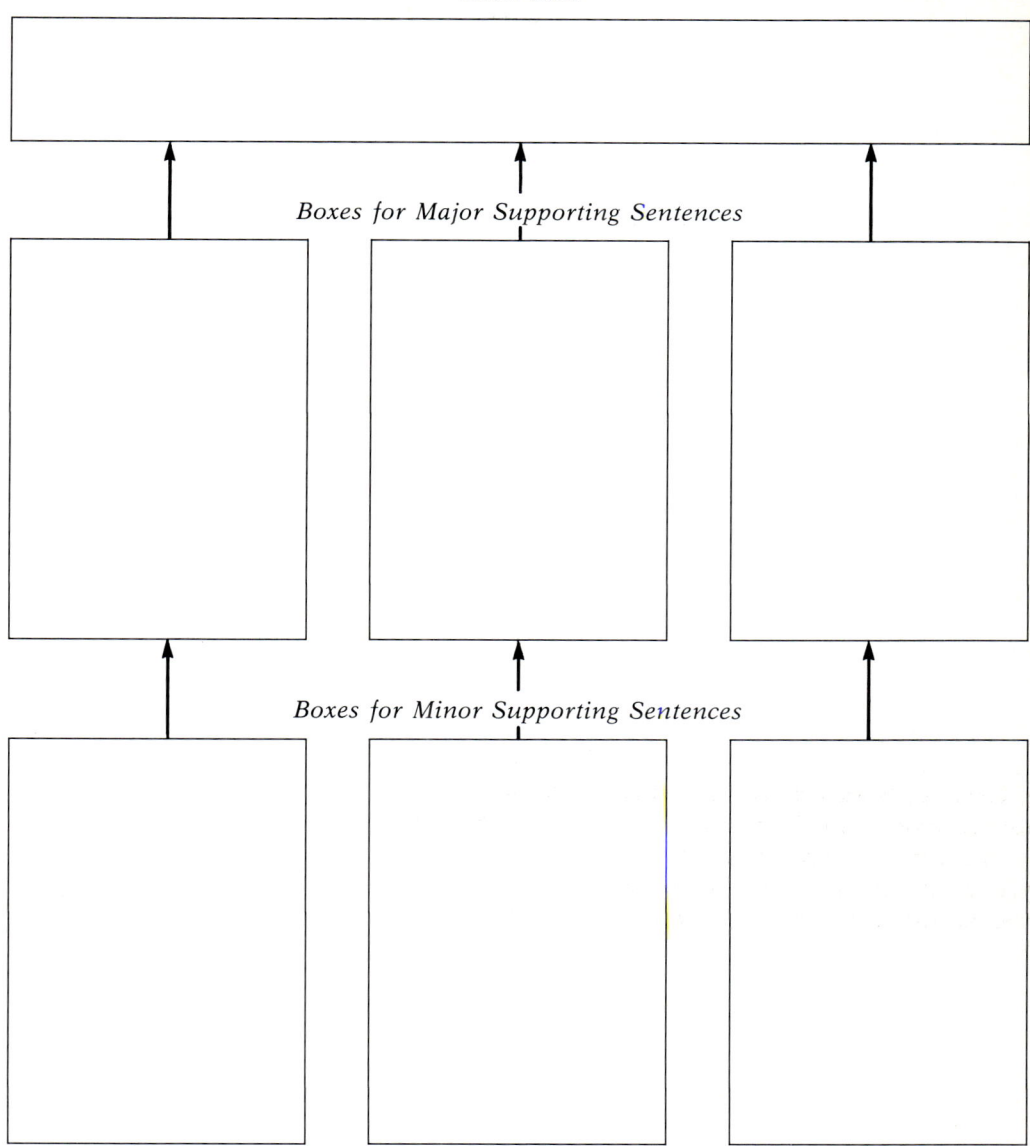

DIAGRAM 4-9

5. For centuries people have been fascinated with the theory that advanced civilizations lived for a while and then disappeared into the sea. The Greek philosopher Plato wrote of Atlantis, the great island believed to have sunk beneath the water in a single day. In the eighteenth century several writers discovered the story of Atlantis and attempted to prove that it had existed. It has been proposed even up to the present day that vanished civilizations lie somewhere beneath the Pacific.

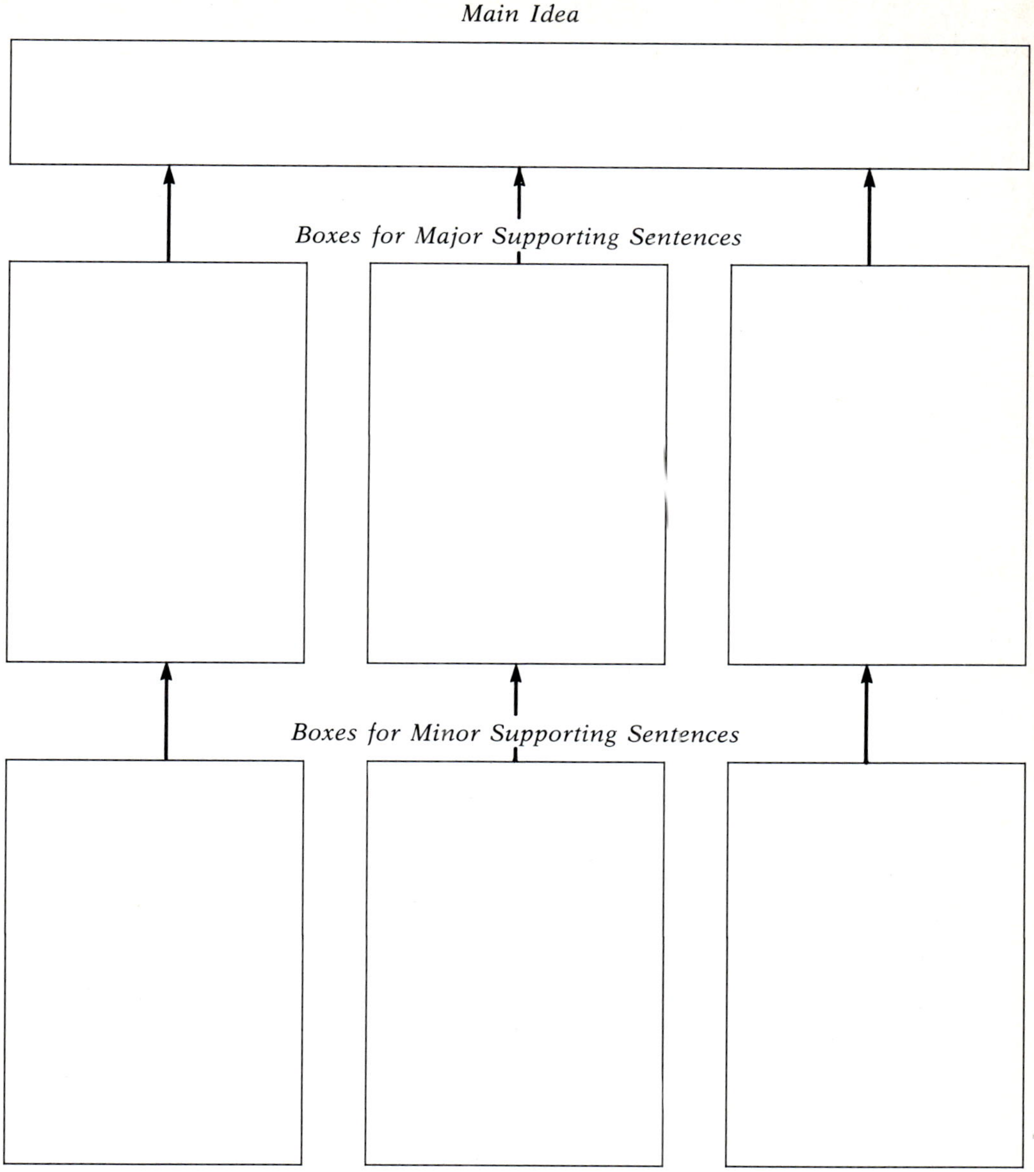

Main Idea

Boxes for Major Supporting Sentences

Boxes for Minor Supporting Sentences

DIAGRAM 4-10

REVIEW TEST: CHAPTER 4

The following pages will test your mastery of Chapter 4.

Directions: All the paragraphs in the following test lack several sentences. Some lack topic sentences as well as major and minor supporting sentences. Others lack only supporting sentences. You are to select the sentences that would correctly fill in the blank spaces.

Note: We suggest that you read all the sentences in the paragraph through. Then read the sentences that could fill in the blanks. Look for the sentence that best fits the context. Two sentences may appear to be equally correct, but actually one will be more appropriate than the other. Use context clues from the paragraph to help you decide.

1. [1] _____ [2] At the present time production workers are just about fifteen percent of the labor force. [3] _____ [4] Although robots employed in industry at the present time are limited to the simplest tasks on the assembly line, those of the future will be aided by the intelligence of computers. [5] _____ [6] Today at the Massachusetts Institute of Technology, computerized robots can play games, all kinds of games from tic-tac-toe to checkers. [7] Fifty years from now, robots may stand in an assembly line that produces more robots. [8] _____

   (a) The word *robot* actually means "worker." It was first used in a Czech play called *R.U.R.*
   (b) Within fifty years factories may be filled not with people but with robots.
   (c) The dream of building a mechanical human being goes back hundreds of years.
   (d) Able to see and touch, they will also be capable of making more complex decisions.
   (e) However, *robotics* may reduce that number to a little less than 5 percent.
   (f) This will be necessary if the request for mechanical people grows to the expected proportions.

2. [1] _____ [2] First of all there is the outer ear. [3] It collects sound waves and directs them into the auditory canal. [4] _____ [5] The second area, or middle ear, contains three small bones. [6] _____ [7] The middle ear is connected to the throat by a small tube known as the *eustachian tube*. [8] The inner ear con-

tains the actual hearing apparatus. [9] This is a small, shell-like organ filled with fluid and nerve endings. [10] It is called the *cochlea*. [11] _____ [12] The ear is a truly complex structure.

   (a) The structure of the ear is almost as complex as that of the eye.
   (b) The human ear is a complicated structure that can be divided into three main parts.
   (c) Untreated infections in the ear can lead to temporary, or even permanent, deafness.
   (d) At the very end of the canal is a membrane called the ear drum or tympanum.
   (e) They are called the hammer, anvil, and stirrup.
   (f) When these nerve endings receive vibrations from the fluid in the cochlea, they transmit them directly to the hearing portion of the brain.

3. [1] Puzzles have always been popular with people of all ages. [2] However, probably no puzzle in the history of games has ever been as popular as the famous Rubik's Cube. [3] _____ [4] Those who could not tolerate the suspense probably went out and bought any one of the numerous books that provides the correct solution. [5] Others just twisted and turned until they figured out how to do it themselves. [6] _____ [7] France even has a cube contest. [8] _____ [9] The winner gets a cash prize. [10] Erno Rubik, the cube's inventor, is apparently not content with the cube's success; he has invented another brain-twister. [11] _____ [12] With time it may become more popular than the original Rubik's Cube.

   (a) Millions of people have frantically twisted and turned the bright blocks in an effort to find a solution to the cube's mystery.
   (b) *Cube Games* is a paperback that features more than ninety puzzles.
   (c) Some just gave up.
   (d) Some people even have cube key rings; that way they practice any time they have a spare moment.
   (e) Contestants try to see who can solve the cube in the shortest amount of time.

(f) The Magic Snake, successor to the cubes, is a sphere that can be twisted into different shapes.

4. [1] Fish are members of the vertebrate family. [2] Because they are cold-blooded animals, they cannot regulate the temperature of their bodies. [3] _____ [4] If fish are placed in freezing water, their temperatures sink. But place them in warm water, and the opposite occurs. [5] Fins and gills distinguish fish from other animals. [6] _____ [7] Fish usually have scales all over their bodies. [8] The scales themselves are colorless, but the skin color of the fish can shine through, making the scales appear to possess beautiful and exotic patterns.
[9] _____ [10] Some fish are easily caught and then sold. [11] Trout and bass, for example, are popular entries on restaurant menus. [12] _____ [13] As one might guess, the shark does not fall into either category.

(a) Warm-blooded animals, if conditions are normal, have a constant body temperature.

(b) Instead body temperature depends upon their surroundings.

(c) Fins function for fish like the arms and legs of other animals.

(d) More important than beauty, the color of a fish provides protection, and many fish hide from enemies by quietly blending into their environment.

(e) Fish lay eggs by a process known as spawning.

(f) Other fish, like goldfish, are kept as pets.

5. [1] _____ [2] Although the movement has been called the Harlem renaissance, it extended far beyond the boundaries of the Manhattan community. [3] Across the Atlantic, the French embraced black music and dance, and Josephine Baker became, almost overnight, the toast of Paris. [4] In America poets like Claude McKay, Jean Toomer, Countee Cullen, and Langston Hughes were known and read. [5] White Americans discovered the blues, and paid willingly to hear the music that could be found only in the black community. [6] Black periodicals like *The Crisis* and *Opportunity* printed the poems of both established and aspiring poets, awarding cash prizes to the most talented. [7] _____ [8] Museums opened exhibitions of African art, and the leading artists of the time bought and imitated African sculpture. [9] _____ [10] In

drama Ridgely Torrence, Paul Green, and Eugene O'Neill wrote plays that placed black people, for the first time, on center stage. [11] _____

(a) Zora Neale Hurston, friend and co-worker of Langston Hughes, became interested in black culture, and began to study the ways of Voodoo.

(b) Particularly fascinated by African art was Pablo Picasso; today the masks he made during that period are worth a fortune.

(c) Thanks to them, even major publishing houses began to open their doors to black writers.

(d) In 1923 Albert C. Barnes founded a museum devoted to the exhibition of black artists.

(e) One of O'Neill's plays, *The Emperor Jones* (1920), became an American classic.

(f) In the years following World War I, black America became the focus of a literary and artistic revolution.

6. [1] In October of 1957 the Russians burst into the space age with the launching of a satellite that became world famous as *Sputnik*. [2] Awed by the Russian breakthrough America made intense efforts to improve satellite technology. [3] Since that time the United States has begun to rival the Russians, launching its own share of satellites. [4] _____ [5] With the technological advances scientists expect, satellites will be used even more in the future. [6] Fifty years from now, they may pave the way for portable telephones, small as a wrist watch. [7] _____ [8] The military, which already makes extensive use of satellites, will continue to do so in the future. [9] At present, the United States military employs satellites for intelligence gathering. [10] _____ [11] Although they possess no satellites of their own, third world countries have still laid claim to precious air space. [12] _____

(a) If they are able to launch a satellite in the future, they do not want to discover that all usable orbits* have been taken.

(b) Hundreds of American satellites have been successfully propelled into the air.

(c) *Sputnik II* contained a dog called Laika; Laika survived an entire week in space.

*orbits: the path of a satellite as it moves around another body

(d) Owners of pocket calculators may use satellite communications to tap into faraway data banks.

(e) In the future, observation satellites will be particularly attentive to Soviet Union military operations, and plans are already underway to increase the satellites in reconnaissance.*

(f) If areas in space, like the Van Allen radiation belt, cannot be permanently occupied by satellites containing human beings, robots may be employed.

7. [1] For most people, snakes are an object of intense fear. [2] Few are as fearless as the Hopi Indians, who perform ritual dances with live rattlesnakes in their mouths. [3] _____ [4] If they are examined without prejudice, snakes prove to be fascinating and relatively harmless members of the reptile family. [5] _____ [6] Although most people think their skins are slimy and wet, quite the opposite is true. [7] _____ [8] Although most snakes are hatched in eggs, some are born alive. [9] Like adult snakes, the babies can go a long time without food or water. [10] Unfortunately the deadliest snakes are the most beautiful. [11] _____

(a) A python can swallow a whole pig.

(b) But, in fact, most snakes are hated and feared without good reason.

(c) Like other reptiles, they are cold-blooded, and their temperatures change with the environment.

(d) The cobra, when it extends its hood before striking, is an awesome sight.

(e) Their skins are cool and dry, pleasant to the touch.

(f) The coral snake, for example, found in parts of the South, has brilliant black, red, and yellow markings.

8. [1] For centuries, the shroud of Turin has been a mystery to Christians and non-Christians alike. [2] So far the many tests performed upon the shroud have only served to increase its mysterious reputation. [3] A fourteen-foot piece of linen fabric, the shroud is believed to have been the cloth in which Jesus of Nazareth was wrapped after his death on the cross. [4] Normally it lies hidden behind an iron grill on a Turin altar, but in 1978 an exhibition was

*reconnaissance: the survey made of a region in order to determine military force

held to celebrate the four-hundredth anniversary of the shroud's discovery. [5] _____ [6] Markings on the shroud reveal the faded image of a naked man laid out for burial. [7] _____ [8] From all indications he died by crucifixion. [9] Although some claim to have discovered flecks of paint in the shroud, others maintain that an artist's fakery is not possible. [10] _____ [11] For a while experts were puzzled when special photographs of the shroud revealed bulges around the eyes. [12] _____

(a) In the sixteenth century, the shroud was scorched by a fire that spread through the chapel.

(b) Officially the shroud belongs to the exiled king of Italy.

(c) The image of the man shows no brush strokes, and it grows blurry at any distance less than two feet.

(d) The mystery was solved when someone pointed out that the Romans placed coins over the eyes of the dead.

(e) During this time scientists were given the chance to examine the cloth.

(f) Strongly built with regular features, his face is partially covered by a beard.

9. [1] Just about fifty years ago, John Steinbeck wrote a novel called *The Grapes of Wrath*. [2] In it he depicted the sorrows and trials of the Joads, a family of migrant workers. [3] _____ [4] Public response to the work was strong and when the book became a film, it grew even stronger. [5] _____ [6] Some are even worse off than they were when Steinbeck wrote *The Grapes of Wrath*. [7] Every year the Department of Labor receives complaints about improper recruitment or failure to pay the minimum wage, but charges are hard to prove, and workers are frequently frightened into silence. [8] Housing provided for the workers is often substandard. [9] Meals belong to the same category, barely meeting nutritional standards. [10] _____ [11] Owners of farms that employ migrant workers are not always present at the work site, and that leaves workers in the hands of crew leaders. [12] _____

(a) More than one crew leader has abused that responsibility.

(b) Henry Fonda played the lead in *The Grapes of Wrath*, and it is still considered one of his best roles.

(c) Prices for necessities are so high a worker may end up owning his employer by the end of the season.

(d) When Steinbeck wrote *The Grapes of Wrath*, there were no laws protecting the rights of migrant workers, and they suffered because of it.

(e) Consequently workers continue to live in substandard housing.

(f) Unfortunately, half a century has made little difference, and migrant workers still live under poor, sometimes horrible, conditions.

10. [1] The Galapagos are volcanic islands located just about six hundred miles from South America's Pacific coast. [2] Hardly the place to spend a summer vacation, they still have begun to attract growing numbers of tourists. [3] _____ [4] For example in the past humans have not exactly benefited the animal population. [5] Sailors who landed on the islands frequently hunted and killed those animals who had not learned to avoid human beings. [6] _____ [7] The huge tortoises were considered splendid souvenirs. [8] People who settled on the islands usually brought animals with them. [9] _____ [10] Even the tourists, spending a quiet weekend can injure the island's fragile ecology.* [11] They do not realize that killing a stray spider can cause harm. [12] _____

(a) Unfortunately, the domestic animals ended up destroying the same vegetation needed to support the wild animal population.

(b) The islands were discovered in 1535, and since that time they have been used by pirates, whalers, and convicts.

(c) Spiders are needed to keep other troublesome pests under control.

(d) The animals who live on the islands are surprisingly tame.

(e) However, for the Galapagos, tourism may create a problem.

(f) In addition to hunting, they also captured thousands of giant tortoises.

*ecology: the relationship between organisms and their environment

Review Test: Chapter 4

A huge tortoise from the Galapagos.

Chapter 5

Learning More About Sentence Functions

Most of the paragraphs you have dealt with up to this point consisted mainly of topic sentences and supporting sentences. However, as this chapter will illustrate, paragraphs do contain other types of sentences.

In this chapter we will introduce four different types: (1) **sentences that provide a transition or make a connection between ideas,** (2) **sentences that provide an introduction,** (3) **sentences that give emphasis to an important point,** and (4) **sentences that provide a conclusion.**

We will also introduce a note-taking format that requires you to use everything you have learned up to this point.

SENTENCES CAN MAKE TRANSITIONS

We can't explain what a transitional sentence is before we've explained what the word *transition* means. Briefly, when we talk about transitions, we are talking about those words or phrases used to link sentences or paragraphs together. The following examples should illustrate what we mean. The first example contains two sentences. No transition links them together:

> He was terribly anxious to get married. The thought of spending the rest of their lives together sent cold shivers up and down his spine.

Those two sentences don't make much sense together. If he's scared, why is he so anxious to get married? Look at the second example. The addition of a single word, a transitional word, makes things clearer:

> He was terribly anxious to get married. *Nevertheless*, the thought of spending the rest of their lives together sent cold shivers up and down his spine.

With the addition of a single transitional word, the relationship between the two sentences becomes clearer. The young man does, indeed, want to get married, but that feeling does not make him forget all his fears. With the help of the transitional word, it is easier to follow what the author had in mind.

Remember then that *trans* is Latin for "across." In a way, that's what transitions do; they help you get "across" from one idea to another. They help you see the relationship between different ideas so that you can follow the author's train of thought.

Transitional sentences work much the same way transitional words do. They link ideas or facts together. They show how two statements are connected so that you don't end up wondering what the sentence before had to do with the one that came after. The following is an example of how transitional sentences are used to link paragraphs together:

> In 1922 Lord Carnarvon and Howard Carter made a discovery that shocked and delighted the entire world of archaeology: They found the fabulous tomb of King Tutankhamen. Two rooms of the tomb had been attacked by grave robbers, but the third room had been left untouched for thousands of years. The room contained not only the mummy of the eighteen-year-old king but also hundreds of priceless objects that provided valuable information about the ancient Egyptian culture.

Transitional Sentence
> *Unfortunately, the story does not end with the discovery.* Following the opening of the tomb, stories of the "curse of the Pharaohs" began to circulate, and many believed that the curse was beginning its awful work. Lord Carnarvon died suddenly, and for some that was proof enough. But even more amazing, as time went on more than twenty people connected with the tomb died under mysterious circumstances.

In the preceding example each paragraph contains a main idea. The first paragraph is concerned with explaining what was so important about the discovery of the tomb; the second explains why many thought the curse was coming true. The author wants you to move smoothly from the first idea to the second and therefore provides the transitional sentence italicized in the paragraph.

This sentence links the ideas in the two paragraphs together. It refers to what was said in the first paragraph and at the same time signals that some new development will be described. The transitional sentence emphasizes that the discovery and the curse are two parts of the same story.

We said in the opening of this section that transitional sentences could also be used to link sentences in the same paragraph together. The following paragraph contains an example.

<blockquote>
Many believed that the death of several individuals who had been involved with the discovery of the tomb was positive proof that the curse did exist, but there were those who wanted to prove that such talk was nonsense. In 1933 a German professor of archaeology wrote a paper on the curse in which he tracked down all the reports of the deaths connected with the tomb. According to his research many of the people who had supposedly died as a result of their entrance in the tomb had actually never set foot in it.
</blockquote>

Transitional Sentence — *The professor was not alone in his refusal to believe in the curse.* Shortly afterwards Howard Carter took up his pen to argue against what he considered foolish rumors.

The italicized sentence is a transitional one, and it is used to show the relationship between the professor already mentioned and Howard Carter. Note how the sentence manages to refer back to the professor and at the same time point ahead to someone else, Carter, who shared his opinion.

Before we go on to the next section, we'd like to give you an example of a particularly important kind of transitional sentence. This is the transitional sentence which totally reverses the author's original line of thought. We can use the following paragraph as an example.

Transitional Sentence — Most Americans think of Thomas Jefferson as the perfect statesman, a hero who seldom, if ever, made a mistake. *A closer reading of history, however, does not confirm this view of Jefferson.* Jefferson was not without his flaws, both personal and political. He was, after all, a man who spoke out against slavery but kept slaves of his own. The very same man who wrote ringing phrases about human equality did not like it if women were too opinionated and forgetful of their place. A proud man, Jefferson was sick at heart when not only he himself but others around him questioned just how well he had governed Virginia during the Revolutionary War.

The first sentence of the sample paragraph would lead you to believe that the rest of the paragraph will maintain that Jefferson was a perfect hero. However, the next sentence, a transitional sentence, reverses the initial train of thought. It tells us that this view of Jefferson is actually quite far from the truth. Obviously the author is going to challenge or question what has just been said.

The real main idea of the paragraph appears in the third sentence, "Jefferson was not without his flaws, both personal and political." This is the main idea that will actually be developed in the rest of the paragraph.

When you read, you should keep an eye open for transitional words, phrases, or sentences that will, in different words, tell you that the author is going to reverse or turn around what was just said. Being aware of the transitional words or phrases will make it easier to follow the writer's train of thought.

The following exercise will introduce you to a number of transitional words and phrases and explain how they are used.

EXERCISE 1

Directions: The following transitions have been grouped together according to their function. For example, all transitions that reverse the writer's train of thought appear together.

moreover, likewise, too, furthermore, again, also, similarly, in addition, in the same vein, by the same token	These transitions indicate that the writer will continue to develop an idea already introduced.
but, and yet, nevertheless, still, on the other hand, although, however, on the contrary, in spite of that fact, unlike, granted that, to be sure, instead	These transitions usually indicate that the writer is reversing the train of thought previously introduced.
in support of, for example, first, first of all, as an example, for instance, to illustrate	These transitions usually indicate that the author is going to give specific reasons or illustrations to support an idea already introduced.

in summary, in brief, in short, on the whole, to sum up, finally, in conclusion	These transitions usually indicate that the author is drawing the paragraph or essay to a close and is going to briefly summarize what has already been said.
thus, therefore, in brief, in short, on the whole, to sum up, finally, in conclusion, ultimately	These transitions usually indicate that the author is drawing the paragraph or essay to a close and is going to briefly summarize what has already been said.
again, as we have said, it has already been mentioned, it has been noted, to reiterate*	These transitions usually indicate that the author wants to repeat a point that has previously been made.

Practice Exercise: Read through the following sentences. Then fill in the blank between the sentences with a transitional word or phrase that will clarify the relationship between the ideas contained in the sentences.

1. Spain, following the death of Francisco Franco, was rocked by political protest. *For example*, thousands of men and women in the northern city of Vittoria took to the streets in response to a call for a general strike.

Explanation: Since the second sentence provides specific illustration for the first, we have added the transitional phrase, *for example*. This phrase makes it clear that the thousands of men and women who responded to the call for a general strike are an example of the political protest mentioned by the author.

Do the rest of the exercises in the same manner.

1. The earthquake in Guatemala reduced hundreds of buildings to rubble. _____ , millions of dollars were needed for reconstruction.

*to reiterate: to repeat

2. George Washington was much admired as a soldier. In his private life, _____ , it has been claimed that he was proud and demanding.

3. Thomas Jefferson was a great statesman. _____ , he was a talented architect and inventor.

4. The preceding paragraphs have given several concrete examples of Senator Moore's failure to answer the committee's questions. _____ , I can say only that Senator Moore must have something to hide.

5. Amnesty International is a worldwide organization dedicated to helping men and women who have been unjustly imprisoned. _____ , the organization regularly publishes the names and addresses of political prisoners and asks that letters requesting prisoners' release be addressed to the proper authorities.

6. _____ in the preceding paragraphs that Ralph Ellison's *Invisible Man* is a work of genius, and time will not decrease its importance.

7. When Rachel Carson first wrote in *Silent Spring* that human beings were destroying the environment, she was laughed at. Time, _____ , has proved her right.

8. The famous anarchists* were innocent of the crime of which they were accused, and the evidence against them was extremely flimsy; _____ they were executed.

9. He had been continuously abused as a child. _____ _____, he grew up to be a bitter and violence-prone adult.

10. In general, early American architecture was developed by men who had little formal training in architecture. Samuel McIntire, _____, one of the earliest and finest architects, was a woodcarver, and Thomas Jefferson, the designer of Monticello,* was educated as a lawyer.

EXERCISE 2 **Practice Exercise:** In this exercise we ask you to identify transitional sentences. If the paragraph contains a transitional sentence, put the number of that sentence in the blank that follows. If the paragraph does not contain a transitional sentence, fill in the blank with an *X*.

1. [1] The traditional attitude toward cancer is one of fearful acceptance: The disease is viewed as a deadly and unpredictable fact of life. [2] But recently research has tended to change that attitude. [3] Cancer, rather than being the mysterious disease with causes that are unknown, may be far more predictable than anyone has been led to believe; in many cases cancer may be caused by human beings themselves. [4] For example, in the last decade scientists

*anarchists: men and women who do not believe in any form of government

*Monticello: Jefferson's estate near Charlottesville, Virginia, famous for its beauty

have discovered that cigarettes, clearly a human invention, cause lung cancer, one of the most deadly forms of the disease. [5] Estrogens, hormones freely given to women suffering from symptoms of menopause, are under suspicion because they may prove to cause cancer of the uterus; and DES, a drug given to pregnant women sometime in the 1950s, has caused cancer in the daughters of several women who took the drug.

Sentence ___2___ is a transitional sentence.

Explanation: We have put the number 2 in the blank. The first sentence tells us of the traditional attitude toward cancer. The second sentence is a transitional sentence, which tells us that the paragraph is going to show how that attitude has changed. The transitional sentence prepares us for the main idea of the paragraph: The causes of cancer may not be so mysterious and unpredictable; human beings themselves may be one of the major causes.

Do the rest of the exercises in the same manner.

1. [1] The character of Sherlock Holmes is for many people more reality than fantasy. [2] Visitors come to visit his imaginary rooms at 221 Baker Street, and letters asking his advice still arrive. [3] Actually these occasional visitors and letter writers are not the only ones who take the fictional detective seriously. [4] There are Sherlock Holmes societies in many countries in the world, and articles tracing the youth of Holmes appear now and then in journals of detective fiction. [5] Once in a while a half-serious article debating an important question is published: did Holmes go to Cambridge or Oxford?

    Sentence _____ is a transitional sentence.

2. [1] For a century, any man or woman accused of a crime has been allowed to place a plea of insanity before the court. [2] But that legal tradition may soon disappear. [3] In the last decade, the insanity defense has come under increasing attack by critics who claim it has been terribly abused. [4] As a result Idaho has abolished the plea altogether whereas several other states have begun to consider drastically modifying the number of possible cases where the insanity defense may apply. [5] Although the idea behind such a defense — that society should not punish those unable to

control illegal behavior—is sound in theory, in reality it presents several serious, possibly insoluble problems. [6] On the most obvious level, the plea of insanity has been used by criminals anxious to avoid the consequences of their crimes. [7] Feigning mental illness, they have escaped a jail sentence. [8] But even where no trickery is involved, it is a complicated matter to identify mental illness. [9] Ideally psychiatrists are the experts who can be called in to label behavior sane or disturbed, but frequently it is the experts who disagree. [10] For example, during the trial of John W. Hinckley, the man who attempted to assassinate President Ronald Reagan, some psychiatrists claimed Hinckley was suffering from severe schizophrenia while others insisted he was legally sane.

Sentence _____ is a transitional sentence.

3. [1] Movie stars were never more adored or imitated than they were in the thirties and forties. [2] When a beautiful platinum-blonde woman named Jean Harlow became a box-office hit, women all over the country dyed their hair platinum-blonde in imitation of their heroine. [3] By the time the forties rolled around, women were no longer sporting platinum hair, but they were wearing a peek-a-boo hair style just like the one Veronica Lake had worn in the film *The Glass Key*. [4] And women were not the only ones who imitated their favorite stars. [5] Sales of T-shirts dropped when a bare-chested Clark Gable appeared in the 1934 film *It Happened One Night*. [6] Men even began lighting their cigarettes differently after seeing Paul Henreid in a film called *Now Voyager*. [7] It was considered the height of sophistication for a man to put two cigarettes into his mouth, light them both, and hand one to the woman he was with, all the while looking deeply into her eyes.

Sentence _____ is a transitional sentence.

4. [1] Human beings, convinced of their superiority over the animal kingdom, are seldom disturbed about the pain and death they bring to other species. [2] For example, South American birds, desired by zoos, pet shops, and private collectors, are frequently packed into small boxes and flown to foreign countries. [3] Many of the birds, however, do not survive the trip but instead die of suffocation.* [4] And birds

---

*suffocation: cutting off the supply of air

are not the only victims. [5] Hunters in search of baby orangutans shoot the mothers who are hiding in tree tops and wait for the babies to fall to the ground. [6] Many of the babies cannot be caught and fall to their death. [7] Seals, prized for their skins, which make lovely winter coats, are brutally slaughtered by hunters who club and skin them almost immediately. [8] Sometimes the seals are skinned alive because a hunter was not skillful with his club.

Sentence _____ is a transitional sentence.

5. [1] The Tyrannosaurus, a large meat-eating dinosaur, sometimes measured forty feet from nose to tail. [2] It carried its huge body kangaroo-style on its tail and legs. [3] According to some authorities, this huge beast could actually leap through the air; however, this idea is treated with skepticism* by many. [4] It is more likely that the Tyrannosaurus spent its time wading in swampy waters in search of the lizards that were a staple of its diet.

Sentence _____ is a transitional sentence.

SENTENCES PROVIDE INTRODUCTIONS

MR. HAYES   Ladies and gentlemen, I am very proud to present our speaker for tonight. Recently returned from a voyage through the Bermuda Triangle, she is the only member of the original crew who managed to return alive. Ladies and gentlemen, Dr. Helen Rhys.

DR. RHYS   Thank you very much for the kind introduction, Mr. Hayes. As you all know, the topic of my speech tonight is the Bermuda Triangle. However, I do not intend to discuss my own voyage through this strange and mysterious region since you can read about it in my forthcoming book, which will shortly be on sale at all local bookstores. Instead, I would like to discuss the mysterious disappearances that have occurred in this region for more than a century. Above all, I'd like to explain the causes of these disappearances.

*skepticism: a doubting or questioning attitude

An introduction is almost always part of a public speech. Someone gets up before the main speaker and gives a brief idea of who is going to talk and what they are going to say. More than anything else, the person giving the introduction tries to get the audience interested in what is going to be said. For example, you'll notice in the preceding dialogue that Mr. Hayes talks about the speaker's trip through the Bermuda Triangle, even though this is not the topic of discussion. He mentions the trip in order to spark the audience's enthusiasm.

Paragraphs also contain introductions; that is, they begin with a sentence, or sometimes several sentences, that introduce the topic and attempt to trigger the reader's interest in the paragraph. Usually the ideas contained in the introductory sentences are not developed in the paragraph. Take, for example, the following paragraph:

> Everyone knows that dreams are of no importance. At least, that's what we tell ourselves when we are reluctant to examine the sometimes frightening messages contained in our dreams. However, we probably all know, even if we don't admit it, that we can't dismiss our dreams, not even the seemingly silly ones. Even if we wanted to, the writings of two of the most famous men in the history of psychology, Sigmund Freud and Carl Gustav Jung, remind us again and again that dreams help us understand who and what we really are. Freud, for example, believed that in our dreams we could find our hidden wishes, wishes we could not admit to anyone, not even to ourselves. Jung studied not only the dreams of his patients but also his own dreams to better understand his hidden desires and motives.

After reading the entire paragraph, we know that the topic is Freud's and Jung's attitude toward dreams. However, after reading just the first two sentences of the paragraph, we knew that it was going to deal with dreams. This is an example of what we mean when we say that introductory sentences help introduce the topic.

Introductory sentences also help trigger interest in a paragraph. For example, the first sentence tells us that dreams don't mean anything, but the second sentence makes it clear that we pretend dreams are unimportant because we fear the messages they contain. The author hopes we will continue reading to discover the real importance of dreams.

As you noticed, the ideas contained in the first two introductory sentences were not developed throughout the paragraph. As a matter of fact, the third sentence, a transitional one, reversed the train of thought originally introduced; it told us that the author was about to contradict what had just been

Carl Jung reminded us that dreams help us understand who and what we really are.

said. Occasionally introductory sentences will provide additional information about the topic or main idea of the paragraph (for example, the date or place of an event described in the topic sentence); but they will seldom contain ideas that are developed throughout the paragraph.

Paragraphs with an implied main idea, as well as paragraphs with no main idea, almost never include introductory sentences. In general, these paragraphs consist almost exclusively of supporting sentences.

The following exercises will give you more practice working with paragraphs that begin with an introductory sentence.

EXERCISE 3

Practice Exercise: The following paragraphs may or may not contain an introductory sentence (or sentences). Read through each paragraph; if there is one or more introductory sentences, fill in the blank that follows with the appropriate number (or numbers). If there is only a topic sentence, place an *X* in the first blank and write the number of the topic sentence in the second blank.

1. [1] The French Revolution had unleashed a storm of demands for liberty and freedom all over Europe. [2] With the fall of Napoleon, however, war and revolution were over, and the rulers of Europe were determined to forever destroy the dream of revolution. [3] After 1815 liberal writers were viewed with distrust, and their books were censored or banned altogether. [4] Nationalist movements* were forbidden, and earlier promises of political freedom broken. [5] The five great powers of Europe—Austria, France, England, Prussia, and Russia—united to stamp out any revolutionary movements that appeared on the continent.

   Sentence __1__ is an introductory sentence.

   Sentence __2__ is a topic sentence.

Explanation: The second sentence in the paragraph is the topic sentence. The first sentence in the paragraph is an introductory sentence; it appears at the beginning of the paragraph and contains an idea that is not developed throughout the paragraph.

Do the rest of the exercises in the same manner.

1. [1] Today the idea of a union is no longer shocking; it is the most natural thing in the world for men and women to get together and demand better pay and better working conditions. [2] Few remember that there was a time when a bitter war was waged against unions and union organizers. [3] In the nineteenth century unions were forbidden by law, and those who tried to form them could be tried for conspiracy. [4] Blacklists were a powerful weapon used to ensure that union organizers or strike leaders would never be hired

---

*nationalist movements: people who band together to release their country from the rule of another country

again. [5] Rumors were spread claiming that union organizers were foreigners who intended to destroy America.

Sentence _____ is an introductory sentence.

Sentence _____ is a topic sentence.

2. [1] Compared to the politically active sixties, the eighties has emerged as a remarkably quiet period in American history. [2] Even on formerly volatile* college campuses, most students are more interested in studying than organizing. [3] There is, however, one clear exception. Still apparently fueled by the energy that first made them prominent activists in the sixties, gay organizations have established themselves on college campuses all over the country. [4] Accepted by many large universities in a way unheard of twenty years ago, they offer a variety of services to gay men and women on campus, offering everything from legal advice to job counseling. [5] Often, particularly on coed campuses, there are separate organizations for gay men and lesbian women, but the two groups usually work together to sponsor cultural events. [6] Although some heterosexual students are disturbed by being confronted with men and women who are openly homosexual, it is the parents, the offspring of a far different generation, who usually respond with anxiety. [7] Some parents have insisted their children withdraw from schools that support gay organizations of any kind. [8] But so far, no one has suggested that the universities return to the days of discrimination, when to be gay meant a life spent in hiding.

Sentence _____ is an introductory sentence.

Sentence _____ is a topic sentence.

3. [1] The Industrial Workers of the World (IWW), an international labor organization founded in 1905, did not have many successes; public distrust and a lack of organization combined to destroy the fledgling labor movement. [2] One victory, however, stands out in the annals of IWW history: the 1912 textile workers' strike in Lawrence, Massachusetts. [3] The strike began when employers decided to enforce a cut in wages; the workers reacted with rage, and the IWW quickly moved in to help organize a strike. [4] IWW leaders William Haywood and Elizabeth Gurley Flynn arrived in

*volatile: explosive

Sentences Provide Instructions 211

Lawrence, and their fiery rhetoric* combined with a particularly brutal offensive launched by the employers helped unite the striking workers. [5] Meanwhile the IWW soup kitchens helped keep the workers from starving during the two months it took to win the strike.

Sentence _____ is an introductory sentence.

Sentence _____ is a topic sentence.

4. [1] In 1871 the *New York Herald* sent Henry Morton Stanley to Africa in search of David Livingston, the English missionary.* [2] Stanley faced sickness, unfriendly natives, and starvation to find the missionary and won himself a reputation as one of the bravest men in the world. [3] Since that time history books have emphasized the heroic side of Stanley's personality, but Stanley was by no means always a hero; on the contrary, he could be both cruel and dishonest. [4] When his real adventures were questioned or greeted with skepticism, he made up fantastic stories that were little more than outright lies. [5] Like most men who had suffered a great deal, he considered the world a dangerous battleground where only the strongest and most brutal could survive. [6] To protect himself, he used violence the way other people raise their voices. [7] Any one who didn't obey orders or who seemed to be a threat was beaten or perhaps even shot.

Sentence _____ is an introductory sentence.

Sentence _____ is a topic sentence.

5. [1] In the nineteenth century a monk named Gregor Mendel discovered the basic rules, or laws, of heredity,* but his discovery was totally ignored. [2] From 1857 to 1865 Mendel had carefully crossed different varieties of garden peas and studied the results of the crossbreeding. [3] When he had finished his studies, he read an account of his experiments to a society of naturalists,* all of whom remained completely uninterested in his discoveries. [4] Articles published about his work were met with the same lack of interest. [5]

*rhetoric: persuasive use of language

*missionary: one who is sent to do charitable work

*heredity: the transmission of characteristics from parents to offspring

*naturalists: people who study plants and animals

It was not until sixteen years after Mendel's death that three European scientists who had made similar discoveries decided to investigate his work.

Sentence _____ is an introductory sentence.

Sentence _____ is a topic sentence.

SENTENCES PROVIDE EMPHASIS

BOB   It's not right to make a decision without thinking about all the consequences. You should always think how decisions will affect not just yourself but other people too. If you do things without thinking about how they're going to affect others, you are behaving irresponsibly.

ALAN   After a while you just can't worry about the consequences; you just have to act. You have to stop thinking about what will happen and go ahead with what you want to do. I really believe you have to stop thinking about consequences and do what you think is right.

As the dialogue illustrates, people repeat themselves. However, much of the time they repeat themselves on purpose. They believe they have something important to say, and to emphasize their idea, they repeat it two or even three times.

Bob, for example, says first that one should always think of the consequences of a decision before acting. Then, using different words, he repeats the same idea two more times. He wants to make sure that Alan hears and understands what he has to say.

Alan, on the other hand, is not ashamed to use the same tactic. He claims that a person should forget the consequences and act. To make his point heard and understood, he too repeats the same idea three different ways.

Writers also use repetition. Frequently if they have a point they want to emphasize, they repeat it. Take, for example, the following paragraph:

Those who claim that what has happened in the past is unimportant are making a serious mistake. Those of us living in the present cannot afford to forget the past. We cannot turn our eyes away and look only to the future. To do so would be to deny that we can learn from the failures and victories of those who have gone before.

The main idea of the paragraph is expressed in the first sentence. The second sentence, which we call an *emphatic sentence*, simply repeats the same idea in different words. The third sentence, again an emphatic sentence, repeats the idea once more. It is not until the fourth sentence that we are given a sentence containing new information.

Here we should point out that emphatic sentences used to restate or repeat what has come before will often appear at the very end of a paragraph. In this case the author uses them not only to emphasize a point but also to conclude the paragraph. By repeating an idea that has already been introduced, the author signals to the reader that he or she is finished presenting new information and is drawing the paragraph to a close. We can use the following paragraph as an example:

> Perhaps one of the greatest hoaxes in the history of archaeology was the discovery of the Piltdown man. In 1912 Charles Dawson claimed that he had found the missing link between humans and the apes; he had discovered the skull of a creature that appeared to be half man and half ape. Scholars the world over were delighted with his find and convinced that it was truly the missing link. It wasn't until forty-one years later that modern research revealed the truth: The skull consisted of a recent human skull and the jawbone of a female orangutan. The scientific world had been badly fooled, and it had taken almost half a century to discover it.

In the sample paragraph the main idea appears in the first sentence where we learn that the discovery of the Piltdown man was one of the greatest hoaxes in the history of archaeology. The rest of the paragraph, up until the last sentence, is concerned with supporting the main idea. We learn more about the hoax and how successful it was. The last sentence in the paragraph, however, does not add anything new about the hoax; it simply repeats, in different words, what we already know: the scientific community had been the victim of a hoax.

The last sentence in the paragraph is an emphatic sentence that serves a dual function: It emphasizes an important point in the paragraph and indicates that the author is finished supporting the main idea of the paragraph. When you read, you should make an attempt to figure out which sentences provide new information and which simply repeat, in different words, what came before. Often you'll discover that there is less new information in the paragraph than you may have thought. Once you know which sentences offer new information and which ones simply provide emphasis, you can concentrate on those offering new ideas.

The following exercises will give you more practice recognizing emphatic sentences.

EXERCISE 4

Practice Exercise: Some of the following paragraphs contain emphatic sentences. Read each paragraph and fill in the blank that follows. If the paragraph does not contain an emphatic sentence, fill in the blank with an *X*.

1. [1] America in the eighteenth century did not pay much attention to her poets. [2] Most of the poets who wrote at that time were little read and quickly forgotten. [3] Phillis Wheatley, however, was an important exception: Her poems were widely read and acclaimed. [4] Brought to America as a slave, Wheatley learned English quickly and, having learned it, began writing poetry. [5] Although she wrote on a variety of subjects, Wheatley's poetry tended to embrace religious themes, a characteristic that furthered its popularity. [6] Her poems won such a wide audience that samples of them were sent to England where they were once again highly praised.

   Sentence ___2___ is an emphatic sentence.

Explanation: The first sentence in the paragraph is an introductory sentence which tells us that eighteenth-century America did not pay a great deal of attention to its poets. The sentence that follows simply offers another version of the same idea; therefore, we call the second sentence an emphatic sentence.

Do the rest of the exercises in the same manner.

1. [1] Little is known about the life of black poet Countee Cullen, and a certain degree of mystery surrounds his childhood and early youth. [2] He himself spoke very little about the past, and most accepted his desire for privacy. [3] When he was pressed to talk about his life, Cullen occasionally gave conflicting accounts but refused to clarify the resulting confusion. [4] The poet disliked talking about his early life, and took every precaution to keep the past a secret. [5] Of the little that is known, it is clear that Cullen

began writing in high school, where friends and teachers applauded his talent. [6] Upon entering college, he sent several poems to some of the newly founded black periodicals. [7] The poems were accepted, and Cullen's reputation was established.

Sentence _____ is an emphatic sentence.

2. [1] Frederick Douglass, the black abolitionist* leader, was a man of great personal courage. [2] In his youth Douglass was severely beaten by a notorious* slave breaker. [3] Finally driven beyond his endurance, Douglass rebelled and beat his tormentor who never dared lay a hand on the young slave again. [4] At the age of twenty-one, Douglass decided to make a final break for his freedom, and armed with false papers, he got on a train bound for New York. [5] When the train stopped, Douglass got off a free man.

Sentence _____ is an emphatic sentence.

3. [1] In the second century B.C., the famous general Hannibal of Carthage decided to launch an attack on Rome. [2] Starting from Spain, he led his men across the Pyrenees Mountains and the Rhone River. [3] From the Rhone to the Alps, Hannibal was forced to do battle with several hostile tribes; but using his famous elephants to charge and kill, he was able to defeat his enemies. [4] Once he had crossed the Alps and entered the Po Valley, Hannibal fought three major battles with the Romans and won all three. [5] But somehow complete victory eluded Hannibal, and after fifteen years of fighting, he took what remained of his army back to Carthage. [6] In the end even the mighty Hannibal was unable to defeat Rome.

Sentence _____ is an emphatic sentence.

4. [1] The story of Solomon and the queen of Sheba appears in the Bible and the Koran, and it is part of the legends of Syria and Egypt. [2] It is a story that has been told and retold. [3] Although there are several versions of the story, all of them do agree on several basic points. [4] According to all accounts, Sheba was a beautiful young queen who journeyed to Solomon, the king of Israel, to test his wisdom.

*abolitionist: one who fought against slavery

*notorious: widely known, usually because of disagreeable or evil actions

[5] Solomon is said to have fallen in love with the young queen and she with him. [6] After bearing Solomon a son, Sheba returned to her own country.

Sentence _____ is an emphatic sentence.

5. [1] Richard Wright, author of the novel *Native Son,* was one of the most eloquent* speakers for the black men and women of his generation. [2] *Native Son* describes the life of Bigger Thomas, a young black man who commits murder out of rage and fear. [3] Based partly on Wright's own experience and partly on a real murder case, the book shocked the American public. [4] However, it was also highly praised for its realistic description of the problems facing black men and women in America. [5] Financially and artistically successful, the book was acclaimed abroad, especially in France where Wright spent the last years of his life.

Sentence _____ is an emphatic sentence.

SENTENCES PROVIDE A CONCLUSION

An author need not always use an emphatic sentence to draw the paragraph to a close; instead, he or she may use what we are calling a *concluding sentence.* **A concluding sentence comes at the end of a paragraph and describes the result or outcome of a problem or state of affairs mentioned in the paragraph.** Occasionally a concluding sentence will also describe what happened to a person, place, or idea with the passage of time. The following paragraph contains an example of a concluding sentence:

In 1692 Salem, Massachusetts, was the scene of a series of witchcraft trials. The trials began when two young girls, who appeared to be taken with fits, began accusing several men and women in the town of trafficking with the devil. The girls' accusations were believed, and before the townspeople came to their senses, nineteen men and women had been hanged and hundreds of others were cruelly tortured and imprisoned. Following the Salem experience, witchcraft trials practically disappeared from the colonies.

The topic of the paragraph is witchcraft trials in Salem, and the topic sentence of the paragraph tells us that in 1692

*eloquent: well spoken, persuasive

Salem was the scene of a series of trials. All the remaining sentences in the paragraph, except for the last one, tell us more about the Salem trials. The last sentence, however, does not tell us more about what happened during the trials; instead, it tells us what happened throughout the colonies after the Salem experience. The last sentence is a good example of a concluding sentence. It does not support the main idea, and it describes the outcome of an event described in the paragraph.

Concluding sentences, according to our definition, do not support the main idea of a paragraph. A sentence that supports the main idea would be considered a supporting sentence. See, for example, the following paragraph:

> To this day almost nothing is known of what happened to the first colonists to arrive at Roanoke Island, North Carolina. On May 8, 1587, three vessels carrying 151 colonists left England. They arrived at Cape Hatteras on July 22 and cruised up what is now called Pamlico Sound until they reached Roanoke Island. John White, governor of the colony, stayed only a month, and then on August 27 he sailed again for England. White was unable to return to the colony until 1591. When he did reach the island, he found the fort in ruins and no trace of the colonists.

In the preceding paragraph the last sentence describes what happened to the colony with the passage of time: It simply disappeared. At first glance, then, it seems to be a concluding sentence. But since the sentence still supports the main idea—nothing is known about the fate of the first colonists—we would call it a supporting rather than a concluding sentence.

Note here that paragraphs without a main idea seldom contain concluding sentences. Supporting sentences in paragraphs without a main idea simply provide different kinds of information about the topic. Usually a final sentence (or sentences) describing the result or outcome of something mentioned in the paragraph would add to the description of the topic and therefore be considered a supporting sentence.

The following exercises will give you practice working with concluding sentences.

EXERCISE 5   **Practice Exercise:** The following paragraphs may or may not contain a concluding sentence. Read through each paragraph and then choose the letter of the sentence which best decribes the final lines of the paragraph.

1. Whether or not a war should have been fought can always be debated. The prowar forces can always come up with a

reason why a war should be waged; the antiwar forces are perfectly able to prove the opposite. But there was one war that everybody agreed had to be fought; that was World War II. In the face of Hitler's murder of millions of human beings, few people were willing to question the need to stop him. And anybody who thought he could be persuaded by peaceful means just had to look at the promises he had broken when dealing with England and Russia. Perhaps during no other war has there been such complete agreement that the enemy had to be fought.

(a) The last sentence in the paragraph is a supporting sentence.

((b)) The last sentence in the paragraph is an emphatic sentence.

(c) The last sentence in the paragraph is a concluding sentence.

Explanation: The last sentence of the paragraph restates an idea that is presented in the topic sentence: In World War II most people agreed that Hitler had to be fought. Since the final sentence repeats something already said, we have circled sentence *b*.

Do the rest of the exercises in the same manner.

1. Dogs clearly have their drawbacks. Forever chasing the mailman, they also shed fur and have fleas. But without doubt, they also have their virtues. In addition to acting as guardians of both people and property, they are a source of devoted and unconditional affection. At present, the virtues of dogs are being touted by more than just their masters, for research has indicated that dogs may be of use in a variety of therapeutic programs. For example, homes for the aged have begun to employ pets as surrogate relatives so that elderly men and women who no longer possess any family can still take comfort in the daily visits of a friendly dog. By the same token, it has been shown that men and women suffering from mental illnesses characterized by emotional withdrawal frequently respond to the tail-wagging, overtures* of dogs. Although devoted cat lovers

*overture: an act, offer or proposal of friendship

may cry "foul," it appears that cats, with their independent natures, are simply too unreliable to be effective.

(a) The last sentence in the paragraph is a supporting sentence.

(b) The last sentence in the paragraph is an emphatic sentence.

(c) The last sentence in the paragraph is a concluding sentence.

2. Human beings like to think of themselves as the only animals who possess total control over all their actions. This is an attractive thought, but it is, nevertheless, not based on fact. A strong emotion such as fear can cause reactions that are totally beyond human control. For example, it is well known that human beings tend to tremble when frightened; the trembling is involuntary and ceases only when the danger is past. Similarly, children and adults have been known to urinate when placed in fear-producing situations.

(a) The last sentence in the paragraph is a supporting sentence.

(b) The last sentence in the paragraph is an emphatic sentence.

(c) The last sentence in the paragraph is a concluding sentence.

3. The Civil Rights Bill was submitted to the United States Congress by President Kennedy in June, 1963, and eventually passed the Senate in June, 1964. After a long debate, the longest in the Senate's history, the bill was carried by seventy-three votes (forty-six Democrats, twenty-seven Republicans) to twenty-seven votes (twenty-one Democrats, six Republicans). The terms of the bill were: (1) voting qualifications had to be the same for blacks and whites; (2) white and black workers had to have the same chance to be hired, and there could be no discrimination in pay or advancement; (3) public places (for example, restaurants, buses, and shops) were to be open to all no matter what the color of their skin.

(a) The last sentence in the paragraph is a supporting sentence.

(b) The last sentence in the paragraph is an emphatic sentence.

(c) The last sentence in the paragraph is a concluding sentence.

4. In 1865, French chemist Louis Pasteur believed that he had found a vaccine to combat rabies, but he was fearful of using it on human beings. Finally, the decision to use the vaccine was forced upon him. On July 6, 1885, a young boy named Joseph Meister was brought to Pasteur for treatment; the boy had been bitten on the arms and legs by a rabid dog. Pasteur consulted with several physicians who assured him that the boy would die. It was only then that Pasteur decided to use his vaccine. Meister lived to become gatekeeper of the Pasteur institute and committed suicide fifty-five years later when the Nazis tried to force their way into Pasteur's burial place.[1]

(a) The last sentence in the paragraph is a supporting sentence.

(b) The last sentence in the paragraph is an emphatic sentence.

(c) The last sentence in the paragraph is a concluding sentence.

5. For more than a decade, there has been a debate about just how much the violence on television contributes to the violence that plagues much of America. Many people involved with raising or educating children have complained about the effect of television violence on youthful behavior. Television executives, however, for their part, have insisted there was absolutely no proof to support the idea that television viewing encouraged children either to participate in violent crimes or to treat them lightly. However, the release of a recent report from the National Institute of Mental Health, shows this position is no longer tenable.* According to the report, there is overwhelming evidence to support the theory that television contributes to aggressive and violent behavior. In addition, the report, compiled during ten years of research, cites other damaging effects brought about by the exposure to television violence. Among these effects are a distrust of other human beings and a confusion about reality. Given the results of this careful and cautious report, it will be difficult in the future for television networks to

[1]Rene Dubos, *Pasteur and Modern Science* (New York: Doubleday, 1960), p. 122

*tenable: capable of being defended

claim that there is little or no evidence of a relationship between violence on television and violence in the street.

(a) The last sentence in the paragraph is a supporting sentence.

(b) The last sentence in the paragraph is an emphatic sentence.

(c) The last sentence in the paragraph is a concluding sentence.

TAKING NOTES

The ability to read a paragraph and identify the function of every sentence is important because it will help you take complete notes. After reading a paragraph, you can sift out the important sentences from the unimportant. See, for example, the following paragraph:

> The very name "bog people" sounds like the title of a horror movie. Despite the name, however, the bog people are not the main figures in a new film. The bog people were discovered in the nineteenth century when it was found that chemicals in the bogs of Scandinavia had preserved corpses that were thousands of years old. The bodies had changed so little that workmen, upon finding a corpse, thought that a recent murder had been committed. According to research following the discovery of the corpses, the bog people had been human sacrifices who were offered up to an earth goddess. After being strangled or stabbed, their bodies had been deposited in the bogs and the soil-acids contained in the waters of the bogs had managed to preserve them for thousands of years. Some specimens were so well-preserved that it was possible to see the stubble of a beard on their faces.[2] Although the bog people are the stuff of which horror movies are made, it was nature, not man, who invented them.

The first sentence in the preceding paragraph is an introductory sentence. The second sentence makes a transition and points ahead to the direction the paragraph will take. We do not reach the topic sentence, then, until the third sentence where we learn that chemicals in the Scandinavian bogs helped to preserve corpses that were thousands of years old. The rest

[2]P.V. Glob, *The Bog People* (Great Britain: Faber and Faber, 1969), p. 52

of the paragraph, with the exception of the last sentence, consists of major and minor supporting sentences. An emphatic sentence concludes the paragraph.

Although the paragraph is made up of eight sentences, we need pay attention to only five of them to take complete notes. By briefly summarizing the main idea and the support for the main idea provided by the author, we can produce notes that contain everything of importance:

Topic: Bog people

Main Idea: Chemicals in the bogs in Scandinavia have preserved corpses for thousands of years.

Support:

1. Bodies have changed very little.
2. Bog people were human sacrifices.
3. Bodies were deposited in bogs and soil acids in waters had preserved them.
   (a) Some specimens were so well preserved one could see the stubble of a beard.

The sample paragraph consists of a topic, main idea, and support for the main idea. Our notes reflect a shortened version of the paragraph and contain the topic, main idea, and support.

Those ideas taken from major supporting sentences have been put into brief sentences and numbered. The idea taken from the one minor supporting sentence has been put into a brief sentence and marked with a letter. The sentence marked with a letter is indented and appears under the numbered sentences. This organization indicates the relationship between major and minor supporting sentences. Minor supporting sentences develop the major ones and are less important.

If we were dealing with a paragraph containing a concluding sentence, our notes would look slightly different.

> For a long time scientists who wanted to study the behavior of chimpanzees have been faced with several problems. Chimps live in very dense forests, and it is often difficult and dangerous to reach them. Moreover, chimps, in spite of their resemblance to humans, do not welcome human visitors. Frequently at the sight of strangers, they make angry gestures and threatening noises. On occasion they have seriously injured unexpected intruders. Scien-

tists interested in studying chimps must face the prospect of spending not months, but years, in the jungle before the chimps begin to accept their presence. Jane Goodall, author of *In the Shadow of Man,* a book on chimps, had to spend four years in the jungles of Tanzania before she was able to make detailed and repeated observations. Her research, however, was well worth the effort since her findings have contributed to an understanding not only of chimpanzees, but also of humans.

Topic: Study of chimps

Main Idea: The study of chimps is difficult.

Support:

1. Chimps live in dense forests and are difficult to reach.
2. They are not friendly to observers.
   (a) Chimps make hostile gestures and noises.
   (b) They have injured intruders.
3. Scientists must spend several years among chimps.
   (a) Jane Goodall, author of *In the Shadow of Man,* spent four years in jungles of Tanzania.

Conclusion: Her research contributed to better understanding of chimps and humans.

The idea contained in the concluding sentence has also been put into a brief sentence although this sentence is not numbered. Concluding sentences that describe the outcome or result of something described in the paragraph do not usually contribute to the support of the main idea and therefore can be separated from the sentences that do provide support.

Before we go on to the exercises, we'd like to point out that your own notes need not be labeled. We used labels to help identify the different parts of a paragraph and to indicate what parts should be included in your notes. Similarly, you may not want to separate the topic of the paragraph from the rest of your notes; that too is perfectly acceptable since the topic of a paragraph will usually appear in the notes on the main idea and supporting sentences.

Also, when taking notes, you may want to use fewer sentences and more phrases. If you decide to use phrases rather than sentences, however, you should be sure to use phrases that will not be meaningless when you return to the notes a few weeks later. Notes should make you independent of the text and should be as complete as possible.

If you prefer to shorten your notes and use phrases, we would suggest the following method: put the main idea into a sentence, and use phrases for support and conclusion. We can use the following paragraph and sample notes as examples:

> For centuries, man has considered himself superior to his ancestor the ape. Humans can, after all, communicate while the best the ape can do is give mating calls or signal that bananas are ahead. Unfortunately, for those who treasure the superiority of man, recent research may be bearing bad news. At the Institute of Primate* Studies in Norman, Oklahoma, chimps have learned to talk in a way once considered impossible for any creature except man. Using sign language, the chimps have learned to express their emotions and to ask questions. Some have even managed to invent words. Upon seeing two swans, one bright chimp who didn't know the word "swan" promptly invented the phrase "water-birds."[3]

The first two sentences in the paragraph are introductory sentences. The third sentence is a transitional sentence that signals the new direction of the paragraph. The fourth sentence in the paragraph is the topic sentence, and it is here we learn that chimpanzees at the Institute of Primate Studies have learned to talk. The remaining sentences provide support for the main idea, and we learn to what degree the chimps were able to express themselves in sign language.

The paragraph has seven sentences, but we have to pay attention to only four of them to make complete notes:

Main Idea: At the Institute of Primate Studies in Norman, Oklahoma, chimps have learned to talk.

Support:

1. Ask questions; express emotions.

2. Invent words.

    (a) One chimp invented phrase "water-birds."

In the preceding notes the short phrases make sense because the main idea has been clearly stated. After reading the sentence containing the main idea, we can mentally fill in

---

*primates: monkeys, apes, and humans

[3]Eugene Linden, *Apes, Men and Language* (New York: Saturday Review Press, 1970), p. 111

Taking Notes 225

the phrases used to take notes on the supporting sentences. We know immediately, for example, that it is the chimps who ask questions and make up words.

In the following pages you are asked to read and take notes on several paragraphs. Make sure your notes include the main idea of the paragraph, support given for that main idea, and any result or outcome described in the last sentence of the paragraph.

EXERCISE 6   **Practice Exercise:**   Read and take notes on each of the following paragraphs.

1. The work of American author F. Scott Fitzgerald was profoundly influenced by the women in his life. For example, Genevra King, an early sweetheart of Fitzgerald's was one of the models for his most famous female character, Daisy, the heroine of *The Great Gatsby*. But Genevra King was not the only woman who found her way into Fitzgerald's novels. His wife, Zelda, was the inspiration for the lovely and neurotic Nicole in the book *Tender is the Night*. Zelda herself complained at one point in their marriage that Fitzgerald wrote down what she said in private conversations in order to use her words in his novels.

Topic: Models for Fitzgerald's female characters

Main Idea: The work of author F. Scott Fitzgerald was influenced by the women in his life.

Support:

   1. Genevra King one of the models for Daisy in *The Great Gatsby*

   2. Fitzgerald's wife Zelda inspiration for Nicole in *Tender Is the Night*
      (a) Zelda complained husband wrote down what she said privately in order to use her words in novels

Conclusion: _____

Explanation: The paragraph consists of five sentences, but only four are important to your notes. The first sentence provides the main idea of the paragraph, and sentences 2, 4, and 5 offer support for the main idea. Sentence 3 is a transitional sentence.

Do the rest of the exercises in the same manner.

1. Mystery writer Samuel Dashiell Hammett (1894–1961) had a rather unusual childhood and youth. At the age of thirteen, he quit school and began a series of jobs that included newspaper boy, messenger, clerk, timekeeper, machine operator, and dock worker. While other young people were working at a university or beginning a new career that was to last the rest of their lives, Hammett was beginning a job that was to provide him with information for the detective stories which made him famous: He was learning to become a detective for the Pinkerton Detective Agency. In his twenties, Hammett finally turned to writing mystery stories full time. Several of his novels produced during this period (*The Glass Key, The Thin Man,* and *The Maltese Falcon*) have become classics of American mystery fiction.

Topic: _____

Main Idea: _____

_____

Support: _____

_____

_____

_____

_____

_____

Conclusion: _____

_____

2. Humans frequently tend to be callous when it comes to dealing with members of the animal kingdom. But in the case of two talking chimps, Nim and his brother Ally, this tendency clearly reversed itself. When Nim and Ally were shipped to a laboratory for research on hepatitis, their human friends expressed both sympathy and outrage. Because both chimps had learned sign language in a program at the University of Oklahoma, their supporters insisted that the chimps would suffer terribly by being isolated in cages. In addition, the chimps' original teacher, Herbert Terrace, argued that use of the chimps in experiments would be a terrible waste: "Why should a chimp with lots of social skills be used for research..."[4] As a result of the outcry, plans are under way to find the animals a good home, and they will not have to take part in any scientific experiments.

Topic: _____

Main Idea: _____

_____

Support: _____

_____

_____

_____

_____

_____

Conclusion: _____

_____

[4]"Newsmakers," *Newsweek,* June 7, 1982, p. 52.

Evita and Juan Perón, the rulers of Argentina during the fifties.

3. Evita Peron was the wife of Argentine dictator Juan Peron, and before her death from cancer, she ruled the South American country alongside her husband. The poor of Argentina adored Evita because she listened to their troubles and promised to do what she could to help. When no help was forthcoming, the poor just assumed that the beautiful Evita was too busy helping someone else. The people of Argentina loved Evita because she would journey through the shabby villages of Argentina and give out small sums of money to anyone who reached out a hand. They did not begrudge her the vast sums of money she spent on her own spectacular wardrobe. In return, Eva claimed to love the people who worshipped her, and she was always start-

ing magnificent projects that would one day benefit the men and women of her country. Unfortunately, she usually lost interest in the projects before they were completed.

Topic: _____

Main Idea: _____

_____

Support: _____

_____

_____

_____

_____

_____

Conclusion: _____

_____

4. Recently there was an attempt to remake the 1932 horror classic *King Kong,* and millions of dollars were spent to recreate what had been a low budget, enormously successful thriller. But like so many others, this remake attempt failed miserably, and the thirties' classic remains unsurpassed. Somehow the beauty and the beast theme, so moving in the earlier film, seemed ridiculous in the modern version so that audiences laughed at scenes meant to be touching. Despite modern special effects, the new Kong could not match the old ape's mixture of gentleness and aggression. Instead he looked like what he was, a monstrous special effect; thus, it was difficult to mourn his death as audiences had once mourned Kong's. Previous attempts to follow up on the success of *King Kong* have met a similar end. In 1933 the original *King Kong* production crew filmed *Son of Kong, 33,* but the movie was quickly made and just

as quickly forgotten. The original *King Kong* can simply not be imitated, and Hollywood should abandon all attempts to remake this horror classic.

Topic: _____

Main Idea: _____
_____

Support: _____
_____
_____
_____
_____
_____

Conclusion: _____
_____

5. Many Americans have begun to take an interest in magical or supernatural happenings. One reason for this increased interest can be traced to the attention members of the scientific world have begun to pay supernatural happenings; witness, for example, the interest shown Israeli magician Uri Geller. For many Americans scientific interest or approval can be taken as positive proof since they believe that scientists cannot be fooled like "ordinary" men and women. And yet the truth may be just the opposite. According to an article in *Technology Review*, scientists may be easier to fool than most people.[5] Living in a world where every attempt is made to produce accurate results, scientists are not prepared for the magician's sleight of hand. In the

[5]Martin Gardner, "Magic and Paraphysics," *Technology Review*, June 1976, p. 43

laboratory every attempt is made to ensure that things are what they seem, but the world of magic is exactly the opposite, and every attempt is made to fool the audience.

Topic: _____

Main Idea: _____

_____

Support: _____

_____

_____

_____

_____

_____

Conclusion: _____

_____

REVIEW TEST: CHAPTER 5

PART A

The following pages will test your mastery of Chapter 5.

1. What four types of sentences were introduced in this chapter?

2. What are the functions of these four sentences?

3. How can understanding the function of these sentences help you to take notes?

4. Complete notes on a paragraph should contain three pieces of information. What are they?

5. To take good notes, do you have to write complete sentences?

_____

_____

_____

_____

PART B

Directions: The paragraphs in the following test lack several sentences. They may lack transitional and introductory sentences, as well as those that conclude and support. You are to select the sentences that would correctly fill in the blank spaces. At no time will you have to add a topic sentence.

Note: We suggest you first read through all the sentences in the paragraph. Then read the sentences that could fill in the blanks. Two sentences may appear to be equally correct, but one will actually be more appropriate than the other. Look for the sentence that best fits the context. Use the context clues in the paragraph to help you decide.

1. [1] _____ [2] Come the night they put their heads on the pillow and doze off in a matter of minutes, waking rested and refreshed in the morning. [3] _____ [4] For some fifty million Americans, falling asleep without frustration or anxiety is an impossibility. [5] They suffer from what doctors call *sleep disorders*. [6] The term can mean a variety of things. [7] _____ [8] It can also mean that they sleep too much, dozing off continuously during the day, even after a good night's sleep. [9] In some cases the term refers to constant nightmares, sleep-walking, and even bed-wetting. [10] Probably the worst disorder is loss of breath during the sleep period. [11] _____ [12] Although in the past doctors have taken complaints of sleep problems lightly, this practice has changed greatly within the last ten years. [13] Most physicians now recognize that such complaints frequently indicate some kind of physical or mental disorder and they react accordingly by reorganizing the patient's sleep habits. [14] _____

(a) Millions of Americans try to combat their sleep problems by taking sleeping pills.

(b) To many, sleeping is as natural as breathing.

(c) In the long run, sleeping pills lose their effectiveness; they may even be dangerous.

(d) It can mean, for example, that they cannot fall asleep, and often don't until early morning, just before it's time to wake up.

(e) As soon as the sleeper dozes off, he or she stops breathing and has to wake up in order to breathe.

(f) But others, numerous others, tell quite a different story.

(g) Sleep disturbances can usually be cured.

(h) In severe cases, they may recommend a sleep clinic where doctors specialize in the treatment of sleeping disorders.

2. [1] Some people take vitamins for illness. [2] _____ [3] For anemia they swallow vitamin B. [4] When winter and the common cold arrive, they quickly consume huge quantities of vitamin C. [5] _____ [6] Certainly the use of vitamins can be beneficial, but taken in large quantities, they can also be dangerous. [7] _____ [8] They fail to realize that vitamins can build up within the body creating dangerous side effects. [9] Too much vitamin C for example can lead to the formation of kidney stones. [10] _____ [11] Excessive use of vitamin D can lead to kidney damage, and vitamin A may cause not cure skin problems. [12] _____ [13] In fact they may do some harm.

(a) However, they may not be doing themselves all that much good.

(b) To heal wounds or cure acne, they may take vitamin E or A, sometimes both.

(c) A sore and discolored tongue may indicate vitamin deficiency.

(d) Unfortunately many people believe that if one vitamin is good, two are better.

(e) While a daily vitamin supplement is undoubtedly beneficial, there is no evidence that large doses of vitamins do much good.

(f) For many years Adele Davis was a leading exponent of

the theory that vitamins, especially in large doses, could help cure illness.

(g) Similarly large doses of vitamin E can reduce the blood's clotting ability.

(h) Those who believed fervidly in Adele Davis's advice were deeply disappointed when she died of cancer.

3. [1] _____ [2] Illnesses like pneumonia, scarlet fever, and syphillis were no longer so terrifying as they once had been. [3] Although still dangerous, they could be controlled by the prompt administering of antibiotic drugs. [4] _____ [5] While the drugs are still useful, they have begun to pose a problem. [6] Prescribed too easily and taken too readily, they no longer guarantee a cure because many bacteria have become resistant. [7] In addition, new bacterial strains requiring even more powerful antibiotics have developed. [8] As a result scientists have begun to warn that if antibiotics continue to be used indiscriminately* people will again be threatened by incurable diseases. [9] This problem is greatest in the underdeveloped countries where powerful antibiotics do not even require a prescription. [10] _____ [11] While it may be possible to limit prescriptions, it is difficult to control the amount of antibiotics contained in animal feed. [12] Eventually they turn up in the meat products prepared for human consumption. [13] Until this situation is brought under control, Americans will, sometimes unknowingly, continue to take too many antibiotics. [14] _____

(a) A half a century ago when antibiotics were first introduced, many hailed them as miracle drugs.

(b) Penicillin, made from blue-green mold, was one of the major breakthroughs in the discovery of antibiotics.

(c) Today antibiotics are not viewed with quite the same optimism.*

(d) Many doctors prescribe antibiotics when less powerful drugs would take longer but be just as effective.

(e) Doctors have begun to look for alternatives to the use of antibiotics.

*indiscriminately: casually, without care
*optimism: positive outlook

(f) If the situation is not controlled, the miracle drugs may prove to be a disaster.

(g) Many patients request that doctors prescribe antibiotics because they cannot afford a lengthy illness.

(h) However, even developed countries, like the United States, face a problem.

4. [1] _____ [2] *The Three Faces of Eve* was a successful book and a highly acclaimed film. [3] The same is true of *Sybil*, another best-selling work turned into a movie. [4] Allegedly taken from real life, both books detail the struggle of two women who tried desperately to fuse their conflicting personalities. [5] _____ [6] Perhaps the most bizarre case to date is that of William "Billy" Milligan, a young man found guilty of rape. [7] _____ [8] When Milligan was tried, doctors testified that he had as many as ten different personalities all possessed with very different talents. [9] Hospitalized after the trial, Milligan revealed ten more very distinct selves, and it appeared that at least twenty-four different people inhabited the body of one young man. [10] _____ [11] Christine is a shy and charming little girl. [12] _____ [13] Ragen is aggressive and skilled in the martial arts. [14] A number of Milligan's selves show artistic talent, and doctors say that one, "the teacher," is a competent artist.[5] [15] At one point it appeared that Milligan's personalities had united into one complete individual, but they soon fragmented. [16] Milligan, however, has not given up hope. [17] _____

(a) Milligan's story was also turned into a successful book called *The Lives of Billy Milligan*.

(b) In *Sybil*, Sally Field made her reputation as a dramatic actress.

(c) With the help of psychiatrists, Milligan believes he can one day resume a normal life.

(d) At times Milligan appears relaxed and normal, but these periods are usually followed by a violent outburst.

(e) Although no one really understands either its cause or cure, people have always been fascinated by the pheno-

[5]"Treating the 24 Faces of Billy" *Newsweek*, October 12, 1981, p. 21

menon* known in layman's terms* as *split personality*.

(f) But split personality is not just confined to women; men have also suffered from it.

(g) Others are not so pleasant.

(h) Some of the personalities are cheerful and affectionate.

5. [1] Although it frequently goes undiagnosed, clinical depression is, at the present time, one of the major illness in America. [2] _____ [3] Instead they assume they are going through a bad time or feeling a little blue; they fail to notice that their entire attitude toward life is slowly changing. [4] _____ [5] Once cheerful people may get little pleasure out of life and have no expectations for a better future. [6] _____ [7] Added to this basic pessimism* are a variety of seemingly unimportant symptoms. [8] Sleep is poor and early morning waking typical. [9] Headaches are frequent, and there may be problems with digestion. [10] There is usually a host of unexplained aches and pains, with no medical cause. [11] Tears may come suddenly and without reason. [12] Because the person suffering from depression has little control over his or her behavior, the advice to "cheer up" or "look on the bright side" is useless. [13] In fact they can further increase the depressive's sense of inadequacy. [14] _____ [15] The outlook is far from hopeless and 90 percent of the patients treated with antidepressants recover completely.

(a) Depression is not just a bad mood; it is also a biologically based illness that can be cured with the use of antidepressant medication.

(b) Many people suffer from depression without realizing that they are seriously ill.

(c) However, the news about depression is not all bad.

(d) Wina Sturgeon's *Conquering Depression* is an excellent book on the subject.

(e) Depression is another piece of evidence to prove that the mind and body are not really separate.

*phenomenon: occurrence

*layman's terms: language that a person without advanced training or skill could still understand

*pessimism: negative outlook

(f) Because the peak of the depression comes on slowly, many people do not notice how much their lives have altered.

(g) Nothing makes them happy, and they always expect the worst.

(h) Antidepressants were discovered some time in the early 1960s.

6. [1] There was a time when video games were a rarity, an interesting idea that might, or might not, become popular. [2] _____ [3] They have conquered the market, and people of all ages have become devoted fans. [4] Although teenage boys are, by and large, the games' most numerous patrons, girls have also begun to show an interest, and some games are being designed with them in mind. [5] Atari was the first company to invent a spectacularly successful video game, but competitors quickly followed suit. [6] _____ [7] Yet in spite of the games' phenomenal success, there are many who object to them. [8] Some critics insist that it is dangerous for teenagers to play for hours, wasting both time and money. [9] As a result, some states have limited access to the amusement arcades where the games are played. [10] Only adults, eighteen years or over are allowed in. [11] _____ [12] They maintain that video games, if played correctly, can help improve math and reading skills. [13] _____ [14] In a world increasingly dominated by computer technology, this would seem to be a desirable benefit. [15] _____ [16] Many companies are already trying to tap the home market; they have designed cassettes that can be used with the family television set. [17] In the future every home with a television set may be equipped to play video games.

(a) *Missile Command* and *Asteroids* are popular video games designed to be played at home.

(b) Despite praise or criticism, one thing is clear, video games are a tremendous success, and they will be around for a long time to come.

(c) Today, however, there is no longer any doubt about the future of computerized video games.

(d) Opponents of video games insist they encourage players to see the world as one huge battleground.

(e) At the present time there are over a hundred video games with many more ready to come off the drawing board.

(f) Pac Man, by Atari, has proven to be popular with girls as well as with boys.

(g) Supporters of the games insist that such precautions are unnecessary.

(h) In addition, young people become familiar with computers, something their parents never learned.

7. [1] _____ [2] Since that time people from all over the world have confirmed the existence of the mysterious, whirling ball of light. [3] _____ [4] In at least two of his plays, William Shakespeare referred to the superstitions surrounding the comet's appearance. [5] _____ [6] When Halley realized that three comets appeared just about seventy-six years apart, he decided that there really was only one comet, making several visits. [7] As a result of his discovery, Halley predicted the comet would return in 1759. The prediction was accurate, and from then on the comet bore his name. [8] _____ [9] For most people Halley's discovery put an end to the belief that comets announced a coming

The mysterious, whirling ball of light known as Halley's comet.

disaster or the death of royalty. [10] _____
[11] As recently as 1973, when the comet Kohoutek was expected, a few people claimed that the world would undergo a disastrous conflict. [12] _____ [13] Kohoutek came and went with most totally unaware of its existence. [14] Like Kohoutek most comets are not as spectacular as Halley's, and many are visible only through high-powered telescopes.

(a) American writer Mark Twain was convinced that his birth and death were linked to the appearance of Halley's comet.

(b) Still, for some, the superstition survived.

(c) Halley was a friend and disciple of scientist Isaac Newton.

(d) Giotto, the fourteenth-century Italian painter, put the great comet into one of his pictures.

(e) However, it wasn't until the seventeenth century that astronomer Edmund Halley discovered the comet's peculiar orbit.

(f) The Chinese were first to sight Halley's comet, and the earliest report is dated as far back as the third century B.C.

(g) Naturally nothing of the kind happened.

(h) But Halley died in 1742 before he could see his prediction come true.

8. [1] In the early forties and fifties, television seemed to have a bright future. [2] _____ [3] Given the right programming, it could help broaden the interests of a huge American audience, providing access to people, places, and ideas not normally encountered in everyday life. [4] Live shows were particularly important, and television built public awareness about issues of national importance. [5] The Kefauver crime investigations, the McCarthy hearings, and the 1948 and 1952 nominating conventions were all televised, and TV seemed ready to fulfill its extraordinary promise. [6] _____ [7] Today, except for a few isolated programs, television has done little to educate or inform the American public. [8] Instead each new season brings a host of comedy shows, complete with "canned" laughter. [9] _____ [10] Those that remain tend

to rely on sexual innuendo* or slapstick for their humor. [11] Crime shows are another staple on television, and they reveal even less imagination. [12] Few offer more than the traditional good guy versus bad guy format. [13] What they lack in imagination they make up in violence. [14] Many of the movies shown on television are usually considered too poor for distribution in theatres. [15] _____ [16] Even good films are frequently ruined by constant interruptions for commercials. [17] Criticized for their selections, programmers maintain they supply the audience with what it wants. [18] _____ [19] They only get to choose between terrible programs and those that are a little less than terrible.

(a) But in fact audiences are never really given a chance to choose better television programs.
(b) In the early days of the medium, nationally known playwrights wrote some superb television scripts.
(c) Many saw it as a powerful educational and cultural tool.
(d) At one point Hollywood was convinced that television meant death to the movies.
(e) They are only run on television because they are not too expensive.
(f) Unfortunately that early trend has not continued.
(g) Most of them disappear after a season or two.
(h) In the early days, Milton Berle was television's most popular comedian.

9. [1] Today no one would deny the genius of Albert Einstein, but oddly enough his boyhood offered little or no glimpse of the brilliance that marked his adult life. [2] _____ [3] Few guessed that, already at the age of twelve, the boy was beginning to think about the mysteries of the universe. [4] _____ [5] As an adolescent he was an indifferent student who could not adjust to the rigorous discipline of German high school. [6] When his teachers suggested his presence was not desirable, Einstein obligingly left school, prepared to pursue his own program of study. [7] _____ [8] He was forced to return to high school so that he could graduate and enter the Federal

*innuendo: sly hints

Institute of Technology in Zurich, Switzerland. [9] Not surprisingly he found college little better than high school. [10] _____ [11] When he left school, Einstein applied for several jobs, but he was repeatedly rejected. [12] Finally he got an uninspiring job in a patent office. [13] In his spare time, after eight hours of work, he began to develop the theories that were to revolutionize modern science. [14] _____ [15] His former teachers could hardly believe it.

(a) When the Nazis came to power, Einstein was forced to flee the country.
(b) In the end Einstein graduated with the aid of a friend.
(c) However, disciplined as he was, he still needed formal schooling to pursue his scientific interests.
(d) In 1921 Albert Einstein received the Nobel Prize.
(e) As a child he was slow to talk, and his parents feared the boy might be retarded.
(f) All his life Einstein spoke up for causes he believed in.
(g) Most were convinced he was a dull boy who would never amount to much.
(h) When he published his work at the age of twenty-six, he was suddenly looked upon as a brilliant thinker who had revolutionized modern science.

10. [1] _____ [2] Now that many fear for their survival, even more attention is being paid to these mysterious animals. [3] Scientists from all over the world are particularly interested in one facet of whale behavior, the strange phenomenon called *beaching*. [4] _____ [5] Explanations for this seemingly self-destructive behavior vary. It has been suggested that whales, like humans, may commit suicide. [6] Such an explanation might be plausible if isolated whales stranded themselves. [7] _____ [8] Whales frequently strand themselves in large groups, with as many as twenty or thirty whales dying at once. [9] Another theory maintains that whales may be infected by a contagious illness that impairs their normal navigational abilities. [10] _____ [11] The most plausible theory points to the whales' tendency to travel in groups. [12] Should the leader of a herd become ill and swim toward the shore, the rest would follow out of habit. [13] _____ [14] In the future,

with careful observation and study, scientists hope to solve it since the precious animals have already dwindled in number, and everything must be done to increase their chances for survival.

(a) This theory like all the others has never been proved, and beaching whales remain a mystery.
(b) *Cetology* is the study of whales.
(c) In the nineteenth century, the California gray whale was known as the "devilfish."
(d) But this is not the case.
(e) When a whale beaches, it swims toward shore and literally strands itself on a beach where it cannot hope to survive.
(f) Whales are marvelous creatures, and for centuries they have been an object of fascination.
(g) However, examinations of beached whales have never revealed any sign of illness.
(h) One of America's most famous novels, *Moby Dick*, is the story of a man's pursuit of the white whale.

Chapter 6

Identifying Different Types of Paragraphs

In this chapter we are going to talk more about taking notes. But at the same time we are going to introduce several different types of paragraphs, all of which appear repeatedly in your reading. Each type of paragraph has particular characteristics, and being aware of these characteristics can help you find the topic and main idea. It can also help you figure out what to include in your notes.

SEQUENCE OF DATES AND EVENTS

PROFESSOR   Jefferson became president in 1801. He was born in 1743, and during the Revolutionary War he served as governor to Virginia. From 1797 to 1801 he served as vice president of the United States. Jefferson graduated from William and Mary in 1762.

STUDENT   Let me see if I've got this right, Professor. Jefferson was born in 1743 and became president of the United States in 1762. Oh, that just doesn't seem reasonable. He was older than nineteen when he became president. For some reason, I just couldn't seem to follow you.

It is not surprising that the student in the dialogue had difficulty following the lecture on Jefferson. If teachers really gave out dates and events in that fashion, everybody would get confused. Dates and events make much more sense when they are presented in the order in which they happened. See, for example, the following paragraph:

> Thomas Jefferson graduated from William and Mary College in 1762 and was admitted to the Bar in 1767. He became a member of the Second Continental Congress in 1775 and was chairman of the committee that wrote the Declaration of Independence. From 1785 to 1789 he was the United States Minister to France, and from 1790 to 1793 he served as the United States Secretary of State. Jefferson served as vice president from 1797 to 1801, and on March 4, 1801, he was inaugurated as the third president of the United States.

The preceding paragraph consists of a list of events, and the events are given in the order in which they happened. This is what we mean when we talk of paragraphs consisting mainly of dates and events.

You'll notice that each event mentioned marks another step in Jefferson's professional and political career. Therefore, we can call "Jefferson's career" the topic of the paragraph. The sample paragraph does not contain a main idea, at least not one that provides us with any useful information; instead, it simply lists the major events in Jefferson's career.

Now that we know the topic of the paragraph and are sure that we are dealing with a paragraph that lists a sequence of dates and events, we have everything we need to take notes:

Topic: Jefferson's career

Support:

1. 1762: graduated from William and Mary College
2. 1767: admitted to the Bar
3. 1775: member of the Second Continental Congress, chairman of committee that wrote Declaration of Independence
4. 1785–1789: United States Minister to France
5. 1790–1793: served as United States Secretary of State
6. 1797–1801: vice president
7. 1801: inaugurated as president

As our sample illustrates, notes on a paragraph describing a sequence of dates and events should always contain all the events and dates when they occurred. Moreover, the dates and events must be presented in the order in which they happened.

The following sample paragraph also presents a sequence of dates and events, but it contains a topic sentence:

> The years between 1918 and 1945 brought violence and upheaval to the newly formed Polish nation. In 1918 Poland was declared independent, and army officer Józef Pilsudski took control of the government. After 1926 the government became a dictatorship, first under Pilsudski and later, after his death in 1935, under officers loyal to him. The officers, however, were not allowed to rule for long. In 1939 Germany and Russia invaded Poland, and both powers divided up the country. During the war years that followed, the Germans murdered anywhere from three to five and a half million Polish Jews; they killed more than half of the population of Warsaw, and the capital itself was completely destroyed. Warsaw, once one of the most beautiful capitals in Europe, was reduced to rubble.

The topic of the preceding paragraph is "political events in Poland between the years 1918 and 1945," and the main idea is contained in the first sentence: Poland underwent violence and upheaval during the years between 1918 and 1945. All the other sentences, with the exception of the fourth and last sentences, use specific dates and events to support the main idea. The fourth sentence is a transitional sentence, which helps us move from the idea contained in sentence 3 ("officers loyal to Pilsudski took over in 1935") to the idea contained in sentence 5 ("the Germans took over in 1939"). The last sentence is an emphatic sentence which concludes the paragraph and repeats that Warsaw was destroyed during the war.

The paragraph consists of seven sentences, but only five are important to our notes:

Topic: Political events in Poland between 1918 and 1945

Main Idea: Poland experienced violence and upheaval between the years 1918 and 1945.

Support:

1. 1918: Poland declared independent, and Pilsudski takes control.

2. 1926: Government becomes dictatorship.

3. 1935: Pilsudski dies, loyal officers maintain dictatorship.

4. 1939: Germany and Russia invade Poland and divide up the country.

5. 1939–1945: Germans murder 3,000,000 to 3,500,000 Polish Jews.

6. Warsaw destroyed.

If you look at the sample notes above, you'll see one date that does not appear in the paragraph; this is the date for the end of World War II. It does not appear because the author assumes you know the dates of World War II. If you are reading and it is clear that the author expects you to know certain dates, make sure to look them up and add them to your notes.

Sometimes an author will not give the exact date of an event but will instead give enough information so that the reader can figure out when the event occurred. If you run across a paragraph where the author uses this method to introduce dates and events, be sure to use the information provided and figure out the correct dates.

For example, had our sample paragraph contained the concluding sentence, "Two years after the war was over and the Nazis had been driven out, the Russians took control of Poland," we would have added the date 1947 to our notes.

In the following exercise we ask you to take notes on several paragraphs that describe a sequence of dates and events. Your notes should include all the dates and events mentioned in the paragraph. Again, once you are taking notes on your own, we would not expect you to label everything. We only use labels in the exercises to clearly illustrate what you need to include in your notes.

EXERCISE 1

Practice Exercise: Read and take notes on each of the following paragraphs.

1. The son of a Spanish immigrant, Fidel Castro was educated at a Roman Catholic school in Santiago, and from 1945 to 1950, he attended the University of Havana. In 1947 he participated in an unofficial raid on the Dominican Republic, and in July 1953 he organized an attack on the army barracks in Santiago. The attack was not successful, and Castro was sentenced to fifteen years in prison. In 1955 Castro was released from prison, and the following year he went to Mexico to build a Cuban revolutionary movement. In December 1959 he returned to Cuba, and in January 1960 he led a successful attempt to overthrow dictator Fulgencio Batista.

Topic: Fidel Castro's Career

Main Idea: _____

Support:
1. 1945–1950: attended University of Havana
2. 1947: took part in unofficial raid on Dominican Republic
3. July 1953: organized attack on army barracks in Santiago
4. 1955: released from prison
5. 1956: Went to Mexico to organize Cuban revolution
6. December 1959: returned to Cuba
7. January 1960: overthrew Batista

Conclusion: _____

Explanation: The paragraph did not contain a word or phrase we could use for the topic; therefore, we had to find our own phrase: "Fidel Castro's career." Since there was no topic sentence in the paragraph, nor was a main idea suggested, we did not fill in the second blank. We did, however, list all the events given in the paragraph, and, most important, we listed them in the same order in which they were presented.

Do the rest of the exercises in the same manner.

1. In 1954 Dag Hammarskjold arrived at the United Nations to assume the post of secretary general, and it was little more than a year before he successfully undertook the task of securing the release of eleven airmen who had been shot down in the Korean War and imprisoned by the Chinese. Two years later, in 1956, Hammarskjold reported on the rebellion in Hungary and at the same time collected a United Nations Emergency Force to deal with the Suez crisis. In 1961 violence broke out in the Belgian Congo, and

Hammarskjold flew to Leopoldville, capital of the Congo, to work out a compromise between the warring forces. On the afternoon of September 17, 1961, the secretary general left the Leopoldville airport to meet with one of the leaders of the Congo, but his plane crashed and burst into flames nine and a half miles from where he hoped to land. The cause of the crash has remained a mystery.

Topic: _____

Main Idea: _____
_____

Support: _____
_____
_____
_____
_____
_____
_____

Conclusion: _____
_____

2. Indira Gandhi began her political career in 1938 when she joined India's Congress Party. She was active in the party for many years and in 1959 was elected president of the Indian National Congress. Five years later, in 1964, she was appointed minister of information and broadcasting, and on January 19, 1966, Mrs. Gandhi became leader of the Congress Parliamentary Party. Shortly after, on January 24 of the same year, she took office as prime minister. In November 1969 she survived an attempt to force her out of office and was reinstated as prime minister. Two years later, in 1971, her position as party leader and prime minister was confirmed when the March elections gave her a clear victory.

Sequence of Dates and Events 251

Topic: _____

Main Idea: _____
_____

Support: _____
_____
_____
_____
_____
_____

Conclusion: _____
_____

Indira Ghandi, the prime minister of India for many years.

3. John W. Hinckley's attack on President Ronald Reagan undoubtedly reminded Americans of the political assassinations that have plagued the United States since John F. Kennedy's death in 1963. Yet few Americans are aware that long before the death of Kennedy, United States leaders were haunted by the threat of assassination. In 1835, the first presidential assailant, Richard Lawrence, claimed he was the King of England, and tried to assassinate Andrew Jackson, but his gun misfired. Every schoolchild knows that Abraham Lincoln was shot and killed by John Wilkes Booth in 1865. But not everyone remembers that the twentieth President of the United States, James Abram Garfield, was killed by Charles J. Guiteau in a Washington railroad in 1881. No sooner had America entered the twentieth century in 1901 than anarchist Leon Czolgosz shot and killed President William McKinley in Buffalo, New York. Twelve years later, John Schrank aimed a gun at presidential candidate Theodore Roosevelt, believing that he had masterminded McKinley's death. In 1933 President Franklin Delano Roosevelt escaped death when Guiseppe Zangara shot but missed, killing instead the mayor of Chicago. Less than twenty years later, President Harry S. Truman also escaped an assassination attempt by radical members of the Puerto Rican Nationalist movement.

Topic: _____

Main Idea: _____
_____

Support: _____
_____
_____
_____
_____

Conclusion: _____
_____

Sequence of Dates and Events

4. Gregor Rasputin, the Russian monk, was an influential member of the tzar's court from 1905 until 1916, and during that time he managed to discredit not only himself but the tzar's authority as well. Rasputin first acquired prominence in 1905 when it was discovered that Alexei, the tzar's son, suffered from hemophilia.* Because he appeared able to heal the boy through hypnosis, Rasputin became the tzarina's closest confidante. By 1911 Rasputin was so confident of his powers that he began to interfere in political affairs. At the same time, members of the court became aware that he had a penchant* for liquor and women; thus rumors began to circulate concerning his negative influence over the czar's family. In 1914, when Russia entered World War I, it was commonly believed that Rasputin was a German agent, and two years later he was murdered.

Topic: _____

Main Idea: _____
_____

Support: _____
_____
_____
_____
_____
_____

Conclusion: _____
_____

*hemophilia: a hereditary disease that principally affects males but is transmitted by females
*penchant: an inclination or liking for someone or something

5. The son of a rector, architect Christopher Wren was born in 1632 in Wiltshire, England. Early in life he displayed an interest in science, and by 1653 when he received his master's degree from Oxford, he had produced more than fifty different inventions, theories, and experiments. Becoming a professor of astronomy in 1657, Wren was among the founders of the Royal Society, and he seems to have come to architecture almost by accident. After the Great Fire of 1666, he prepared a plan for the reconstruction of London, and was invited to join the Royal Commission for the rebuilding of the city. In his position as surveyor general of works, Wren was in charge of all royal and government building in London. Soon he found himself with commissions to design the city's new churches, and it was this chance that secured him his place in European architecture. Wren died in 1723 and was buried in St. Paul's Cathedral. Walking tours of Wren's churches are still popular in today's London.

Topic: _____

Main Idea: _____

_____

Support: _____

_____

_____

_____

_____

_____

Conclusion: _____

_____

SEQUENCE OF STEPS

Some paragraphs consist mainly of a *sequence of steps*. These paragraphs explain how to do something, how something functions, or how something develops. The following paragraph is an example of what we mean:

> The first step in growing bean sprouts is to purchase some tiny green mung beans from a health food store. Then line the bottom of a pot with pebbles and place a layer of beans over the pebbles. Next put enough water over the beans to wet them thoroughly. Cover with a damp black cloth and place in a warm spot. Make sure that the spot for the beans is fairly warm because the correct temperature is important to the sprouting of the beans. Once the beans have been settled in a warm spot, they must be rinsed daily with fresh water. In eight days they should have sprouted and can be used as a nutritious addition to salads and cooked vegetables.

The sample paragraph describes a sequence of steps to follow in growing bean sprouts. Every sentence, except the fifth (a minor supporting sentence) and the seventh (a concluding sentence), contains a step necessary to grow bean sprouts. We can say then that growing bean sprouts is the topic of the paragraph.

Clearly, there is no topic sentence in the paragraph, but the sentences do combine to suggest a main idea that can be stated in a sentence: "There are seven steps necessary to growing bean sprouts." In this case the suggested main idea does contain useful information; it is important to know how many steps have to be completed to grow the sprouts.

Now that we know the topic and main idea of the paragraph and are sure that the paragraph describes a sequence of steps, we have everything we need for our notes that would look something like this:

Topic: Growing bean sprouts

Main Idea: There are seven steps necessary to grow bean sprouts.

Support:

  1. Purchase tiny mung beans.

  2. Line bottom of pan with pebbles.

  3. Place layer of beans over pebbles.

  4. Wet beans thoroughly with water.

5. Cover beans with damp black cloth.
6. Put in warm spot.
    (a) Warmth important
7. Rinse daily.

Conclusion: Nutritious addition to salads and cooked vegetables.

As our sample notes illustrate, notes on a paragraph describing a sequence of steps should always indicate the process or activity explained in the paragraph and list all the given steps in the correct order.

If you look carefully at the sample notes, you'll notice that there are seven steps listed as well as a brief version of the main idea and conclusion. Thus it looks as if the paragraph contained nine rather than six sentences. We mention this because it illustrates an important point: when you are taking notes, you can, if you wish, divide the ideas contained in a single sentence. For example, in the previous paragraph, two sentences (the second and the fourth) contained two steps rather than one. Since separating the steps makes it clearer how many there are and what they are, we have listed them separately rather than together as they appear in the paragraph.

The following paragraph also describes a sequence of steps. This paragraph, however, contains a topic sentence:

> There are three basic stages involved in the development of identical twins. Their growth begins when the father's sperm pierces the egg of the mother. The fertilized egg then splits and divides into equal halves, each half receiving exactly the same number of chromosomes* and genes.* The halves of the egg then develop into two babies who are of the same sex and who are identical in all hereditary traits such as hair color and eye color.

The topic of the paragraph is the development of identical twins, and the topic sentence tells us that there are three stages of development. Once we know exactly what the three stages consist of, we are ready to take notes.

*chromosomes: bodies that consist of hundreds of clear, jelly-like particles strung together like beads. They carry the genes.
*genes: the elements responsible for the transmission of hereditary characteristics, such as hair color and eye color

Topic: Development of identical twins

Main Idea: There are three stages in the development of identical twins.

Support:

1. Father's sperm pierces mother's egg.
2. Fertilized egg splits and divides into equal halves; each half receives same number of chromosomes and genes.
3. Halves of egg develop into two twins of the same sex, identical in all hereditary traits such as hair color and eye color.

We have included in our notes the topic, main idea, and all the stages described in the paragraph. Moreover, the stages are ordered just as they were in the sample paragraph. This last point is an important one. If you are taking notes on a paragraph describing a sequence of steps, be sure to maintain the correct order.

The following exercise will provide more practice working with paragraphs consisting mainly of a sequence of steps or, as they are frequently called, *stages*.

EXERCISE 2 **Practice Exercise:** Read and take notes on the following paragraphs.

1. In spring, the stickleback, a small fish found in both fresh and salt water, goes through a strange courtship ritual. With the coming of the spring months, the male stickleback begins to look for a place where he can build his nest. Once he has found one, he grows aggressive and fights off all invaders. After finishing the nest, he goes off in search of a female. When he finds one, he leads her to the nest, and she enters it. The male then hits the tail of the female forcing her to deposit her eggs. Once she lays the eggs, the female swims off, and the male enters the nest.

Topic: Courtship of the stickleback

Main Idea: In spring the stickleback goes through a strange courtship ritual.

Support:

1. Male stickleback looks for place to build his nest.

2. Finding one, he grows aggressive.
3. After finishing the nest, he looks for female.
4. Leads her to the nest which she enters.
5. Male hits female's tail forcing her to deposit eggs.
6. Once eggs are laid she swims off and male enters the nest.

Conclusion: _____

Explanation: Since our notes contain the topic, main idea, and all the steps described in the paragraph, we have everything of importance.

Do the rest of the exercises in the same manner.

1. Nature is capable of extraordinary trickery in the attempt to preserve species life. For example, a rare species of South African orchid is able to survive only because certain beetles, living in the same area, cannot distinguish a female beetle from a flowering orchid. Early in spring when the ground first thaws, the male beetles emerge from the earth, just a few weeks before the females appear. Immediately they begin looking for a mate. Because orchids in the area produce an aroma like the sex attractant of the female, the males assume they have found their female partners. Possessed of poor eyesight but with an excellent sense of smell, the beetles spend the next few weeks fertilizing the orchids. Somehow, almost automatically, the beetles know when the real females have arrived, and they abandon their flower-mates in order to perpetuate their own species.

Topic: _____

Main Idea: _____

_____

Support: _____

_____

Conclusion: _____

2. The first act of a newly hatched queen bee is to seek a mate. Three to five days after hatching, she will attempt her first flight, flying far from the hive to avoid inbreeding.* When she is far enough, the queen produces a scent that attracts drones from distant hives. Once a drone arrives, mating takes place at an altitude of about fifty feet. Following the mating, the queen flies home to lay her eggs. A queen who does not mate by the time she is two weeks old will never mate and will remain barren.*

Topic: _____

Main Idea: _____

Support: _____

*inbreeding: to reproduce by continued mating of closely related individuals
*barren: without offspring, incapable of reproduction

___

___

Conclusion: ___

___

3. Human digestion begins when we use our teeth to cut and grind food. As we chew, saliva moistens and softens food so it can be easily swallowed. After being swallowed, the food passes into a tube that connects the mouth and stomach; this tube is called the *esophagus*. After the food reaches the stomach, muscles in the stomach wall mix it together, and combine it with a gastric juice that consists mostly of water and hydrochloric acid. The gastric juice reduces the food to a liquid that can pass into the small intestine. The passage takes about eight hours. During this time, enzymes break down the food even more, preparing it for absorption into the blood stream.

Topic: ___

Main Idea: ___

___

Support: ___

___

___

___

___

___

Conclusion: ___

___

4. Many years ago orange growers in Brazil discovered that one tree had somehow produced seedless oranges. The growers, in an attempt to reproduce oranges without seeds, decided to make use of a process called *grafting*. One small twig was taken from the branch that had produced the seedless oranges, and the twig was fitted into an ordinary orange tree. After the slit into which the twig had been inserted was carefully bandaged, the parts of the tree began to grow together. Within a short time, oranges began to grow on the grafted twig and, as the growers had hoped, they contained no seeds.

Topic: _____

Main Idea: _____

_____

Support: _____

_____

_____

_____

_____

_____

Conclusion: _____

_____

5. The eggs of the king salmon hatch in fresh-water streams, but within a year after hatching, the young salmon head out to sea. During their journey they are destroyed by their natural enemies, the bear, duck, and raccoon, and by the polluted waters containing the wastes of factories and cities. Only a small proportion of the salmon actually reach the sea. Those who do stay anywhere from four to six years

and then begin their journey back to a river like the one in which they hatched. Here they lay thousands of eggs that will hatch and go through the same life cycle. Once the adult king salmon have laid their eggs, life is over for them. They change color and become slimy. Slowly, they float downstream with their tails forward. In a matter of days, they are dead.

Topic: _____

Main Idea: _____
_____

Support: _____
_____
_____
_____
_____
_____
_____

Conclusion: _____
_____

LISTS OF CHARACTERISTICS

In the first two sections, we dealt with paragraphs in which the order of information was very important. Had the order been changed, the paragraphs would have been confusing. In this section we are dealing with paragraphs in which the order is not particularly important. As a matter of fact, as we will show, the order can be rearranged without any resulting confusion. We'll begin with the following paragraph:

> The prehistoric elephant bird, also known as the roc bird, lived in Southern Madagascar. Standing around nine to ten feet high, the bird was unable to fly and weighed close to 1,000 pounds. This enormous bird also had enormous eggs. One specimen, still preserved in the British Museum in London, has a circumference of twenty-eight inches and is seven times larger than an ostrich egg.[1]

The elephant bird is the precise topic of the paragraph. It is impossible to find a more precise one since we have to choose one that allows us to include all the different facts mentioned in the paragraph.

As you have probably already noticed, the paragraph does not contain a topic sentence, nor does it contain a main idea. The paragraph is concerned mainly with listing the major characteristics of the elephant bird, not with stating or suggesting a main idea.

Now that we know the topic of the paragraph and are sure that the paragraph simply lists the major characteristics of the elephant bird, we have everything we need for our notes:

Topic: Elephant bird

Support:

1. Known as roc bird
2. Lived in South Madagascar
3. Flightless
4. Nine to ten feet high and weighed around 1,000 pounds
5. Enormous eggs
    (a) One specimen 28-inch circumference and seven times larger than ostrich egg

Notes on a paragraph that simply lists the major characteristics of a person, place, or event require a clear statement of the topic and a list of all the characteristics mentioned in the paragraph.

---

[1] Norris McWhirter and Ross McWhirter, *Guinness Book of World Records* (New York: Bantam Books, 1975), p. 107

At this point we want to illustrate what we claimed previously: order in paragraphs that do little more than list the major characteristics of a person, place, or event is not particularly important. See, for example, the following paragraph:

> The British Museum in London houses an enormous egg, one that has a circumference of twenty-eight inches. This large egg once belonged to an equally large bird, the elephant, or roc-bird, a prehistoric inhabitant of Southern Madagascar. Standing anywhere from nine to ten feet high, the elephant bird must have cut an impressive figure, especially considering that he weighed around 1,000 pounds.

In the first sample paragraph the author begins by telling where the elephant bird lived, how much it weighed, and how tall it was; the paragraph ends with some details about the egg specimen housed in the British Museum. In the second sample paragraph the order of the characteristics is reversed. But as you see, it doesn't make much difference.

The following exercises will give you more practice reading and taking notes on paragraphs that consist mainly of a list of characteristics.

EXERCISE 3

Practice Exercise: Read and take notes on the following paragraphs.

1. The Mennonites are a sect of Protestant Christians who were named after Menno Simons, a religious reformer who lived in the sixteenth century. Members keep apart from the rest of the world and are opposed to taking oaths, holding public office, or performing military service. Several Mennonite settlements exist in eastern Pennsylvania and in parts of the midwest.

Topic: Mennonites

Support:

    1. Named after Menno Simons, religious reformer who lived in the sixteenth century

    2. Keep apart from the rest of the world

    3. Opposed to taking oaths, holding public office, performing military service

    4. Settlements exist in eastern Pennsylvania and parts of the Midwest

List of Characteristics 265

Explanation: We can say that our notes are complete because they contain the topic and all the characteristics of that topic presented in the paragraph.

Do the rest of the exercises in the same manner.

1. *Poor Richard's Almanack,* published between 1732 and 1757, contained information about the weather, tides, and holidays. Anyone who wanted to know the winter forecast or the date of the next eclipse consulted "Poor Richard." Benjamin Franklin published the almanac and was responsible for the jokes and proverbs that made the book so popular. The almanac sold around a thousand copies a year and was widely read by the colonists. After 1757 *Poor Richard's Almanack* was taken over by another publisher, and Franklin was no longer involved in its publication.

Topic: _____

Support: _____

_____

_____

_____

_____

_____

2. Some $375,000,000 a year is being paid to practitioners called "psychoquacks," who masquerade under a weird assortment of scientific-sounding titles. They claim cures which range from stopping a patient from biting his nails to curing alcoholism. Psychoquacks are not licensed to practice psychiatry, psychoanalysis, or clinical psychology; they usually have no preparation in these specialized health professions. Most psychoquacks have forged credentials or receive their degrees from schools with questionable reputations. One or two correspondence courses in psychology often complete the training offered by these

schools. There are more than twenty-five thousand psychoquacks in the United States.²

Topic: _____

Support: _____
_____
_____
_____
_____
_____

3. *Apache* was the name given to the Indian tribes who inhabited the southwestern part of the United States and parts of northern Mexico. The Apaches were excellent hunters and riders, and they had little trouble outwitting the white settlers who were flooding their lands. Many tribes lived on the outskirts of white settlements for more than a hundred years and managed to remain completely independent. Probably the most famous Apache is Geronimo, the Apache chief who led a series of rebellions.

Topic: _____

Support: _____
_____
_____
_____
_____
_____

²From *Focusing on Health* by Jessie Helen Haag. Copyright ©1973 by Steck-Vaughn Company. Reprinted by permission.

4. Under the leadership of George Fox, the Quakers began preaching in seventeenth-century England. After being persecuted in their own country, they migrated to New England where they finally found a home in 1681. During meetings, Quakers do not speak out or preach. Instead they meditate quietly listening for the word of the Lord. All Quakers consider themselves members of the holy priesthood, and each and every Quaker possesses the ability to hear the voice of God. Because they refuse to swear oaths or bear arms, the Quakers organized the American Friends Committee. The purpose of the committee is to do relief work during both war and peace. The Quakers also have an extensive missionary program in Asia, Africa, and America. Quakers no longer wear special clothing or address one another with special pronouns ("thee" and "thou"), but their original beliefs have changed very little since they first organized in England. At the present time there are about 130,000 Quakers in America.

Topic: _____

Support: _____

_____

_____

_____

_____

5. In 1841 a group of men and women, led by minister and literary critic George Ripley, decided to form a cooperative farm* in West Roxbury, Massachusetts. The members of the farm hoped to pursue their intellectual studies and learn about life in the country. The colony, known as Brook Farm, never numbered more than one hundred, but it stirred a great deal of interest and drew visitors from all over the country. Several famous figures in American literature

*cooperative farm: a farm owned and worked jointly by a group of people

were involved in the experiment, among them writers Margaret Fuller and Nathaniel Hawthorne. Poet and critic Ralph Waldo Emerson was also interested in the colony although he was skeptical about its success. In 1846 Emerson's skepticism proved to be well founded, and Brook Farm was abandoned.

Topic: _____

Support: _____

_____

_____

_____

_____

COMPARISONS

SALESPERSON	This foreign import is also much more economical in terms of gas. It needs much less gas than the American model.
CUSTOMER	I know, but it's also much less comfortable; I like to be able to move my legs when I ride in a car.
SALESPERSON	But don't let that sidetrack you into forgetting that these little cars are a lot cheaper. You have to pay through the nose for the leg room in those cars.
CUSTOMER	Yes, but it's not as cheap as it used to be, and the price is climbing all the time.
SALESPERSON	That's just one more reason to buy it now!

Dialogues like the preceding one are certainly familiar; after all, people make comparisons all the time. They talk about the similarities and differences between two things usually in order to decide which one is better. Comparisons, however, are not just part of conversation; they also appear in writing. We can use the following paragraph from a previous chapter as an example:

> Daphne du Maurier's short story "Don't Look Now" is a masterpiece of suspense; it is unfortunate that the film made from the story was not nearly as good. Du Maurier's story is suspenseful and mysterious, but it is also logical. One understands, for example, why the woman in the cape murders the architect. The movie, however, seems determined to avoid any logical explanation of the architect's death. One never understands why the woman in red chooses to attack a man she'd never seen before. It is regrettable that the film chose to ignore du Maurier's logical explanation of the mystery.

You'll notice that every sentence in the paragraph, with the exception of the emphatic sentence used to conclude the paragraph, contributes a new point to a comparison of the story "Don't Look Now" with the movie bearing the same name.

However, although you can easily see that the paragraph contains several comparisons, you may not be sure what the point of these comparisons is. We can explain by listing the similarities and differences mentioned in the paragraph:

Differences:

1. Story is a masterpiece, but film is not nearly as good.

2. Story is suspenseful, mysterious, and logical, but film is not logical.

3. In the story the reader understands why the woman in the cape kills the architect; in the film the reason is not so clear.

The first thing you'll notice about the list is that only differences are listed; no similarities appear. Furthermore, in each comparison, the story fares better than the film.

The next thing you should notice is that one comparison is clearly more general than the others. The comparison in item 1 tells us that the story was better than the film, but no specific details are given. We don't know why the story was better. The remaining comparisons in our list, however, are more specific and explain exactly what advantages the story had over the film.

Since we know that the main idea of a paragraph is the one developed by the rest of the sentences, we know that the comparison in item 1 must contain the main idea of the sample paragraph. But that means we've found the main idea without finding the topic. The question still remains: What is the topic? Is it the story or the book?

We know that the story can't be the topic since the film is mentioned just as much. By the same argument, the film cannot be the topic. As our list illustrates, both the story and the film are repeatedly mentioned because they are repeatedly compared. Since that is the case, it is obvious that the comparison of the book and the film is the topic; this is the subject to which the author continuously returns.

We now know the topic and main idea of the paragraph, and we know that the paragraph deals with comparisons. We are ready then to take notes:

Topic: Comparison between short story "Don't Look Now" and the movie

Main Idea: Film was not nearly as good as the short story.

Support:

1. Story suspenseful, mysterious, and logical:
   (a) Reader understands why woman in cape murders architect.

2. Movie avoids logical explanation:
   (a) Viewer never understands why architect is murdered.

As our sample notes indicate, notes on paragraphs that consist mainly of comparisons should always contain a clear statement of the two things being compared and a summary of all the similarities and differences mentioned.

Before we ask you to take notes, we'll use the following paragraph to give you another example of a paragraph consisting mainly of comparisons:

During the Civil War black and white soldiers fought equally hard, but black soldiers received less pay. While many white soldiers were getting thirteen dollars a month, black soldiers were getting only seven. It was claimed that both black and white soldiers could receive officers' commissions, but in reality, few black soldiers were ever promoted.

In the sample paragraph two groups are compared, black soldiers and white soldiers. We learn not only about the similarities between them but also about the differences. The next question is: what about the main idea? Is there a topic sentence or a suggested main idea in the paragraph? Again we'll answer that question by making a list of comparisons.

Similarities: Both fought equally hard.
Both could become officers.

Differences: Black soldiers paid less.
Black soldiers were not given officer's commissions.

Here, unlike the list we drew up from the previous sample paragraph, there is no one comparison that sums up all the others. But even a quick look at the comparisons tells us that a main idea is implied: There was discrimination against black soldiers during the Civil War. This main idea is not stated in a topic sentence, but it is clearly implied. When two groups work equally hard, but one is treated worse, there is clearly discrimination involved.

Now that we know the topic, main idea, and the differences, we are ready to take notes:

Topic: Comparison between black and white soldiers during the Civil War

Main Idea: Black soldiers were discriminated against during the Civil War.

Support:

1. Black and white soldiers fought equally hard, but black soldiers received less pay.
   (a) White soldiers got thirteen dollars a month while blacks got only seven.
2. Blacks and whites could become officers, but few blacks were promoted.

The following exercises will give you more practice working with paragraphs that consist mainly of comparisons between people, things, or events.

EXERCISE 4   **Practice Exercise:** Read and take notes on the following paragraphs.

1. Between the ninteenth and twentieth centuries, the huge area in America known as the Great Plains underwent startling changes. At the beginning of the nineteenth century, there were few settlements, and one could walk for miles without seeing a house. By the end of the century settlements were springing up all over, and more and more men and women were seeking their fortunes in the section that had been known as the "Great American Desert." In 1800 the plains had been covered by herds of buffalo. These huge, dumb animals were the natural cattle of the plains, and the Indian tribes living on the plains hunted them because their flesh could be eaten and their hides made into clothing. By 1900 the tribes of Indians, among them the Apache, Sioux, and Navajo, who had roamed freely over the plains in pursuit of the buffalo were enclosed in reservations.

Topic: Comparison between Great Plains at the beginning of the nineteenth century and at the end

Main Idea: The Great Plains changed greatly in the years between the nineteenth and twentieth centuries.

Support:

1. Beginning of nineteenth century, few settlements and houses
2. End of nineteenth century, settlements springing up all over
3. 1800: plains had been covered with buffalo
    (a) Natural cattle hunted by Indians who ate flesh and used skins for clothing
4. By 1900 tribes of Indians — Apache, Sioux, and Navajo — had been enclosed in reservations.

Conclusion: _____

Explanation: Our notes are complete because they contain the main idea and list the differences between the Great Plains before and after the turn of the century.

Do the rest of the exercises in the same manner.

1. Between 1890 and 1900, millions of people from the southern and eastern parts of Europe left their own countries in search of a new one, one that would give them peace and security. With this dream in mind, they immigrated to America, but unfortunately, the land they entered was for many a far cry from what they had imagined. The new immigrants had hoped to find a comfortable place to live where they could settle and live out the rest of their lives. But the cities to which they came were not prepared to house so many new arrivals, and many immigrant families ended up living in ugly tenements that were poorly supplied with light, heat, and water. They had dreamed of finding work, work that would make them independent and, if possible, rich. They found instead that jobs were scarce. Frequently they were forced to take jobs for which they were not suited, jobs that left them exhausted and depressed. Many immigrants found that instead of the warm welcome they had expected, they were treated as outsiders with funny customs and an even funnier way of speaking.

Topic: _____

Main Idea: _____

_____

Support: _____

_____

_____

_____

Conclusion: _____

_____

2. The Africanized or so-called *killer bees* are scheduled to appear in the United States sometime around 1990, and their projected arrival has aroused much speculation and fear. However, a lot of the anxiety surrounding the killer bees is unfounded. In many ways, they resemble the familiar honeybee. Their venom, for example, is not more toxic than that of the honeybee. In fact, it is less toxic than the venom of a yellow jacket or wasp. Although movies have tended to play up the vicious nature of the bees, they are actually no more destructive than bees that now inhabit American gardens. What does distinguish the Africanized bee from the ordinary honeybee is its determined defense of territory. Disturbed, the bees will mount an attack that can continue for days, and they will pursue an intruder whereas honeybees will quickly give up. With this problem in mind,

Between 1890 and 1900, millions of men and women immigrated to the United States in search of the American dream.

beekeepers have been forced to build hives far away from the vicinity of human beings.

Topic: _____

Main Idea: _____

_____

Support: _____

_____

_____

_____

_____

_____

Conclusion: _____

_____

3. William Edward Burghardt Du Bois became the main spokesman for blacks opposed to the policies of Booker T. Washington. Both men wanted full equality for blacks, but they proposed different means to reach that goal. Washington's mild approach stressed opportunities rather than grievances, jobs rather than rights, and self-improvement rather than demands for better conditions. Du Bois's approach was the militant* one of Frederick Douglass. He insisted that real economic gain for blacks would not be possible without political rights, full access to public accommodations, and equality in funds spent for education. Although challenged by Du Bois, Washington remained the dominant figure in the black movement from his Atlanta Compromise speech until his death in 1915. Even so,

*militant: aggressive

W. E. B. Du Bois became one of the main spokesmen for blacks in the early part of the twentieth century.

Du Bois's militancy became the inspiration and basis for the civil rights movement throughout the twentieth century.[3]

Topic: _____

Main Idea: _____

_____

[3]Reprinted with permission of Allyn and Bacon, Inc., from *The Black American in United States History* by Edgar A. Toppin. Copyright © 1973 by Allyn and Bacon, Inc.

Support: _____
_____
_____
_____
_____
_____

Conclusion: _____
_____

4. In the summer of 1982, a movie called *Conan, the Barbarian* arrived at local theatres. Featuring bodybuilder Arnold Schwarzenegger, the film was an extraordinary success as audiences, composed largely of teenagers, thrilled to Conan's exploits, which included a love affair with a flaming witch and a battle with a forty-foot snake. As is frequently the case with such fictional superheroes, Conan's original creator, Robert Ervin Howard, lived a life far different from the one he invented for the printed page. In contrast to Conan, who takes the world by storm, Howard lived most of his life in a small town in Texas. Where the barbarian uses muscle, the writer, a shy and quiet intellectual, liked sports but fought his battles with a typewriter rather than his fists. Unlike his wildly passionate creation, Howard was enamored of neither women nor battle. He led a quiet life as a reasonably happy, married man. If he loved anything deeply, it was his mother, whose death sent him into a depression from which he never quite recovered.

Topic: _____
Main Idea: _____
_____
Support: _____
_____

_____

_____

_____

Conclusion: _____

_____

5. When Gerald Ford, the thirty-eighth president of the United States, came to office, he was fond of emphasizing his resemblance to one of his famous predecessors, Harry S. Truman. Like Ford, Truman had been a vice president who became president only by chance. Truman took over when Franklin Roosevelt died in office, a circumstance that resembled Ford's own ascent to the presidency when Richard Nixon resigned from office. Truman, like Ford, was not an intellectual, and he tended to exaggerate his lack of learning, insisting that he was just a simple man with simple tastes. Ford also liked to emphasize that both he and Truman came to office at a difficult time. Truman led the nation during the final months of World War II, and Ford entered office after the nation had been faced with the Watergate scandals.

Topic: _____

Main Idea: _____

_____

Support: _____

_____

_____

_____

_____

Conclusion: _____

_____

CAUSES AND EFFECTS

ANN   My brother went into analysis because he felt so nervous.

BETTY   I think it's the other way around; your brother is really nervous since he went into psychoanalysis.*

    The two women in the dialogue talk about two events: the nervousness of Ann's brother and his decision to go into psychoanalysis. They both agree that the two events have something to do with one another, that one event happened because the other happened before. However, they disagree about which event came first and which followed. They are not sure whether Ann's brother was nervous and decided to go into psychoanalysis or whether he became nervous after entering psychoanalysis.

    We are dealing here then with two events, one of which happened because the other came before; in this case we say that a *cause-and-effect relationship* exists between the two. We call the event that came first the *cause* and the event that followed after the *effect*. Ann and Betty then agree that a cause-and-effect relationship exists between the brother's entry into psychoanalysis and his nervousness, but they cannot agree on which is the cause and which is the effect.

    However, we did not introduce this dialogue to figure out whether the nervousness of Ann's brother came before or after his entrance into psychoanalysis. We introduced it to illustrate what we mean when we talk about a cause-and-effect relationship, and to stress that knowing a cause-and-effect relationship exists between two events does not always tell you which is the cause and which is the effect.

    Many of the paragraphs you run across in your reading do deal with cause-and-effect relationships. Therefore, we will talk about such paragraphs in detail in this section so that you will know how to read and take notes on them.

    Since cause-and-effect relationships can be somewhat complicated, we will use diagrams throughout this section. They will help simplify our explanation. Diagrams 6–1 and 6–2, for example, illustrate the preceding dialogue. Ann's argument is illustrated in Diagram 6–1. Betty's argument is illustrated in Diagram 6–2.

*psychoanalysis: a type of therapy making use of techniques developed by Sigmund Freud, such as dream interpretation and free association

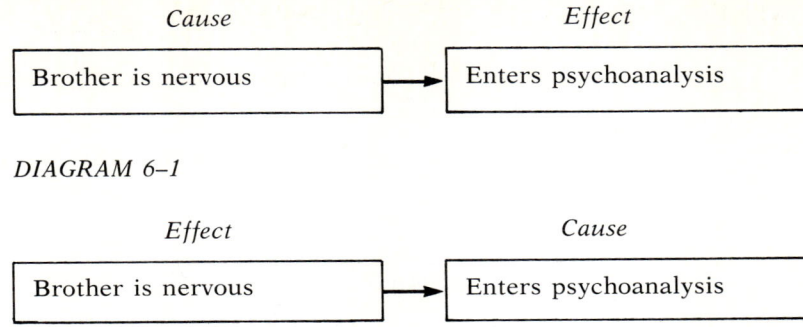

DIAGRAM 6–1

DIAGRAM 6–2

In the following paragraph there is less confusion about which events can be labeled "causes" and which can be labeled "effects":

> The election of Ulysses S. Grant to office brought with it a train of corruption and scandal that has not been equalled under any other president's administration. The Grant years were those when Jay Gould, Jim Fisk, and Daniel Drew manipulated the gold and stock exchange for their own private profit. Boss Tweed and friends were at the height of their power and were happily engaged in robbing New York. Congress spent most of its time figuring out how to vote higher salaries for its members.

The first sentence in the sample paragraph describes a cause-and-effect relationship. We learn that the election of Grant (first event) brought about a train of corruption and scandal (second event). The rest of the sentences give specific examples of corruption and scandal. Diagram 6-3 illustrates the cause-and-effect relationship between the events described in the sample paragraph.

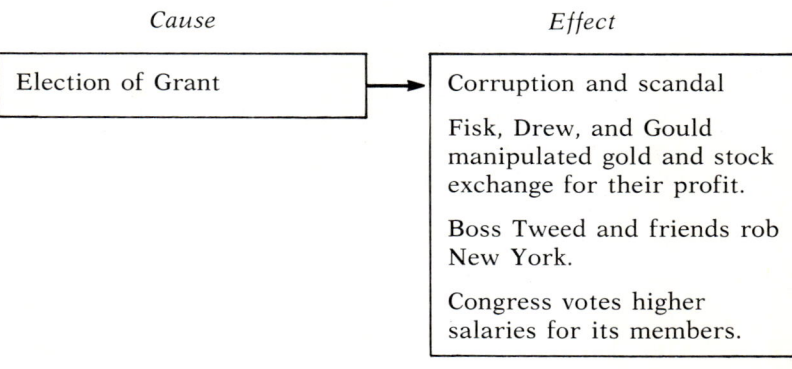

DIAGRAM 6–3

Notice that Diagram 6–3 gives us a clue to the topic of the paragraph. It tells us that the paragraph returns again and again to the effects of Grant's election. This is the subject the author repeatedly mentions, and we can then say that the effects of Grant's election are the topic of the paragraph.

We can also use Diagram 6–3 to figure out if there is a topic sentence in the paragraph. If we look at the list contained in the box labeled "effect," it is clear that the last three items are all specific examples of corruption and scandal. "Corruption and scandal" is the general phrase that sums up all three examples presented in the paragraph. Now we have to see if there is a sentence that contains this phrase. It doesn't take very long to locate that phrase in the first sentence of the paragraph. This sentence must be the topic sentence because, as we know from Diagram 6–3, it is developed throughout the paragraph.

Now that we know the topic and main idea of the paragraph and are sure that we are dealing with a paragraph that describes a cause-and-effect relationship, we are ready to take notes:

Topic: Effects of Grant's election

Main Idea: Grant's election brought with it corruption and scandal.

Support:

1. Gould, Fisk, and Drew manipulated gold and stock exchange for their profit.
2. Boss Tweed and friends robbed New York.
3. Congress voted higher salaries for its members.

Clearly, notes taken on a paragraph devoted to describing cause-and-effect relationship should contain all the causes and effects introduced in the paragraph.

At this point, we want to introduce another paragraph, one that emphasizes causes rather than effects:

Growing numbers of well-to-do Americans are making the decision to move abroad. They find it impossible in America to walk the streets at night without fear of being raped, mugged, or murdered, nor do they see a way to escape the poisonous air of the cities. They maintain that even American food has become increasingly dangerous to eat. Last but not least, they insist that they are sick of the pace of American life, a pace that leaves no time for relaxation or pleasure.

If we diagram the cause-and-effect relationship in this paragraph, we end up with the results in Diagram 6–4.

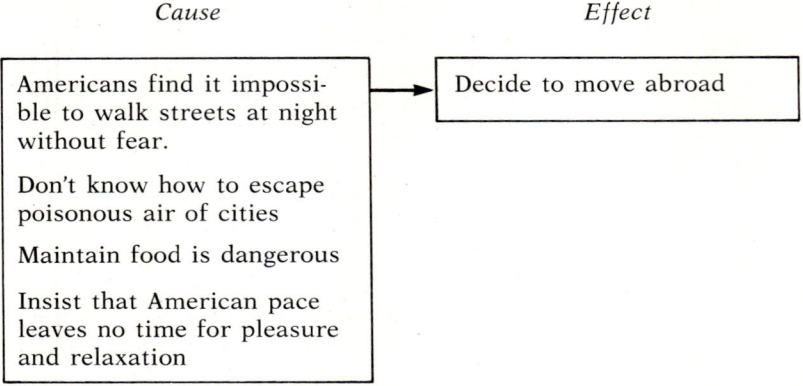

DIAGRAM 6–4

Diagram 6–4 tells us that this paragraph, unlike the first one, does not emphasize the effects of an event. It emphasizes the causes of one. It also tells us that there is no one cause given that is general enough to sum up all the others. But if we look at the list of causes again, one general one does emerge: growing numbers of well-to-do Americans are leaving because they are dissatisfied with life in America. Our diagram then should look like Diagram 6–5:

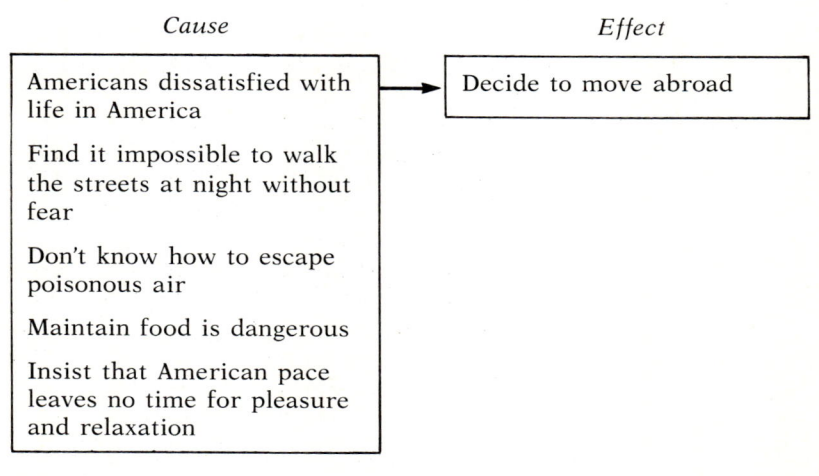

DIAGRAM 6–5

We can use Diagram 6–5 to figure out what the topic of the paragraph is: the diagram shows us that the paragraph keeps coming back to the causes for Americans' flight. Therefore, we can say that causes for well-to-do Americans' decision to move is the topic of the paragraph.

Diagram 6–5 can also help us figure out if there is a topic sentence in the paragraph. For example, it tells us that the paragraph lists several specific causes for Americans' decision to move abroad; all the causes are equally specific, and no more general one is given. Thus the paragraph cannot contain a general sentence that sums up the cause-and-effect relationships described in the paragraph. However, based on the causes and the effects listed in the diagram, we can infer the following main idea: Wealthy Americans are moving abroad because they are dissatisfied with conditions in America.

Now we are ready to take notes:

Topic: Causes for well-to-do Americans' decision to move

Main Idea: Well-to-do Americans move abroad because they are dissatisfied with America.

Support:

1. Find it impossible to walk streets at night without fear

2. Don't know how to escape poisonous air

3. Maintain food is dangerous

4. Insist American pace leaves no time for pleasure

Before introducing the exercises, we'll rewrite the last paragraph and make it a bit more complicated; we want you to see a paragraph that contains what we are calling a *chain of causes:*

> Growing numbers of well-to-do Americans are making the decision to move abroad. They find it impossible to walk the streets at night without fear of being raped, mugged, or murdered; nor do they see a way to escape the poisonous air of the cities *since that same air is beginning to pollute the countryside.* They maintain that even American food has become increasingly dangerous *because of the enormous number of chemical additives.* Last but not least, they insist that they are sick of the pace of American life, a pace that leaves no time for relaxation or pleasure.

If you look at the italicized additions in the paragraph, you'll see that they further explain the causes for the

Americans' decision to move abroad. If we add these additions, our diagram would look like Diagram 6–6.

With additions, the main idea of the paragraph is not altered, but as we said before, the causes are explained in greater detail. They are shown to be not only the cause of some event but also the effect of another event. Thus the diagram contains what we call a chain of causes. As you can see from Diagram 6–6, the sample paragraph contains two of these chains as shown in Diagram 6–7.

Notice that if you read the diagrams against the direction in which the arrows point, they illustrate a chain of effects

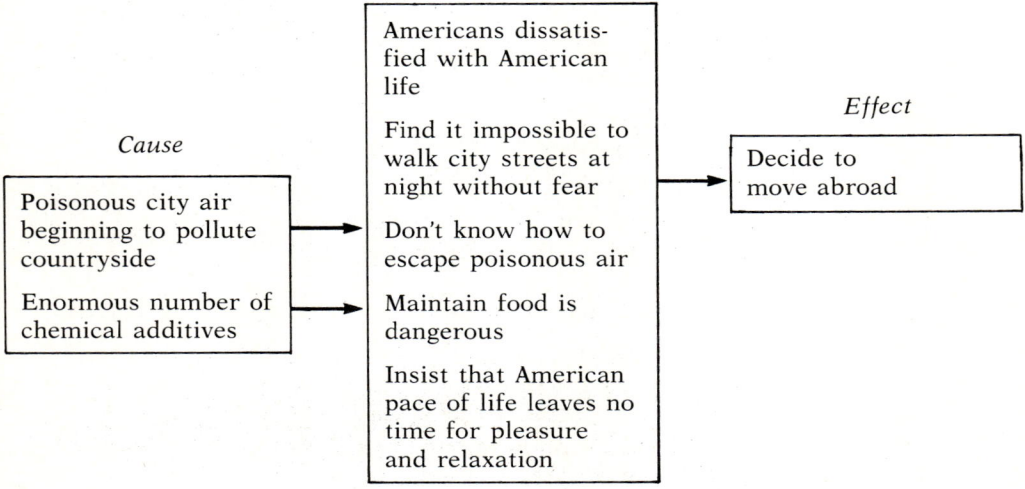

DIAGRAM 6–6

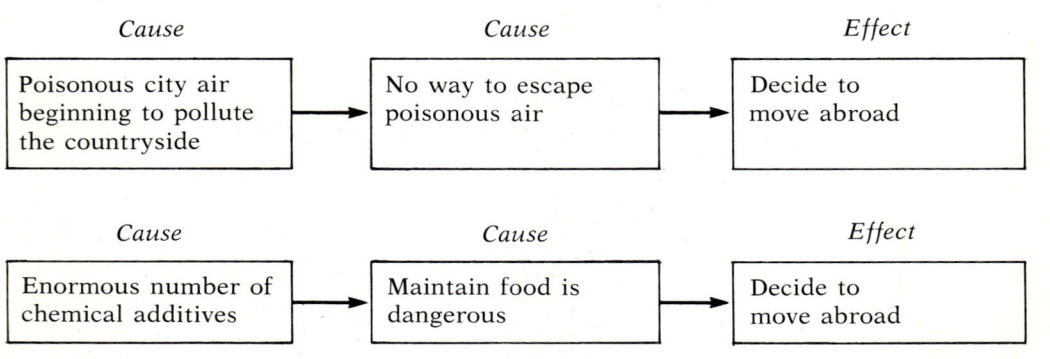

DIAGRAM 6–7

resulting from one cause. However, it doesn't make much difference if you refer to the events as a chain of causes or a chain of effects; the relationship between them remains the same.

If you are taking notes on a paragraph that contains a chain of causes or effects, those chains should be included in your notes:

Topic: Causes for Americans' decision to move abroad

Main Idea: Americans are moving abroad because they are dissatisfied with America.

Support:

1. Americans afraid to walk streets at night
2. Can't escape poisonous air because it pollutes city and countryside
3. Food dangerous because of number of chemical additives
4. Insist American pace too fast

In the following exercises you are asked to read and take notes on paragraphs that describe a cause-and-effect relationship; some describe chains of causes or effects. After reading each paragraph, make sure you can identify the cause-and-effect relationship described in the main idea; list all the causes and effects given in the paragraph and identify any chains of causes or effects; then you are ready to take notes.

EXERCISE 5   **Practice Exercise:** Read and take notes on the following paragraphs.

1. It would seem in retrospect that the prohibition laws* of the 1920s actually helped encourage, rather than hinder, illegal activity. Citizens in every section of the country showed nothing but contempt for the laws, and any attempt at law enforcement was met with indifference or hostility. Probably the worst result of the laws was that the control of liquor distribution fell into the hands of organized crime, which led to increased criminal violence throughout the country. Rather than decreasing crime, the prohibition laws actually helped to increase it.

*prohibition laws: laws forbidding transportation, sale, and possession of alcoholic beverages

Topic: Effects of prohibition

Main Idea: Prohibition encouraged illegal activity.

Support:

1. Citizens showed contempt and hostility for enforcement of the laws.

2. Liquor distribution fell into the hands of organized crime causing violence to spread.

Conclusion: _____

Explanation: The effects of prohibition are the topic of the paragraph. The first sentence of the paragraph is the topic sentence, and it tells us that the prohibition laws led to increased illegal activity. The remaining supporting sentences describe the effects in detail, and we have included all the effects in our notes. We have not put the information contained in the last sentence into our notes because this is an emphatic sentence that repeats the idea contained in the topic sentence.

Do the rest of the exercises in the same manner.

1. No one can deny that several events led up to America's rebellion against British domination. However, it is certain that England's use of the Coercive* Acts, acts that the British Parliament passed in order to punish the colonists for the Boston Tea Party, was one of the major causes of America's decision to rebel. The acts closed the port of Boston until the tea that had been destroyed was paid for and took away Massachusetts's colonial charter. Officials who had been elected locally were to be appointed by the King, and a new quartering act specified that British troops would have to be housed in public inns when necessary.

Topic: _____

Main Idea: _____

_____

_____

*to coerce: to bring about by force

Support: _____
_____
_____
_____
_____
_____
_____

Conclusion: _____
_____

2. To secure their political authority and to preserve peace, the Tokugawa shoguns* isolated Japan from the rest of the world in 1639. Christianity was banned. Except for some Chinese and a small Dutch contingent, who lived closely supervised lives in Nagasaki harbor, all foreigners were expelled from Japan. Not only were Christian books barred but also any book, even a Chinese translation, dealing with any Western subject. Japanese were forbidden on pain of death to leave their homeland. Vessels were restricted in size so they could be used only in coastal trade and not in overseas commerce.[4]

Topic: _____

Main Idea: _____
_____

Support: _____
_____

*shoguns: Japanese military leaders who had great power up until 1868

[4]From *Exploring World Cultures* by Esko E. Newhill and Umberto LaPaglia, ©copyright 1974 by Ginn and Company (Xerox Corporation). Used with permission.

_____
_____
_____

Conclusion: _____
_____

3. For three years prior to America's entry into World War I, Americans had wavered in their desire to give up their neutral position; but the Germans' resumption* of submarine warfare and the Zimmerman telegram helped change neutrality into hostility, and America went to war. In the two months that preceded President Wilson's war message, eight vessels had been sunk by German submarines, and forty-eight American lives were lost. The hostility created by the sinking of the vessels was further increased when it was revealed that German Foreign Secretary Alfred Zimmerman had proposed in a message to the Mexican government that Mexico should join with Germany if a German-American war broke out.

Topic: _____

Main Idea: _____
_____

Support: _____
_____
_____
_____
_____
_____

*resumption: the act of beginning or starting again

Causes and Effects 289

Conclusion: _____

_____

4. The emotion of fear sets off many changes in your body. When you become frightened, you breathe more deeply, giving your muscles more oxygen and greater energy. Your heart beats more powerfully so that your blood circulates faster, carrying oxygen to all parts of your body. Your stomach and intestines no longer contract and all digestive action stops. No saliva flows in your mouth and your throat becomes dry. Your face becomes pale because the tiny blood vessels shrink under the skin so that less blood would flow if you were cut. The blood can clot faster so that there would be less bleeding from a wound. The pupils of your eyes enlarge, admitting more light during the emergency. You might be able to perform great feats of strength in this condition.[5]

Topic: _____

Main Idea: _____

_____

Support: _____

_____

_____

_____

_____

_____

Conclusion: _____

_____

[5] From page 214 of *Biology and Human Progress* by Louis Eisman and Charles Tanzer ©1972 by Prentice-Hall, Inc., Englewood Cliffs, N.J. Reprinted by permission.

5. When Elvis Presley, the acknowledged king of rock-and-roll, died he was horribly overweight, addicted to countless drugs, and subject to fits of uncontrollable rage. Exactly what caused Presley to degenerate so terribly is still unknown; there seems in fact to have been no one cause, but

Elvis Presley, one of the great performers of rock-and-roll.

a complicated variety of causes. Throughout his career, Presley longed to be taken more seriously as an actor, but discouraged by his manager Colonel Tom Parker, he never made anything but critical disasters. Films like *Blue Hawaii* made money, but they never made the critics take notice. Devoted to his mother, who protected him throughout his childhood and youth, he was grief-stricken over her death in 1958, and he never quite recovered from her loss. Oddly enough, although he never complained, Elvis's spirit seems to have been damaged by his highly publicized stint* in the army. Upon his return to civilian life, he failed to achieve the promise, personally or professionally, of the pre-Army years.

Topic: _____

Main Idea: _____
_____

Support: _____
_____
_____
_____
_____
_____
_____

Conclusion: _____
_____

CLASSIFICATIONS

The following paragraph introduces the topic "the audience at horror movies." The topic sentence—in this case the first

*stint: a fixed amount of duty performed within a given period of time

sentence—divides members of the audience into three different groups. This is a good example of a paragraph devoted to **classification**:

> The theater audience in a horror movie can be divided into three groups. First of all, there are the gigglers. Members of this group may giggle out of nervousness, or they may find the scenes really funny. Then there are the hand grabbers. This group seems to think they can get through anything as long as there is something to hold. The last group contains the talkers. They always have a comment to make. For example, when the horrible-looking monster comes into view, they turn to a neighbor and say something clever like, "He's certainly cute, isn't he?"

After reading this paragraph, it might seem that it is similar to those paragraphs we introduced in the section on comparisons. The paragraph does, after all, describe the differences between groups of people. But before reaching that conclusion, let's analyze the paragraph more carefully. We can begin by listing all the groups that are described:

1. theater audiences
2. people who laugh
3. people who grab hands
4. people who talk

The first thing you should notice is that only the differences between the last three groups are described. We learn how each group differs in its reaction to horror films. However, no mention is made of the difference between these three groups and the first one. That would, indeed, be difficult to do since the last three groups are all part of the first one. This then is the clue that helps us distinguish the sample paragraph from those given in the section on comparison paragraphs. The sample paragraph does not talk only about the things that are compared. It also talks about the larger group, theater audiences, to which all the other groups in the paragraph belong.

This larger group is in fact the topic of the paragraph since every sentence talks about people who belong to theater audiences. Actually, the whole point of the paragraph is to tell us that the larger group can be divided into smaller groups or, as they are often called, *categories*. This is the main idea of the paragraph, and it is stated in the first sentence. The rest of the paragraph illustrates the division by describing the characteristics of the smaller categories.

We call such a division of a larger group into smaller categories a *classification*. All of the paragraphs within this section deal with the process of classification; that is, they explain how a larger group of similar persons, places, or things can be divided into smaller categories.

Once we know that the paragraph deals with classification, we are ready to take notes:

Topic: Theater audiences in horror films

Main Idea: Theater audiences in horror movies can be divided into three groups.

Support:

1. Gigglers:
    (a) Laugh out of nervousness or amusement
2. Hand grabbers:
    (a) Must hold on to something
3. Talkers:
    (a) Always have a comment to make
        (1) e.g., "movie monster is cute"

As our sample notes illustrate, notes on paragraphs that make classifications should contain the name of the larger group that is being broken down into categories; the names of the categories, if any names are given, and the characteristics of each category.

You'll notice in the sample paragraph that the names of the categories indicate the characteristics of each group. This is not always the case. Sometimes an author does not give each category a name, or else the names may not clearly indicate the characteristics. This is true of the next sample paragraph:

> Studies indicate that human beings use two kinds of memory: short term and long term. When we use short-term memory, we retain information for a very brief period of time. For example, we use short-term memory when we look up a phone number and remember it only long enough to dial. When we use long-term memory, we retain information for a considerable length of time. A young child, for example, may memorize a poem and remember it for the next twenty years.

The topic of the paragraph is "memory," and the topic sentence tells us that there are two kinds of memory, long term and short term. We also learn from the paragraph that each type of memory has its own characteristics. Short-term memory is characterized by the retention of information for a very brief period of time. Long-term memory is characterized by the retention of information for a long period of time.

Now that we know what larger group can be divided into smaller categories, the names of the categories and the characteristics of each category, we have everything we need for our notes:

Topic: Memory

Main Idea: Human beings use two kinds of memory.

Support:

1. Short-term memory: retain information for short period of time
   (a) Look up information in telephone book and remember it long enough to dial
2. Long-term memory: retain information for a longer period of time
   (a) Memorize poem and remember it for twenty years

The following exercise will give you more practice reading and taking notes on paragraphs that deal with classification. Before you take notes, decide what larger group is being divided into categories. See if the categories are named and note the characteristiccs of each separate category.

EXERCISE 6   **Practice Exercise:** Read and take notes on the following paragraphs.

1. Studies indicate that learning can be divided into two categories: incidental learning and intentional learning. *Incidental learning* takes place by chance; there is no clearly defined intention to learn. For example, a student who wants to check if he or she knows the first sixteen presidents of the United States may ask a friend to listen while they are named; during the recitation, the friend may, by chance, also learn the names of the first sixteen presidents. *Intentional learning* takes place when there is a clearly defined purpose present from the very beginning. For example, a student may sit down with a list of the fifty states and their capitals because he or she needs to learn them for a test.

Topic: Learning

Main Idea: Learning can be divided into two categories.

Support:

1. Incidental learning takes place by chance.
   (a) Student who helps a friend learn the first sixteen presidents of the United States may, by chance, learn them too.
2. Intentional learning takes place when purpose is present from very beginning.
   (a) Student sits down with the intention to learn the capitals of fifty states.

Conclusion: _____

Explanation: Learning is the topic of the paragraph. The topic sentence tells us that learning can be divided into two categories and provides the names of the categories: incidental and intentional learning. Since we have listed the larger group, which is divided into categories, and have given the names of the categories and their characteristics, we have everything of importance in our notes.

Do the rest of the exercises in the same manner.

1. *Schizophrenia* is perhaps the worst of all mental illnesses. It can force its victims to sit motionless for hours or torture them with the sound of strange voices. Although after years of research experts remain ignorant of what causes the disease, they have been able to identify its three basic types. *Catatonic schizophrenia* is characterized by extreme immobility. For hours at a time, the victim of this type will remain as if in a stupor, sitting or standing without movement. In contrast, those suffering from *hebephrenic schizophrenia* are practically incapable of quiet behavior; they tend to talk or babble constantly. Perhaps the most well-known form is *paranoid schizophrenia*, which leaves patients believing that they are surrounded by enemies who threaten their lives. At present, no cure for the disease is known, but several drugs have been developed to help control the symptoms.

Topic: _____

Main Idea: _____
_____

Support: _____
_____
_____
_____
_____
_____

Conclusion: _____
_____

2. The human brain is divided into two halves, known as the right and left hemispheres. Although the hemispheres cooperate for many functions, research suggests they control highly different activities. For example, the right hemisphere is more concerned with musical than verbal ability. Thus patients suffering from damage to the right side of the brain may find their ability to recognize formerly familiar melodies severely impaired, at the same time that their speech shows absolutely no evidence of any brain injury. Similarly, many difficult physical tasks show little left hemisphere involvement; it appears that the left hemisphere has enough to do coordinating the abilities to read, write, speak, and do arithmetic.

Topic: _____

Main Idea: _____
_____
_____

Support: _____

_____

_____

_____

_____

_____

Conclusion: _____

_____

3. Most people use repetition to remember what they have read. However, few of us realize that we actually use two different kinds of repetition: active and passive. When we use *active* repetition, we do not simply repeat over and over what we have just read. Instead, without looking back at the text, we see if we can repeat, in our own words, what we have just learned. When we use *passive* repetition, we simply repeat what we see before us in the text. No attempt is made to translate the material into our own words.

Topic: _____

Main Idea: _____

_____

Support: _____

_____

_____

_____

_____

Conclusion: _____

4. There are four ways in which members of the House of Representatives may vote. The most common is the *voice vote*, when members voting for a bill say "yea" and those opposed say "nay." The Speaker judges which side has the most voice votes and announces the result. If any member feels that the Speaker is mistaken, he may call for a *standing vote*, called a "division." In this case, the members stand to be counted for or against a measure. A third method is the *teller vote*. If one-fifth of the members present so demand, all the members of the House pass between "tellers" and are counted as they do so, first those in favor and then those opposed to the measure. The *roll call* is the procedure used for important measures. The Clerk of the House calls the roll, and each of the 435 members responds by answering "yea" or "nay." Roll call voting takes about 45 minutes.[6]

Topic: _____

Main Idea: _____

Support: _____

[6] From *American Government: Continuity and Change* by Allen Shick and Adrienne Pfister. Copyright ©1972 by Houghton Mifflin Company. Reprinted by permission.

Conclusion: _____

_____

5. In the human body, blood circulates through elastic, tube-like canals called *blood vessels*. Consisting of three different types, blood vessels are well-adapted to their functions. The vessels called *arteries* carry blood away from the heart to all parts of the body. The largest artery in the human body is the *aorta*. Because of oxygen, blood in the arteries appears bright red. In contrast, blood in the *veins*, another type of blood vessel, appears purplish because it is no longer carrying a supply of oxygen. Veins carry blood back to the heart, and they contain small valves which prevent the blood from flowing backward. This is important in those parts of the body where the blood has to move against the pull of gravity. The third type of blood vessel is the *capillary*. Capillaries are tiny vessels connecting arteries and veins. Their walls are extremely thin. They have to be so that digested food can pass through them to the cells of the body.

Topic: _____

Main Idea: _____

_____

Support: _____

_____

_____

_____

_____

_____

Conclusion: _____

_____

MIXED PARAGRAPHS

In the preceding pages we introduced several different types of paragraphs and gave you a number of sample paragraphs to analyze. Each sample paragraph illustrated one particular type. However, we should also emphasize that you will frequently encounter what we are calling *mixed paragraphs;* that is, you will run across paragraphs that seem to be a mixture of two different paragraph types. See, for example, the following:

> John Calvin's famous work *Institutes of the Christian Religion* (published in 1536) helped spread the Protestant faith to those countries not already under the sway of Lutheranism; after reading Calvin's book, countless people became Protestants. Although the book owed almost all its ideas to the writings of Martin Luther, it still had a wider appeal than anything Luther had published. While Luther's emphasis on the saving power of faith was difficult for many to accept, Calvin's emphasis on the unimportance of mankind in the face of God's majesty and power was something that people of the sixteenth century could readily grasp.

In the preceding paragraph the author returns again and again to Calvin's book *Institutes of the Christian Religion;* this is the topic of the paragraph. The first sentence in the paragraph, the topic sentence, describes a cause-and-effect relationship, and we learn that many people converted to the Protestant faith after reading Calvin's book. We can say then that the paragraph deals with a cause-and-effect relationship.

However, when the author begins to describe Calvin's book, the paragraph begins to resemble another type of paragraph, one dealing with the comparison of two things. To explain why the book encouraged conversion, the author compares the writings of Luther with those of Calvin. We learn that Calvin's writings had a wider appeal and that Luther stressed the saving power of faith while Calvin stressed the majesty and power of God.

We can say then that the paragraph is a combination of two different types: it describes a cause-and-effect relationship and makes a comparison. This paragraph is a good example of what we have in mind when we talk about a mixed paragraph.

The question now is: how do you take notes on a mixed paragraph? We can answer that question by referring to what you have already learned.

Previously, when you took notes on a paragraph that described a cause-and-effect relationship, you had to make sure that your notes included the cause-and-effect relationship described in the paragraph, all specific causes and effects, and any chains of causes or effects. Those same instructions hold true for the sample paragraph. Your notes, then, will contain the following information:

> Reading Calvin's book caused many people to convert to the Protestant faith.

This sentence contains the main idea of the entire paragraph, and it describes the only cause-and-effect relationship contained in the paragraph. The paragraph does not contain any chains of causes and effects.

However, as we have already mentioned, the paragraph also compares the writings of Luther with the writings of Calvin; therefore, we have to add more information to our notes. Earlier in this chapter when you dealt with paragraphs making comparisons, you had to indicate the two things being compared and list the differences or similarities between the two. Notes on this part of the sample paragraph then would include the following information:

Similarities: The ideas in the works of both were very similar.

Differences: Calvin's writing had a wider appeal than Luther's. People responded to Calvin's emphasis on God's power but did not respond to Luther's emphasis on the power of faith.

Our final notes on the paragraph would look like this:

Topic: Institutes of the Christian Religion

Main Idea: Reading Calvin's book caused many people to convert to the Protestant faith.

Support:

1. Ideas taken from Luther, but Calvin's writings had wider appeal
2. People responded to Calvin's emphasis on God's power but not to Luther's emphasis on power of faith.

Notes on a mixed paragraph present no problem once you are sure what types of paragraphs have been combined. You need only make sure that your notes contain the most important characteristics of each type. For example, the sample paragraph dealt with a cause-and-effect relationship and made a comparison between two things. Our notes, therefore, had to include all the causes and effects described in the paragraph as well as a complete description of the similarities and differences between the two things compared.

The following is another example of a mixed paragraph:

> Increased spells of warm weather and decreased use of a pesticide called Mirex have resulted in a plague of what laymen call fire ants. Indeed, pleasant weather and an absence of pesticides have encouraged whole armies of ants to make their homes in farmers' fields where they can leisurely munch on crops of potatoes and okra. Should a tractor overturn one of their nests, the furious ants swarm over the machine and attack the driver. Using their jaws to hold the victim's skin, they thrust their stingers into the flesh, holding the same position for up to twenty-five seconds. The sting produces a painful burning sensation and is frequently followed by painful infections, which can last weeks and even months. Some victims who were especially allergic to the ants' poison have not survived a fire ant attack.

The topic sentence in the paragraph describes a cause-and-effect relationship, and we learn that warm weather and decreased use of a pesticide called Mirex have resulted in a plague of fire ants. The second sentence, a supporting sentence, describes the same cause-and-effect relationship in more detail, and the remaining supporting sentences contain a sequence of steps that describes a fire ant attack, a disagreeable aspect of the plague. Thus we are dealing with two paragraph types: cause and effect and a sequence of steps.

Our notes, then, would look like this:

Topic: Fire ants

Main Idea: Increased warm weather and decreased use of pesticide called Mirex have resulted in a plague of fire ants.

Support:

1. Whole armies of ants have moved into farmers' fields and are eating potatoes and okra.

2. If tractor overturns nest, ants swarm over machine and attack driver.

3. Sting produces painful burning sensations and can produce infections.

Conclusion: Some especially allergic victims have died foling fire ant attack.

Since we know that our paragraph describes a cause-and-effect relationship and a sequence of steps, we have made sure to include all causes and effects mentioned in the paragraph, and we have listed all the steps in the order in which they occur. You will notice that some of the steps also consist of a cause-and-effect relationship, but they offer no particular problem since by including the steps, we have also included the causes and effects.

EXERCISE 7   **Practice Exercise:** All of the following are mixed paragraphs. Read each one and decide which paragraph types are represented. Then circle the correct types and take notes on the paragraph.

1. In 1911 Benito Mussolini was a socialist* who was firmly opposed to cooperation with the established government; he held an important post in the Italian Socialist Party and was editor and contributor to a socialist newspaper. When rumors of war began to circulate in 1914, Mussolini sided with the majority of his associates who were determined to keep Italy out of the war. By the end of 1914, however, Mussolini had begun to reverse his position on the war and was demanding that Italy begin to take up arms. In the following year Mussolini gave up his post in the Socialist Party to devote himself to the war effort. When the war came to an end, Mussolini gathered together a band of ex-soldiers and adventurers and began to break up communist and socialist meetings. By 1922 Mussolini had bullied King Victor Emmanuel III into giving him a post in the government, and the ex-socialist became the new prime minister.

   ((a)) The paragraph makes comparisons.
   (b) The paragraph describes a cause-and-effect relationship.
   ((c)) The paragraph lists a sequence of events and dates.
   (d) The paragraph lists important characteristics.
   (e) The paragraph lists the steps in a process.
   (f) The paragraph deals with classification.

   Topic: <u>Comparison of Mussolini's career before and after 1914</u>

   Main Idea: <u>Mussolini's career after 1914 contradicted everything he had stood for up to that time.</u>

   *socialist: one who believes that those who produce material wealth should also possess political power

Support:

1. <u>1911: Mussolini a Socialist opposed to cooperation with government. He held important post in Italian Socialist Party.</u>
2. <u>1914: Beginning of 1914, Mussolini against war.</u>
3. <u>1915: Mussolini gave up post in Socialist Party.</u>
4. <u>1919: Mussolini gathered together ex-soldiers to break up meetings of Communists and Socialists.</u>
5. <u>1922: Mussolini became prime minister.</u>

Explanation: The paragraph does not contain a topic sentence, but all the sentences work together to imply one main idea: after 1914 Mussolini's career contradicted everything he had stood for up to that time. The paragraph implies that main idea by describing Mussolini's career before and after 1914, and the reader is forced to compare the differences between the two stages. Once we have the main idea, it is clear that the paragraph deals with comparisons.

However, a series of dates are also given, and these dates signify particular events. We know then that the paragraph describes a sequence of dates and events.

Once we know the types of paragraphs contained in the mixed paragraph, we know that our notes must contain the following information: (1) the two things being compared and the similarities or differences between them and (2) all the dates mentioned and the events accompanying them.

Do the rest of the exercises in the same manner.

1. Hollywood propaganda films of the late thirties and early forties can be divided into three general categories: (1) films that praised America, (2) films that introduced World War II allies, and (3) films that criticized the enemy. Beginning in the late thirties, Hollywood began producing a series of biography films, all of which glorified the American democratic tradition. John Ford's *Young Mr. Lincoln* (1939) and John Cromwell's *Abe Lincoln in Illinois* (1940) were examples of Hollywood's attempt to prove that American democracy gave everyone a chance at success. In the early forties many Hollywood movies offered an introduction to the American allies. Films like *Mrs. Miniver* (1942) and *Journey for Margaret* (1942), for example, presented a sympathetic picture of the British people. During the latter part

of the forties, Hollywood was determined to introduce American audiences to the enemy, and movies like *Hitler's Children* (1943) and *Behind the Rising Sun* (1944) portrayed German and Japanese brutality. Many of the later anti-German and anti-Japanese films have since been criticized because of their distorted and simplistic themes that presented the German and Japanese people as half-mad beasts.

(a) The paragraph makes comparisons.
(b) The paragraph describes a cause-and-effect relationship.
(c) The paragraph lists important characteristics.
(d) The paragraph lists a sequence of steps.
(e) The paragraph lists a sequence of dates and events.
(f) The paragraph deals with classification.

Topic: _____

Main Idea: _____

_____

Support: _____

_____

_____

_____

_____

_____

Conclusion: _____

_____

2. With the sixties, America said goodbye to the puritan morality that made the 1953 movie *The Moon is Blue* shocking because it used words like *virgin* and *mistress*. Although few mourn the passing of such rigid moral standards, many fear the flood of pornography that has resulted from its loss. If

Americans refused to mention pornographic movies in polite society in the fifties, just the reverse is true today. Movies like *The Devil in Miss Jones* and *Deep Throat* are considered pornographic classics, are praised for their humorous approach to success, and still, after a decade, command large audiences. As little as twenty years ago, *Playboy* was considered a rather shocking addition to suburban newsstands, but at the present time, it is being crowded out of the market by a host of competitors, less reluctant to place explicit* sex scenes on the covers of their magazines. When the 1981 movie *Body Heat* appeared on the screen, it was praised for introducing "hard core" sex into a film that was otherwise not pornographic. If the fifties were too rigidly opposed to sex, the sixties and seventies appear to have loosened the floodgates, and the eighties may just have to pay for it.

(a) The paragraph makes comparisons.
(b) The paragraph describes a cause-and-effect relationship.
(c) The paragraph lists important characteristics.
(d) The paragraph lists a sequence of steps.
(e) The paragraph lists a sequence of dates and events.
(f) The paragraph deals with classification.

Topic: _____

Main Idea: _____
_____

Support: _____
_____
_____
_____
_____
_____
_____

*explicit: clear, obvious

Conclusion: _____
_____

3. The oboe is a musical instrument consisting of a cylindrical pipe, which is blown through a double reed. Fragments of wall paintings indicate that the instrument was known to the ancient Egyptians and Sumerians. Traditionally, the oboe has been used to provide musical accompaniment at weddings, funerals, festivals, and parades, and it was once believed that music produced by the instrument could influence the behavior of animals and cure epilepsy, gout, and snakebite. The musical tone of the oboe differs from that of the flute or trumpet, two instruments with which the oboe has frequently been confused. However, the uses and legends associated with the oboe resemble those of the flute and trumpet.

(a) The paragraph makes comparisons.
(b) The paragraph describes a cause-and-effect relationship.
(c) The paragraph lists important characteristics.
(d) The paragraph lists a sequence of steps.
(e) The paragraph lists a sequence of dates and events.
(f) The paragraph deals with classification.

Topic: _____
Main Idea: _____
_____

Support: _____
_____
_____
_____
_____
_____

Conclusion: _____

_____

4. In 1874 Mary Outerbridge brought tennis equipment to American soil. In the same year a court was laid out in the private club to which Miss Outerbridge belonged. Within seven years tennis had become quite popular with the upper classes, and Eugene E. Outerbridge decided to organize the United States Lawn Tennis Association. By 1914 interest in tennis increased, and the nature of the game was beginning to change. Prior to 1914 the game had been considered a delightful, if slightly too strenuous,* pastime, a game to be played by the wealthy in their leisure moments. However, 1914 saw the entrance of young players like Maurice E. McLoughlin, a young tennis champion whose spectacular and aggressive playing style emphasized the speed, endurance, and concentration needed to play the game. By 1915 the national tennis championship had been transferred from the privileged environs of Newport, Rhode Island, to the far less sophisticated West Side Tennis Club at Forest Hills, New York, and tennis was beginning to break free of its role as an upper-class diversion.*

(a) The paragraph makes comparisons.
(b) The paragraph describes a cause-and-effect relationship.
(c) The paragraph lists important characteristics.
(d) The paragraph lists a sequence of steps.
(e) The paragraph lists a sequence of dates and events.
(f) The paragraph deals with classification.

Topic: _____

Main Idea: _____

_____

Support: _____

_____

_____

*strenuous: characterized by great effort
*diversion: pastime

_____

_____

_____

_____

Conclusion: _____

_____

5. The venom of a bee resembles the venom of a snake, and the sting of a bee, like the bite of a snake, can prove dangerous. Unfortunately, while most people react quickly to the bite of a snake, they tend to ignore the sting of a bee, a practice that can prove dangerous. Anyone suffering from the sting of a bee should immediately take the following action: (1) Remove the stinger by brushing it away; do not try to pull it out. (2) Apply any one of the several professional bee sting remedies to the whitish swelling that appears almost immediately following the sting. (3) If the swelling continues throughout the day, call a doctor.

   (a) The paragraph makes comparisons.
   (b) The paragraph describes a cause-and-effect relationship.
   (c) The paragraph lists important characteristics.
   (d) The paragraph lists a sequence of steps.
   (e) The paragraph lists a sequence of dates and events.
   (f) The paragraph deals with classification.

Topic: _____

Main Idea: _____

_____

Support: _____

_____

_____

_____

Conclusion: _____

The following pages will test your mastery of Chapter 6.

REVIEW TEST: CHAPTER 6

Directions: Start by identifying the type of paragraph. Read through the list of possible types and select the correct letter. Then fill in the appropriate blank.

Once you have filled in the blank, you are ready to take notes. Practice making your notes as brief as possible, but make sure you get all the necessary information.

Note: If you choose letter g, mixed paragraph, write down which paragraph types have been combined, for example:

Type: *g, cause and effect, comparison and contrast*

1. Unlike many American bosses, Japanese managers go to great lengths to involve employees in the life of the company. For example, although General Motors actively recruits productivity suggestions from employees and offers up to $10,000 for a proposal that is adopted, the company receives an average of less than one suggestion per employee per year and adopts some one-third of the ideas. At Toyota's main plant near Nagoya, on the other hand, officials receive more than nine suggestions per worker per year and adopt the vast majority.[7]

   (a) sequence and dates of events
   (b) sequence of steps
   (c) list of characteristics
   (d) comparison and contrast
   (e) cause and effect
   (f) classification
   (g) mixed

Type: _____

Topic: _____

Main Idea: _____

---

[7] From "How Japan Does It—And Can We Do It Too" by Christopher Byron. Reprinted from the August 1981 *Reader's Digest*, pp. 64–65. Adapted from *Time*, the weekly news magazine. Reprinted by permission.

Support: _____

_____

_____

_____

_____

_____

_____

Conclusion: _____

_____

2. The making of chocolate is a lengthy and somewhat complicated process, but most agree that this particular product is worth the effort. The chocolate bar begins with a tropical tree, an evergreen called *Theobrama cacao*. The tree bears yellowish flowers and reddish-brown seed pods, but only the pods really interest the chocolate grower. Harvested twice a year, they contain the cacao beans used to produce chocolate. Once the beans have been collected—it takes several hundred to make a pound—they are dried and shipped to chocolate factories. On arrival, the beans are cleaned, roasted, and chopped into bits. These tiny bits and pieces are then turned into a bitter liquid which is mixed with special, usually secret, ingredients. This process can last for several days because the liquid must be stirred into a fine, smooth syrup. After being heated sufficiently, the chocolate is further sweetened and finally decorated. The result can be as simple as the chocolate bar or as complicated as the Easter egg.

(a) sequence of dates and events
(b) sequence of steps
(c) list of characteristics
(d) comparison and contrast
(e) cause and effect
(f) classification
(g) mixed

Type: _____

Topic: _____

Main Idea: _____
_____

Support: _____
_____
_____
_____
_____
_____

Conclusion: _____
_____

3. Anyone who has ever cheered on his or her favorite athlete knows that yelling can produce hoarseness. When a person yells or screams, the vocal cords—two thick, muscular strings—close tightly and create a tremendous amount of air pressure. As they open to let out a sound, the sudden release of air causes the cords to slam together. When the cords hit each other, especially over a long period of time, they can bruise and swell. If this happens, they will not fit together properly. Air then leaks between the cords, and the voice sounds hoarse. Hoarseness is a sign that the vocal cords need rest. Trying to talk to get rid of the hoarseness only makes matters worse, and the cords may begin bleeding. Many vocalists, especially rock singers who shout a lot, suffer from bleeding and irritated cords.

(a) sequence of dates and events
(b) sequence of steps

(c) list of characteristics
(d) comparison and contrast
(e) cause and effect
(f) classification
(g) mixed

Type: _____

_____

Topic: _____

Main Idea: _____

_____

Support: _____

_____

_____

_____

_____

_____

_____

Conclusion: _____

_____

4. For many years now, columnists such as Edwin Newman and William Safire have repeatedly pointed out that the English language appears to be in a bad way. It is littered with pretentious diction, confusing euphemisms,* and obvious mispronunciations. However, no one has attempted to do in depth what writer George Orwell did, almost forty years ago, in his famous essay "Politics and the English

*euphemism: the substitution of a pleasant or inoffensive term for one considered too crude or offensive, e.g, *underarm* for *armpit*

Language." In that essay Orwell attempted to analyze and explain the causes for such a sad state of spoken and written affairs. He attributed careless or vague use of language to an equally careless and vague method of thinking. In short, he argued that men and women who refused to think with care would not speak or write with it either. From this point of view, anyone disturbed by the state of the English language should attempt to reform not the language but the people, and the rest would follow: English would re-emerge as an instrument of communication rather than confusion.

(a) sequence of dates and events
(b) sequence of steps
(c) list of characteristics
(d) comparison and contrast
(e) cause and effect
(f) classification
(g) mixed

Type: _____

Topic: _____

Main Idea: _____

Support: _____

Conclusion: _____

_____

5. Igneous rock is hard and durable. Two common types of igneous rock are *granite* and *basalt*. Both contain several different minerals. In granite we usually find some quartz, mica, and a mineral called feldspar. The quartz in granite is hard and glassy. The other minerals may be pink, gray or black in color. Granite is a very tough stone which is used for heavy buildings. Basalt is a hard, dark-colored rock, which is not quite as strong as granite. After a volcano erupts, basalt is usually formed when the lava hardens. Because of its strength and availability, basalt is used for road construction and other jobs that require wearing ability and hardness.[8]

(a) sequence of dates and events
(b) sequence of steps
(c) list of characteristics
(d) comparison and contrast
(e) cause and effect
(f) classification
(g) mixed

Type: _____

_____

Topic: _____

Main Idea: _____

_____

Support: _____

_____

_____

[8]Reprinted from *The GED Handbook of Basic Science*, copyright 1967, 1972 by Cambridge Book Company (out of print), New York, 1972, p. 95. Reprinted with the permission of the publisher.

_____

_____

_____

Conclusion: _____

_____

6. The thyroid gland is shaped somewhat like the letter *H*, and it is located in front of and on either side of the trachea. It is important in the regulation of energy, and if the gland does not function properly, it can produce several unpleasant side effects. The most common result of thyroid malfunctioning is a condition called *goiter*. This occurs when the thyroid does not receive sufficient quantities of iodine. The thyroid becomes enlarged and swollen. In contrast to its normal state, it becomes distinctly visible as a swelling at the front of the neck. With the addition of iodine to the diet, goiter will usually disappear. Prolonged and serious stress can also cause the thyroid to malfunction, producing the condition known as *hypothyroidism*. When this happens, the thyroid becomes underactive, and there will be a severe decrease in energy. The individual suffering from hypothyroidism will feel tired and listless. In addition, he or she may see a decrease in hair and nail growth. Less common than hypothyroidism is *hyperthyroidism* or an overactive gland. When this happens there is an excess of energy. There may even be a low-grade fever. Both thyroid imbalances are fairly easy to correct with proper rest and medication. In some severe cases, surgery may be necessary.

(a) sequence of dates and events
(b) sequence of steps
(c) list of characteristics
(d) comparison and contrast
(e) cause and effect
(f) classification
(g) mixed

Type: _____

_____

Topic: _____

Main Idea: _____
_____

Support: _____
_____
_____
_____
_____
_____

Conclusion: _____
_____

7. Langston Hughes was born at the turn of the century in 1902. Shortly after his birth in Joplin, Missouri, Hughes's father, James Nathaniel Hughes, moved to Mexico in an effort to escape racial prejudice, but his mother, Carrier Mercer Langston, could not bear the idea of settling in a foreign country. She stayed in the United States but was forced to move constantly in order to stay employed and support her family. Despite the continual moving, Hughes developed a strong interest in poetry, and, at fourteen, he was good enough to be elected class poet when the family settled for a time in Lincoln, Illinois. Upon entering high school in 1916, Hughes was still interested in poetry, and he published his work in the school newspaper. After graduation, he enrolled at Columbia University in 1921, but was still not sure what he wanted to do. However, anxious for adventure, he signed on with a cargo vessel and, in 1923, sailed for Africa. After his return to the States in 1924, Hughes got a job as a busboy in the Waldman Park Hotel. As luck would have it, in 1925 poet Vachel Lindsay visited the Waldman and sat at Hughes's table. The young poet-busboy was able to slip several poems under Lindsay's plate. The next day Lindsay an-

nounced that he had discovered a poetic genius, and less than three years later, Langston Hugues was publishing his work in *Vanity Fair, Poetry,* and *The New Republic.*

(a) sequence of dates and events
(b) sequence of steps
(c) list of characteristics
(d) comparison and contrast
(e) cause and effect
(f) classification
(g) mixed

Type: _____

_____

Topic: _____

Main Idea: _____

_____

Support: _____

_____

_____

_____

_____

_____

Conclusion: _____

_____

8. Europeans play a game called *lotto,* the American form of which is called *bingo.* Once popular with all ages, the game is now played largely by the elderly. It employs a six-by-four-inch card printed with numbers; in the middle of the

card is a blank space called "free play." The object of bingo is to put a small ball or block on a continuous sequence of numbers. The numbers may move horizontally,* vertically*, or diagonally.* Although bingo can be played at home, most bingo games are now run for profit, attracting large numbers of players. If the number of players grows, the proprietor of the game usually increases the prize. When players fill in a row on their cards, they shout "Bingo!" If two players shout at the same time, they divide the win. This practice has influenced the English language, and Americans often use the expression "Bingo!" to express a pleasant or unexpected surprise.

(a) sequence of dates and events
(b) sequence of steps
(c) list of characteristics
(d) comparison and contrast
(e) cause and effect
(f) classification
(g) mixed

Type: _____

_____

Topic: _____

Main Idea: _____

_____

Support: _____

_____

_____

_____

*horizontally: in a straight line from left to right
*vertically: in a straight line from top to bottom
*diagonally: in a straight line from upper left-hand corner to lower right-hand corner

Conclusion: _____

9. Plants manufacture food by a process known as *photosynthesis*. In the plant, tiny bodies called *chloroplasts* contain *chlorophyll*, a green pigment which does most of the work of food production. After the necessary raw materials, water and carbon dioxide, enter the plant, the chlorophyll captures energy from the sun. The captured energy then sets off a chemical reaction which combines the carbon dioxide and water. They then form a simple sugar called *glucose*. Some of the sugar is used to provide the cells with energy while some is stored in the stem and leaves of the plant. In the final stage of photosynthesis, the plant releases pure oxygen into the air where it can be used again by other living things.

(a) sequence of dates and events
(b) sequence of steps
(c) list of characteristics
(d) comparison and contrast
(e) cause and effect
(f) classification
(g) mixed

Type: _____

Topic: _____

Main Idea: _____

Support: _____

_____

_____

_____

_____

_____

Conclusion: _____

_____

10. In 1854 Henry David Thoreau published *Walden*, his much-revised journal of life in the woods surrounding Walden Pond. At the time Thoreau lived there, the pond was owned by poet and philosopher Ralph Waldo Emerson. Heavily wooded and filled with wildlife, almost no one lived in the area near the pond, and Thoreau wrote often about the marvelous sights and sounds human beings could find if they were only brave enough to enter alone. Perhaps the best things about his journal are the wonderful descriptions of nature where Thoreau wrote of warm summer nights, the haunting cry of wild birds, and the taste of fresh fruit. In Thoreau's time, the water in the pond was so clear he dreamed of plumbing its bottom. Pollution didn't exist, and a clever fisherman could catch his dinner, later on, finding blueberries for dessert. However, that was a long time ago, and today's Walden Pond is quite different. The pond is no longer privately owned. It has been a state park since 1922, but it is only recently that hordes of pleasure seekers have begun to descend upon it. Intent on having a good time, they drive motorcycles through the woods, destroying natural paths and banks. The beach is littered with refuse no one has bothered to pick up, and wild animals are no longer readily seen. Officials have had to fine those ready to hunt the few creatures hardy enough to survive the human invasion. Even crime has entered the woods: there have been arrests for everything from illegal entry to rape. Some environmentalists, angry at what is happening, have founded a group called "Walden Forever Wild."[9]

[9]"The Description of Walden Pond," *Newsweek*, October 20, 1981, p. 20

(a) sequence of dates and events
(b) sequence of steps
(c) list of characteristics
(d) comparison and contrast
(e) cause and effect
(f) classification
(g) mixed

Type: _____

_____

Topic: _____

Main Idea: _____

_____

Support: _____

_____

_____

_____

_____

_____

Conclusion: _____

_____

Chapter 7

Reading an Essay

In the following pages we will talk about how to read an essay, and you will see that the same skills you used to read a single paragraph now apply to reading an entire essay. Similarly, you'll learn that taking notes on an essay is much like taking notes on a paragraph.

Read the essay that follows. When you are finished, continue with the rest of the chapter, and we'll explain the function of every paragraph in the essay.

SAMPLE ESSAY

Dangerous Dieting

1

Introductory Paragraph

Pat was always on a diet. Eighteen years old and thin, she maintained that she was simply too fat, and no amount of coaxing could convince her that she was actually dangerously underweight for her height and age. To reduce her already pencil-slim figure, she suddenly began to refuse any food except for a few pieces of toast and some water. At the end of only one month she weighed ninety pounds.

2

Most parents, when their children begin talking about dieting, react just as Pat's parents did. They smile indulgently* and hope that their children won't allow themselves to become too

*indulgently: leniently, without strictness

Topic Paragraph

thin. But in general, they do not worry. In figure-conscious America, it is quite natural for young people to desire a slim figure. However, in Pat's case, and in the case of many like her, dieting is nothing to smile at. It is not a momentary whim that will be pursued and forgotten; instead, it is the symptom of a serious emotional disorder. Doctors call such excessive and irrational dieting *anorexia nervosa* or, because it has been known to lead to death by starvation, the *starvation disease*.

3

Supporting Paragraph

Victims of the starvation disease are usually girls who have no apparent reason to diet. They are not overweight; they are not preparing to take part in specialized sports activities requiring a slender figure; they have not been told to diet by their doctor. They stop eating because, in spite of all evidence to the contrary, they believe they are too fat. Determined to lose the imaginary excess poundage, they refuse to eat more than a few morsels of food. Usually they lose weight rapidly, sometimes more than fifty pounds in a matter of months.

4

Supporting Paragraph

Some teenagers who are obsessed with the need to diet seek psychiatric treatment because they, or their parents, realize that the diet is leading to starvation. Others do not seek treatment but simply begin eating on their own. Still others do not seek treatment, nor do they resume a normal diet; instead, they allow themselves to slowly starve to death.

5

Supporting Paragraph

The actual cause of the starvation disease has not been determined, but one possible cause has been discussed by therapists: Teenagers may be starving themselves to rebel against parental authority. The refusal to eat has traditionally been a young child's weapon against parental discipline since the parent may plead and even demand that the child eat, but the child can refuse and demonstrate his or her power over the situation. Unconsciously, teenagers who diet to the point of starvation may be attempting to teach their parents the same lesson: Control is not in the hands of the parents.

6

Concluding Paragraph

At the present time, research is being undertaken to determine the exact cause of the starvation disease. Federal grants have been distributed, and research is underway at a number of universities and hospitals. Researchers hope to be able to pinpoint what triggers the disease and find out how to bring it to a halt.

INTRODUCTORY PARAGRAPH

Rather than ask you to refer to the essay again and again, we'll begin each section with the paragraph being discussed:

> **1**
>
> Pat was always on a diet. Eighteen years old and thin, she maintained that she was simply too fat, and no amount of coaxing could convince her that she was actually dangerously underweight for her height and age. To reduce her already pencil-slim figure, she suddenly began to refuse any food, except for a few pieces of toast and some water. At the end of only one month she weighed ninety pounds.

The topic of the above paragraph is Pat's diet, and the supporting sentences suggest a main idea: Pat's dieting was excessive and dangerous. However, having found the topic and main idea, we still have to explain why we labeled the paragraph "introductory."

It will make our explanation easier if you think for a moment of what you learned about introductory sentences: introductory sentences introduce the topic of a paragraph. Appearing at the beginning of a paragraph, they contain an idea that is usually not developed in any of the remaining sentences.

The introductory paragraph has much in common with the introductory sentence in a paragraph. It appears at the beginning of an essay and usually contains a main idea that is not developed in the remainder of the essay. For example, in the sample essay we hear no more about Pat and her diet after the second paragraph. The essay was not written to tell Pat's story; rather, her story was meant to trigger the reader's interest in the rest of the essay. Wondering why Pat was so intent on dieting, the reader will continue with the essay.

The introductory paragraph also serves to introduce the topic of the entire essay. After reading the first paragraph, it is obvious that the author intends to say something about dieting, especially excessive dieting.

Material appearing in the introductory paragraph varies depending on the type of essay. Introductory paragraphs in essays appearing in magazines and newspapers frequently contain stories, jokes, or quotations. These are meant to make the reader continue to find out what the story, joke, or quote has to do with the rest of the essay. Essays appearing in textbooks may simply use the introductory paragraph to give an overview of the topic under discussion. If the reader is interested in the topic, he or she will read further.

TOPIC PARAGRAPH

2

Most parents, when their children begin talking about dieting, react just as Pat's parents did. They smile indulgently and hope that their children won't allow themselves to become too thin. But in general, they do not worry. In figure-conscious America, it is quite natural for young people to desire a slim figure. However, in Pat's case, and in the case of many like her, dieting is nothing to smile at. It is not a momentary whim that will be pursued and forgotten; instead, it is the symptom of a serious emotional disorder. Doctors call such excessive and irrational dieting *anorexia nervosa* or, because it has been known to lead to death by starvation, the *starvation disease*.

The topic of the preceding paragraph is teenage dieting, and up until the fourth sentence in the paragraph, it looks as if the main idea is implied: teenage dieting is not a serious matter. However, the fifth sentence, a transitional one, reverses the author's original train of thought. The author is not going to tell us how unimportant dieting is. He is, instead, going to tell us quite the opposite: teenage dieting, when it is excessive, can be the symptom of a serious emotional disorder. This is the idea that will be developed in the remainder of the paragraph and, indeed, in the remainder of the essay.

Perhaps you already noticed in your initial reading of paragraph 2 that the main idea contained in the topic sentence, sentence 6, does not receive much support from the rest of the paragraph. And yet, as we have stressed throughout this text, the main idea of a paragraph will be supported and developed by the other sentences in the paragraph.

The difference here, of course, is that we are dealing with an essay and not a single paragraph. The main idea of the topic paragraph does not go unsupported, but most of the support comes from the other paragraphs in the essay, not from the other sentences in the topic paragraph. This is an important point since it is one of the reasons why the second paragraph receives its label.

It will be easier to explain the function of the topic paragraph if we briefly review the function of the topic sentence. As you know, this is the sentence that contains the main idea of a paragraph and ties the other sentences in a paragraph together.

The topic paragraph of an essay functions much like the topic sentence of a paragraph. Like the topic sentence, the

topic paragraph is the focal point of an essay. It contains the main idea that ties the other paragraphs in the essay together. Almost every other paragraph in the essay develops the main idea contained in the topic paragraph.

Many topic paragraphs contain little more than a topic sentence or suggested main idea. Supporting sentences do not play a key role since support for the main idea of the paragraph will come from the rest of the essay. However, occasionally a topic paragraph will contain supporting sentences that give you a clue as to how the author intends to develop the main idea of the essay. For example, in the topic paragraph of the sample essay, we learn that excessive dieting can lead to death by starvation. This is an idea that will reappear later on in the essay.

SUPPORTING PARAGRAPHS

3

Victims of the starvation disease are usually teenage girls who have no apparent reason to diet. They are not overweight; they are not preparing to take part in specialized sports activities requiring a slender figure; they have not been told to diet by their doctor. They stop eating because, in spite of all evidence to the contrary, they believe they are too fat. Determined to lose the imaginary excess poundage, they refuse to eat more than a few morsels of food. Usually they lose weight rapidly, sometimes more than fifty pounds in a matter of months.

4

Some teenagers who are obsessed with the need to diet seek psychiatric treatment because they, or their parents, realize that the diet is leading to starvation. Others do not seek treatment but simply begin eating on their own. Still others do not seek treatment, nor do they resume a normal diet; they allow themselves to slowly starve to death.

5

The actual cause of the starvation disease has not been determined, but one possible cause has been discussed by therapists: Teenagers may be starving themselves to rebel against parental authority. The refusal to eat has traditionally been a young child's weapon against parental discipline since the parent may plead and even demand that the child eat, but the child can refuse and demonstrate his or her power over the situation. Unconsciously, teenagers who diet to the point of starvation may be attempting to teach their parents the same lesson: Control is not in the hands of the parents.

The topic sentence of paragraph 3 tells us that victims of the starvation disease have no apparent reason to diet while the remainder of the paragraph emphasizes that point and gives an example of how extreme the diet can become.

Paragraph 4 deals with the different ways teenagers react to their compulsive need to diet:

1. Some seek psychiatric treatment.
2. Some begin eating on their own.
3. Some starve to death.

The main idea of the paragraph is not stated in a topic sentence, but it is implied: victims of the starvation disease have three basic reactions to their compulsive need to diet.

The topic sentence of paragraph 5 tells us that some therapists consider rebellion against parental authority to be a possible cause of compulsive dieting. The remainder of this paragraph emphasizes this point and supplies a reason for the therapists' opinion.

Having found the main ideas in paragraphs 3, 4, and 5, however, we still have to explain why we labeled the paragraphs as we did. It will help our explanation if you remember the function of supporting sentences when they appear in a paragraph containing a topic sentence: supporting sentences help illustrate and make more convincing the main idea contained in the topic sentence. **Supporting paragraphs in an essay fulfill a similar function: they help illustrate and make more convincing the main idea contained in the topic paragraph.**

The first supporting paragraph, for example, tells us that victims of the starvation disease have no apparent reason for dieting. This in itself does not prove that excessive dieting is a symptom of a serious emotional disorder, although it does indicate that the teenagers' behavior is somewhat strange. Why do they diet when there is absolutely no reason for it?

It is the last sentence in the paragraph that begins to support the main idea of the essay in earnest because it is here that we are given an illustration of how excessive the diet can be. It consists of little food, and the weight loss is extraordinarily rapid. If this is the kind of diet teenagers go on for no apparent reason, then something is indeed wrong. We begin to understand why excessive dieting is viewed as a symptom of an emotional disturbance.

The implied main idea of paragraph 4 is that there are three basic reactions to the compulsive need to diet. Taken by itself, the main idea of this paragraph does not really support the main idea of the essay. We need to know what the three basic reactions are, and this information comes from the supporting sentences.

We learn, first of all, that some teenagers seek psychiatric help because they realize that dieting is leading to starvation. If the need to diet is so totally out of control that psychiatric help is needed to bring it to a halt, it is clear that the diet is a symptom of much more than a desire to lose weight. The first supporting sentence, then, does help to develop and support the main idea of the entire essay.

The next supporting sentence describes another possible reaction: some teenagers begin eating on their own. Notice that this supporting sentence, while it helps to develop the main idea of paragraph 4, does not do much to develop the main idea of the essay. If the teenagers begin eating of their own accord, excessive dieting does not seem so serious. We draw your attention to this sentence because it is important to realize that not every sentence in the supporting paragraphs will help develop the main idea of the essay.

The final supporting sentence of paragraph 4 does support the main idea of the entire essay. It tells us that some teenagers simply allow themselves to starve to death. This is more evidence that excessive dieting can be the symptom of an emotional disorder.

Paragraph 5 gives a possible cause of the starvation disease; and at first glance, it may not seem as if this paragraph provides any reinforcement for the main idea of the essay. Rebellion against parental authority is fairly common among teenagers and need not indicate any emotional disorder. However, remember the author said that the rebellion is unconscious. That means that if the teenagers are using dieting as a weapon against their parents, they are not aware of it. Not only do they endanger their lives for a cause unknown to them but they have chosen a method of rebellion that cannot possibly solve their problem. In this case excessive dieting, even if it is an act of legitimate rebellion, is a symptom of an emotional disorder.

Paragraphs 3, 4, and 5 have done what they were supposed to do: they have helped illustrate and make more convincing the main idea contained in the topic paragraph.

CONCLUDING PARAGRAPH

6
At the present time, research is being undertaken to determine the exact cause of the starvation disease. Federal grants have been distributed, and research is underway at a number of universities and hospitals. Researchers hope to be able to pinpoint what triggers the disease and find out how to bring it to a halt.

The topic sentence of the final paragraph tells us that research is being undertaken to determine the causes of the starvation disease, and the rest of the paragraph tells us where the research is being undertaken, and gives us some idea of what the researchers hope to find.

You'll notice that the final paragraph of the sample essay does not do a great deal to prove that dieting is a symptom of an emotional disorder. It simply tells us what is being done as a result of the disease's occurrence.

The author's reason for including this paragraph will become clearer to you if you review what you have already learned about concluding sentences in single paragraphs. Remember that concluding sentences appear at the end of a paragraph and are frequently used to present the outcome or result of a problem or state of affairs described in the paragraph.

Concluding paragraphs can fulfill a similar function. Much of the time the authors use them to discuss the outcome or result of something that has been described in the essay. They may also use them to summarize the key points of the essay or to offer an opinion about an idea mentioned in the essay. Occasionally concluding paragraphs will offer a solution for a problem introduced in the essay.

In our sample essay the author uses the concluding paragraph to tell us what consequence the occurrence of starvation disease has had. The author is no longer concerned with proving that excessive dieting is the symptom of a serious emotional disorder. The previous paragraphs have already done that. Instead, the last paragraph is used to tell us what is being done in response to the strange disease's occurrence.

Not all essays contain concluding paragraphs. Some essays just come to a halt after the supporting paragraphs. However, many essays do contain concluding paragraphs, and they are fairly easy to recognize because they do one of the following:

1. Repeat one or several points already made in the essay.
2. Give the result or consequence of something described in the essay.
3. Offer a solution to some problem described in the essay.
4. Offer an opinion about an idea mentioned in the essay.

ANALYZING AN ESSAY

In the last section we went into some detail in order to show you that there are many similarities between the functions of sentences in a paragraph and the function of paragraphs in an essay. Perhaps that comparison gave you a clue to what we would like to emphasize now: when you read an essay, you should look for many of the same things you look for when reading a paragraph.

For example, you should make sure that you know the precise topic of the essay. Frequently, the title of the essay can give you a clue to the topic. Certainly, "Dangerous Dieting" indicated that the sample essay was going to deal with dieting.

However, you should not rely solely on the title to find the precise topic. In addition to using the title, you can do exactly what you did when you wanted to find the topic of a single paragraph: look and see what subject the author returns to again and again. For example, in the sample essay the author refers repeatedly to excessive dieting; thus we chose excessive dieting for the precise topic of the essay.

Once you are sure of the topic of the essay, look carefully for what we have called the *topic paragraph*. As we explained, this is the paragraph that contains the main idea of the entire essay. The main idea of the topic paragraph will usually be contained in a topic sentence, although on occasion the main idea may be suggested by the supporting sentences, and the paragraph will not contain a topic sentence.

Once you think you have found the main idea of the entire essay, check to see if you are correct by carefully examining the role of the remaining paragraphs. If they work to support and develop the main idea you have chosen, then you know that your choice is correct.

When you analyze the supporting paragraphs, don't be content with simply pulling out the topic or main idea. Frequently, as in our sample essay, the supporting sentences will help develop not only the main idea of their separate paragraphs but also the main idea of the entire essay. Make sure you know what information supporting sentences contribute.

Since there are major and minor supporting sentences in a single paragraph, you may have wondered if there are major and minor supporting paragraphs in an essay. The answer is yes. Minor supporting paragraphs refer back to major supporting paragraphs, supplying additional information about an idea already introduced in the major supporting paragraph. They need not refer directly back to the main idea of the essay. Our first sample essay does not contain any minor supporting paragraphs, but you will encounter them in the exercise that follows.

Having found the topic and main idea of the essay and having discovered how the author has chosen to support the main idea, you need only analyze the concluding paragraph and you are ready to take notes.

As we said before, the concluding paragraph will usually do one of four things:

1. Repeat an important point.

2. Explain a consequence.

3. Offer a solution.

4. Offer an opinion.

If the essay does contain a concluding paragraph, you need to discover which function the paragraph fulfills. If it simply restates something already mentioned in the essay, you need not pay any more attention to the concluding paragraph. However, if it explains a consequence or offers a solution, you should make sure you know exactly what consequence or solution the author has described.

Once you have finished analyzing the concluding paragraph, you are ready to take notes.

TAKING NOTES ON AN ESSAY

Using our sample essay, we are going to give you two sets of notes. Both are based on a format already introduced in Chapters 4 and 5; that is, they include the topic, main idea, support, and conclusion. The first set of sample notes is not very detailed. It represents the kind of notes you would take if you were reading the sample essay in order to be prepared to answer questions in class:

Topic: Excessive dieting

Main Idea: Excessive dieting is a symptom of a serious emotional disorder.

Support:

1. Called *anorexia nervosa*, or starvation disease
2. Victims have no apparent reason to diet
3. Three basic reactions to compulsive need to diet:
    (a) Seek psychiatric treatment
    (b) Begin eating again
    (c) Starve to death
4. May be caused by rebellion against parents

Conclusion: Research being undertaken to study starvation disease

As we already mentioned, notes on an essay contain the same basic information as notes on a single paragraph, but since there is more information in an essay, the organization of the notes differs slightly.

Like the notes on a single paragraph, the preceding notes begin with the topic and main idea. In this case, however, the notes begin with the topic and main idea of an entire essay, not of a single paragraph.

Following the notes on the main idea are several short sentences that sum up the supporting sentence in the topic paragraph and the main idea of every supporting paragraph. These sentences are numbered and indented; they take the position previously occupied by notes on the major supporting sentences in a single paragraph.

With the exception of the third supporting paragraph, we did not include information contained in the major supporting sentences. In paragraph 3, however, the main idea alone does not explain very much; therefore, we used brief phrases to summarize information contained in the major sentences. These phrases have been lettered and indented. They take the position formerly occupied by notes on the minor supporting sentences in a single paragraph.

If you were to take notes in order to pass a test, you would have to include more of the information contained in the major and minor supporting sentences:

Topic: Excessive dieting

Main Idea: Excessive dieting is the symptom of a serious emotional disorder.

Support:

1. Doctors call it *anorexia nervosa,* or starvation disease.
2. Victims diet for no apparent reason:
   (a) Stop eating no matter what the scale says
   (b) May lose fifty pounds in a few months
3. Three basic reactions to compulsive need to diet:
   (a) Seek psychiatric help
   (b) Begin eating of their own accord
   (c) Starve to death
4. May be caused by rebellion against parents:
   (a) Refusal to eat commonly used by children to gain control
   (b) Unconsciously, teenagers may be using the same tactics

Conclusion: Research being undertaken to study starvation disease:

   (a) Undertaken at universities and hospitals
   (b) Hope to pinpoint what triggers disease and how to bring it to a halt

The second set of sample notes is far more detailed than the first. Instead of just the main idea of each paragraph, the notes include the information contained in the major supporting sentences. These are the kind of notes you would take if you were reading to prepare for a test.

The following exercise will give you more practice reading and taking notes on essays.

EXERCISE 1

Directions: Read through the practice essay twice. The first time read it through quickly just to get a general idea of what the author is trying to say. Then read it through a second time more carefully. Note the label of each paragraph and see how the paragraphs fulfill the functions we have described on the preceding pages.

The Ebbinghaus Experiments

1

Introductory Paragraph

Introduces the reader to the topic, "Ebbinghaus's experiments with memory," and provides just enough information so that the reader wonders what the experiments were.

1

At the end of the nineteenth century a German psychologist named Hermann Ebbinghaus became interested in the carefully controlled laboratory experiments being used to do research in the fields of physiology* and physics. He was so impressed with the results of these experiments that he decided to introduce similar methods into the study of human memory.

2

Topic Paragraph

Topic sentence of this paragraph contains the main idea of the entire essay. Supporting sentences in the paragraph tell the reader how experiments were performed.

2

Using only himself as a subject, Ebbinghaus devoted six years of research to his experiments. During that time he memorized lists of nonsense syllables, put them aside for specified intervals of time, and then relearned them. *By comparing the time taken to learn the lists with the time taken to relearn them, Ebbinghaus was able to come to several important conclusions about the role of memory in learning; and these conclusions, after nearly a century of research, have been repeatedly confirmed.*

3

First Major Supporting Paragraph

Describes one of the conclusions mentioned in the topic sentence of the preceding paragraph.

3

One important conclusion concerned the rate of forgetting. As a result of his research, Ebbinghaus maintained that the rate of forgetting becomes progressively slower over time. A list of nonsense syllables that Ebbinghaus had learned and then put aside for an hour required more than half the original study time to be relearned; but a list that had been put aside for more than twice that time (9 hours) was not, as one would expect, totally forgotten. The rate of forgetting had slowed down, and only two thirds of the original study time was required to relearn the nonsense syllables.

*physiology: study of how living organisms function

4

| Second Major Supporting Paragraph |

Supports the idea that Ebbinghaus's conclusions have been confirmed.

4

Since 1885 when Ebbinghaus first published his work, investigators have studied the rate of forgetting. They have used not only nonsense syllables but also passages of prose, lists of facts, and excerpts from poetry. Like Ebbinghaus, they have almost always discovered that the rate of forgetting slows down over time; it is rapid at first but becomes slower as the amount of time between learning and relearning increases.

5

| Minor Supporting Paragraph |

Supports the preceding paragraph telling how Ebbinghaus's conclusions have been modified.

5

Modern researchers have, however, pointed out that the rate of forgetting depends on various circumstances. It depends, for example, on the kind of memorizing involved. If two people are given the same passage to memorize, but one is told to remember the exact words, while the other is told to remember only the general idea of the passage, the one told to remember the exact words will forget more rapidly.

6

| Third Major Supporting Paragraph |

Describes another conclusion and supports the idea that Ebbinghaus's findings have been confirmed.

6

Another of Ebbinghaus's conclusions, which modern research has confirmed, but again with certain modifications, is that overlearning during the initial learning period makes relearning at a later time easier. Based on his experiments, Ebbinghaus maintained that the more repetitions involved in the original learning, the fewer repetitions needed for relearning. Investigators who followed have come to similar conclusions but have also concluded that each and every repetition will not produce an equal return in time saved during the relearning period. After a point the repetition of material already memorized does not produce sufficient reward.

7

| Fourth Major Supporting Paragraph |

Describes another of Ebbinghaus's conclusions and supports the idea that his conclusions have been confirmed.

7

Research that followed the Ebbinghaus experiments by more than half a century have also confirmed Ebbinghaus's belief that learning sessions devoted to memorizing are more effective if they are distributed over a period of time. In 1940 an American psychologist, A.P. Bumstead, decided to do a series of experiments to determine whether it was better to have several short learning sessions spaced out over a period of time or one long unbroken learning session. Using only himself as a subject, Bumstead memorized several different poetry selections, spacing his learning sessions at intervals that varied from one hour to eight days. After finishing the experiment, Bumstead concluded that increasing the time between learning sessions actually decreased the amount of time needed to memorize the material.

8

| Concluding Paragraph |

Describes a consequence of Ebbinghaus's work.

8

The preceding paragraphs provide just a brief summary of Ebbinghaus's work, but no matter how brief the discussion, it would not be complete without mentioning one of the most important results of Ebbinghaus's research, one that even he may not have anticipated. Ebbinghaus was a pioneer in the study of human memory, and his work raised questions that are still being studied today.

The following are sample notes on the preceding essay. They are fairly detailed and represent the kind of notes you would take if you knew that you wanted to review the information contained in an essay without having to go back and read it.

In general, we have organized the following notes exactly as we did those taken on the dieting essay. The few additions we did make have been indicated in the margins.

Sample Notes

Important details in introductory paragraph have been included in statement of main idea, for example, Ebbinghaus's first name and period of time when he began experiments.

Topic: Ebbinghaus's experiments

Main Idea: End of the nineteenth century, Hermann Ebbinghaus came to conclusions about role of memory in learning, and these conclusions have been confirmed after nearly a century of research.

Support:

1. Ebbinghaus maintained that rate of forgetting slows down over time.

   (a) List of nonsense syllables Ebbinghaus had learned and put aside for an hour required more than half of original study time to be relearned, but list put aside for nine hours not totally forgotten

Notes on minor supporting sentences have been numbered and indented beneath notes on major supporting sentences.

        (1) Rate of forgetting had slowed down; only two thirds of original study time required to relearn nonsense syllables

2. Since 1855 investigators have studied rate of forgetting.

   (a) Used nonsense syllables, passages of prose, lists of facts, and excerpts from poetry

   (b) Discovered that rate of forgetting slows down

   (c) Researchers point out that rate of forgetting depends on various circumstances:

Topic sentence in minor supporting paragraph treated like major supporting sentence: Sentence has been lettered and indented under notes on main idea of second supporting paragraph.

      (1) Depends on kind of memorizing involved

        (a) Individuals told to remember exactly forget more rapidly than those who need only retain general idea.

3. Modern research has confirmed, with modification, that overlearning makes learning easier.

   (a) Ebbinghaus maintained that much repetition in original learning makes relearning easier.

   (b) Modern research concluded that each and every repetition does not produce equal return in time saved.

4. Later research confirmed conclusion that learning sessions are more effective if distributed over time.

   (a) 1940: Bumstead experiments:

      (1) Bumstead memorized poetry selections and spaced learning sessions.

      (2) Concluded that increasing time between sessions decreased amount of time needed to memorize

No notes have been taken on the conclusion because information contained in concluding paragraph can be inferred from the rest of the notes.

Now it's your turn to analyze an essay. Read through the following essay twice. The first time just try and get a general idea of what the author is trying to say. Then read it through a second time more carefully. Decide what the function of each paragraph is and then label each paragraph just as we did in the sample essay.

Meditation and America

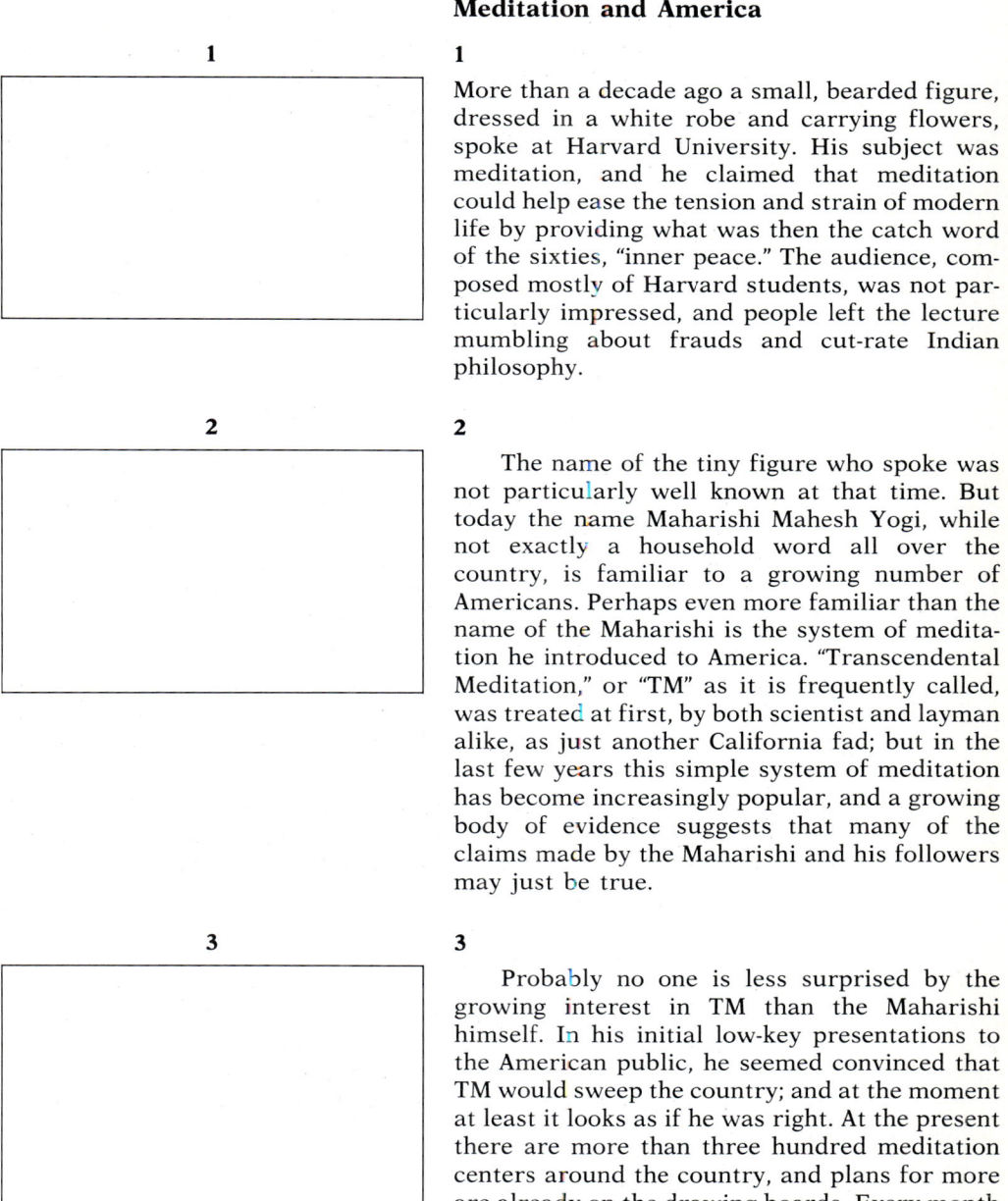

1

More than a decade ago a small, bearded figure, dressed in a white robe and carrying flowers, spoke at Harvard University. His subject was meditation, and he claimed that meditation could help ease the tension and strain of modern life by providing what was then the catch word of the sixties, "inner peace." The audience, composed mostly of Harvard students, was not particularly impressed, and people left the lecture mumbling about frauds and cut-rate Indian philosophy.

2

The name of the tiny figure who spoke was not particularly well known at that time. But today the name Maharishi Mahesh Yogi, while not exactly a household word all over the country, is familiar to a growing number of Americans. Perhaps even more familiar than the name of the Maharishi is the system of meditation he introduced to America. "Transcendental Meditation," or "TM" as it is frequently called, was treated at first, by both scientist and layman alike, as just another California fad; but in the last few years this simple system of meditation has become increasingly popular, and a growing body of evidence suggests that many of the claims made by the Maharishi and his followers may just be true.

3

Probably no one is less surprised by the growing interest in TM than the Maharishi himself. In his initial low-key presentations to the American public, he seemed convinced that TM would sweep the country; and at the moment at least it looks as if he was right. At the present there are more than three hundred meditation centers around the country, and plans for more are already on the drawing boards. Every month countless numbers of men and women sign up to learn how to meditate, and the Maharishi International University is already open and courses are in session.

4

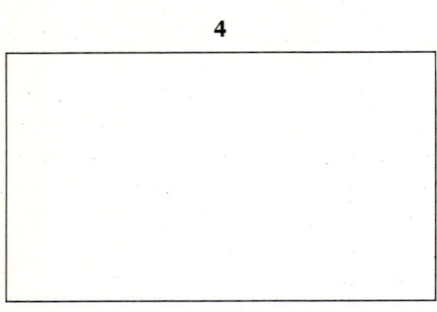

4

Undoubtedly, one reason for the increasing interest in TM is the ease with which meditation can be learned. The initiates simply listen to introductory lectures, pay their fee, and receive a date for the initiation ceremony. On the prescribed date, they arrive carrying a handkerchief, some fruit, and a few flowers. After a short wait they are escorted to the waiting meditation teacher who talks with them briefly and gives them a *mantra*, the word they will use during meditation.

5

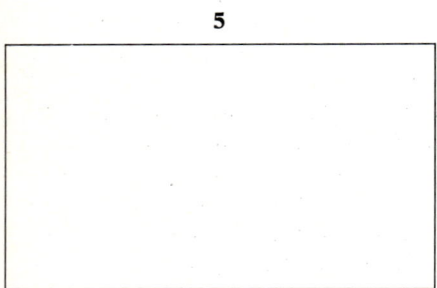

5

The actual meditation begins with the meditators sitting down in a dark and quiet room. They can let their thoughts come and go freely but must mentally come back to the mantra, repeating it silently. At the end of the fifteen or twenty minutes, they slowly cease the meditation and then return to the day's regular activities.

6

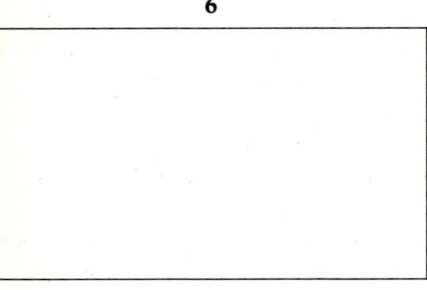

6

Although the ease with which TM can be learned certainly contributed to its success in America, it is still true that the number of celebrities who openly proclaimed the benefits of meditation helped to spark the public's interest. Beginning with the Beatles, who helped make the Maharishi famous, the list has grown, if not more spectacular, certainly longer. Talk show host Merv Griffin praised meditation on nationwide television and invited the Maharishi to be his guest. Singer Peggy Lee credited her weight loss and improved health to meditating, and even the flamboyant* Joe Namath is said to have meditated before a game.

*flamboyant: showy, flashy

7

7

For a number of people, however, it was the research results on TM, not the celebrity interest, that convinced them that TM could improve their lives. Many turned to meditation when research findings seemed to confirm several of the Maharishi's claims. One of the first experiments conducted at the UCLA Medical School indicated that TM can produce a state of rest deeper than sleep, a fact that reinforced the Maharishi's claim that meditation could provide more energy.[1] In a later study neurologists* at Massachusetts General Hospital discovered that alpha waves, which are associated with relaxation, increased during meditation, a finding that lent credence to the Maharishi's claim that TM could reduce anxiety and stress.[2]

8

8

Whatever the reason, the number of people in America who meditate has grown enormously in the last few years, and interest in TM doesn't seem to be waning. Certainly, those who already meditate sound encouraging; they claim that transcendental meditation has improved their lives. They feel calmer and have more energy; or at least they think they do, and that's all the Maharishi ever promised.

Directions: Fill in the following blanks by taking notes on the second essay. If you feel that the concluding paragraph contains no important information, do not fill in the blanks for that paragraph. Any important information in the introductory paragraph should be included in the notes on the topic paragraph.

Topic: _____

_____

[1]Harold H. Bloomfield et al., *TM: Discovering Inner Energy and Overcoming Stress* (New York: Dell, 1975), p. 92

*neurologists: doctors who study the nervous system

[2]"Forty Minutes to Bliss," *Time,* October 13, 1975, p. 74

Main Idea:

Support:

_____
_____
_____
_____
_____
_____
_____
_____
_____
_____
_____

Conclusion: _____
_____
_____
_____
_____
_____
_____
_____

Read and analyze the next essay just as you did "Meditation and America." After you have labeled each paragraph, take notes on the essay.

The Mountain People

1

The Ik are a small tribe located in East Africa. Formerly a society of hunters, the Ik have been forced to become farmers because their government decided that Ik lands were needed for a national park. In the space of less than fifty years, the Ik have been forced to develop agricultural skills they did not previously need, and they have not had much success, especially since the lands they were given receive little rain. Deprived of their right to hunt and unable to support themselves through farming, the Ik have learned what it means to live with constant hunger and starvation.

2

In 1972 anthropologist Colin Turnbull published *The Mountain People*, a book that described the two years he spent living among the Ik. Trumbull's book, although it received good reviews, was not a bestseller like *Jaws*, *The Exorcist*, or *Love Story* because most people who browse through book stores looking for something interesting to read do not turn to the anthropology section. *The Mountain People*, however, deserves a wide and thoughtful audience since the author's description of life among the Ik challenges all of mankind's cherished notions about the inherent* goodness of human beings.

3

Certainly, the book challenges the assumption that children and parents must love one another. The Ik, who are painfully aware of every extra mouth to feed, do not regard their children with joy or even amusement; they know that children expect to be fed, and that is exactly what the Ik cannot or will not do. Children are a troublesome burden to their parents, and at the age of three, they are forced out of the home. Left alone to fend for themselves, the children form small independent groups that keep up a constant search for food; some children manage to survive this way, many do not.

*inherent: essential, natural

4

Quite naturally children who have been treated in this fashion harbor no special love for their parents or grandparents, and Turnbull's book contains numerous examples of starving parents being turned away when they sought help in the homes of their grown-up children. The children maintain that they have to care for themselves and cannot possibly afford to nurse aged parents who can no longer feed themselves. The parents, apparently remembering their own attitude, consider their children's behavior quite natural and go away without making any ridiculous demands for attention and affection.

5

Love, in general, whether it be between man and wife, parent and child, or sister and brother, seems to have disappeared from the life of the Ik. Men care little or nothing for their wives and value them only if they are able to provide food. The women share that practical attitude and quickly abandon a husband who can no longer provide food or money. Brothers and sisters do not protect and guard smaller members of the family; on the contrary older siblings* steal from the younger and take great delight in encouraging the younger children to hurt themselves. A small child who unthinkingly sticks his or her hand into a fire and howls in pain is a source of great amusement to the older children.

6

Sex does not interest the Ik any more than love although prostitution flourishes among the young girls. It is a means of getting food or gifts from neighboring tribesmen who are better off than the Ik. Sex is only interesting if it helps to provide food; otherwise, it requires too much energy.

*siblings: brothers and sisters

7

The need to give or receive companionship is practically unheard of among the Ik, and both men and women prefer to be alone. Alone, they can gobble, without interference, the food they have stolen or found, and they need not waste energy carrying on a conversation. Companionship usually encourages activities like talking and laughing, and, in general, the Ik are too tired to talk and have little to laugh about. Although Turnbull does cite examples of the Ik coming together to work on a common task, it is always evident that each member of the group expects to be paid for his or her contribution; services are not offered out of friendship.

8

Since the publication of *The Mountain People*, a play titled *The Ik* based on the book has been produced in England, France, and Germany. It was enormously successful, and audiences viewed the play with fascination and horror. *The Ik*, however, had little effect on the life of the people it described; the Ik who are still alive spend their days searching for food and fighting starvation.

Directions: Fill in the following blanks by taking notes on the essay. If you feel the concluding paragraph contains no important information, do not fill in the blanks for that paragraph. Important information in the introductory paragraph can be included in notes on the topic paragraph. However, if you think the introductory paragraph contains a great deal of information, treat it as a supporting paragraph and add it to your notes.

Topic: _____

_____

Main Idea: _____

_____

_____

_____

Support:

Conclusion: _____

Read and analyze the next essay just as you did the previous ones. After you have labeled each paragraph, take notes on the essay.

The Other *Little Women*

1

Louisa May Alcott was born in Germantown, Pennsylvania, in 1832 and began writing at the age of sixteen, although her early work, *Flower Fables*, was not published until she was twenty-two. In 1863 she published *Hospital Sketches*, a collection of pieces about her experiences as a volunteer nurse in the Civil War. Her first novel, *Moods*, appeared in 1865 but was not as widely read as the sketches. It was not until the publication in 1868 and 1869 of the two-part novel *Little Women* that Alcott became famous throughout America.

2

Little Women, the story of four adolescent girls, Meg, Jo, Amy, and Beth, who grow up during the Civil War, is still read and enjoyed by young girls today. Modern readers, however, have tended to read the book more critically than previous generations; and for many, Alcott's female characters, with the exception of the determined and aggressive Jo, are lifeless and silly creatures. In general, the girls tend to be vain and foolish, and only with careful instruction, usually from men, are they able to behave like responsible human beings. Even those characters not in need of constant moral instruction are so lacking in vitality* that one wishes they possessed less virtue and more personality.

3

Noting the unflattering image of females in *Little Women*, some critics have assumed that Alcott had simply absorbed the nineteenth-century stereotype of women, a stereotype that stressed the vanity and helplessness of females. Such critics apparently forgot how dangerous it is to assume that characters in a novel must reflect the author's personal opinions and beliefs. Certainly recent research challenges the idea that Alcott totally accepted the nineteenth-century view of women. According to scholar Madeleine Stern, Alcott also wrote thrillers under the pseudonym A. M. Barnard, and the thrillers are peopled with heroines who constantly defy the image of women as shy and frivolous* creatures in need of male guidance in order to survive.

4

The women of the thrillers are usually strong willed, passionate, and clever. They know what they want whether it be revenge, money, or love, and they do not give up easily, even when the most amazing obstacles are placed in their path. For example, Virginie Varens, the heroine of "Plots and Counterplots," is a beautiful Spanish dancer who is determined to marry a rich man. When her first husband is slain, she tracks down his twin brother and proceeds to use all her considerable charm and intelligence to win his heart. In her pursuit Virginie assumes several disguises, spins an amazing number of tall tales, and manages to captivate* everyone except the man she hopes to marry.

*vitality: liveliness
*frivolous: thoughtless, silly
*captivate: charm, win over

5

At the end of "Plots and Counterplots," Virginie finally goes too far, and after driving a lovely female rival to suicide, her deceit and trickery are discovered. When the man whose heart she had hoped to win tells her that he is going to imprison her for the rest of her days, Virginie never loses her wits. And, indeed, while telling him about her sinful life, she manages to take poison rather than allow herself to be locked away. Her last words, "I have escaped," have the ring of triumph, and it is clear that she has outwitted the man who had hoped to see her punished.

6

Madame von Arnheim, the heroine of "The Skeleton in the Closet," is hardly the conscienceless social climber that Virginie Varens is. On the contrary, she is a virtuous widow who appears to live alone and, in the words of her friends, "desires no Adam." Beautiful and dignified, she is held in awe by all her acquaintances, and there is not a trace of nonsense about her, even though she has no husband or father to guide her. Straightforward where Virginie was deceitful, Mathilde von Arnheim keeps only one secret: Her husband is a hopeless idiot who must be guarded and cared for like a child.

7

Although Mathilde is portrayed as a rather sad and lonely figure, it is still she who controls most of what happens in the story. When the hero, Gustave Novaire, a young man who is madly in love with her, is shaken by a sudden burst of thunder, it is Mathilde who comforts him until the moment of fright has passed. Later he too comforts her, but she is trembling only because she is anxious about him, not because she is frightened by the thunder.

8

In the final scene where Mathilde and Gustave discover that they have been kept apart by the jealous schemes of a young man in love with Mathilde, it is again she who takes command of the situation and delivers a harsh rebuke.*

9

Unlike the majority of the nineteenth-century heroines who would have fainted at the mention of words like "opium" and "hashish," the women in Alcott's stories actually experiment with dangerous drugs. Cecil Yorke, the heroine of "A Marble Woman," begins taking opium when it is offered to her as a cure for insomnia. Within a short time she becomes addicted and begins taking opium in the form of candy. After a year of addiction, her secret is discovered by her husband. Cecil readily admits that she has been taking drugs and manages to give them up, but not before she has made it clear to her husband that her addiction started because he forced her to lead a lonely and secluded life.

10

"Perilous Play," published shortly before the second half of *Little Women*, also deals with drugs, although the heroine, Rose St. Just, does not become addicted. Bored with an afternoon's entertainment, Rose and a few friends decide to experiment with hashish. Excited by the effects of the drug, Rose and Mark, an attractive young man, decide to go sailing. Mark, frightened by his violent impulses, hands Rose a knife and tells her to kill him if he does anything rash. Rose, who remains calm even under the influence of hashish, wraps her cloak around her and accepts the knife without a murmur.

*rebuke: criticism

11

When it seems that Mark is about to lose control of the boat, Rose takes over and issues the directions that save them from disaster. When a sudden storm strikes and they are again in danger, it is Rose who spots a passing vessel and rouses Mark long enough to make him shout for help. Together they manage to flag down a ship and are able to reach safety.

12

With the discovery of the thrillers, there may be a tendency to see Alcott as a secret feminist* who hated the role assigned to women. But that is as dangerous as assuming that *Little Women* reflected Alcott's personal feelings about the nature of men and women. What the discovery of the thrillers does do is challenge the assumption* that Alcott was a prisoner of her time and therefore unable to visualize women as anything more than sweet creatures who, with the right guidance, might grow up to know their place.

Topic: _____

Main Idea: _____

Support: _____

*feminist: man or woman concerned with the fight for women's rights

*assumption: idea or statement supposed true without proof or demonstration

Conclusion:

REVIEW TEST: CHAPTER 7

PART A

The following pages will test everything you have learned up to this point.

Directions: Read the essay that follows. When you are finished, turn to the questions. Do not worry about having to reread parts of the essay; this will be necessary in order to answer all the questions.

Essay 1

1. [1] Although admirers called her "Moses" and "General Tubman," Harriet Tubman, the most successful conductor on the Underground Railroad, a secret organization that helped free runaway slaves, was not very impressive at first glance. [2] Tiny and slight, no one noticed her in a crowd. [3] In addition, she had been wounded on the head as a child and suffered from strange, trance-like seizures. [4] Sometimes when she would be waiting on a platform to speak, she would appear to doze off. [5] However, when Tubman roused herself and began to speak, she seemed to grow a foot in height, and no one who heard her ever forgot what she said or what she looked like. [6] Because she was inspired by the righteousness of her cause and schooled in the poetic rhythms and images of black spirituals, Tubman's accounts of slave life and the perils of escape made a powerful impression so that even noisy crowds grew quiet and attentive in order to hear her speak. [7] When the four-foot Tubman talked, no one interrupted.

2. [1] Born in 1820 in Bucktown, Maryland, Harriet Greene was a sickly child, and her mother had to struggle to keep her well; yet despite the burden of slavery, the family worked hard to support and protect one another. [2] Even though Tubman gave several interviews about her life as a child and young woman, facts are hard to verify. [3] There are, for example, no exact records of her birth. [4] However, one item in the woman's life is in no need of further verification, the reputation Harriet Tubman left behind her when she died: thanks to her, hundreds of slaves found their way to freedom and many more survived because of her dedicated activities as a scout and nurse behind the lines during the Civil War.

3. [1] According to Tubman's own account, she decided on her course of action at an early age. [2] Wounded by a slave holder, Harriet prayed for him continuously in the hopes

that he would see the light. [3] But when he came to visit intent only on seeing if she was well enough to sell, the girl realized her prayers were not enough. [4] She decided instead to pray for her own health and bide her time until she knew, for sure, how to make an escape. [5] Little did she know how long the wait would be.

4. [1] During the fifteen years that followed, Tubman worked much of the time in the fields, growing strong enough to do the work of a man. [2] Her body did not break under the strain, even though her old wound still troubled her now and then. [3] Although Harriet Greene married and became Harriet Tubman around 1844, she did not forget her vow to escape. [4] Fortunately her docile appearance did not reveal the rebellious spirit within. [5] Quiet as she seemed, she was still waiting for the right moment. [6] Finally a dream decided her fate. [7] For in a dream she saw herself and a friend being sold away from their families. [8] Almost in answer she dreamed again. [9] This time she saw herself flying over great distances until exhausted she fell into the midst of friendly faces who helped her cross the river into freedom. [10] Years later when the dream had come true, Tubman claimed that the people who helped her in reality were the same ones she had seen in her dreams.

5. [1] The dream encouraged Tubman to make her escape. [2] Accompanied by her two brothers, she followed the North Star, hoping it would guide them to safety. [3] When they grew hungry and the way seemed hopeless, Tubman's two brothers gave up and went back. [4] But she refused. [5] No matter how exhausted she became, she would not return to being a slave. [6] She preferred dying to giving up, even though she had left her husband behind. [7] Spending long nights alone in the woods, Tubman traveled hundreds of miles until she arrived in Philadelphia a free woman. [8] The time was 1849, and she was little more than thirty years old.

6. [1] Although initially Tubman went to work as a servant to feed and clothe herself, she was determined to bring freedom to the rest of her family. [2] Before long she made contact with members of the Underground Railroad, learning through them the necessary names of people and places that guaranteed safety during the flight to freedom. [3] With her knowledge of the underground network, Tubman returned to her home to bring back her sister and her sister's children. [4] One year later, in 1851, she made

a second trip, helping her brothers make good their escape. [5] Finally in the same year, she returned for her husband, only to find that he had a new family. [6] Content to stay where he was, her husband did not want to escape. [7] Although she had to swallow her anger, Tubman decided to do without a husband, and she brought out a neighbor's family instead.

7. [1] The rescue of her family was just about Tubman's last personal act. [2] From that point on, she devoted herself to the elimination of slavery. [3] During the next decade she traveled back and forth between free and slave states, making about twenty secret journeys in all. [4] By the end of the ten years, she was personally responsible for the escape of over three hundred men, women, and children. [5] Her devotion to the freedom of black people earned her the name of "Moses." [6] This was the name slaves used when they wanted to make contact with the woman they believed could save their lives. [7] Because some of her escapes were so extraordinary, and because she was still subject to strange seizures, there were those who thought Harriet Tubman had magical powers. [8] But those who had traveled with her knew otherwise. [9] To them it was clear her success came from no magical source: it was the result of brains, daring, and ingenuity. [10] Magic had nothing to do with it.

8. [1] Tubman's rescues were planned with enormous attention to detail, and she flatly refused to take any chances that might endanger her or her charges. [2] If, for example, wanted notices were posted describing the number and appearance of her group, she would see to it that the group changed. [3] If the description said one man and two women, she would dress one of the women in the party in men's clothes, thus avoiding her pursuers. [4] When she had any doubts about any member of her party, she acted on them and refused to take any man, woman, or child she did not trust completely.

9. [1] In addition to her work on the Underground Railroad, Tubman was active as a soldier in the Civil War, and acting as a Union agent, she made reconnaissance missions behind Confederate lines. [2] Traveling by herself and dressed as an old woman, she walked country roads collecting information about troop movements and supply sources. [3] Eventually she began to lead guerrilla raids into enemy territory. [4] Although the raids were enormously

successful, Tubman received little or no reward. [5] When the government did finally award her a pension, it was as a private citizen not as a public soldier.

10. [1] Tubman also worked as a nurse, moving among the freed slaves whom the war had left rootless and frightened. [2] Because she knew about the healing properties of

Thanks to Harriet Moses Tubman, hundreds of slaves found their way to freedom.

herbs, she provided natural medicine when necessary drugs were in short supply. [3] If she could do nothing else, she at least tried to provide food, and she would distribute baked goods to her hungry brothers and sisters. [4] At the same time she tried to teach them to make pies or cakes that could be exchanged for much-needed money and medical supplies.

11. [1] By the time the Civil War came to an end, Tubman was around forty-four years old, and famous for her exploits. [2] The Queen of England sent her an honorary medal and an invitation to visit the mother country. [3] Unfortunately her own government was not so generous. [4] Members of Congress refused to take up her request for monetary support. [5] Only the newly organized Freedman's Association paid her a salary to help orient newly liberated men and women. [6] Because Tubman had married again after she learned of her first husband's death, she finally received a pension, not for her own activities as a soldier, but for her husband's.

12. [1] For the rest of her life Tubman continued to work for her people, constantly trying to raise money and supplies for men and women who had to start life all over again. [2] Despite her slender resources she was able to find a home for those who were homeless after the war. [3] Her own home became a meeting place for the many who hoped to make a new life now that slavery was a thing of the past. [4] Although Tubman was able to spend the last years of her life without pressing worries about money, she never stopped working. [5] When she died somewhere around the age of ninety-four, she had no regrets about the way she had spent her life. [6] She had found freedom not only for herself but for the countless men and women who never knew her name, but called her simply "Moses."

Questions

1. Does essay 1 contain an introductory paragraph? If you answered yes, what is the number and function of that paragraph?

2. What is the function of sentence 7 in paragraph 1?

_____

_____

3. What is the number of the topic paragraph? _____
   a. What is the main idea of the topic paragraph?

_____

_____

   b. Is that idea expressed in a topic sentence? _____

   c. If your answer is yes, what is the number of that sentence?

   _____

4. Give three pieces of information from the supporting paragraphs which the author uses to make the main idea convincing.

_____

_____

_____

5. Does the essay contain any minor supporting paragraphs? If your answer was yes, list the number of all supporting paragraphs.

   _____   _____

   _____   _____

   _____   _____

6. Paragraph 2 contains two transitional words or phrases that you learned about in Chapter 4. What are they? What is the function of each?

7. Is the main idea of paragraph 5 expressed in a topic sentence? If your answer is yes, what is the number of that sentence?

   _____

   a. Paragraph 5 has what type of organization?
      1. Comparison and contrast
      2. Classification
      3. Cause and effect

8. Paragraph 8 begins with two sentences:
   a. Tubman's rescues were planned with enormous attention to detail, and she flatly refused to take any chances that might endanger her or her charges.
   b. If, for example, wanted notices were posted describing the number and appearance of her group, she would see to it that the group changed.

   Which sentence is the topic sentence? _____

   Briefly explain why you chose this sentence.

   _____

   _____

9. Does essay 1 have a concluding paragraph, or does it come to a halt with a supporting paragraph?

   _____

   _____

10. Select the title that best reflects the contents of this essay. It should be neither too general nor too specific, but

precise enough to cover all the important parts in the essay.

a. Harriet Tubman's Life Under Slavery
b. Harriet Tubman's Life as a Soldier
c. Harriet Tubman's Fight Against Slavery

PART B

Directions: Read the essay that follows. When you are finished, turn to the questions. Do not worry about having to reread parts of the essay; this will be necessary in order to answer all the questions.

Essay 2

1. [1] Sigmund Freud, the father of psychoanalysis, was born in 1856 in a part of Czechoslovakia then known as Freiberg, Moravia. [2] Son of Jakob and Amalia Freud, Sigmund was the first of eight sons and his mother's favorite. [3] When by 1860 it was clear that his father's wool business was not flourishing, the family moved to Vienna, Austria, where it was hoped prospects would be better. [4] Family fortunes did improve enough so that in 1873 young Sigmund was able to begin his medical studies. [5] But he did not complete them until 1881, taking three years longer than most students to receive his degree. [6] A good student but uncertain about the future, Freud could not easily settle on a choice of career. [7] Much as he liked scientific research, it was clear that there were few positions available for a young and relatively poor scientist. [8] As a result, Freud decided to become a specialist in neuropathology.* [9] In 1883, he began studying with Theodor Meynert, one of the great brain specialists of the nineteenth century. [10] Between 1885 and 1886, Freud studied in Paris. Here his interest in the use of hypnotism as a treatment for mental illness was encouraged by the work he saw going on in the locked wards of French hospitals.

2. [1] But it was not until Freud joined forces with friend and colleague Josef Breuer that he began to make the

*neuropathology: study of the diseases affecting the brain, spinal cord, and nerves

discoveries that were to revolutionize psychology. [2] It was at this point that Freud, spurred on by Breuer, began to put together the theory of human development called *psychoanalysis*, and each discovery led to a new and more important one. [3] Above all, it was Breuer who told Freud about the puzzling case of Anna O., a woman who appeared to suffer from a split personality. [4] Although Anna could speak English, she could only understand German. [5] Troubled by hallucinations during the day, at night she grew calm. [6] At times she was extraordinarily fluent, but at other times, she forgot the simplest words. [7] Perhaps her severest symptom was her *hydrophobia* or fear of water. [8] For more than six weeks, she refused to drink even a single glass. [9] However, placed under hypnosis and encouraged to remember the circumstances under which her fears began, Anna began to recover. [10] In a strange way, the simple act of remembering appeared to aid her recovery. [11] Through studying Anna's case, Freud was able to formulate some of the ideas about the human mind central to his new theory. [12] During the next ten years, he continuously worked on the basic concepts discovered through the study of Breuer's patient Anna O. [13] The use of free association, the importance of dreams, the function of repression, and the existence of the unconscious all found their roots in this single case.

3. [1] For example, Freud had learned from Anna that her fear of water had been triggered by a childhood incident, remembered only under hypnosis. [2] Therefore, he argued that unpleasant or frightening memories were never really forgotten. [3] Instead, they were repressed or pushed out of consciousnes until something forced them to resurface. [4] Repression, then, worked like censorship. [5] It covered, hid, or deleted those things the individual found painful or threatening. [6] But unlike censorship, it could not permanently eliminate what was unpleasant or frightening. [7] As Anna O. had shown, repressed memories returned. [8] To explain how thoughts or ideas could be repressed or forgotten Freud insisted that there was more to the mind than consciousness. [9] There was, in fact, something he termed the "unconscious," a part of the mind always kept hidden. [10] In Freud's view no one could ever fully answer the simple question: "What's on your mind?" [11] No one really knew.

*decipher: to read and figure out something difficult or unclear

4. [1] Initially Freud believed that only hypnosis could help uncover the contents of the unconscious. [2] However, because of difficulty guiding patients into the trance state, he invented the technique of free association. [3] When his patients reported a memory, he would ask them to say anything that came to mind, no matter how trivial. [4] By paying attention to all the associations that emerged, he hoped to unlock what the memory meant in the unconscious part of the mind.

5. [1] This method became even more important in 1886 when Freud's father died. [2] Because he was disturbed by the many unpleasant and overpowering emotions he felt, Freud decided to explore his own unconscious. [3] Becoming both patient and doctor, he used free association to understand the origin of his own feelings. [4] At the same time he began to write *The Interpretation of Dreams*, the book still considered his masterpiece. [5] By recording both memories and dreams, Freud hoped to decipher* his unconscious wishes.

6. [1] It was during this period that Freud became even more convinced of the importance of dreams, for he decided that sleep lifted the normal desire to censor unpleasant thoughts and feelings. [2] Thus, the study of dreams could provide a way into a part of the mind usually kept hidden. [3] Although some of Freud's theories about dreams have been disproved, much current dream research has supported him. [4] Dreaming, for example, does seem to be a crucial human activity, and one of the reasons we fall asleep may be in order to dream. [5] Dreams, in fact, appear to be central to a sense of physical and mental well-being.

7. [1] By the time Freud finished his analysis, he was more determined than ever to explore the human unconscious, and during the next decade he used free association with a number of patients. [2] Many of the case histories* he wrote up during this period have become classics in the study of psychology. [3] Above all they serve to illustrate an idea that had become basic to Freud's thinking, the idea that no human being was reasonable without a struggle. [4] Having analyzed himself and numerous others, Freud was convinced that the mind had a powerful irrational side, that men and women often did things contrary to common sense. [5] Afraid of heights, for example, a person would

*case histories: detailed studies of individual patients

Sigmund Freud claimed "dreams are the royal road to the unconscious."

still be drawn to the edge of a high building. [6] By the same token, patients would burst into laughter when discussing a serious, even a tragic situation. [7] From Freud's point of view, such seemingly bizarre* behavior occurred when the irrational, unconscious side of a human being took over. [8] Similarly, when a man or woman failed to get well, despite proper care and medication, Freud suggested that illness might be fulfilling a hidden need.

*bizarre: strange, unreasonable

8. [1] From this perspective, even jokes became something more serious than innocent fun. [2] Instead they were attempts to express unconscious and unpleasant feelings in acceptable ways. [3] Under the protection of humor, individuals could laughingly say something they would never dare to say seriously; they could reveal their true feelings without being punished. [4] In particular Freud loved a joke by the German poet and writer Heinrich Heine: "One must forgive one's enemies, but not before they have been hanged." [5] He used it to illustrate how a joke could undermine traditional statements about the importance of forgiveness.

9. [1] Despite objections to his theories, Freud's reputation grew. [2] By the late twenties many famous celebrities were traveling to Vienna to be analyzed by the great Doctor Freud. [3] When in 1933 Freud discovered he had cancer of the jaw, he still continued his work and research. [4] However, when the Nazis invaded Austria in 1938, he was forced to flee to England, where he spent the final months of his life. [5] After much pain, for which he refused medication, Sigmund Freud died at the age of 83. [6] Today his theories, though widely disputed, are still considered important and valuable contributions to the study of human behavior.

Questions

1. Paragraph 1 has which type of organization?

    a. sequence of steps
    b. list of dates and events
    c. list of characteristics

2. What is the number of the topic paragraph? _____

    a. What is the main idea of the topic paragraph?

    b. Give three pieces of information that the author uses to support the main idea.

3. Paragraph 2 has which type of organization?

   a. cause and effect
   b. comparison and contrast
   c. sequence of steps

4. Paragraph 6 contains three transitional words and phrases. List them along with their functions.

5. What is the relationship between sentences 4, 5, and 6 in paragraph 7?

   a. They are all major supporting sentences that serve to illustrate the main idea of the paragraph.
   b. Sentences 5 and 6 provide emphasis for sentence 4.
   c. Sentences 5 and 6 are minor supporting sentences that serve to illustrate sentence 4.

6. Are there any paragraphs in the essay that do not contain a topic sentence? If the answer is yes, please list the number or numbers of those paragraphs:

   _____

   _____

   _____

7. Does the essay contain a concluding paragraph or does it come to a halt with a supporting paragraph? If your answer is yes, what is the function of the concluding paragraph?

8. Select the title that best reflects the contents of this essay. The title should be neither too general nor too specific.

   a. The Discovery of the Unconscious
   b. The Life of Sigmund Freud
   c. Freud's Discovery of Psychoanalysis

9. Given the title you have chosen, which paragraphs contain the least information necessary to complete notes?

   _____

10. If you were reading this essay just to be prepared for class, your notes would be fairly brief. In the following blanks, give your idea of what essential parts those notes should contain:

Topic: _____

_____

Main Idea: _____

_____

Support: _____

_____

_____

_____

_____

_____

Conclusion: _____

_____

_____

Chapter 8

Reading a Textbook

In the following pages, we'll introduce and explain surveying, a four-step reading skill that will help you get the most out of your textbooks. We'll also talk about the organization of chapters in a textbook, and you'll see that reading textbook chapters has much in common with reading a single paragraph or an essay. At the end of the chapter, we'll talk about the need to review what you have read and show you that the format previously introduced for note taking is still useful, even when you are dealing with an entire chapter rather than a single essay or paragraph.

SURVEYING

The following four steps make up the reading skill called *surveying.* **The purpose of surveying is to give you advance knowledge about something you are planning to read.** A good survey can tell you what topic is under discussion and what the author plans to say about that topic.

Step 1: Read the Title, the Headings, and the First Paragraph

Up to now, the first thing you had to do—whether analyzing a paragraph or an essay—was to find the topic. Finding the topic is also the starting point for understanding a chapter in a textbook.

In the tests that concluded the preceding chapter, we asked you to choose appropriate titles of the essays, titles neither too general nor too specific but precise enough to sum up the major portion of each essay. It is clear then that the **title** provides an important clue to the topic of an essay. The same is true for a textbook chapter, and you should always look at the title first.

Even more informative are the **headings** that separate the chapter into sections. We can use an excerpt taken from a meteorology textbook to illustrate what we mean (Figure 8–1).*

CHAPTER OUTLINE

THUNDERSTORMS
Thunderstorm Activity
Stages of a Thunderstorm
Lightning
Thunderstorm Climatology

TORNADOES
Tornado Activity
Formation of Tornadoes
Tornado Climatology
Fighting Back at Tornadoes

HURRICANES
Hurricane Activity
How Hurricanes Are Produced
Breeding Ground for Hurricanes
The Naming of Hurricanes
Effects of Hurricanes

OTHER DISTURBANCES
Waterspouts
Whirlwinds
Blizzards
Cold Waves

SUMMARY, KEY TERMS, QUESTIONS

WEATHER IN THE NEWS

Most of the time the weather is like unobtrusive background music in our lives. We dress for rain or heat or snow when we leave home in the morning, and manage to stay fairly comfortable throughout all four seasons of the year. Only occasionally does the weather take over and dominate our lives, rendering us helpless, destroying property and lives, or simply dislocating the neat patterns that we have set up for our lives. Let's examine the origins and cycles of activity of serious storms.

We have already seen that cyclonic wind patterns are capable of producing various types of severe storms, although not all cyclonic wind patterns do so. These storms are called by many—often

FIGURE 8–1

The title of this chapter is "Storms," and that title, combined with the chapter outline of major headings, allows us to infer the main idea for the entire chapter: "There are several major types of storms."

Like the title and the headings, the first paragraph in the chapter provides useful information. Read through this first paragraph of the chapter on "Storms" to see what we mean:

> Most of the time the weather is like unobtrusive background music in our lives. We dress for rain or heat or snow when we leave home in the morning, and manage to stay fairly comfortable throughout all four seasons of the year. Only occasionally does the weather take over and dominate our lives, rendering us helpless, destroying property and lives, or simply dislocating the neat patterns that we have set up for our lives. Let's examine the origins and cycles of activity of serious storms.*

In this case, the first paragraph specifies even further the author's intent. The chapter will deal with the causes and effects of serious storms: "Let's examine the origins and cycles of activity of serious storms." Thus, without finishing one page of text, we already have a good idea of the direction the author is going to take.

Step 2: Use the Headings to Raise Questions About the Chapter

Usually you can get a good impression of the author's ideas about a topic simply by reading the headings that divide the text into short sections. The chapter on storms just discussed, for example, is divided into sections by what we call *major* and *minor* headings. The heading "Thunderstorms" is considered a major heading; "Thunderstorm Activity" is a subheading or minor heading under the major topic. **To an alert reader, major headings signal that the author is introducing a new idea about the topic of the chapter. The minor headings indicate that the author is continuing to develop an idea already presented.**

In our sample chapter, the major heading "Thunderstorms" immediately reveals the first type of storm the author plans to discuss. The minor headings "Thunderstorm Activity" and "Stages of a Thunderstorm" indicate the author's intention to

*From *Meteorology: The Earth and Its Weather* by Joseph S. Weisberg. ©1981 by Houghton Mifflin Company. Used by permission.

describe in some detail what happens during a thunderstorm. It is not until the second major heading "Tornadoes" that the author changes direction and introduces a new kind of serious storm. Major and minor sections of a text work together just like major and minor sentences: major headings introduce new ideas whereas minor headings provide additional explanation of an idea already presented.

As we have already suggested, you can make use of the major and minor headings to anticipate the contents of a chapter. However, you can also use them to focus your concentration. After reading the headings, use words like *what, why, how, when,* and *where* to form questions about the material. Then as you read, look for answers to your questions. In Figure 8–1, for example, the minor heading "Effects of Hurricanes" is listed under "Hurricanes." If you want to read that section efficiently, you should have a question in mind when you begin reading, such as "What are the effects of hurricanes?" This technique—of asking yourself questions based on the headings—will help you increase your comprehension. If you have questions about a chapter in mind as you read, you'll find that those portions of the text providing the answers seem to stand out. Moreover, questions can help you decide if you are really understanding the material. If you read through any major section of a chapter and are not able to answer one question about that section, you know that you have been reading—but not understanding.

Step 3: Read the Final Paragraph; Look at Key Terms and Final Questions

The final paragraph of a chapter will frequently be a concluding paragraph; that is, the author will use it to summarize important ideas or to suggest possible solutions to problems described earlier in the text. Reading the last paragraph of a chapter can usually help you identify some of the key ideas presented throughout the chapter.

Some chapters in textbooks end with several paragraphs under the heading *Review* or *Summary*. If you are reading a text that provides a summary or review at the end of each chapter, read all the paragraphs that fall under that heading. They should give you a clear idea of the major ideas and terms presented in the chapter.

Also important are those words usually listed at the beginning or end of the chapter; this is the vocabulary needed to understand the subject of the chapter. You may want to jot them down so that you are prepared when their definitions appear in the text.

Figures 8–2 and 8–3 show excerpts from the same chapter already introduced. They contain a summary, a list of key terms, and questions. Look at how much information you can obtain just from these two pages:

SUMMARY

Severe storms are most often produced by unstable air masses. Thunderstorms, tornadoes, and hurricanes are the commonest forms of cyclonic activity. They come about because of interactions between air masses and the energy entering the systems, which creates instability.

Lightning—also associated with thunderstorm activity—takes many forms. It results from the buildup of electrical charges on various parts of the Earth and the clouds.

Each storm forms in a specific way. Some storms form in specific localities, as well. Hurricanes, in particular, do this. Each storm passes through a certain cycle of activity, and dies when energy is no longer fed into the system. Other factors, such as entrainment and friction, dissipate the energy available to the storm system.

KEY TERMS

Eye	Lightning
Tropical disturbance	Thunder
Tropical depression	Pilot leader
Tunderstorm	Step leader
Tornado	Suction vortex
Hurricane	Typhoon
Tropical storm	Cyclone
Squall line	Easterly wave
Cumulus stage	Waterspout
Mature stage	Whirlwind
Entrainment	Blizzard
Dispersal stage	Cold wave

FIGURE 8–2

The first paragraph of the summary in Figure 8–2 already tells you something about the causes of storms: "Severe storms are most often produced by unstable air masses." Similarly, the list of key terms tells you what words will be important to an understanding of storms, their causes and effects. Even the questions in Figure 8–3 provide useful information. Question 3, for example, tells you immediately that hurricanes "follow a curved path across the earth's surface."

You should also try jotting down shortened versions of final questions. Then when you begin reading and run across

QUESTIONS

1. What is a thunderstorm? Describe the development of each stage, including the process of entrainment.
2. Explain how hurricanes are formed. Why do they arise in specific source regions? Why don't they occur elsewhere?
3. Why do hurricanes generally follow a curved path across the Earth's surface?
4. Why do hurricanes begin to dissipate as they cross land masses?
5. What is a tropical disturbance? A tropical depression?
6. Describe the growth of a hurricane. Enumerate the events that take place during its appearance and growth.
7. Compare a tornado and a hurricane.
8. Where in the North and South Atlantic Oceans do semipermanent anticyclones exist? What importance do they have in summer? In winter?
9. In what way did the various systems for naming hurricanes arise?
10. Today, fewer people die from the effects of severe storms than used to be the case in the past. Explain why.
11. At times, tornadoes seem to cause selective damage along their paths. Explain why.
12. How are thunderstorms related to convective processes?
13. Why are cumulonimbus clouds and thunderstorms almost synonymous? Describe the process of formation of cumulonimbus clouds.
14. Describe the way that lightning is formed between any two possible sites of discharge. List the sites of possible discharge.
15. What are the most frequent sites of thunderstorm activity?

FIGURE 8–3

an answer, write down the page number and a brief note next to the question. Again, keeping in mind questions while you are reading will help you spot the answers to those questions and help you decide whether or not you are understanding everything you should.

Step 4: Go Back and Read the First Sentence of Every Paragraph

We already said that reading the headings in a chapter can usually tell you two things:

1. what the author intends to say about the topic of the chapter
2. how the author supports those ideas

Reading the first sentence of every paragraph can provide even more information about the author's ideas, but the information will usually be more specific. We can use the following sample paragraph to illustrate what we mean:

> **THUNDERSTORMS**   **Thunderstorms** are local disturbances produced when clouds undergo rapid, intense convective movements resulting in the formation of cumulonimbus clouds. These storms bring about a variety of precipitation: rain, hail, sleet, and ice, as well as lightning and thunder. They are accompanied by gusty winds. Figure 8-1 shows the stages of thunderstorm activity. We shall examine these stages in a bit more detail.[2]

The first sentence of the paragraph following the major heading *Thunderstorms* adds to your knowledge of the chapter. You already knew the author was going to talk about thunderstorms. But, in addition, you now know what causes them.

Reading the first sentence of every paragraph also can give you clues to the way an author presents material. As you move from paragraph to paragraph, you can check to see if the author uses underlining, lists, italics, or illustrations to emphasize important points. Knowing that an author favors a particular method of emphasis can help you when you are reading because you'll find it easier to pick out the important passages.

Before we introduce the first exercise, we want to make an important point about surveying. Even if you decide to use different steps when you survey, your purpose should still be the same: try to get as much advance information about the chapter as you can. Find out what topic is under discussion, what ideas are presented about that topic, and how those ideas are supported. In short, focus your reading. It will help improve speed, comprehension, and retention.

EXERCISE 1   **Directions:** Survey the textbook pages in Figures 8–4 to 8–6. Then see if you can answer questions 1 through 4. Survey according to the steps outlined on the previous pages.

Note: We suggest you read the questions before you survey. You'll find that the answers seem to stand out if you know what you are looking for.

---

[2]Weisberg, *Meteorology*, p. 210

THUNDERSTORMS   **Thunderstorms** are local disturbances produced when clouds undergo rapid, intense convective movements resulting in the formation of cumulonimbus clouds. These storms bring about a variety of precipitation: rain, hail, sleet, and ice, as well as lightning and thunder. They are accompanied by gusty winds. Figure 8-1 shows the stages of thunderstorm activity. We shall examine these stages in a bit more detail.

THUNDERSTORMS

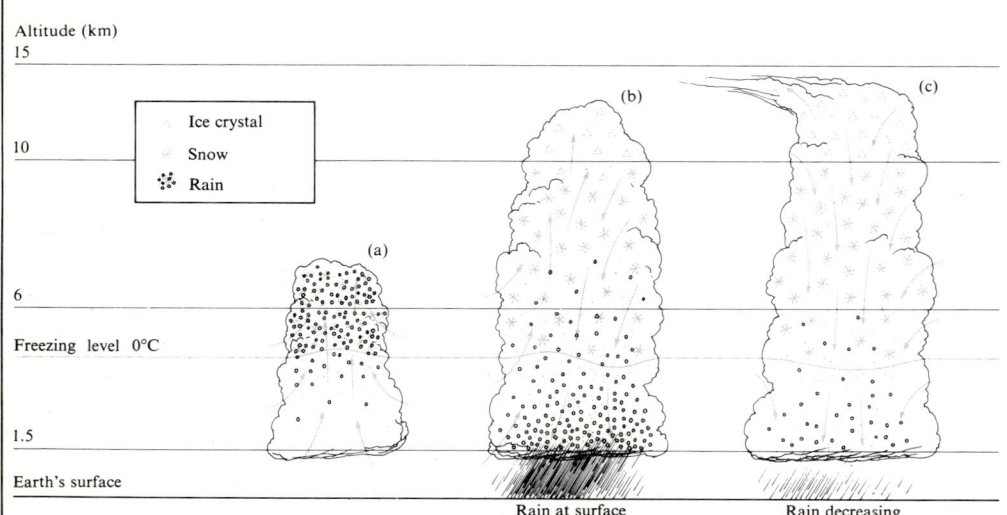

FIGURE 8-1 The stages of a thunderstorm: (a) cumulus stage, (b) mature stage, (c) dispersal stage

Thunderstorm Activity

The commonest breeding ground for a thunderstorm is a region of unstable, often moist, air that is being heated by the surface of the Earth. This sort of heating is particularly rapid over land masses in the summer. As the air is heated, it decreases in density. And as it does so, it generates a convection current. This causes air to rise and, as it rises, to cool. Because air at upper levels is cooler than air at the surface of the Earth, the convective activity increases in intensity and force.

Several local factors may be responsible for initiating a thunderstorm: (1) A rising air mass. (2) Thermal convection in an air mass on the Earth's surface. (3) Orographic uplift. (4) Advection of low-level warm air.

Although meteorologists do not yet know all the causes of all types of thunderstorms, they understand enough to be able to determine the major events that take place during a thunderstorm, and the consequences thereof.

Most thunderstorms move from the West and Southwest in a generally Northward direction. Most are not very large. They vary

FIGURE 8–4

212
STORMS

in size from about 0.5 km to about 10 km (0.3 to 6 mi) in diameter. They average about 1 km (0.6 mi). Often several thunderstorms are grouped along lines called **squall lines,** which consist of strong winds and storms along a line of intense convection. These squall lines usually precede a cold front.

The thunderstorm itself, during its intense, mature stages, is marked by strong, rapid updrafts and downdrafts. Sheetlike rain often falls. During the downdraft stages, winds vary from light to heavy. These drafts can approach gale force; winds of 112 km/hr (70 mi/hr) are common.

The thermal instability of the air feeds the storms and intensifies their accompanying turbulence. Radiational cooling of the cloud formations at the upper levels increases the strong convection currents. In addition, radiation of heat from the ground or from the accompanying frontal system causes some heating of the cloud base.

Mechanical processes can also enhance the formation and intensity of the storm. Cold air masses along the ground force warm air upward. In mountainous terrain, orographic uplift accomplishes the same thing.

As the storm builds, water vapor condenses and releases latent heat. This huge amount of heat energy feeds the convection processes and further boosts the storm's intensity. Warm, moist air is rapidly forced upward past the condensation level. Cumulus clouds form. The thunderstorm is on its way.

Stages of a Thunderstorm

A thunderstorm goes through three stages: it builds, it rapidly expends its energy, and it dies as quickly as it came. Each stage is marked by distinctive events.

1. The **cumulus stage** is marked by a single updraft from the ground level. Vertical clouds begin to form and build in height. The updraft that initiates this stage causes a ground-level low-pressure center to form, with little or no wind in it. Near the end of this stage, converging surface winds appear, and move into the center of the system. As air enters from the sides of the system, it moves upward and out of the system at progressively higher levels. No rain falls at this point, but, at the upper levels, condensation occurs, with the release of immense amounts of latent heat. The rising air cools quickly, at a rate that exceeds that of normal adiabatic cooling. Thus the very cold air releases large amounts of latent heat rapidly.

2. The **mature stage** is the most active stage of the thunderstorm. It is marked by the beginning of precipitation, which initiates

FIGURE 8–5

213
THUNDERSTORMS

downdrafts. Cooler, drier air moves from the periphery through the clouds toward the center of the system. This influx of cooler, denser, environmental air, called **entrainment,** intensifies the downdrafts. Strong vortexes may result, which may cause tornadoes to develop. In large thunderstorms, ice forms in the upper levels of the clouds. These clouds may reach a height of 8 km (5 mi) or more.

Violent updrafts and downdrafts sweep through the storm cells. Warm air near the Earth's surface feeds the upward motion of the air, while precipitation causes the colder downdrafts. Rain, and occasionally hail, falls. Downdrafts are strong. The adjacent colder air pushes in along the ground toward the center of the system. By now, a towering cumulonimbus cloud system has formed. Lightning and thunder are frequent. Mature cells or regions of updrafts and downdrafts develop; their effects may be felt for miles. This is the most violent stage of the storm.

3. The **dispersal stage** is marked by downdrafts that occur over the entire cell, which is what ultimately defuses the thunderstorm. Updrafts no longer feed the storm, so it is cut off from its source of warm, moist air. Precipitation soon slows and comes to a stop. Clouds evaporate, since no more moisture is being added to the system. The winds change from a converging to a diverging path. End of thunderstorm.

Lightning

Ever since Benjamin Franklin, scientists have been investigating the exact nature of **lightning.** It is the most spectacular show that the atmosphere puts on. Lightning results from a build-up of electrical charges in (a) neighboring parts of a cloud, or in (b) portions of the Earth that are adjacent to a charged region of the atmosphere. The charges seem to build up most frequently when violent updrafts of air sweep through a cloud. When the water droplets and ice crystals in the clouds fall and collide with other droplets in supercooled water vapor, they accumulate regions of like electrical charges (Figure 8-2 on page 214).

When there is a discharge of electricity between adjacent positive and negative fields, lightning occurs. One common theory about the origin of lightning is that, as the larger droplets of water in a cloud break apart, they accumulate electrical charges. Small droplets, which are near the center of the cloud, accumulate negative charges (electrons). Larger droplets, which are near the outermost regions of the cloud, are left with positive charges.

Another theory about lightning is that positive charges build up on ice crystals near the top of cumulonimbus clouds, while in the

FIGURE 8–6

Surveying 381

1. What are the three stages of thunderstorm development?

2. What is the commonest breeding ground for a thunderstorm?

3. Check off any one of the following devices the author uses to emphasize major points or terms.
    a. lists with numbers or letters
    b. underlining
    c. boldface type
    d. diagrams
    e. colored ink
    f. illustrations

4. What is the most active stage of the thunderstorm?

READING

Each chapter in a textbook usually deals with one topic, with each major section in the chapter helping to develop a general idea about that topic. Athough major sections have main ideas of their own, all of these ideas should reinforce the general main idea (or ideas) of the entire chapter.

To a degree, reading a textbook chapter is much like reading an essay. Only there is much more material to organize. As you read through a chapter, you have to maintain an *overview;* you cannot concentrate on each major section as if it were an essay separate from the rest of the chapter. While you are reading, you must always keep the following in mind: how does each section deepen your knowledge of the chapter topic and main idea? Do the major sections, in fact, combine to suggest more than one general main idea about the topic? Is there a clear relationship between the sections, or are they presented as separate attempts to develop the overall main idea?

To illustrate what we mean, we'll use our sample chapter and some simple diagrams. From our survey, we already inferred a general main idea that controls the chapter: "There are several major types of storms." *Thunderstorms* is the first major heading; it introduces a particular kind of storm while the paragraph following that heading defines thunderstorms in more detail and provides a cause: "Thunderstorms are local disturbances produced when clouds undergo rapid, intense, convective movements resulting in the formation of cumulonimbus clouds." The minor heading following the major one introduces *Thunderstorm Activity*, and provides more specific information about characteristics and causes. If we diagram the relationship so far expressed within the chapter, it will look like this (see diagram 8–1):

Main Idea of Entire Chapter

> There are several major types of storms.

↑

Main Idea of First Major Section

> Thunderstorms are local disturbances produced when clouds undergo rapid, intense, convective movements resulting in the formation of cumulonimbus clouds.

↑

Main Idea of First Minor Section

> The commonest breeding ground for a thunderstorm is a region of unstable, often moist, air that is being heated by the surface of the earth.

DIAGRAM 8–1

    As the diagram suggests, the first major section is devoted to the development of the general main idea. It does not introduce any material that would force us to include another overall main idea; we do not have to change or expand our original impression based on the survey. Let's look at the second major section, and see if that demands a revision of our initial idea:

TORNADOES   **Tornadoes** are closely related to thunderstorms. Both arise from strong cumulonimbus systems. Both are small in scope and local in origin. In fact, tornadoes are among the smallest storms in size, but the most destructive in the regions in which they strike. Every minute of its existence, a tornado has energy equivalent to that of our most powerful bombs.[3]

---

[3]Weisberg, *Meterology*, p. 217

Again, the major section confirms the general main idea, but this time the storm under discussion is the tornado, and the author does indicate a relationship between tornadoes and the thunderstorms just discussed: "Tornadoes are closely related to thunderstorms." If we continued our diagram, it would look like something like this:

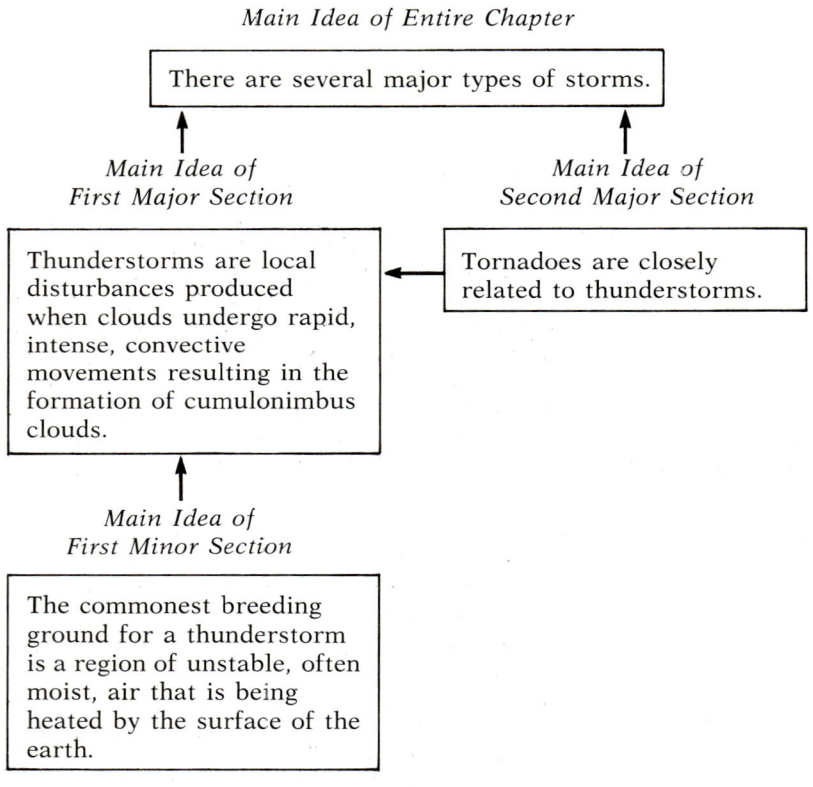

DIAGRAM 8–2

Obviously we do not intend for you to keep diagrams in your head. However, we do ask you to continuously **think about the way major and minor sections relate to and develop the main idea of the chapter.**

In the following exercise, we ask you to read the sample selection and fill in the empty blocks of the diagram:

EXERCISE 2 **Directions:** Survey and read the following textbook excerpt. Then fill in Diagram 8–3.

HURRICANES	Extreme cyclonic activity, as we have said, centers around systems of very low pressure, around which winds move in a violently twisting path. The name for such activity varies. These storms are called **typhoons** in the Pacific Ocean, **cyclones** in the Indian Ocean region, and **hurricanes** in the West Indies. The name hurricane has its origin in the word *huracan*, which was the name of the storm god of the ancient Mayans. Even earlier, Caribbean Indians used a similar name to describe evil spirits. Indians even in prehistoric days expressed their terror of hurricanes in their folklore, and no wonder. Winds would increase to violent proportions, bringing death and destruction. Suddenly they would stop blowing and there would be a calm period. Then violent winds would begin again, but *from the opposite direction*, again causing severe damage. These strange events led the Indians to believe that the storm was the result of some supernatural being venting its rage on the unfortunate population.
Hurricane Activity	As we know, hurricanes, typhoons, and cyclones all result in violent winds moving about the calm center, or eye, of a storm. Seen from above on satellite photos, the storm appears to be a flattened, spiral form. The strong winds that spiral around the eye, or vortex, of a hurricane create the visual effect of a hollow spool, with circular edges marked by twisting winds and cloud formations. The center of the storm is clear and calm. Air is sucked into the sides and rapidly forced out of the upper regions of the storm cell. The effects of these winds are felt for several kilometers above the face of the Earth.

FIGURE 8–7

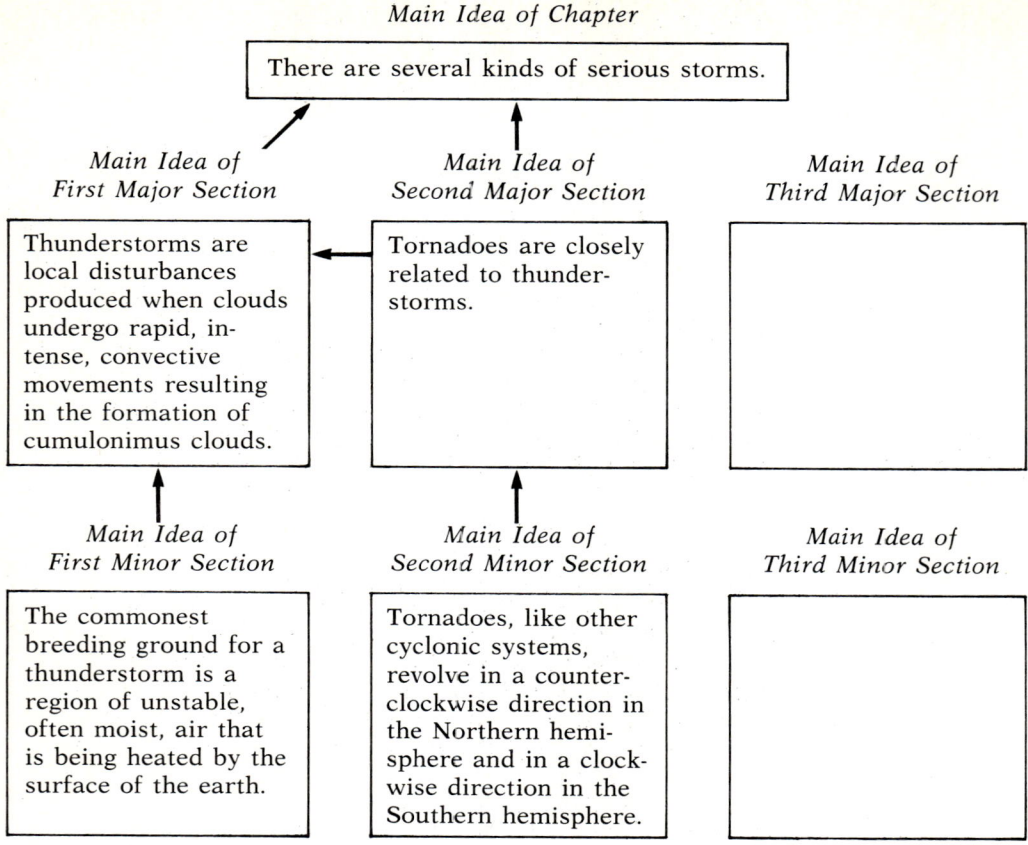

DIAGRAM 8-3

WRITING

Unfortunately, most people don't write in their textbooks. They think that books should be preserved without a mark on them, that a textbook should look the same at the end of the semester as it did at the beginning. This idea, a holdover perhaps from borrowing books at the local library, is a mistaken one. Marking important words, sentences, or even entire passages can help you remember what you read. Similarly, jotting down your own questions or thoughts in the margin of your text will help you understand what you've read. You'll know where you agree with the author and where you don't. You'll know which points are clear and which ones are not.

We'll use the following list of symbols to mark a section from our sample text (see Figures 8–7 to 8–8):

_____ Underlining indicates that information is important.

R, ex R and *ex* indicate examples or reasons given in support of a previous statement. These symbols can be used instead of underlining when the reasons and examples are easily understood and possibly not too important since similar ones could be supplied by common sense.

○ Circles indicate key terms that should be remembered.

[ ] Brackets are used for important passages that are much too long to be underlined.

? Question marks signal that something is still unclear and needs explanation.

* Asterisks indicate that a portion of the text may reappear as a test question.

When you mark your textbooks, you may well want to invent your own list of symbols, but whatever the code, you should have the following goals in mind:

1. You'll want to draw attention to important information so that when you reread, you'll know what parts of the text are especially important.

2. You'll want to note points that are unclear so that you can clarify them.

3. You'll want to indicate the relationship between ideas.

Before we go on to the next exercise, we want to make several important points before marking your text. First of all, remember to mark or write in your text after you have finished reading. Don't just pick up your text and start circling and underlining. **Survey, read, and then mark.**

To write in your text, you need to think about what you've read. You cannot decide immediately what is important and what is not. Marking a text without reading it first can produce crowded pages that emphasize the unimportant and ignore the important. If at any point you find that your pages are becoming so heavily marked that you can't read them with ease, you should immediately transfer notes and questions to a notebook. You don't want to obscure important points in your text; you want to highlight them. That is the purpose for marking your textbook in the first place.

When you mark your texts, be sure to underline only those words and phrases that communicate the most important ideas. You should be sure not to underline everything; instead, rely on those key words and phrases that convey the idea contained in the sentences. For example, take the following paragraph:

> The name *hurricane* has its origin in the word *huracan*, which was the name of the storm god of the ancient Mayans. Even earlier, Caribbean Indians used a similar name to describe evil spirits. Indians even in prehistoric days expressed their terror of hurricanes in their folklore, and no wonder. Winds would increase to violent proportions, bringing death and destruction. Suddenly they would stop blowing and there would be a calm period. Then violent winds would begin again, but from the opposite direction, again causing severe damage. These strange events led the Indians to believe that the storm was the result of some supernatural being venting its rage on the unfortunate population.[4]

We have underlined only those words necessary to communicate the ideas contained in the topic and supporting sentences because, as usual, these sentences contain the most important information. If we returned to review this paragraph to study for a test, we would be able to read just those words and phrases we have underlined and still be able to understand the main idea, as well as the support provided for it. The same does not hold true, however, for the following paragraph:

> The name hurricane had its origin in the word *huracan*, which was the name of the storm god of the Ancient Mayans. Even earlier, Caribbean Indians used a similar name to describe evil spirits. Indians even in prehistoric days expressed their terror of hurricanes in their folklore, and no wonder. Winds would increase to violent proportions, bringing death and destruction. Suddenly they would stop blowing and there would be a calm period. Then violent winds would begin again, but from the opposite direction, again causing severe damage. These strange events led the Indians to believe that the storm was the result of some supernatural being venting its rage on the unfortunate population.

If we were to read only the underlined words and phrases in the paragraph, we would not understand at all what the

[4]Weisberg, *Meteorology*, p. 224

author wanted to say. Reading just the underlined words and phrases, we could never discover the origin of the word *hurricane*, and it would appear that the storm was a supernatural being venting its rage. That's not at all what was said in the paragraph, but that's what careless underlining can lead us to believe.

Equally useless is the following paragraph, where no attempt has been made to use underlining for emphasis. Almost every sentence in the paragraph has been underlined, making everything of equal importance. If we returned to read this paragraph to review for a test, we would end up simply rereading the entire text, rather than selected points:

> The name hurricane has its origin in the word *huracan*, which was the name of the storm god of the ancient Mayans. Even earlier, Caribbean Indians used a similar name to describe evil spirits. Indians even in prehistoric days expressed their terror of hurricanes in their folklore, and no wonder. Winds would increase to violent proportions, bringing death and destruction. Suddenly they would stop blowing and there would be a calm period. Then violent winds would begin again, but from the opposite direction, again causing severe damage. These strange events led the Indians to believe that the storm was the result of some supernatural being venting its rage on the unfortunate population.

Underlining is an important device for emphasizing key points and illustrating relationships between ideas, but careless underlining can do more harm than good. The following exercise will help you develop skill in underlining.

EXERCISE 3   **Directions:** Figure 8–8 contains the excerpt we marked as an example, along with two additional paragraphs. Devise your own code and mark all three paragraphs.

HURRICANES

Extreme cyclonic activity, as we have said, centers around systems of very low pressure, around which winds move in a violently twisting path. The name for such activity varies. These storms are called **typhoons** in the Pacific Ocean, **cyclones** in the Indian Ocean region, and **hurricanes** in the West Indies.

The name hurricane has its origin in the word *huracan*, which was the name of the storm god of the ancient Mayans. Even earlier, Caribbean Indians used a similar name to describe evil spirits. Indians even in prehistoric days expressed their terror of hurricanes in their folklore, and no wonder. Winds would increase to violent proportions, bringing death and destruction. Suddenly they would stop blowing and there would be a calm period. Then violent winds would begin again, but *from the opposite direction*, again causing severe damage. These strange events led the Indians to believe that the storm was the result of some supernatural being venting its rage on the unfortunate population.

Hurricane Activity

As we know, hurricanes, typhoons, and cyclones all result in violent winds moving about the calm center, or eye, of a storm. Seen from above on satellite photos, the storm appears to be a flattened, spiral form. The strong winds that spiral around the eye, or vortex, of a hurricane create the visual effect of a hollow spool, with circular edges marked by twisting winds and cloud formations. The center of the storm is clear and calm. Air is sucked into the sides and rapidly forced out of the upper regions of the storm cell. The effects of these winds are felt for several kilometers above the face of the Earth.

FIGURE 8–8

TAKING NOTES

When you took notes on paragraphs and essays, you included the topic, main idea, support, and conclusion. Basically, when reading a chapter in a textbook, you will have to include the same information. However, there is a second method for taking notes that is more appropriate to longer reading selections. As you grow accustomed to taking notes, you will rely on this method more than the first.

The key words in using this method are *condense* and *summarize*. This means, whenever you can, reduce sentences to a few words and reduce paragraphs to a few sentences or phrases. You will still use letters, numbers, and identation to indicate relationships, but less so since you will be more interested in combining than separating.

In the following example, we supply the original paragraph. Compare it with the sample notes:

THUNDERSTORMS **Thunderstorms** are local disturbances produced when clouds undergo rapid, intense convective movements resulting in the formation of cumulonimbus clouds. These storms bring about a variety of precipitation: rain, hail, sleet, and ice, as well as lightning and thunder. They are accompanied by gusty winds. Figure 8-1 shows the stages of thunderstorm activity. We shall examine these stages in a bit more detail.

Notes: 1. Thunderstorms—local disturbances with hail, sleet, ice, lightning, wind

As we said before, numbers are still important to indicate relationships. Here we use the number 1 to indicate that the thunderstorm is the first storm discussed in the chapter. Notice now what we eliminated from the original paragraph. First of all, we included only those words necessary to communicate the author's ideas. Everything else has disappeared. This is the same principle you already learned for underlining. Notice too that we left out any reference to the cause of thunderstorms even though the paragraph does talk about it. Since causes are explained more thoroughly later on, we did not deal with them here. Like underlining, note taking is done *after* the first reading; that way you can eliminate repetition.

Here is another sample excerpt, a slightly longer one than the previous one. Again our goal is the same, to restate briefly all important points:

TORNADOES	**Tornadoes** are closely related to thunderstorms. Both arise from strong cumulonimbus systems. Both are small in scope and local in origin. In fact, tornadoes are among the smallest storms in size, but the most destructive in the regions in which they strike. Every minute of its existence, a tornado has energy equivalent to that of our most powerful bombs.
Tornado Activity	Tornadoes, like other cyclonic systems, revolve in a counterclockwise direction in the Northern hemisphere and in a clockwise direction in the Southern hemisphere. People in the American Midwest call them "twisters." A good name, but it doesn't nearly give an apt description of the violence, destruction, and fear generated by these cyclonic winds (Figure 8-4).
	As we said earlier, tornadoes are small by comparison with other storms. On the average, a tornado has a diameter of less than a few hundred meters. The average tornado covers a path about 25 km (16 mi) long and makes contact with the ground for only a few minutes. However, there are occasional supertornadoes. On May 26, 1917, a tornado struck Illinois and Indiana, leaving a path of destruction 469 km (293 mi) long. It lasted for 7 hours and 20 minutes, even though it had a forward speed that was about average for most tornadoes.
	The energy contained in a tornado—even though the tornado is small in scope—is unimaginably enormous. Houses are shattered. Cars are blown end over end. Pieces of wood have been found driven through metal, and straw through wood as though the straw were a nail. A 1931 tornado in Minnesota lifted an 83-ton railroad car containing 117 passengers, carried it about 30 meters, and dropped it intact into a ditch. All the passengers survived.

FIGURE 8–9

Notes: 2. Tornadoes—like thunderstorms, also arise from strong cumulonimubus systems, both small in scope, local in origin, tornadoes small but destructive, move counterclockwise in Northern hemisphere and clockwise in Southern, called "twisters" in midwest, average diameter: 25 km. (16 mi.), lasts only minutes, exception: supertornadoes, e.g. Illinois and Indiana, May 26, 1917, 7 hr. 20 min., tornadoes have enormous energy, e.g. lifted 83-ton railroad car (1931)

Notice here how much material we combined that had originally been separated. Because almost all the details given in the four separate paragraphs fall into the category "characteristics of the tornado," we put them all together, separating the individual details with nothing more than commas. Thus we reduce four separate paragraphs into a much shorter piece of text.

Although we have not used any, in time you will develop your own shorthand. This will further reduce your notes. For example, having introduced the subject of tornadoes, we could have used a *T* to indicate repetition of that word. By the same token, *railroad* could have been written *RR*. **Developing your own shorthand is fine. Just make sure you can understand it when you review for a test a month later.**

In the following exercise, we present some sample paragraphs and ask you to take notes according to this method.

EXERCISE 4 Directions: Read the following selection and then complete the notes we have begun.

OTHER DISTURBANCES

There are other atmospheric disturbances that are closely related to tornadoes and thunderstorms. They have different names and occur in various places, but they all result from the instability of air masses and the interactions of land, air, and water. Here are some of them.

Waterspouts

Waterspouts usually occur in the Gulf of Mexico and the Western regions of the Atlantic and Pacific Oceans. Some are tornadoes that move from land onto water. Others are similar to tornadoes, except that they take place over an open expanse of water (Figure 8-10). That is, they result from instability of the air over the water. However, unlike tornadoes, they are more often fair-weather occurrences. They achieve only a few thousand meters in height. In addition, waterspouts are extremely short-lived; often they last only a few minutes.

Whirlwinds

Whirlwinds, also called "dust devils," are swirling ground-level masses of air that are neither as extensive nor as violent as tornadoes. They usually occur in summer, when warm land surfaces heat the air rapidly and trigger small cyclonic activity. They are generally only a few hundred meters high. They are also short-lived and local, although they may enlarge as air converges and flows upward.

Blizzards

Blizzards are composed of extremely cold, snow-bearing winds, which pick up snow from the ground and blow it along in a dense mass, curtailing visibility. The U.S. Weather Bureau defines blizzards as snow that reduces visibility to less than 150 m (500 ft), with winds that travel more than 50 km/hr (32 mi/hr), and with low (often below freezing) temperatures. Snowdrifts may pile up many feet deep, as they did in the Great Blizzard of '88 that buried houses up to three stories tall. Blinding, heavy snow is especially hard on cities. For example, the blizzard that hit the Northeastern United States in February of 1978 paralyzed transportation and communications for days and caused millions of dollars of damage throughout New England and the mid-Atlantic states (Figure 8-11).

Cold Waves

Cold waves are a rapid drop in temperature within a 24-hour period—a drop so sharp that crops must be specially protected. They result from North winds that sweep out of an anticyclone, bringing low temperatures and causing surface temperatures to plummet sharply. Snow, sleet, and cold rain (which often freezes on contact) may accompany these waves. A cold wave that is quite common in South America is called the **pampero.**

FIGURE 8-10

Notes: 3. Other storm-like disturbances.

    a. Waterspouts—occur Gulf of Mexico and Western regions of the Atlantic and Pacific. Some are tornadoes, some similar but happen over water, usually fair weather, last a few minutes, few meters in height

    b. _____

    c. _____

    d. _____

REVIEWING

When we talk about reviewing, we have the following steps in mind:

1. Using your notes, list the main ideas of each section.

2. Without looking at your notes or text, see if you can remember how the author supported those ideas.

3. When you are finished, check your notes to see what you have left out.

Too often when we read and have the text before us, everything the author says seems perfectly clear. Problems only begin to arise when, without the text, we attempt to restate the author's main points and discover that we have not understood as much as we thought. Reviewing is an important step, one you should not forget. It is important because it can tell you what you really learned from your reading.

Reviewing after you have read a chapter and taken notes on it will help you decide what sections you need to reread; it will also tell you which of the author's ideas are really clear to you. You can then concentrate on those that have given you some difficulty in your review.

EXERCISE 5 **Directions:** The following sentence sums up the selection you just read and took notes on. Write down everything you remember about the support given for this idea. We have filled in the first blank for you.

There are four major storm-like disturbances

1. Waterspouts — Gulf of Mexico and Western regions of Atlantic and Pacific

_____

2. _____

3. _____

4. _____

Once you are finished, look back at the sample section, *Other Disturbances,* and see if you have left out any important information.

The following exercises contain different kinds of textbook selections. We present these selections to give you practice with the skills covered in this chapter and to introduce you to the variations that can exist in the organization of textbooks.

Reviewing 397

Whenever a selection differs markedly from the one we used as a sample throughout the chapter, we have indicated the difference at the end of the selection.

EXERCISE 6   **Directions:** The selection in Figures 8–11 to 8–16 has been taken from an economics textbook. Using the five steps we introduced, survey the entire selection. Then answer the questions that appear below.

After you have completed the survey and answered the questions, look carefully at the captions since it is here that we have indicated how this section differs from the one used throughout Chapter 8.

2

What is the outlook for the economy?

The older generation has not been a "do-nothing" group. Those who belong to what is now called the "older generation" lived through the Great Depression and World War II. Their outlook on life has been influenced by the human tragedy and economic waste which they witnessed. They did their utmost to insure that the present generation lived in a better world than theirs was when they were young. Much has been accomplished, but much remains to be done.

Poverty still exists in the United States. Since the early 1930's, programs of public welfare, aid to dependent children, old-age benefits, and unemployment insurance have helped millions of people. Private and public pension plans also have been developed for retired workers. Fewer people live in dire poverty, and each year more people attain middle-class standards of living. Nevertheless, an estimated 40 million Americans still live at a level which the Bureau of Labor Statistics terms below the "poverty line." There are millions of people, both urban and rural, white and nonwhite, who lack adequate food, clothing, housing, and education, and who do not receive the medical care they need. In an affluent society, the gap between "haves" and "have-nots" should be narrowed.

Solving the problem of poverty will involve increased production, more equitable allocation of goods and services, and a rethinking of government taxing and spending policies. Anyone able to work must be educated or trained so that his skills may be used to best advantage. Minimum wages and payments to those unable to work must be tied to the cost of living.

Many people cannot afford adequate health care. Medicare and government-sponsored health insurance have brought hospitalization, medical treatment, drugs, therapy, and home health care within the reach of most elderly citizens. Public welfare provides some hospital and medical benefits to others, while private hospitalization and medical insurance (Blue

HIGH UNEMPLOYMENT RATE FOR TEENAGERS
In recent years, the unemployment rates for sixteen-to nineteen-year-olds has remained the highest of any age group. The following table, based on statistics from the Labor Department, suggests the scope of this problem.

	males	females
1950	12.8	12.0
1955	11.7	10.6
1960	15.3	14.2
1965	14.3	16.5
1970	14.6	12.3
1973	14.0	10.7

It seems likely that the high unemployment rate for teenagers will continue. Thirty-four million new young workers looking for jobs will enter the labor market in the 1970's. While the proportion of teenagers will decline slightly from 8.7 to 8.3 per cent, their numbers will continue to rise. In 1960, there were 5.2 million teenagers in the work force. By 1968 there were 7.1 million, and by 1980 there will be 8.3 million.

The rise in the teenage population during the 1960's is attributed to the post-World War II "baby boom." Whereas the annual growth rate has been 3.9 per cent, it is expected to drop to 1.3 per cent by 1980. Thus the teen-age population will gradually decline.

Most teenagers are unemployed because they lack work experience and education, and because there are too few jobs available for unskilled workers.

FIGURE 8–11 From *The American Economy: Analysis, Issues, Principles,* by Roy J. Sampson, William P. Mortenson, and Ira Marienhoff, pp. 451–452 ©1975 by Houghton Mifflin Company. Used by permission.

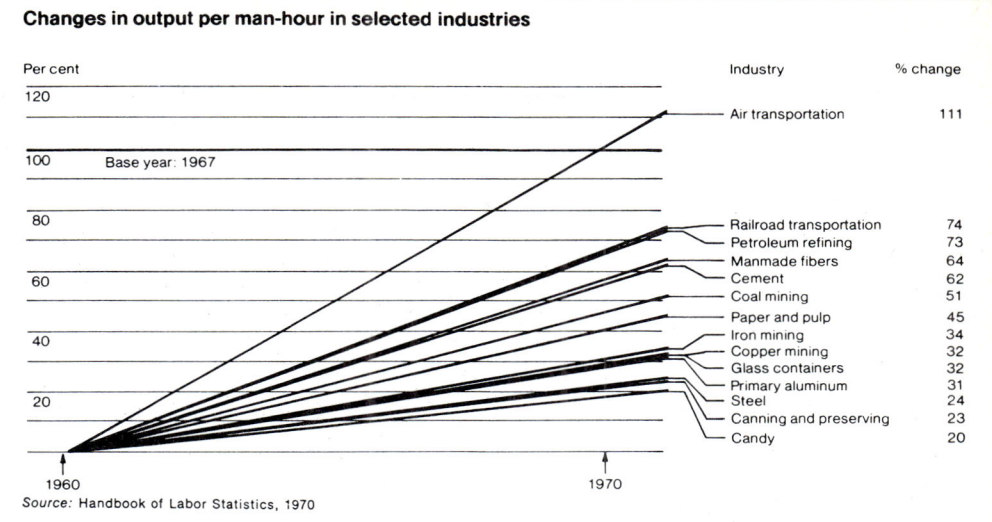

Cross, Blue Shield, and various other private plans) cover millions of Americans. These programs provide some form of medical or hospital insurance for about half of the population, but even for this half the amount may not be adequate to cover serious or prolonged illnesses.

Many dreaded diseases, such as polio, smallpox, diphtheria, typhus, scarlet fever, malaria, typhoid, and tuberculosis have almost been eliminated in this country and greatly reduced in other parts of the world. Even the "childhood diseases" of measles, mumps, and whooping cough no longer present serious problems, and ways of preventing or treating many other ailments have been much improved. The average life-expectancy of a newborn child in this country is more than half again that of a child born in India. Today an American is more likely to die of ailments associated with old age than with youth.

Social progress has lagged far behind technological advances. Achievements in science

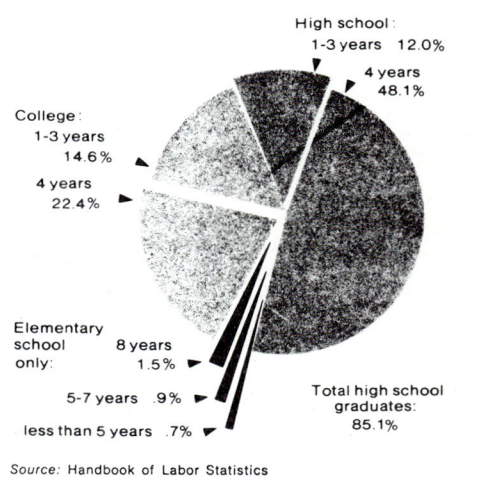

FIGURE 8–12 From *The American Economy: Analysis, Issues, Principles,* by Roy J. Sampson, William P. Mortenson, and Ira Marienhoff, p. 453, ©1975 by Houghton Mifflin Company. Used by permission.

and technology have been notable. In addition to advances in medical and biological sciences, the past half-century has witnessed the development of computers, transistors, lasers, synthetics, nuclear energy, jet-driven air transport, space navigation, and many other examples of applied technology which people take for granted. But during this period also were developed atomic-powered submarines, hydrogen bombs with multiple warheads, and long-range missiles for delivering the bombs.

Technological advances and better educated workers have greatly increased per capita output while reducing the average work week. On the other hand, greatly increased production has created shortages of some natural resources, and has contributed to the pollution of air, land, and water. The great migration from rural to urban areas has helped bring about traffic congestion, slums, and housing problems and high crime rates in the cities. Only a beginning has been made toward correcting many of these social ills.

High productivity and consumption create problems as well as affluence. Critics of the American way of life often point out that this country, with but 6 per cent of the world's population, uses about one-third of the world's resources. But they often neglect to point out that this country also accounts for one-third of the world's production (as measured by GNP's). It might be argued that instead of "exploiting the rest of the world" by its high level of consumption, the United States is being exploited by the rest of the world. The nation's long-sustained favorable balance of trade shows that more goods are shipped out of this country than into it. Americans are not living "high on the hog" at the expense of other nations. Quite the contrary. Peoples in many lands would live less well if the United States produced less.

Yet there is another side to this coin. In any discussion of the consumption of the world's resources, it should be recognized: (1) that some resources are not renewable; and (2) that as developing countries increase their production, each of them will increase its consumption of these resources. One might ask what would happen if people in many other lands began to produce and consume at the same rate as people in the United States. Would not greatly increased worldwide production and consumption lead to the depletion of important natural resources and create serious ecological problems?

Racism continues to plague American society. Racial discrimination and prejudice exist in this country, as they do in all countries having large racial minorities. This is one of mankind's most deeply-rooted and troublesome social problems. In this country, the older generation has broken down the principal legal barriers to integrated education and minority voting rights. Some progress has been made also with respect to housing and employment. But much more remains to be done.

In 1968, the President's National Advisory Commission on Civil Disorders (the Kerner Commission) issued a report about the racial crisis in American cities. Subsequently the Commission issued follow-ups of its original report confirming its earlier observations. The report concluded:

1. The nation is rapidly moving toward two increasingly separate Americas.

Within two decades, this division could be so deep that it would be almost impossible to unite: a white society principally located in suburbs, in smaller central cities, and in the peripheral parts of large central cities; and a Negro society largely concentrated within large central cities. . . .

2. In the long run, continuation and expansion of such a permanent division threatens us with two perils.

The first is the danger of sustained violence in our cities. The timing, scale, nature, and repercussions of such violence cannot be foreseen. But if it occurred, it would further destroy our ability to achieve the basic American promises of liberty, justice, and equality.

The second is the danger of a conclusive repu-

FIGURE 8–13 From *The American Economy: Analysis, Issues, Principles,* by Roy J. Sampson, William P. Mortenson, and Ira Marienhoff, p. 458, ©1975 by Houghton Mifflin Company. Used by permission.

diation of the traditional American ideal of individual dignity, freedom, and equality of opportunity. We will not be able to espouse these ideals meaningfully to the rest of the world, to ourselves, to our children. . . .

3. We cannot escape responsibility for choosing the future of our metropolitan areas and the human relations which develop within them. It is a responsibility so critical that even an unconscious choice to continue present policies has the gravest implications.[1]

The report made specific recommendations for arresting the process of alienation between the races. Most of their recommendations were economic in nature. They included:

Consolidating and concentrating employment efforts.
Opening the existing job structure.
Creating one million new jobs in the public sector in three years.
Creating one million new jobs in the private sector in three years.
Developing urban and rural poverty areas.
Encouraging business ownership in the ghetto.[2]

Methods of implementing each of these recommendations were also proposed.

The environment must be cleaned up. Pollution of air, water, and land has gotten out of hand in many parts of the country. The great majority of communities have not solved the problem of disposing of garbage, sewage, and solid waste materials. Rats thrive in dumps. Chimneys and cars spew noxious and dangerous fumes that threaten the lives of trees, plants, and humans. Unsightly billboards and junkyards and a growing amount of litter deface highways and recreational areas. Industries, government agencies, and individual citizens continue to pollute Planet Earth as though they believed living space to be unlimited and the environment indestructible. The long-range economic and social costs of this neglect may be catastrophic.

Cities are confronted with difficult environmental problems. In the large cities a great many people are crowded together, often in substandard housing. City sanitary services, geared to smaller communities, often are inadequate. There are, therefore, serious problems of pollution, traffic congestion, and fire hazards, as well as risks of epidemics—all aggravated, if not caused, by overcrowding. Schools find it difficult to meet the needs of all pupils, and there are high rates of crime and delinquency. Because high-income families and many businesses have moved to suburbs, city income from taxes is not sufficient to meet growing urban needs.

A leading newspaper provided a frightening account of what a breakdown of public services would mean to New York City. The sidewalks were strewn with rubbish because the men who operate the municipal sanitation service were on strike. They had asked for money which the city could not pay. Fires were breaking out in various parts of the city. Alarms sounded in the fire stations, but no apparatus moved because firemen were also on strike. Crimes and looting spread even more quickly than the fires. Where were the police? On strike. The article went on to point out that the only exaggeration in this description of a big city threatened with anarchy and collapse was the timing of the strikes. They did not occur simultaneously. Moreover, the article suggested that still other public services were similarly deteriorating in the nation's largest cities, including telephone, postal, and public transportation systems.

The situation in rural areas also needs to improve. Poor environment, poor people, and poor public services are problems in rural America as well as in the cities. There are rural slums and rural poor, less visible only because they are less concentrated. Many farmers do not have enough land for a profitable operation, and many rural workers lack the education and work skills needed to make a living in the cities.

[1] *Report of the National Advisory Commission on Civil Disorders* (Washington, D.C.: U.S. Government Printing Office, 1968), pp. 225–226.
[2] *Ibid.*, p. 233.

FIGURE 8–14 From *The American Economy: Analysis, Issues, Principles,* by Roy J. Sampson, William P. Mortenson, and Ira Marienhoff, p. 459, ©1975 by Houghton Mifflin Company. Used by permission.

Moving to the city is often a will-o'-the wisp.

Big farmers make a good living from their crops, livestock, and government subsidies, whereas small farmers and agricultural laborers make up the rural poor. Only recently have some farm workers been unionized. Unprofitable farming eventually should be eliminated (along with government agricultural subsidies), but the persons involved in such operations must be provided with opportunities for necessary retraining to earn a living in other occupations.

There is a danger that economic power will rest in too few hands. In any free enterprise system, the successful tend to drive out or to take over the less successful. Corporations grow larger and some of them become amazingly diversified. Economists and Presidents have warned against a "military-industrial complex" and the influence it exerts over government spending. Both the economy and the lives of most Americans may be increasingly controlled by the "Five Bigs" of contemporary society—Big Agriculture, Big Business, Big Government, Big Labor, and Big Military.

"Bigness" in itself is not necessarily either good or bad. In some operations, efficiency increases with size; in other operations, being small may be an advantage. Bigness should evolve in business when it is efficient, provided that it does not ignore and threaten the rights of the smaller business.

Big Labor implies that it needs bigness to bargain effectively with Big Business. Big Military seems necessary for the nation's security; Big Government to cope with the ever-growing problems and needs of society. At times consumers of goods and services may feel that they too need to organize and grow big!

Developing countries must be helped to raise their standard of living. For humanitarian as well as other reasons, the inhabitants of the world's less-developed nations must live better. World peace depends upon international good will and trust, and the hope for a better way of life. Anarchy may well characterize the behavior of people who know that others live well while they themselves starve. Military adventures may be used by dictators who seek to unify their underprivileged subjects by directing their hatred against a scapegoat.

As citizens of the world's richest nation, Americans necessarily must play a leading role in furthering international prosperity and peace. This goal, however, cannot be achieved by one nation. All the economically developed countries of the world must somehow be united in an effort for the common good of mankind. And the developing nations themselves must be encouraged to co-operate in the task of helping themselves.

This may be the next generation's most important and most difficult problem. The very future of civilization, and even of mankind itself, may depend upon how successfully the problem of helping developing nations to achieve economic maturity is solved.

Too rapid population growth is a major contributing factor to many difficult problems. Economic reasons help to explain why peoples in developing countries tend to have large fami-

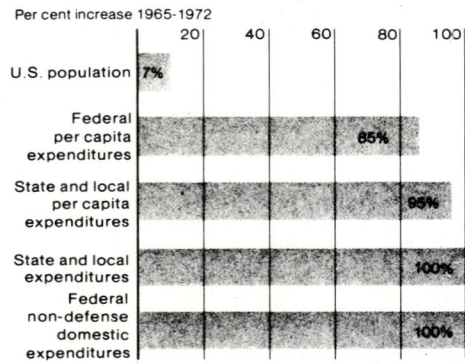

Public costs soar as U.S. population grows

Per cent increase 1965-1972

	20	40	60	80	100
U.S. population	7%				
Federal per capita expenditures				85%	
State and local per capita expenditures				95%	
State and local expenditures					100%
Federal non-defense domestic expenditures					100%

Source: Statistical Abstract

FIGURE 8–15 From *The American Economy: Analysis, Issues, Principles,* by Roy J. Sampson, William P. Mortenson, and Ira Marienhoff, p. 460, ©1975 by Houghton Mifflin Company. Used by permission.

lies. Many hands may be needed to do the work. Parents can look forward to a more secure old age if several grown-up children can look after them. And in earlier times, deaths among children were so high that comparatively few survived to maturity.

In developed countries social values and religious beliefs are factors that influence the size of families. But whatever the reasons, too rapid population growth carries important economic implications for any society, whether developing or developed.

Gloomy predictions have been made that the world's population may double three times within a century. Some experts predict that such population growth will exhaust food, fuel, and other resources. Optimistic statements have also been made that the world can easily support several times its present population. Which is right? The truth probably lies somewhere between these two extremes.

Certainly some habitable regions are thinly populated, and the underwater resources of the oceans have barely been tapped. Increased scientific knowledge, better production methods, and perhaps different consumption habits should make possible a much more efficient use of food and other resources.

Yet the earth's resources, including usable land, are limited. Already many parts of the world are so overpopulated (and underproductive) that hunger and want are the constant companions of millions of people. Most of these poor people cannot move to more hospitable lands. Some form of population control seems to be the best path towards a better way of life. This approach already is being encouraged in India. In the United States, a "thinly populated" country, some people feel that such problems as poverty, pollution, and urban congestion grow out of this country's "population explosion."

CHECK UP

1. Why is there poverty in this country? What can be done about it? About health care?

2. Why are high productivity and consumption a boon for a nation? What problems may they create?

3. What problems were identified in the Kerner Commission Report? What economic recommendations were made in it?

4. What causes contributed to the current problems of this country's big cities? To the pollution of the environment?

FIGURE 8–16 Many textbooks feature graphs and charts. You should look over all graphs and charts during your survey and pay attention to them when you read. They usually illustrate key points made in the text.

From *The American Economy: Analysis, Issues, Principles,* by Roy J. Sampson, William P. Mortenson, and Ira Marienhoff, p. 461, ©1975, by Houghton Mifflin Company. Used by permission.

Questions

1. From your survey how would you answer the question, what is the outlook for the economy?

_____

_____

_____

_____

2. What have critics of the American way of life pointed out about the population of this country and its use of the world's resources?

3. According to the chapter have racial problems in America been solved?

4. Do people living in rural areas share some of the problems of people living in the cities?

5. According to the chapter can we view the earth's resources as unlimited?

6. How does the author describe the relationship between technological advance and social progress?

7. In a free-enterprise system, what is the relationship between the successful and unsuccessful?

EXERCISE 7   **Directions:** Figures 8–17 to 8–18 consist of a short selection from a biology text. We have begun to mark it according to the system introduced on page 387. After you have read the selection, continue marking it where we have left off.

In case you have forgotten it, here is a list of the symbols we used to mark our sample selections.

    _____   Important information is underlined. Complete sentences are not underlined, only those necessary words and phrases.

    R, ex   When supporting sentences contain reasons or illustrations that are easily understood, we use the symbols R and ex. In this way we avoid excessive underlining, which can make the page too crowded. These symbols can also be combined with underlining to better express the relationship between ideas.

    ○   Key terms are circled.

    [ ]   Important passages too long to be underlined are put in brackets.

    ?   Question marks appear next to material that is unclear.

    *   We use asterisks to indicate that a portion of the text may reappear as a test question.

Parasitism

Since it <u>illustrates</u> the <u>extent to which organisms</u> may <u>evolve specializations</u>, parasitism, from an evolutionary point of view, is one of the most interesting interactions between species. <u>Most parasites</u> are *host-specific*; they <u>live on</u> only <u>one species of host</u> and <u>cannot survive on another</u>. Basically, we may <u>divide parasites into two classes</u>: *ectoparasites* (*ecto* outer), such as <u>fleas, lice</u> and many bacterial and fungal infections; and *endoparasites* (*endo* inner), such as <u>intestinal nematodes, flatworms</u>, and bacterial parasites. <u>Endoparasites</u> are usually the <u>most highly evolved</u>, since they <u>are adapted to a very specialized environment</u>. This kind of specialization may be somewhat disadvantageous, however, since it presents problems to the parasite species in getting from one host to another. As an evolutionary solution to this problem, many endoparasites are adapted to two hosts. One of the hosts is called the *primary host* and is the one in which the parasite matures and reproduces. The other is called a *vector* (or *secondary host*) and transports the immature stages of the parasite from one primary host to another. You may recall our discussion of the Myxoma virus in the Australian rabbit population. (See fig. 13.1 for a parasite life cycle.)

2

The human parasites that cause the extremely debilitating disease *schistosomiasis* illustrate the complexity a parasite's life cycle may reach. The disease is caused by at least three species of blood flukes of the family Schistosomatidae. *Schistosoma haematobium* is found in most of Egypt, in Iraq, parts of Israel and Jordan, and Portugal; *S. mansoni* is found in Egypt north of Cairo, in Africa, and in the West Indies and parts of South America (possibly as a result of the slave trade); and *S. japonicum* is found in Japan, Taiwan, China, the Philippines, and Malaysia. The life cycle of each species differs slightly, but in general, the adult schistosome lives in the blood vessels near the intestines. When ready to reproduce, it migrates to the intestines and lays its eggs in the capillaries of the intestinal wall. The eggs are deposited in such quantities that they cause the capillaries to

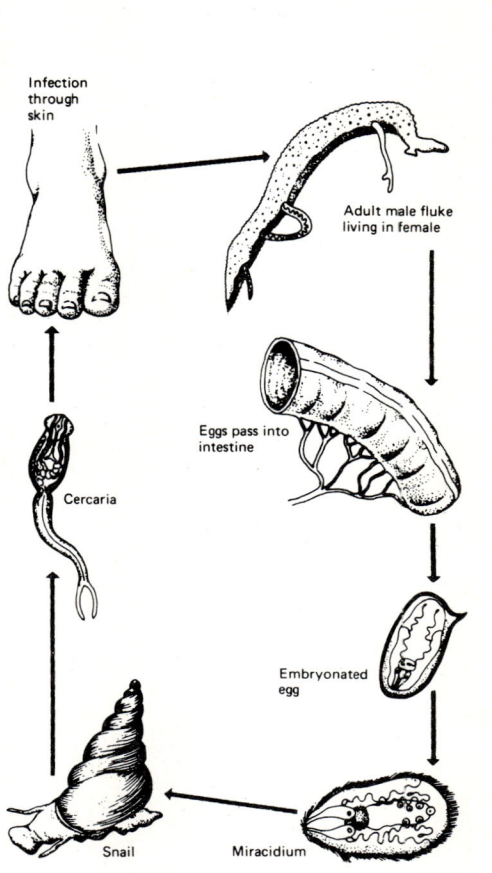

FIGURE 13.2 As described in the text, schistosomiasis involves a parasite with a very complex life cycle. The parasite reproduces sexually within the human, and again asexually within a secondary host, a snail. This results in a tremendous reproductive potential, which is required to insure that the species finds enough hosts to survive. The disease may be chronic, but it often leads to death. *(After Barnes.)*

FIGURE 8–17 From *Biology: Evolution and Adaptation to the Environment*, by Mahlon G. Kelly and John C. McGrath, p. 390, ©1975 by Houghton Mifflin Company. Used by permission. Figure 13.2 after Barnes: *Invertebrate Zoology*, third edition, ©1974 by W.B. Saunders Company, Philadelphia.

rupture and expel the eggs into the intestinal tract itself, whence they reach the outside of the body in the feces. If the feces are not diluted with water, the eggs will die in a few days. If the feces are diluted but the water is treated in a sewage plant, the cycle will also end. However, in many of the countries where the schistosome is common, human wastes are not well-treated or are used as fertilizers (particularly in rice paddies). If the eggs reach a body of water, whether it be a rice paddy, an irrigation ditch, or a river, they will hatch in a short time (from a few minutes to about sixteen hours). The tiny, ciliated larvae that hatch can live in the water for up to twenty-four hours. They swim about until they encounter a snail of a certain species. The larvae bore into the snail and make their way to a digestive gland in the innermost part of it. Once in the snail, they reproduce asexually and are capable of enormous population explosions. One species of snail harboring *S. mansoni* was observed to discharge an average of 3500 schistosomes daily, and the offspring of one larva was found to exceed 200,000. The immature schistosomes are discharged from the snails in "puffs," and the new individuals enter the water, where they can survive for two to three days. Should they come into contact with a human being while in the water, they attach themselves to the skin and digest their way into the blood stream. They are then carried through the heart, lungs, and liver to the intestines, where they remain to mature and begin the cycle anew (see fig. 13.2). While in the heart, lungs, and liver, they sometimes lay eggs which can accumulate and produce tumors. The disease, which is not itself usually fatal, frequently so weakens the human host that he may die of some other cause normally considered insignificant.

FIGURE 8–18 Biology texts frequently contain illustrations which outline the steps in a process. Attention should be paid to these illustrations since they usually help explain the key passages from the text.

From *Biology: Evolution and Adaptation to the Environment*, by Mahlon G. Kelly and John C. McGrath, p. 392, ©1975 by Houghton Mifflin Company. Used by permission.

EXERCISE 8 **Directions:** The sample selection in Figures 8–19 to 8–20 is titled "Government: Policeman and Partner of Business," and the entire chapter deals with the way government influences and aids business.

Read through the selection and note how we have marked the pages. When you are finished, complete the notes we have begun. Remember to **condense** and **summarize**, using letters, numbers and indentation to indicate relationships.

Protection through Enforcement of Contracts

The pattern of protection of people in business dealing has taken many other forms. Perhaps the most important to business have been the various laws that are designed to clarify various forms of contracts and make them enforceable. A moment's reflection will make us see that most of business—buying, selling, borrowing money, hiring people, or getting materials—depends upon a system of agreements and understandings. Contracts serve to make these arrangements clear and to spell out the obligations of each party. If contracts were not enforceable, business as we know it would not be possible. Modern business is therefore dependent upon laws designed to clarify the various forms of contracts and make them enforceable.

Matters of contract terms have traditionally been left to the states. Since state laws have tended to differ, one of the most important developments of recent years has been the enactment of uniform state laws following the Uniform Commercial Code devised by the American Bar Association in 1952 and approved by all states except Louisiana. This complex piece of legislation spells out in detail the nature and handling of contracts in business sales and purchases.

Safeguarding Workers

ex We also have laws that seek to protect workers by setting a floor under wages, limiting hours of work, and regulating conditions of work. One of the most far-reaching of these laws has been the federal law protecting the right of workers to join labor unions. This law has had the effect of encouraging and strengthening unions.

Protecting Consumers

Other laws and regulations are designed to protect buyers. Laws enforcing fair competition serve to some extent to protect the unwary buyer from being duped by the slick-talking seller. In recent years, the *ex* authority of the Pure Food and Drug Administration to protect consumers of foods and drugs has been greatly expanded. Other laws in the broad category of consumer protection include the many state and *ex* national laws regulating security transactions, which are designed to protect investors against unscrupulous sellers of securities and which will assure that all sellers give adequate and accurate information to buyers.

FIGURE 8–19 Reprinted with permission from *A Practical Introduction to Business* by Harold Koontz and Robert M. Fulmer (Homewood, Ill.: Richard D. Irwin, Inc., 1975 c.), p. 69.

Aids to Business

Still other patterns of government involvement have arisen from the various kinds of aid that government has extended to business. Long before 1900, these included tariff protection against foreign competition; the provision of patents, trademarks, and copyrights; the getting of standards of correct weight and measures; land grants to railroads to encourage their construction; services for farmers; and assistance in foreign trade.

The maintenance of a sound monetary system has been important to business, as have the laws governing the setting up of corporations and those protecting investors in case a business becomes bankrupt.

Perhaps the most direct and important of all government supports to business are the many programs of financial aid and support. These include: [the guaranteeing of bank loans for the purchase of homes and the financing of defense facilities; subsidies to American ocean shipping companies; the construction of highways and airports; direct subsidies to farmers; the establishment of the National Railroad Passenger Corporation, or Amtrak, to take the burden of intercity passenger service off the railroads; and the giving of grants to communities for improving public transportation.]

These programs, it should be pointed out, also result in government controls on business. Governments, whether national, state, or local, do not extend aid without attaching strings limiting the way it may be spent and who is entitled to it.

Government Ownership

Another pattern of government influence may be seen in the many instances of government ownership. To be sure, in most cases government enters into business when private businesses either will not or cannot respond to a public need. Whether it be the United States Postal Service, the Alaska Railroad, the Panama Canal, the Tennessee Valley Authority that provides for flood control and electric power generation, government-owned airports or highways, national parks and forests, or government-owned public housing, the effect is the same. These government enterprises all set rules for those who use their services, buy from them, or sell to them.

FIGURE 8–20 Headings explain what subject will be discussed in the paragraph or paragraphs that follow.

Reprinted with permission from *A Practical Introduction to Business* by Harold Koontz and Robert M. Fulmer (Homewood, Ill.: Richard D. Irwin, Inc., 1975 c.), p. 70.

Main Idea: Government has influence in business world.

1. laws to clarify and make contracts enforceable: uniform state laws following Uniform Commercial Code (American Bar Association, 1952) spell out nature and handling of contracts

2. laws protecting workers cover: (a) wages, (b) conditions, (c) hours, (d) federal law protecting right to join unions

3. laws to protect buyers: (a) fair competition, (b) authority of Pure Food and Drug, (c) state and national laws regulate security transactions

4. _____

_____

5. _____

_____

REVIEW TEST: CHAPTER 8

The following test will review everything covered in the preceding chapter:

1. In the correct order, list the four steps necessary to a complete survey.

   _____

   _____

   _____

   _____

2. What is the purpose of surveying?

   _____

3. Please fill in the blank in the following sentence:

   During your reading, it is important to keep a mental _____ of the entire chapter.

4. What is the basic purpose for marking your textbook?

   _____

   _____

5. Should you mark your textbook while you are completing your first reading or after you have finished? Please explain your answer.

   _____

   _____

6. Headings in a textbook can help you anticipate what the author is going to say. How else can they be of use?

   _____

   _____

7. What are the two key words to remember when taking notes?

8. Most authors will use illustrations, lists, or italics to indicate what?

9. What is the purpose of reviewing?

10. What are the steps in a review?

Chapter 9

Critical Reading

BRENDA	I think it is a good idea to stop the production of nuclear energy.
ELLEN	I'm surprised! Yesterday you told me exactly the opposite: you insisted that the world was not in danger from nuclear energy. What made you change your mind?
BRENDA	I read another pamphlet, and it gave me a real scare.
ELLEN	But why do you believe the second pamphlet more than the first one? Because you read it later?
BRENDA	I really don't know. I guess because this pamphlet just kept on emphasizing how much danger we are all in.
ELLEN	Come on! You have to read these things more critically.

If we assume Brenda possesses the reading skills introduced in the previous chapters, then we can safely assume that she understood what she read in the two pamphlets on nuclear energy. Yet, because the authors of the pamphlets obviously put forth different opinions about the merits of nuclear energy, she has a problem: she cannot decide which author she should believe. Unlike Ellen, who has developed the ability to evaluate what she reads, Brenda has not mastered enough *critical reading skills* to do so.

Critical reading skills are extremely important since much reading matter, particularly newspapers, magazines, and advertisements, attempts to influence your thinking and behavior. In general, there is nothing wrong with this; it is only wrong if you allow yourself to be unknowingly influenced, if you passively absorb other people's opinions without trying to find out if they are truly sound or not.

Up to this point in the text, we have concentrated largely on reading in order to understand an author's ideas. This is an important step by itself. And it is also a good introduction to critical reading since you can't evaluate how ideas are presented until you know what they are. In this chapter we ask you to use your old skills and learn some new ones as we introduce several of the basic skills necessary to critical reading.

FACTS AND OPINIONS

To different degrees, much of what we read is composed of both *facts* and *opinions*. The two usually go together. Facts are statements about people or things that describe their characteristics or their behavior. We consider a statement to be a fact only when its truth is well-known or can be established by direct observation or recourse to other sources such as books and magazines, witnesses, or experts. The following sentences are examples of facts:

> In 1981 the largest hotel in Kansas City, the Hyatt Regency, contained an atrium that was four stories high and was crossed by several bridge-like skywalks. On July 17, 1981, two of these skywalks crashed down during a party that was attended by more than one thousand guests. As a result of the collapse, 114 people died, and more than 200 were injured.

Each of the above sentences records several facts since their truth can be established by consulting newspapers and magazines, or actual witnesses to the accident.

Opinions, in contrast, express an author's feelings, beliefs or judgments about a particular topic. Representing a personal point of view, they are not facts themselves and, therefore, cannot be labeled true or false. We can, however, talk about opinions as *justified* or not. The following example explains what we mean:

> The hotel catastrophe in Kansas City just shows how incompetent most architects and engineers are. They shouldn't be allowed to design anything unusual since they cannot predict the consequences of what they are doing.

In response to the Hyatt Regency disaster in Kansas City, the author of the above sentences has developed some strong opinions. Such definite opinions, however, raise two important questions: (1) did the author attempt to justify those opinions with supporting facts? (2) should you consider making these opinions your own? In the present case, the answer to both questions is no. The paragraph contains only opinions except for the brief reference to the catastrophe having taken place in Kansas City which, taken by itself, is not sufficient to condemn architects and engineers in general. To be taken seriously, opinions must be supported by relevant facts. A more successful attempt to use facts in support of an opinion appears in the following paragraph:

> The National Bureau of Standards investigated the Hyatt Regency acccident in Kansas City. It was discovered that the original design of the skywalks had been changed at a later date. As a consequence the loads these structures could carry was greatly reduced. A second study by the International Conference of Building Officials concluded that the Kansas City building inspection procedures at the time of construction revealed various shortcomings. This suggests that the design of buildings, especially if they incorporate novel features and are used by large crowds, should be carefully evaluated by independent agencies with adequate resources and procedures.

The author does not give an opinion until the last sentence where a suggestion is made for future construction of buildings like the Hyatt Regency. Unlike the previous example, the author does not simply present an opinion as if that were enough proof in itself. The first three sentences in the second example all contain facts used to persuade you that the final opinion is sound.

Note, too, that the author helps you distinguish between fact and opinion by starting the last sentence with the words "This suggests..." When you read you should always be on the lookout for words that signal opinions. The following are just a few of the most important ones: possibly, conceivably, perhaps, appears, seems, suggests, believes, thinks, and feels.

The following exercises will give you more practice distinguishing facts from opinions.

EXERCISE 1 **Practice Exercise:** Read each of the sentences carefully. Then label them *F* for fact, *O* for opinion, or *B* if the sentence contains both.

1. Measles has an incubation period of seven to fourteen days.
   ___F___

Explanation: We labeled this sentence *F* because the statement can be checked easily by referring to a medical doctor or textbook.

Do the rest of the exercises in the same manner.

1. The Supreme Court should reintroduce prayer into the schools.

   _____

2. Within ten years, computers are going to replace teachers.

   _____

3. From full moon to full moon, the lunar cycle is about 29.5 days.

   _____

4. Sylvester Stallone has made millions of dollars on *Rocky*, *Rocky II*, and *Rocky III*; can *Rocky IV* be far behind?

   _____

5. The battle of the Alamo, where frontier hero Davy Crockett died, took place on February 23, 1836.

   _____

6. Soap operas are pure junk.

   _____

7. An extraordinary and imaginative film, Steven Spielberg's *E.T.* earned several million dollars in the first weekend of its American debut.

   _____

8. Diet pills called "starch blockers" were recalled by the Food and Drug Administration for further testing; that probably means they were a health hazard.

   _____

Facts and Opinions 417

9. Some experts suspect that the universe may be only half as large and half as old as is generally believed.

   _____

10. The "local color" movement in American literature began after the Civil War and continued right up until the turn of the century.

    _____

EXERCISE 2

Practice Exercise: Read through the following paragraphs consisting of numbered sentences. After you have finished, we ask you to identify each sentence in the paragraph according to whether it is fact, opinion, or a mixture of both. Again, you can use the labels *F, O,* or *B*.

1. [1] Worse than the common cold, backaches hinder, disable, even cripple millions of people every year. [2] Backache is no respecter of age, and in recent years, the teenage athlete Tracy Austin and the Supreme Court Justice William H. Rehnquist have been treated for back troubles. [3] Although there are drugs to relieve the pain of backache, they are not a cure; they simply relieve the symptoms. [4] Every year in the hope of the cure, around 200,000 people undergo back surgery. [5] But in 20 percent of all cases, surgery fails completely, and patients are left with their symptoms intact.

   (1) __B__   (2) __F__   (3) __F__   (4) __F__   (5) __F__

Explanation: Every sentence is labeled according to whether it contains a fact, opinion, or mixture of both. Sentence 1, for example, is labeled *B* because it begins with an opinion—not everyone would consider the backache worse than the cold—and ends with a fact—you can check medical records to see if millions of people do indeed suffer.

Do the rest of the exercises in the same manner.

1. [1] Cookbooks produced in America during the early forties and fifties show a varied collection of recipes rich in butter, milk, and eggs. [2] But such cookbooks are clearly a thing of the past since many Americans have become aware of the need to reduce the large amounts of fat they consume. [3] According to the recent study produced by the American

Heart Association, there is much evidence tying fatty foods to diseases of the heart like arteriosclerosis.* [4] Saturated fats raise the level of cholesterol in the blood, and cholesterol in turn directly contributes to hardening of the arteries. [5] Aware of the changing times, even such formerly staunch supporters of cream and butter like Craig Claiborne and Julia Child have begun to publish recipes that avoid both.

(1) _____ (2) _____ (3) _____ (4) _____ (5) _____

2. [1] There is no sport that can rival the game of soccer. [2] Certainly America's tedious national pastime, baseball, cannot compare with it. [3] Even on its best days, baseball lacks the speed and grace of soccer. [4] Every four years, teams from all over the world compete for the world cup in soccer. [5] It is time for America to join the rest of the developed nations, like England, France, West Germany, and Italy, in the competition for the World Cup. [6] That would be a truly international game of champions unlike the "World" Series, which contains only American teams.

(1) _____ (2) _____ (3) _____ (4) _____ (5) _____

3. [1] Orcas, or "killer whales" as they are more commonly known, are extraordinary creatures. [2] Inhabitants of the cold seas, they are huge, black and white mammals with enormous, jagged teeth that make them highly successful predators. [3] In turn, none of the other ocean creatures are capable of preying on them. [4] Some years ago, *Orca, the Killer Whale*, was a financially successful movie starring Richard Harris. [5] But if the film is remembered at all, it is not because of Harris and his whale companion, rather the film has probably gone down in history as the movie in which Bo Derek made her screen debut.

(1) _____ (2) _____ (3) _____ (4) _____ (5) _____

4. [1] The atmosphere of Venus is approximately ninety times greater than Earth's. [2] Temperatures near the planet's surface are as high as 900 degrees Fahrenheit. [3] The planet nearest Earth, Venus, is shrouded in clouds and is, there-

---

*arteriosclerosis: more commonly known as hardening of the arteries, which occurs when walls of the arteries begin to thicken

Orcas, or "killer whales," are highly successful predators.

fore, not highly visible. [4] Several attempts, however, have been made to explore the planet's surface, particularly in the Soviet Union. [5] The Soviets have landed several robot crafts on Venus, and at least one has been able to collect soil samples and transmit color pictures.

(1) _____   (2) _____   (3) _____   (4) _____   (5) _____

5. [1] In the annals of public health, what some critics now call the "swine flu affair" may go down as one of the federal government's greatest disasters. [2] In 1976, federal health authorities made a concentrated effort to immunize the public against an influenza epidemic they knew might never arrive. [3] The concern was great because the so-called *swine flu* virus seemed to resemble a virus believed to have caused a deadly outbreak of flu in 1918. [4] After the government spent over $100 million, the flu never came. [5] But several people who had the shot to prevent flu came down with a rare illness called the *Guillain-Barré syndrome*. [6] The disease appeared to be linked to some part of the immuni-

zation experience, and more than $9 million in damages were paid to those who contracted the paralytic disease. [7] As a result of the swine flu affair, two high-ranking federal officers were dismissed from their posts.

(1) _____ (2) _____ (3) _____ (4) _____ (5) _____

(6) _____ (7) _____

FAULTY ARGUMENTS OR FALLACIES

Look again at the passage (p. 414) used in the previous section, in which the author tries to convince readers that most architects and engineers are incompetent. The attempt failed because only one instance of bad work by such professionals was mentioned; that was certainly not enough evidence to prove the author's point. Another example of a similarly unsuccessful attempt is illustrated in the following sentences:

> This newspaper alone describes three separate cases of welfare fraud. Government welfare is a rip-off of the tax-paying public.

There is no way in which three, or even thirty, cases of individual fraud can prove anything about the entire system of public welfare. Many more well-documented examples would be needed to make this conclusion at all credible. Attempts of this kind, in which an insufficient number of facts are used to arrive at a more general conclusion or opinion, occur so frequently that they have been given a special name: they are called *hasty generalizations*. Although it is important, as we pointed out in Chapter 2, to make general statements based on specific facts, such judgments should be made with care. **They should depend on a large body of concrete evidence, and if they do not, you may want to think twice about their value.**

In addition, be wary about generalizations using words such as *always, never,* and *all.* They are particularly questionable because very few generalizations hold true all of the time. While it is certainly correct to state that all human beings possess a brain, should you just as readily state the following?

> At least three quarters of my married friends are divorced or separated; no marriage can survive these days.

While it might be appropriate, based on the evidence, to say that divorce is a growing problem in American society, it is hardly justifiable to insist that *every* marriage is doomed to fail.

Hasty generalizations represent a specific type of poor or faulty judgment; that is, they represent an argument that fails because it uses irrelevant or insufficient information to make a point. Such arguments are also referred to as *fallacies*. The ability to discover fallacies is important to critical reading.

Along with hasty generalizations, there are numerous other types of faulty arguments or fallacies, but we cannot deal with all of them here. Instead, we will concentrate in the following discussion on the two that occur most frequently, the *attack on the person* and the *appeal to the emotions*.

An attack on the person occurs when someone does not give reasons for disagreeing with an opinion or idea, but instead attacks the life, career, or background of the person speaking or writing. The following is an example:

> Although Professor X insisted during a hearing that defense spending by the government must be cut, I cannot take seriously the proposals of someone who is an acknowledged draft dodger.

The issue at hand is a cut in defense spending. Yet the author does not deal with that question at all, but instead attacks the person proposing the cut. However, the professor's military career is not relevant to defense spending, which is the subject that should be criticized.

Occasionally, there are cases where a person and a position are so closely linked that an attack on one does, indeed, implicate the other. Take, for example, the following memorandum:

> Ms. Miller, I was very impressed with your suggestion for revising our bookkeeping procedures. But it has been brought to my attention that your past record contains two convictions for embezzlement. I am afraid that must influence my final decision.

In this example, it makes sense to challenge Ms. Miller's proposal on the basis of her past conduct although the proposal should be evaluated on its own merits before being completely discounted.

An appeal to the emotions is a fallacy that occurs when the speaker or writer tries to persuade by playing on the audience's emotions instead of by supplying the audience with reasons. Imagine reading the following speech for the defense:

The defendant is accused of serving liquor to those under the age of eighteen, thereby contributing to the delinquency of minors. Yet this is a man with two children of his own, a family man who has worked hard for over twenty years to earn a decent living. Only by the sweat of his brow has he managed to put enough bread on the table to feed those hungry mouths.

This is a case where the defense should either convince the jury that the accused is not guilty or else explain the circumstances of the crime. The man serving liquor, for example, may not have known the age of the people drinking. But no argument or explanation of this type is used; instead there is an attempt to arouse pity by evoking the image of a man who has struggled to make a living for his children. The intention is to stir up enough emotion so that the members of the jury do not think clearly about the crime itself.

Certainly, appeals to the emotions are not restricted to jury trials. They occur any time that someone thinks emotion might be more effective than fact. In 1982, for example, when Argentina invaded the Falkland Islands, there were many speeches like the following:

> This is an open act of vicious aggression on the part of Argentinian military forces, one that will not be tolerated by a people whose history testifies to England's honor and greatness. We are ready to answer force with force, and we will not flinch from once again taking up arms in the name of freedom.

Here the author might have justified the need for war by arguing that British residents of the islands were not safe under Argentinian rule. This at least would have been an attempt to give reasons for the assertion that war was necessary. There is, however, no suggestion of a reason in this brief illustration: the entire emphasis of the paragraph is the arousal of strong patriotic emotions.

The following exercises will give you more practice analyzing these basic errors in reasoning.

EXERCISE 3

Practice Exercise: Read each paragraph; then decide if it contains an error in reasoning. If it does, circle the letter of the error in the paragraph.

1. The name of the poet Ezra Pound has again been suggested as a candidate for a posthumous literary award. The suggestion has caused an uproar among many members of the

literary community, and there are those who insist that Pound's name be withdrawn because of his treasonous behavior during World War II when he made broadcasts for the Fascists.*

(a) hasty generalizations
(b) attack on the person *[circled]*
(c) appeal to the emotions
(d) no error

Explanation: As the excerpt makes clear, this is an award for literary ability. Therefore, an attempt to deny it would have to address the question of Pound's skill as a poet. To attack instead his political past is to be guilty of an error in reasoning, in this case, the attack on the person.

Do the rest of the exercises in the same manner.

1. There have been many complaints about cuts in social services. It has been pointed out that the cuts were both unnecessary and unfair. That is, however, quite untrue. If money has been withdrawn, it has been withdrawn with good reason. This is a country built on the self-reliance of the individual, and the pioneer spirit of the past was not fueled by money from the government. That spirit must live again.

   (a) hasty generalization
   (b) attack on the person
   (c) appeal to the emotions
   (d) no error

2. The recent exhibit of Pablo Picasso's paintings should never have taken place. This is a man who was notorious for his affairs with many different women, and his personal life revealed a mean and grasping spirit. Yet we honored this same man in one of our country's finest museums. That exhibit should have been closed the day it opened.

   (a) hasty generalization
   (b) attack on the person
   (c) appeal to the emotions
   (d) no error

*Fascists: Italians who sided with Hitler in W.W.II.

3. A costly and complicated federal program, the distribution of food stamps has been severely criticized in the past as too expensive and too inefficient. Recently, food stamp fraud has been documented in at least four different states in the United States. Given the evidence of fraud, where the individuals using food stamps were far from needy, it is a good idea to consider limiting, perhaps even abolishing, the program.

   (a) hasty generalization
   (b) attack on the person
   (c) appeal to the emotions
   (d) no error

4. Edwin Wilson and Frank Terpil, two ex-agents of the Central Intelligence Agency, have been proven to be training terrorists in the service of the Libyan government. Dangerous and dishonest men, they are using their knowledge of CIA techniques to further the interests of a government that has expressed hostility toward the United States. They prove, conclusively, that the agents of the CIA bear more watching than the spies and criminals they presume to investigate.

   (a) hasty generalization
   (b) attack on the person
   (c) appeal to the emotions
   (d) no error

5. When, in 1980, Islamic fundamentalists known as the Shiite Muslims overthrew the Shah of Iran, they complained bitterly of persecution by the Shah. Angry at the United States for its support of the ex-leader they publicly recounted the many abuses suffered during the Shah's reign. Unfortunately, past oppression has not encouraged charity and humanity in the fundamentalists. They too have begun to persecute those less powerful, and the Bahais, members of an Islamic sect more liberal than the Shiite Muslims, have been driven from their homes and forced to hide in the mountains of Iran. At least 100 Bahai leaders have been killed, and 200 members are reported missing.

   (a) hasty generalization
   (b) attack on the person
   (c) appeal to the emotions
   (d) no error

CONNOTATIONS OF WORDS

People who write do so with purpose or intention; they have a reason for using the printed page. Frequently their reason is to persuade readers that they should adopt a particular opinion or share certain ideas. Much of the time, as you have already learned, writers provide facts to support opinions or ideas. However, there are more subtle techniques that can be used to persuade an audience. Becoming aware of these techniques will enhance your critical reading skills; thus the remainder of this chapter will introduce some of the most important ones.

As you probably know, words convey information. But they don't all do it in the same way. Some words simply refer to facts or ideas. They suggest no value judgments, and they do not arouse emotions on the part of the reader, either positively or negatively. Other words, however, do more: they suggest certain attitudes or trigger specific associations and feelings, thus affecting in some way the reader's reactions.

Take, for example, the words *rye bread*. For most people, they simply stand for bread made from a specific type of grain. For immigrants from certain parts of Europe, too, the words have precisely this meaning. But, in addition, they can also suggest very specific associations: they can create strong memories of the country left behind or trigger feelings of homesickness, since good rye bread, a staple of some European diets, is not readily available in the United States. We can say, then, that for those people, the words *rye bread* have specific *connotations*.

Authors are aware of the connotations associated with certain words, especially if they know their audience well, and they use them quite deliberately to make their writing persuasive or convincing. In the previous section, highly connotative language was always used when writers or speakers tried to appeal to emotions in order to make their ideas acceptable and believable. **Thus it is not always what we say but *how* we say it that influences people.** Assume, for example, that you want to encourage a friend to change an opinion. Your choice of words will be important to your success. Compare the following approaches, noting the positive and negative connotations of the words used.

a. I know how stubborn you are, but in this case you've got to get that idea out of your thick skull.

b. I know how firm of purpose you are, but in this case you have to modify your opinion.

Chances of success with sentence *a* are not good. Many people would react angrily to being told they are stubborn and have a thick skull. Sentence *b*, in contrast, contains words with favorable associations. It is considered good to be firm of purpose, and the word *modify* does not have to indicate a drastic change. This second approach could meet with success.

Here is another example that will illustrate the use of connotative language. Imagine two different descriptions of the same book, one from a book review meant to encourage purchase, the other from a review meant to discourage potential readers:

a. *The White Hotel* by D. M. Thomas is a highly imaginative novel; reading it, I entered into a dream world, filled with the most extraordinary and unique fantasies.

b. *The White Hotel* by D. M. Thomas is a highly unrealistic novel, filled with the most extraordinary and eccentric fantasies. Reading it, I felt as if I were having a weird nightmare.

In the first excerpt, phrases like *highly imaginative* and *unique fantasies* are used because they have positive associations that might persuade someone to buy the book. In the second excerpt, the author has a very different intention in mind and employs, therefore, phrases like *highly unrealistic* and *eccentric fantasies* because they usually have negative connotations.

When you read, you would do well to think about the connotations of the words used. If you do, you will be less likely to be influenced without being aware of it.

As we already indicated, some words do not possess connotations. The words *of, the, where, table,* and *curtains,* for example, seldom arouse emotions of any kind. They make connections, show relationships, and name objects. They do not represent ideas, and they evoke neither positive nor negative responses. We say, then, that these words have only *denotations:* **these are explicit definitions that can be found in any dictionary.** All words have denotations, but they do not necessarily have connotations.

Moreover, the connotations of words may be *personal* as well as collective. By personal we mean that they may be based on individual experience. Take, as an example, the word *dentist.* For people who have had many unpleasant experiences visiting the dentist, this word has strong negative connotations, and they would easily understand the following sentence: "It was worse than a day at the dentist's." But for those who have never spent time having dental work done, the sentence would not make much sense. For them, the word *dentist* arouses no emotional response at all.

In general, when you read, an author will draw on words with connotations shared by the intended audience. Therefore, be wary of assuming that your personal reactions to words are the ones the author has in mind. Instead, assume that he or she is drawing on a more general rather than a strictly individual experience.

EXERCISE 4

Practice Exercise: In each exercise, there are three sentences that say almost the same thing. Choose the sentence that attempts to eliminate almost all connotations.

1. (a) He weighs 120 pounds and he's 6 feet tall.

   (b) He's skinny.

   (c) He's slender.

Explanation: We chose sentence *a*. That is the only sentence where the words do not evoke strong positive or negative connotations. In contrast *skinny* has negative connotations whereas *slender* has positive ones.

Do the rest of the exercises in the same manner.

1. (a) She wore a colorful sweater.

   (b) She wore a red and green turtleneck.

   (c) She wore a flashy sweater.

2. (a) He is so blunt.

   (b) No one has ever caught him in a lie.

   (c) He has always been very honest.

3. (a) She is a liar.

   (b) She has a great imagination.

   (c) She failed the lie detector test.

4. (a) She is happy.

   (b) She laughs a lot.

   (c) She is silly.

5. (a) The car is an antique.

   (b) The car was bought in 1948.

   (c) The car is old.

EXERCISE 5

Practice Exercise: In each sentence, choose the word with either a neutral or positive connotation.

1. Your hair is quite <u>fine</u>/thin.

Explanation: We have underlined *fine,* because most people react positively to being told they have *fine* hair, but they react negatively if their hair is labeled *thin.*

Do the rest of the exercises in the same manner.

1. He is an enthusiastic/fanatical believer.
2. "I won't," she answered/retorted.
3. You're a slow/thorough reader.
4. That plan is foolhardy/daring.
5. I think she's a drudge/hard worker.
6. What a weird/unique idea.
7. The room is a little damp/clammy.
8. The vase is very brittle/fragile.
9. She is very ambitious/pushy.
10. He is thrifty/stingy.

TONE AND MOOD

Paying attention to the connotations of words is particularly important in helping you understand what is not explicitly stated in the text. For example, it can help you understand the author's use of *tone* and *mood,* two very important aspects of writing that are normally implied rather than stated. To begin with, *tone* is like tone of voice; it **reflects the attitude the author takes toward the material.** Tone can be light-hearted or angry, optimistic or pessimistic.

Identifying the author's tone can tell you much about the author's purpose. If the tone is angry or critical, the author may be attempting to discourage you about a particular person or idea. In contrast, a happy or approving tone may reflect the desire to encourage support or belief for a cause or individual. The following paragraphs will illustrate what we mean:

a. Senator X is everything a statesperson should be. An eloquent speaker, she has the ability to choose the right word at the right moment. Filled with determination as she is, she will undoubtedly be elected governor.

b. Senator X is a true politician. A smooth talker, she knows just what to say and when to say it. Devoured by ambition as she is, she undoubtedly will be elected governor.

In paragraph *a* the author obviously takes an approving tone toward the subject of Senator X, and the words *statesperson, eloquent,* and *determination* are meant to have a favorable effect on the reader as well, persuading him or her to support the senator. In contrast, paragraph *b* employs the words *politician, smooth talker,* and *devoured by ambition* to produce a critical or pessimistic tone, one clearly meant to diminish voter support.

When an author openly takes a stance in writing, implying a particular attitude through the creation of tone, we call it *subjective reporting*. In this type of writing, the author suggests a personal involvement, using language that appears to reflect his or her attitude. However, this is not always the case: authors do not always assume a particular tone. Instead they may attempt to eradicate all evidence of a personal opinion. This is called *objective reporting*. The difference between these two types of reports will become clearer if you compare a front-page news article with an editorial in your local newspaper. The purpose of the news article is to inform, and every attempt is made to eliminate evidence of authorial tone in contrast to the editorial where the author's point of view is clearly evident.

In general, objective reports employ less connotative language than reports that are subjective. But they still rely on words with connotations to communicate something about the mood or feeling surrounding the topic under discussion. We can take the following paragraph as an example:

Members of the union leadership met yesterday with management to debate what they called the "union-busting tactics" of their employers. When a representative of management spoke, she was greeted with a prolonged silence that ended in catcalls and whistles on the part of the workers. Clearly the audience was not pleased with her proposals. When the meeting ended, union and management left together in stony silence.

We might say that the mood of this meeting, as described by the writer, is ominous or angry. Phrases such as *catcalls* and *stony silence* indicate an unpleasant, bitter atmosphere although this is nowhere explicitly stated. The author employs these connotative words to create the appropriate mood of the meeting; however, they are not an indication of personal attitude. We do not know how the author feels about the subject.

When you read, you should always be alert for the way in which an author uses connotative language to convey tone or mood since both provide vital information. **Tone can provide a clue to the author's purpose whereas mood can tell you something about the circumstances surrounding the topic.**

EXERCISE 6

Practice Exercise: Decide if the author employs a certain tone or conveys a particular mood. Then label the paragraph *S* for a subjective report or *O* for an objective report.

1. Americans have always lusted for heroes, and lacking them, we have been driven to invent them. Such was certainly the case with the man born Joel Hagglund but christened Joe Hill. A poet and songwriter, Hill's name first came to the public's attention when he wrote a series of songs that were adopted by the early American labor movement. His name, however, only became a household word when he was arrested for armed robbery and murder. According to the legend, Hill never committed the murder, and he was executed in an attempt to destroy the labor movement. Although it is true that Hill was tried and convicted on circumstantial evidence, it is equally true that his story contained numerous contradictions and loopholes. At his best, he was a man unfairly tried and convicted; at his worst he was a criminal who boldly proclaimed himself innocent. But in neither case was he a legendary hero, and the tendency to eulogize him is a misguided attempt to create a hero where none existed.

   <u> S </u>

Tone and Mood 431

Explanation: The author of the paragraph employs a skeptical tone. The use of the plural pronoun *we*, along with highly connotative language, such as *lusted* and *misguided attempt* tells you this is an example of subjective reporting.

Do the rest of the exercises in the same manner.

1. At the present time cognitive* psychology offers the promise of a scientific breakthrough. While, for more than half a century, it has been unfashionable to theorize about the inner workings of the mind, more and more attention is being paid to the work of cognitive scientists who hold that the functions of the brain, and ultimately the human mind, can be scientifically investigated. Despite the fact that much research still needs to be done, scientists have already begun to explore the complexities of memory and speech acquisition. By all accounts, it appears that the most sophisticated modern computer is no match for the intricacies of human thinking. Experiments have shown, for example, that even very small children can perceive complicated patterns and anticipate cause-and-effect relationships.

   _____

2. Fifty years ago, parents could lean over the back fence and chat companionably with other adults who had the same family problems. Today things have changed, and we live in a highly urbanized society where it becomes harder and harder to meet our neighbors. Many single parents feel particularly isolated in their home; they lack the easy camaraderie* an earlier generation enjoyed. As a result many have turned to public and private support groups where they can talk over problems and exchange information. Parents who feel unable or unwilling to cope by themselves can find a wide variety of services in these parent centers, including health information, crisis intervention, family counseling, and financial advice. For a long time it has been assumed that only children needed the support of their peers. As a result, the emphasis has been on the creation of counseling centers and meeting places for young people. It's about time we thought of parents as well.

   *cognitive: having to do with thinking, reasoning, and knowing
   *camaraderie: friendship, companionship

They too need the guidance and friendship available in a peer group.

———

3. Perhaps the most irritating thing about soap operas is their insistent distortion of reality. Were programs like "Guiding Light," "Search for Tomorrow," or "General Hospital" used to introduce the earth to the population of another planet, those extraterrestrial* beings would be convinced that two out of every four people on earth are doctors, who almost never spend any time in the operating room, preferring instead the intimacies of the hospital lounge where they can continue romantic conversations uninterrupted. In the same vein, no one on a soap ever has a simple problem, like a sick relative or a tough job. Somehow the Mafia is always involved, or if not the Mafia, then some bizarre members of a Satanic cult, determined to destroy an entire neighborhood in suburbia. Real life is tough enough. Why do they have to make everything more complicated?

———

4. William Howard Taft was the twenty-seventh president of the United States, and, by all accounts, his presidency was undistinguished. A huge bear of a man, Taft did not inspire confidence; even his own mother did not support his candidacy. Instead she publicly maintained that the White House would be a mistake for her son's career. Taft himself is said to have claimed that any party nominating him would make a "great mistake." Once in office, Taft proved to be as incompetent as he had predicted, and he managed to alienate an old friend and mentor, Theodore Roosevelt. Roosevelt was so outraged at Taft's conservation policy, he decided to challenge his one-time friend when time for re-election came. Although Roosevelt did not win, he managed to split the Republican party sufficiently so that Woodrow Wilson was elected. Taft was not surprised at his loss, and he accepted defeat graciously.

———

*extraterrestrial: beyond earth

Tone and Mood   433

William Howard Taft, the twenty-seventh president of the United States, failed to inspire confidence.

5. The Japanese have accustomed themselves to the presence of robots in the work place. More than two-thirds of all industrial robots, in fact, are found in Japan. Although robots are not capable of assembling finished products, they can do the many simpler tasks that lead up to that stage, and they have proven to be a boon to their employers, increasing worker productivity by a substantial amount. For their part Japanese workers are relaxed about the rise in the robot population. Most contracts guarantee the average worker employment until the age of fifty-five. In addition, the majority of workers participate in some kind of profit-sharing plan, with the result that robot productivity only increases the worker's paycheck.

EXERCISE 7   **Practice Exercise:** Read each paragraph carefully, and decide which words help create the dominant tone or mood. Then fill in the blanks with words that maintain the correct tone or mood.

1. Haiti is a small Caribbean country of astonishing beauty, but it is also a land of heartbreaking poverty. Unemployment plagues more than 50 percent of the population, and the annual income is pitifully low, less than $300 per year. It is no wonder, then, that many Haitians want to leave their island home. A large number want to escape to America, but unfortunately America does not welcome them. According to officials, economic devastation does not entitle Haitians to political asylum in the United States. As a result, many who enter this country illegally are returned to their homeland to face the consequences. Although no one is really sure what those consequences are, it is clear that the government of Haiti is not pleased with those who have tried to flee its shores, and those returned may face ___severe___ reprisals. If Haitian refugees are not allowed political asylum in this country, they will be returned to a life of ___misery___ and ___fear___.

Explanation: The tone of the paragraph is sympathetic to the plight of the Haitians. The words *plagued* and *heartbreaking* indicate a sympathetic tone. In addition, the author clearly suggests that political asylum for the Haitians should be considered. Used in this context, the words *fear, misery,* and *severe* all have strong negative connotations, thus maintaining the author's tone and purpose.

Do the rest of the exercises in the same manner.

1. Early in his career, Sigmund Freud desperately dreamed of making a new medical discovery. He thought he had fulfilled his dream when he happened upon a drug called *cocaine*. Initially the drug seemed almost magical in its powers, and Freud enthusiastically prescribed it for a variety of ailments, even sending some to his wife. But his enthusiasm soon dimmed, as he began to regret his initial optimism. Particularly painful to him was the loss of a young and gifted colleague who apparently took an overdose of the drug. Freud also discovered that the wonderful "high" produced by ingestion of the substance could lead, even more quickly, to _____ depression and painful death. He was also faced with increasing evidence that cocaine could produce vivid and _____ hallucinations. Eventually, Freud learned to view his exciting discovery as a personal and professional _____.

2. When Americans began settling this magnificent country, they had an optimistic and winning spirit. Nothing could stand in their way. But today's Americans have grown weak and apathetic.* They no longer believe in the _____ of the American dream, and they are ready to give in to Russian aggression. It is not impossible, however, to regain the spirit of the past. We just have to retrieve our _____ and fight for them, refusing to take second place to any other nation. Americans can easily _____ their dreams if they would only stop giving in to defeat.

3. Half a century ago, the average consumption of coffee was a little over three cups per day, but that statistic has changed; the average adult now drinks a little over one cup of coffee per day. The reason is simple: most Americans are anxious to avoid the unpleasant and sometimes dangerous effects of too much caffeine. Although for years many people relied on caffeine to wake them in the morning or give them a quick pick-up in the afternoon, it is precisely this mood-altering effect that has made experts more than a little suspicious. It appears that caffeine consumption can cause a variety of _____ side effects, among them: insomnia, anxiety, depression, diarrhea, heartburn, and muscular tension. Almost as _____ as the side effects are the symptoms of withdrawal, symptoms like headache, drowsiness, nausea, and irritability. It's time that Americans realized caffeine is not a harmless stimulant. On the contrary it is a drug that bears watching. Taken in large quantities, it can have _____ effects on mind and body.

4. In the world of comedy Richard Pryor is without peer. The promise of his early work has finally matured into genius. When Pryor walks out on stage in movies like *Richard Pryor in Concert* and *Richard Pryor, Live on the Sunset Strip*, the audience comes alive with _____ and enthusiasm, and the star does not fail them. His comic monologues are masterpieces filled with _____ and originality. In addition, his ability to imitate everything from lions to five-year-old children is astonishing. He has the vision of the great painters, and he manages to select just the right details to evoke not just a personality but a way of life. In the world of comedy, Pryor is the acknowledged _____.

*apathetic: showing little emotion or feeling

5. More than any other time in history, America is plagued by the influence of cults, exclusive groups that present themselves as religions devoted to the worship of a single individual. Initially most Americans were not terribly concerned with the growth of cults, but then in 1979 more than 900 cult members were _____ slaughtered in the steamy jungles of a small South American country called Guyana. The reason for the slaughter was little more than the wild, paranoid fear of the leader, the Reverend Jim Jones, who called himself father and savior. Since that time, evidence has increased that another cult leader, the Reverend Sun Myung Moon, has amassed a large personal fortune from the purses of his followers, male and female "Moonies," who talk of bliss while peddling pins and emblems preaching the gospel of Moon. Cults with their hypnotic rituals and their promises of ecstasy are a _____ to American youth, and it is time to implement* laws which would allow for a thorough _____ of their movements.

*implement: to provide or ensure

REVIEW TEST: CHAPTER 9

PART A

The following pages will test your mastery of Chapter 9.

1. What are the characteristics of a factual statement?

2. What are the characteristics of an opinion?

3. What are some of the words that signal the introduction of an opinion? List at least three.

4. Each one of the following three sentences represents a different kind of statement. One fact, one opinion and one a mixture of both. Using the letters, *F*, *O*, or *B*, identify them correctly.

    (a) Every year approximately twenty million readers spend 200 million dollars on the purchase of paperback romance novels. _____

    (b) Of all the writers of romance, British author Barbara Cartland has to be the worst. _____

    (c) Rosemary Rogers is probably the most successful author of paperback romances; her highly profitable *Sweet Savage Love* first appeared on bookshelves in 1974. _____

5. Would you say that the opinion expressed in the following paragraph is justified? Please explain your answer.

    On May 13, 1917, three shepherds in Fatima, Portugal, claimed to have seen the Virgin Mary. Thus, the legend of the miraculous Lady of Fatima began. It appears that the legend is still thriving today. In May of every year, an average of 300,000 people make the pilgrimage to the village of Fatima in order to celebrate rituals honoring the Virgin's first appearance. Because many of the people who make the journey are poor and ailing, the town has established clinics to treat those who are ill or in pain after the long trip. Even knee pads are provided for the travelers since many, as an act of devotion, travel the last mile on their knees.

_____

_____

_____

_____

PART B

Directions: Check off any informal fallacies you discover in the following paragraphs.

1. Mr. Allen has recommended that the laws restricting the sale of pornographic literature be strictly enforced. This argument is based on his belief that such literature abuses women and damages sexuality. Let me only point out in this column that Mr. Allen has been known to both gamble and drink. It is ironic, therefore, that he stands now as a representative of public morality.

    (a) hasty generalization
    (b) attack on the person
    (c) appeal to the emotions
    (d) no error

2. In contrast to the traditional assumptions, it appears that the non-union shops have better benefits than those with unions. During the last month, the Rand company of Boston has surveyed fifteen different industrial companies in North and South Carolina. In ten of the fifteen cases, workers who were not unionized actually had better employee benefits than those who were members of a union. Although their wages were slightly lower, non-unionized workers had better health care and more than the average number of paid sick days. This proves that unions are no longer necessary as they were twenty or thirty years ago.

    (a) hasty generalization
    (b) attack on the person

(c) appeal to the emotions

(d) no error

3. Jane Fonda is once again an acknowledged superstar, acclaimed by critics and fans alike. Everyone appears to have forgotten the politics Miss Fonda so boldly expressed in the seventies. Above all, they have forgotten that the actress publicly took the side of North Vietnam during a time when her own country was helping wage a war against that Communist country. It does not seem fair, therefore, to offer Miss Fonda awards, adulation,* and acclaim when there are many actors and actresses just as talented who are, in addition, possessed of the appropriate patriotic spirit.

(a) hasty generalization

(b) attack on the person

(c) appeal to the emotions

(d) no error

4. For several decades it has been assumed that ailments like gastritis, ulcers, and colitis were related to emotional tension and anxiety. Repeated studies suggested, for example, that individuals who were hard-working and highly conscientious had a greater tendency to develop gastrointestinal* ailments. Recently, however, a leading university published a one-year study in which there seemed to be no relationship between the presence of such ailments and emotional stress or personality type. It appears that existing notions about emotional factors contributing to these illnesses need to be revised.

(a) hasty generalization

(b) attack on the person

(c) appeal to the emotions

(d) no error

5. In the last year, the state legislature approved the allocation of more than fifty thousand dollars for the improvement of city jails. This decision was ill-timed, ill-conceived, and above all misguided. The men and women inside those jails are guilty of robbery, rape, and murder. As free individuals, they were a menace to society, and they have been placed

*adulation: praise, flattery in excess

*gastrointestinal: pertaining to the stomach and intestines

in prison in order to be punished. They are not meant to be living in a rest home.

(a) hasty generalization

(b) attack on the person

(c) appeal to the emotions

(d) no error

PART C

1. How would you define the connotations of words?

_____
_____
_____
_____

2. How can recognizing connotative language help you in critical reading?

_____
_____
_____
_____

3. Do all words possess connotations?

_____

4. Read through the following brief movie review. Then pick the letter that best describes the tone:

   a. critical and unsympathetic

   b. critical but sympathic

   Sissy Spacek's new movie *Raggedy Man* is a <u>quiet</u>, <u>simple</u> film in which nothing much happens until the end. Not meant to be an action film, the movie is a character study, centering on the life of Nita Longley, a war widow trying to raise two young children in a small town. Although the idea is <u>hardly an original one</u>, Spacek is a powerful actress, and she gives the part all she's got. Sometimes, in fact, her performance is so perfect, it threatens to overpower the <u>modest</u> film. Still audiences, composed largely of <u>young people</u>, seem to like this <u>low-budget</u> movie, and they <u>cheer</u> their enthusiasm when it ends <u>with</u> Nita triumphant.

Please replace each of the underlined words to significantly alter the tone. You need not rewrite the entire paragraph. Just list the replacement for the underlined words.

_____

_____

_____

_____

_____

5. The author of the following paragraph evokes a certain mood when describing a meeting. Read through the paragraph; then decide what mood you think the author evoked:

   Recently several hundred psychiatrists met to debate whether or not homosexuality should be deleted from the standard list of mental illnesses. Even after hours of energetic, sometimes excited, discussion, members of the group remained polarized in their views. Whereas some insisted that homosexuality was absolutely not a mental illness, others insisted just as doggedly that homosexual tendencies indicated a neurotic disorder. Pale and tired after hours of wrangling, the departing members of the medical profession refused to discuss their meeting.

   _____

Appendix

BORROWED WORDS AND PHRASES

As you already learned in Chapter 1, English has borrowed from other languages. In the following pages we present more borrowed words, exclusively from Latin and French. Although the expressions contained in this list are seldom part of ordinary conversation, they do appear in scholarly writing or speech. If you learn them now, you avoid being confused or puzzled when they appear in texts or lectures. *Note:* When these words appear in print, they are underlined or placed in *italics*. This indicates that they are still considered foreign words. Since they do come from other languages, you should look these phrases up in your dictionary: in many cases you will have to learn the correct pronunciation.

Latin

1. *ad hoc* — literally, "toward this"; refers to something devised or created for a particular situation or purpose.

2. *ad infinitum* — literally, "to infinity"; suggests that someone or something will continue indefinitely.

3. *a posteriori* — literally, "from the subsequent"; indicates that reasoning is based on experience, that one may argue from facts to general principles.

4. *a priori* — literally, "from the previous causes"; indicates that reasoning is based on theories or general principles rather than experience or factual knowledge.

5.	*bona fide*	literally, "in good faith"; means that something is genuine or authentic.
6.	*in loco parentis*	literally, "in the place of the parent"; indicates that some group or institution substitutes for absent parents.
7.	*in toto*	literally, "in sum" or "as a whole"; indicates that something should be taken totally or altogether.
8.	*prima facie*	literally, "on first appearance"; refers to a first impression formed before any closer inspection.
9.	*non sequitor*	literally, "it does not follow"; points to an irrelevant or illogical conclusion or statement.
10.	*quid pro quo*	literally, "something for something"; indicates an equal exchange.

French

11.	*carte blanche*	literally, a "blank card"; signifies unrestricted power or unconditional authority.
12.	*déjà vu*	literally, "already seen"; refers to the experience of going through something that seems to have happened before.
13.	*double-entendre*	literally, "double meaning"; indicates that a word or phrase has two meanings, one of which has sexual overtones.
14.	*entrée*	literally, "entrance"; can refer to the main course of a meal; can also indicate the right of entrance to a select group.
15.	*idée fixe*	literally, "fixed idea"; suggests that an idea has become an obsession.
16.	*fin de siècle*	literally, "end of the century"; refers to the end of the nineteenth century and suggests a climate of extreme sophistication and boredom.

Borrowed Words and Phrases

17. *noblesse oblige* — literally, "nobility obligates"; signifies that responsible behavior is considered the obligation of all aristocrats.

18. *nom de plume* — literally, "pen name"; means the same as "pseudonym."

19. *raison d'être* — literally, "reason for being"; refers to the sole or essential reason for existence.

20. *vis-à-vis* — literally, "face to face"; can indicate two things or persons that are opposite or corresponding; can also mean "in relation to."

EXERCISE 1

Directions: Fill in the blanks with one of the Latin or French words introduced in the previous list.

1. I have such a feeling of _____ ; it is as if all this had happened to me before.
2. The _____ evidence suggests that he is guilty, but we won't know for sure until we can look more closely at all the facts.
3. They decided to form an _____ committee to elect a president.
4. Even after almost a century, Vienna still has a certain _____ charm.
5. Since his wife's death, that child is his _____
6. George Eliot was the _____ of Mary Ann Evans, the famous english novelist.
7. _____ is the motto of my very proper and very aristocratic uncle.
8. An aspiring young artist, she arrived in New York hoping for an _____ into the most talented circles.
9. His original belief in the importance of regular exercise has become an _____ ; even if he is tired or ill, he always spends at least two hours working out.

10. I am so bored after two hours; I really believe this lecture may continue _____ .

11. I don't understand how that follows; to me what you say is a complete _____ .

12. We want a straightforward _____ agreement; we will accept a cut in wages if management will increase our benefits.

13. I don't like her jokes. They always contain some sly, little _____ .

14. Is he a _____ member of that exclusive club?

15. _____ , Plato argued that realm of perfect forms existed even though human senses could perceive little more than a poor imitation of that world.

16. For years schools tried to act _____ , but at the present time they have just about given up; they could not give the same level of care provided in the home.

17. When I offered you the use of my home, I did not give it to you _____ .

18. If that's what an individual membership costs, what will it cost if we take the group _____ ?

19. You will have to argue the existence of God _____ .

20. _____ the Calvinist tradition in America, Ralph Waldo Emerson was clearly a rebel.

WORDS THAT CONFUSE

The following pages contain a number of words that cause confusion mainly because their spelling and pronunciation are either exactly the same or very similar. For example, take the two words *alter* and *altar*. The word *alter* means "to change," while the word *altar* refers to a platform usually found in a church. They are two different words with two different meanings. But because the words look and sound so much alike, it is not uncommon to see an error like the following: "He refused to altar a word in his speech." Obviously whoever wrote that sentence was confused about the two words *alter* and *altar* and ended up making a rather silly error.

However, before we go on to the words themselves, we should point out that they can cause confusion with reading as well as writing. For example, take the following sentence: "They refused to support the consul." The word *consul* in this sentence refers to a single person, not a group of people *(council)*, but many people would not be at all sure of that because they are not sure about the difference between the two words *council* and *consul*.

To avoid the kind of confusion just described, study the lists that follow.

List 1

1. *accent* — (1) a particular way of speaking, "He had a noticeable Southern *accent*"; (2) spoken or written emphasis on a particular letter or syllable, "The *accent* is on the last syllable of the word"; (3) to emphasize, "He *accented* the last syllable."

   ascent — upward climb or advancement, "The long *ascent* up the mountain had made him very tired."

   assent — agreement, "She readily gave her *assent* to the plan even though it was risky."

2. *accept* — to receive, take what is offered, "He could not *accept* the gift."

   except — all but, "Everyone went *except* the teacher."

3. *access* — a way of approach or admittance, "He didn't have *access* to the office."

   excess — a larger amount than needed, "He tried desperately to lose the *excess* weight."

4. *advice* (rhymes with mice) — recommendation or suggestions, "The lawyer refused to accept *advice* although he had lost his last three cases."

   advise (rhymes with wise) — to make recommendations and suggestions, "He *advised* her to try for a scholarship."

5. *affect*   to influence, "Unfortunately, his actions will *affect* us all."

effect   (1) result, "The *effect* of the accident was painful to see"; (2) to cause or bring about, "He hoped to *effect* change once he was elected."

6. *aisle*   a passageway between rows of seats, "The usher stumbled as he went down the *aisle*."

isle   a small island, "He dreamed of being abandoned on a desert *isle*."

7. *allusion*   reference, "He knew better than to make an *allusion* to the judge's past."

illusion   false idea or belief, "He had no *illusions* about his physical strength."

8. *alter*   to change, "She refused to *alter* one word of what she had written."

altar   platform in a church, "The statue was placed on the *altar*."

9. *angel*   a winged spirit, "Over the altar they hung a picture of an *angel*."

angle   (1) the figure formed by two lines coming from a common point, "The student had to draw a right *angle*"; (2) to fish with a hook and line, "She had been *angling* for more than an hour."

10. *birth*   beginning of life, "The *birth* of the child was celebrated all over the land."

berth   bed built into a train or ship, "The train was so packed he couldn't even get a *berth*."

EXERCISE 2   **Directions:** Underline the correct word in each of the following sentences.

1. His (assent, ascent, accent) told us that he must be a foreigner.
2. From her point of view, there was an (excess, access) of violence on television.
3. He tried to (advise, advice) his client, but she was not interested in listening to him.

4. The (assent, ascent, accent) up the curving staircase had worn him out.
5. She liked him because he did not make one single (allusion, illusion) to his enormous wealth.
6. Somehow he managed to (assent, ascent, accent) all the wrong syllables when he spoke.
7. Only top officials had (access, excess) to the special file.
8. They didn't pay much attention to his (advise, advice).
9. He refused to give his (assent, ascent, accent), even though he knew that refusing could be dangerous.
10. The (effects, affects) of the storm could be seen everywhere.
11. The movie had absolutely no (effect, affect) on her.
12. He could not sleep in the uncomfortable (birth, berth).
13. All the objects on the (altar, alter) had been destroyed.
14. They were not pleased about the (birth, berth) of the child.
15. Life had helped her to get rid of many of her (illusions, allusions).
16. There was not enough room for two people to walk up the (aisle, isle).
17. She did not want to make any (illusions, allusions) to his lack of education.
18. The candidate could only (effect, affect) change once the election was over.
19. It was a lush, tropical (aisle, isle).
20. She decided to place the furniture at right (angels, angles).
21. He couldn't (except, accept) money he hadn't earned.
22. They were all going to go (except, accept) the teacher.
23. The (angels, angles) smiling in the heavens were beautifully painted.
24. After a few moments the teacher gave his (assent, ascent, accent).

25. After a struggle we moved the boulder aside and gained (access, excess) to the cave.

List 2

1. *capital*   (1) major city of a state or nation, "Hartford is the *capital* of Connecticut"; (2) supply of wealth, "He didn't have enough *capital* to start a business."

    capitol   (1) a building where a legislature meets, "The members were in the *capitol*"; (2) building in Washington, D.C., where Congress meets.

2. *cereal*   breakfast food made from grain, "Hot *cereal* was not exactly his favorite breakfast."

    serial   novel or drama presented in short episodes, "The next episode of the *serial* would not be presented until the following week."

3. *cite*   to quote or mention, "He *cited* three different authorities to prove his point."

    sight   the ability to see, "The poor animal slowly lost its *sight*."

    site   location, piece of land, "The company could not find a suitable *site* for the new building."

4. *coarse*   (1) not smooth, "The poor woman wore clothes of *coarse* material"; (2) crude, vulgar, "After a few drinks, his language became very *coarse*."

    course   (1) body of studies, "What *courses* are you taking next semester?"; (2) way of behaving, "What *course* does the lawyer intend to follow?"; (3) path or route, "The *course* of the river was winding and dangerous."

5. *conscience*   sense of right and wrong, "Even after the murder, his *conscience* did not bother him."

    conscious   aware of things outside oneself, "He was barely *conscious* after the accident."

6. *consul* — an official representing his or her country in a foreign country, "The honorary *consul* had been kidnapped."

   council — a group of people appointed or elected to make decisions or discuss issues, "The town *council* was under fire from the townspeople."

   counsel — (1) to give recommendations or advice, "The priest tried to *counsel* the young married couple"; (2) recommendations or advice, "They had come to him for *counsel* because they trusted him"; (3) attorney, "The *counsel* was fired after the first day of the trial."

7. *decent* — (1) proper, in good taste, "She hoped that the child would learn some *decent* manners"; (2) good, honest, "He had been a *decent*, hardworking man all his life."

   descent — (1) downward movement or slope, "The *descent* was exciting but dangerous"; (2) family origin, "He was interested most of all in the *descent* of man."

   dissent — disagreement, "There was a great deal of *dissent* among the members."

8. *device* (rhymes with *mice*) — gadget, handy invention, "It was a strange *device*; no one knew what it was used for."

   devise (rhymes with *wise*) — to think of, come up with, "He had *devised* a plan to help him escape."

9. *dual* — double, "The actor was asked to play a *dual* role."

   duel — fight between two people, "In almost every western there is a *duel* between two gunfighters."

10. *dyeing* — coloring, "They were able to make a fortune simply by *dyeing* and selling T-shirts."

    dying — losing life, coming to an end, "He feared *dying* during the night."

EXERCISE 3

Directions: Underline the correct word in each of the following sentences.

1. The (site, cite, sight) of the building had been completely ruined by the heavy rain.
2. His (conscious, conscience) did not bother him a bit.
3. The new (council, counsel, consul) sat in her room waiting for the message to arrive.
4. He did not (cite, site, sight) enough references.
5. She left because there was too much (dissent, decent, descent) among the members.
6. She hoped to make a great deal of money with the new (device, devise).
7. They had come to him for (council, counsel, consul), but he was unable to help.
8. The prisoners wanted to (device, devise) a plot to escape.
9. The loss of his (sight, site, cite) had severely depressed him.
10. The (descent, decent, dissent) was slippery and dangerous.
11. The newly elected members of the (council, counsel, consul) were not happy with the vote.
12. All his life he had been a (descent, decent, dissent) hard working man, but it had not helped him in the slightest; he was as poor as ever.
13. She had to play the (dual, duel) role of mother and father.
14. The monk wore a robe made out of (coarse, course) cloth.
15. The teacher asked them to learn the (capitals, capitols) of all fifty states.
16. Her parents said she should decide which (coarse, course) to take before the semester started.
17. The children hated (cereal, serial) for breakfast.
18. Many people still question human beings' (descent, decent, dissent) from the animal kingdom.

19. It was an excellent (cereal, serial); each episode was more exciting than the one before.
20. The men and women sitting in the (capital, capitol) building were concerned with the problems of the poor.
21. The (dual, duel) was fought early in the morning.
22. He was not at all (conscious, conscience) of the impression his clothes made on other people.
23. (Dying, Dyeing) is probably the one thing everyone fears.
24. The mother tried to (council, counsel, consul) them about the danger they were in.
25. The coat looked worse after they finished (dying, dyeing) it.

List 3

1. *elicit* — to draw out or forth, to bring about a response, "The teacher tried to *elicit* a response from the class."

   illicit — not permitted, improper, "The whole town was talking about their *illicit* affair."

2. *eminent* — well known, respected, "The *eminent* lecturer did not arrive on time, and the crowd became angry."

   imminent — about to happen, "The departure of the refugees was *imminent*."

3. *farther* — greater distance, "The group planned to walk much *farther* than he desired."

   further — more, in addition, "The grant gave them enough money to study the problem *further*."

4. *formally* — according to accepted rules and regulations, "He was *formally* dressed for the occasion."

   formerly — previously, happening before, "*Formerly* he had been president of the company."

5. *holy* — sacred, worthy of worship, "The crowd became silent when the *holy* man entered."

	holey	full of holes, "The *holey* old sweater was the only thing he owned."
	wholly	completely, totally, "That solution is *wholly* inadequate."
6.	*irrelevant*	not appropriate or related to a particular situation, "The lawyer tried to prove that the new evidence was *irrelevant*."
	irreverent	disrespectful, "She knew it was *irreverent* to whistle, but she did it anyway."
7.	*its*	indicates ownership, "The horse broke *its* leg."
	it's	contraction* of *it is*, "*It's* too late to go to the show."
8.	*later*	after the usual or expected time, "The show started *later* than they had expected."
	latter	the second of two things mentioned, "She tended to agree with the *latter* statement."
9.	*lessen*	to decrease, "The doctor hoped to *lessen* the pain with the use of drugs."
	lesson	something to be learned, "Try as he might, he could not memorize the *lesson*."
10.	*loose*	(1) not tight, "The movie star wore a *loose*-fitting robe for his role as a prophet"; (2) free, "Above all, he was not allowed to set the dog *loose*."
	lose	(1) to misplace, "He didn't want to *lose* the tickets"; (2) to suffer defeat, "They could not afford to *lose* the first game of the season."

EXERCISE 4   **Directions:** Underline the correct word in each of the following sentences.

1. They hoped to do (further, farther) work on the subject.

---

*contraction: a shortened word or words formed by omitting a letter or letters

2. The (imminent, eminent) historian was not invited back to lecture.
3. He hated to dress (formally, formerly).
4. The (holy, holey, wholly) objects had been placed on the altar.
5. No one had expected the plane to go (further, farther).
6. I only agreed with the (latter, later) part of his speech.
7. She had (formally, formerly) been called Elliot before her marriage.
8. After months of dieting, his clothes had become (loose, lose).
9. The judge was furious with his (irreverent, irrelevant) behavior.
10. He swore that he would come (later, latter).
11. (It's, its) not too late to try.
12. The announcer claimed that the tornado was (imminent, eminent), and the population had only a few minutes to flee.
13. The child was too tired to study the day's (lesson, lessen).
14. Somehow he failed to (elicit, illicit) a single response.
15. His comments were absolutely (irreverent, irrelevant); they had absolutely no bearing on the case.
16. How did the horse manage to break (it's, its) leg?
17. Their (elicit, illicit) behavior was a well-known scandal.
18. Shivering, she wrapped the (holy, holey, wholly) blanket around her shoulders.
19. His statements were (holy, holey, wholly) inaccurate.
20. The team hated to (loose, lose) the game.
21. He tried to (lessen, lesson) his rival's chance of winning by spreading false rumors.
22. The child was careful not to (loose, lose) his last quarter.

23. It was necessary to walk (further, farther) down the road to catch a glimpse of the estate.
24. The teacher sent the (irreverent, irrelevant) student directly to the principal's office.
25. The storm damaged the roof of the house and shattered (it's, its) windows.

List 4

1. *marital*   refers to marriage, "After twenty years of *marital* bliss, his wife died."

   marshal   one who enforces rules or laws, "The *marshal* led them before the court."

   martial   refers to war, "He had a great deal of training in the *martial* arts."

2. *medal*   an award or prize made of metal, "He did not want to accept the *medal*."

   meddle   to interfere, "He made a vow not to *meddle* in his daughter's life."

   metal   substance that has a shine, conducts electricity, and may be combined with other substances, "They had searched long and hard for the precious *metal*."

3. *miner*   one whose job it is to take minerals from the earth, "After being a *miner* all his life, his health was not very good."

   minor   (1) lesser in importance or amount, "That's only a *minor* problem; you're lucky it's not worse"; (2) a person who is not yet legally adult, "*Minors* are not allowed to drink here."

4. *moral*   (1) good and honorable, "The judge was a *moral* man, and he refused to take the bribe"; (2) lesson of a story, "It was easy to see what the *moral* of the story was."

   morale   confidence or spirit, "The *morale* of the troops was very low after the last battle."

5. *patience*   ability to bear stress and strain, ability to

	wait, "A chess player needs a great deal of *patience*."
patients	people suffering from illness, "The doctor had too many *patients* and was unable to treat all of them properly."
6. *personal*	private, "They did not discuss their *personal* problems."
personnel	group of workers employed at the same place, "The *personnel* in the company was not satisfied with the new order."
7. *pore*	(1) to study carefully, "He *pored* over the books for several hours"; (2) a tiny opening in the skin, "He seemed to be sweating from every *pore*."
pour	to make something liquid flow, "The child *poured* the water into the sand."
8. *principal*	(1) chief, most important, "The union leader was the *principal* suspect"; (2) the head of a school, "The *principal* was very popular with everyone in the school."
principle	rule or basic truth, "He needed to understand two basic *principles* to solve the problem."
9. *profit*	gain, "The company claimed to have made almost no *profit* on the investment."
prophet	a spokesperson for a religion or cause, "The *prophet* claimed that God spoke through him."
10. *quiet*	silent, "They were told to be *quiet* because they were in a hospital zone."
quit	to stop, "After several tries, she managed to *quit* smoking."
quite	really, "I tell you he is *quite* mad."

EXERCISE 5 **Directions:** Underline the correct word in each of the following sentences.

1. It was his policy not to (meddle, metal, medal) in the personal affairs of his business partners.

2. He hated any story that had a (moral, morale) in it.
3. He had a happy marriage and was therefore quick to praise the (martial, marital) tie.
4. After seeing fifty (patients, patience) in one day, she was enormously tired.
5. They were really (quite, quiet, quit) angry with him.
6. The troops sang a rousing (martial, marital) hymn as they went into battle.
7. After what he had suffered in the war, the (meddle, metal, medal) they had awarded him meant little or nothing.
8. You need (patients, patience) to learn to play chess.
9. The children were surprised to see that the new (principle, principal) was so young.
10. Thousands of prospectors had come in search of the precious (meddle, metal, medal) that was said to lie beneath the earth.
11. He had tried to (quite, quiet, quit) smoking several times, but he had never succeeded.
12. The (principle, principal) behind the theory was difficult to understand.
13. The reporters wanted to know everything about the politicians's (personnel, personal) life.
14. The (prophets, profits) were not as large as the company expected.
15. Sitting on the cosmetic counter were about fifteen different types of (pour, pore) cleansers.
16. A (moral, morale) person would have refused the bribe.
17. After a meeting the (miners, minors) decided to go on strike.
18. The troops sang in an effort to lift their (moral, morale).

19. The (prophet, profit) standing on the mountain was the center of all eyes.
20. The accountant (poured, pored) over the books looking for an error.
21. The head of the firm did not have a very good relationship with the (personnel, personal).
22. Can you (pour, pore) me a glass of wine?
23. No one could take him seriously; it was such a (miner, minor) problem.
24. He was said to be a friendly young man, although very (quite, quiet, quit) and rather shy.
25. The (principle, principal) speaker at the high school graduation was the state's newly elected governor.

List 5

1. *respectfully* — showing special consideration or appreciation, "The jury rose *respectfully* as the judge entered."

   respectively — in the order given, "Smith Jones, and Brown were each mentioned *respectively*."

2. *stationary* — to be in a fixed position, unable to move, "They had built the platform so that it would be *stationary*."

   stationery — paper used in writing letters, "The *stationery* looked expensive."

3. *straight* — not curving, "The child was too young to draw a *straight* line."

   strait — (1) a narrow passage of water, "The plane approached the Bering *Straits*"; (2) difficulty, "His parents wrote to find out exactly what kind of *strait* he was in."

4. *than* — used in comparisons, "The young dog had grown taller *than* his mother."

then	(1) at that time, "He was only a lieutenant *then*"; (2) therefore, "It is clear *then* that the solution to the problem is not known."
5. *thorough*	complete, careful, "He always did a *thorough* job."
threw	form of the verb *throw* which indicates the action is not going on in the present, "The catcher *threw* the ball."
through	(1) by means of, "*Through* lies, he had managed to enter the hospital"; (2) in one side and out the other, "She walked *through* the door"; (3) among, "They walked *through* the flowers."
6. *to*	(1) toward, "She threw the ball *to* the catcher"; (2) used before a verb form, "They hoped *to* sing in the concert."
too	(1) more than enough, "The child had put on *too* much weight"; (2) also; "The family pet wanted to go *too*."
two	the number 2, "The *two* men hoped to win the lottery."
7. *vain*	(1) proud, conceited, "She was not the slightest bit *vain* about her looks"; (2) hopeless, "They made a *vain* attempt to free her."
vein	a vessel that brings blood to the heart, "One blue *vein* stood out on his forehead."
8. *ware*	something that can be sold or marketed, "The merchant was forced to display his *wares* in the street."
wear	to carry on one's body, "They were asked to *wear* formal clothes for the dance."
where	(1) in what place, "I don't know *where* the telephone book is"; (2) from what place, "*Where* did you get that book?"
9. *waive*	to put aside, to give up, "Fifty freshmen were able to *waive* the composition course."
wave	to move back and forth, "The leaves of the tree *wave* as the wind blows."

10. *your*   indicates possession or ownership, "That's *your* problem," she said angrily.

     you're   contraction of *you are*, "You're not serious."

EXERCISE 6

Directions: Underline the correct word in each of the following sentences.

1. The department store had put its most expensive (stationary, stationery) on sale.
2. The trees were taller (then, than) she remembered.
3. They took the test to see if they could (waive, wave) the basic math course.
4. They were forced to go (threw, through) the back entrance.
5. Everyone bowed (respectfully, respectively) when the queen entered the room.
6. The merchant had arranged his (wares, wears) so that they caught the customers' attention.
7. The sailor (waived, waved) the flag to signal the other ship.
8. Her mother wanted to know (where, wear, ware) they were all going.
9. (You're, your) not really going to do that.
10. For a child, she had much (to, too, two) much money to spend.
11. He tried (to, too, two) sing, but the notes were terribly off key.
12. Do you really want to go (then, than)?
13. In a fury the waiter (threw, through) the dishes on the floor.
14. He had to remain (stationary, stationery) for the entire play.
15. Is that (you're, your) hat or somebody else's?
16. The (to, too, two) players concentrated only on the game.

17. The clothes those children (where, wear, ware) are always soiled.
18. A needle was placed in her (vain, vein) to draw a blood sample.
19. After too many drinks, he could not walk a (straight, strait) line.
20. They made a (vain, vein) attempt to rescue the drowning boy.
21. She didn't want to write about the terrible (straight, strait) she was in.
22. The army, navy, and marines (respectfully, respectively) were mentioned in the speech.
23. Jeff was invited (to, too, two) but he declined our invitation.
24. The (vain, vein) young man spent hours admiring himself in the mirror.
25. The ship passed slowly through the dangerous (straight, strait) and anchored safely in the harbor.

RECOGNIZING THE UNFAMILIAR WORD

When you read, you run across words you don't know. Everybody does. The important question is: What do you do when you see an unfamiliar word? Do you ignore it and try to pretend it isn't there? When you are in school, you probably do what most people do: You ask somebody to pronounce the word and tell you what it means.

If you favor this method, you may have discovered more than once that an unfamiliar word was actually familiar; that is, you knew it when you heard it. It was only in print that the word was unfamiliar.

If this happens frequently, you probably have a problem common to a great many people: You have a large listening vocabulary and a much smaller sight vocabulary. Thus you can recognize many words when you hear them, but when these same words appear in print, they become unfamiliar.

Fortunately, this is a problem that can be remedied. One way to remedy it is to learn or review the following:

1. The relationship between speech sounds and the letters of the alphabet
2. The rules for breaking words into syllables

SPEECH SOUNDS AND THE LETTERS OF THE ALPHABET

Before people could write, they could speak, and the spoken word was the only way people communicated with one another. But there came a time when people wanted to preserve what they had said, and they invented symbols to represent the sounds they made when speaking. In short, they invented an alphabet.

When we talk about the English alphabt, we are referring to those twenty-six letters that represent the different speech sounds in our language. For example, if someone were to hold up a chart with the letter *t* on it and ask you to make the sound represented by that letter, you would put your tongue up against the roof of your mouth and force a stream of air around your teeth and tongue. That is, you would respond to the letter *t* with a particular kind of sound.

All this may sound very easy. After all, you've known how to make the sound represented by the letter *t* ever since you were a child. But actually, it's not all that simple because many letters of the alphabet represent more than one sound. Think for a minute about the words *gun* and *large*. Both words contain *g*'s, but the sounds you make in response to those letters are quite different.

In the following pages we'll talk more about the relationship between speech sounds and letters of the alphabet. We'll focus on those letters that can be particularly confusing because you do not always respond to them with the same speech sound. We'll also concentrate on those letters that are easy to associate with speech sounds; whenever you see them in print, you almost always respond with the same speech sound.

VOWEL AND CONSONANT SOUNDS

What is a vowel? We'll bet your answer was something like this: "The vowels are *a, e, i, o, u* and sometimes *y*." That is correct; however, there is a reason why those particular letters are called *vowels* and not *consonants*.

A, e, i, o, u and sometimes *y* are only letters of the alphabet. They have been called *vowels* because they stand for a particular kind of sound. When you see one of these letters in a word, you make what we call an open sound. That is, you don't use your teeth, tongue, or lips to close off the stream of air used to make the sound. For example, if you wanted to, you could make an *o* sound (as in *bone*) for as long as you wanted. You would only have to stop when you ran out of breath.

The same is not true of consonants. Try making a *t* sound (as in *sit*) for a long time. You can't do it. The letters we call *consonants* stand for or represent sounds that can be made only if you use your tongue, teeth, or lips to close off the stream of air.

The letters of the alphabet then are called *vowels* and *consonants* because of the sounds they represent. Vowels or vowel letters stand for open sounds. Consonants or consonant letters stand for closed sounds.

Consonants

Usually you know almost immediately what sound to give a consonant letter even though it is clear that consonant sounds change slightly with each word you pronounce. For example, the sound you make when you see the *b* in the word *cab* is slightly different than the sound you make for the *b* in the word *bit*. The difference in the sounds, however, is not that great, and we can say that almost every consonant letter stands for only one speech sound.

Note that we said *almost* every consonant letteer. Some consonant letters do represent more than one sound. In the following pages we'll cover a few of the most important ones.

c Let's say you saw the word *curds* written somewhere. How would you respond to the letter *c*? Would you sound it like the *c* in the word *cent*, or would you sound it like the *c* in the word *cat*?

Actually there is a rule that can help you decide what sound to give the letter *c*; it may not work each and every time, but it will work most of the time: When *c* is followed by *i, e,* or *y*, try first sounding the *c* as it is sounded in the word *cent*. If the letter *c* is followed by any other letter, sound it like the *c* in the word *cat*.

PRACTICE 1 Say the following words aloud. You will not know all of them, but that is not important at this time. What is important is that you should be able to pronounce all these words if you keep in mind what you just learned about the letter *c*.

What sound to give the letter *c* will probably be your only problem. Pronouncing the remainder of each word will probably not give you any difficulty. If you do have any trouble, you can use the rhyming words printed in parenthesis as clues.*

Put an X next to any word that gives you trouble. Check to see if you have pronounced every word correctly. Pay special attention to those words you marked with an X.

curt (hurt)	cid (did)	coop (loop)	celt (belt)
cyst (list)	cad (mad)	cast (fast)	cot (hot)
cult	cog (hog)	city	carp (harp)
cite (bite)	cell (bell)	cant (ant)	colt (bolt)

g When you see the letter *g* in a word, you can respond with one of two sounds, the sound of *g* in words like *gem* and *gin*, or the sound of *g* in words like *gas* and *good*. Once again, you should look at the letter following *g* to decide which sound to make.

If the *g* is followed by *i*, *e*, or *y*, sound it like the *g* in the words *gin* or *gem*. If it is followed by any other letter, sound it like the *g* in the words *good* and *gas*.

Again like all the rules we'll introduce, this one cannot be used each and every time. Try it first. If it doesn't work, then switch to another sound.

For example, let's say you saw the word *gave* in print and didn't know it. You would first try sounding the *g* like the *g* in the word *gem*. However, when you tried to pronounce the word with that sound of *g*, you wouldn't come up with a familiar word. That doesn't mean you should give up. Instead, you would sound the *g* in the word *good*. This time you would recognize the familiar word *gave*.

---

*We do not include a rhyming word where (1) the word to be sounded is undoubtedly part of your vocabulary, (2) the only available rhyming word would be equally unfamiliar, or (3) the rhyming word would give away the pronunciation of the unfamiliar word.

PRACTICE 2 Say the following words aloud. You will not know all of them, but that is not important at this time. What is important is that you will be able to pronounce all the words on this list if you keep in mind what you have just learned about the letter *g*.

Put an X next to any word that gives you trouble. Check to see if you have pronounced all the words correctly. Pay special attention to the words you have marked with an X.

gent (went)	gam (ham)	gash (mash)
gad (mad)	gene (bean)	gull (skull)
gym	page	gip (tip)
large	gaff (laugh)	gap (lap)
gags	gist (fist)	gongs

y: As you already know, the letter *y* is sometimes counted as a vowel and sometimes as a consonant. In this section we are dealing with *y* only when it is counted as a consonant. Whenever y appears at the beginning of a word, it is counted as a consonent and sounded like the *y* in the word *yes*.

PRACTICE 3 You probably do not know every word on this list, but with the help of the word in parenthesis and your knowledge of the way the *y* is sounded when it appears at the beginning of a word, you should be able to pronounce most of the words. Put an X next to any word that gives you trouble. Check to see if you have pronounced every word correctly. Pay special attention to those words marked with an X.

yes	yaws (jaws)	yock (lock)	yin (pin)
yep (pep)	yell (bell)	York	yen (pen)
yap (map)	young	you	yip (lip)
yelp (help)	yore (bore)	yowl (owl)	yon (on)

Consonant Teams

Some consonants frequently appear together in words while others do not. For example, you'll often see the consonants *b* and *l* standing side by side, but you'll never see the consonants *w* and *x* next to one another.

We call those consonants that frequently appear next to each other *consonant teams,* and together they usually signal

Vowels and Consonant Sounds

that you must respond with a sound somewhat different from the sound you make when the consonants are separated from one another.

Since consonant teams do appear in a great many words, it is a good idea to become familiar with the way they are *usually* sounded. We italicized the word *usually* because we want to stress that you will not always respond to consonant teams with the same sound.

Consonant teams	Sample words
bl	black, blue, blind
cl	clap, click, clean
gl	glove, glass, gland
fl	flip, flop, flat
pl	play, place, plan
gr	groan, grin, grill

Note: The preceding consonant teams are sounded much as they are in the list of sample words, especially when they appear at the beginning or middle of words. When they appear at the end of words, they are less likely to be sounded as they are in the sample words.

PRACTICE 4 You know most of the words on the following list. Read through the list to hear how the consonants are sounded when they are part of a team and when they are not. Put an X next to any word that give you trouble. Check to see that you have pronounced every word correctly. Pay special attention to those marked with an X.

back	cap	luck	lend	fad	gip
lack	lap	puck	bend	lad	rip
black	clap	pluck	blend	flat	grip

PRACTICE 5 Read through the following list of words. They all begin with consonant teams, and the teams should be sounded as they were in the sample word list. Put an X next to any word that gives you trouble. Check to see if you have pronounced all the words correctly. Pay special attention to those marked with an X.

blur (fur)   plum (sum)

clack (black)   flick (lick)

gloom (room)   glade (made)

gloss (loss)   clot (hot)

flare (care)   clink (link)

flirt (dirt)   greed (seed)

bloom (room)   grope (rope)

blot (lot)   flog (hog)

Here are some more consonant teams with which you should be familiar. Again if these consonant teams appear at the beginning or middle of unfamiliar words, they are usually sounded as they were in the sample list.

Consonant teams	Sample words
sl	sleep, slap, slip
br	break, broad, bread
cr	crack, creep, cross
dr	drive, drip, drill
fr	freeze, from, fry
tr	trip, trap, troop

PRACTICE 6 You know most of the words on the list. Read through the list to hear how the consonants are sounded when they are part of a team and when they are not. Put an X next to any word that gives you trouble. Check to see that you have pronounced every word correctly. Pay special attention to those marked with an X.

bush	fat	sap	dip	tap	can
rush	rat	lap	rip	rap	ran
brush	frat	slap	drip	trap	crank

PRACTICE 7 Read through the following list of words. They all begin with consonant teams, and the consonant teams should be sounded as they were in the sample word list. Put an X next to any word that gives you trouble. Check to see if you have pronounced all the words correctly. Pay special attention to those marked with an X.

slung (hung)   frap (rap)   frit (bit)

slang (rang)   frock (rock) trump (dump)

Vowels and Consonant Sounds

breed (need)   crave (brave)   droop (loop)

crank (rank)   crest (rest)   troll (roll)

slur (fur)   drat (cat)   crass (grass)

PRACTICE 8   Some of the italicized words in the following sentences may be unfamiliar to you, but you should be able to pronounce them if you sound the consonant teams just as you have in the previous exercises. You can also make use of the rhyming word at the end of each sentence. Put an X next to any word that gives you trouble. Check to see that you have pronounced every word correctly. Pay special attention to those words you marked with an X.

1. The doctor said his condition was *grave;* They did not expect him to recover.   (rave)
2. A cable car in Britain is called a *tram.*   (ram)
3. She couldn't stand the blouse because it had a lot of *frills;* she liked plain blouses.   (kills)
4. As he approached the hive, he could hear the *drone* of the bees.   (bone)
5. The actress was made up as an aged *crone;* her hair had been whitened, and wrinkles had been painted on her face.   (bone)
6. He was a *brash* young man; nothing could disturb him, and he always had the right word at the right time.   (cash)
7. The woman tried to *plead* for her life, but the killer refused to listen.   (bleed)
8. Every time he tried to *glide* on skates, he fell down.   (side)
9. They didn't exactly *flock* to see the new movie; as a matter of fact, only three people bought tickets.   (lock)
10. The *sloop* had been washed up on shore without a sign of its crew.   (loop)
11. There was exactly one *clove* left in the spice jar.   (drove)
12. He didn't take long to *blurt* out the whole sad story.   (hurt)

PRACTICE 9

Read the following sentences aloud and think of a word that would fit the blank and make sense. Then see if you can find a consonant team that would, if added to the letters in the blank, form the word you thought of or another word that would also fit the rest of the sentence.

Consonant Teams: bl, cl, gl, fl, pl, gr, sl, br, cr, dr, fr, tr

1. He tried to _____asp the gun, but his hand was too weak.
2. The leader would not allow the _____oop of boys to go up the mountain.
3. The child was a _____ail little thing, pale and thin from not eating.
4. He could not study because of the sound of the _____ill.
5. On top of the _____isp lettuce was a mound of mushy tuna fish.
6. The _____isk wind blew her hat off.
7. All the men were shot once their _____ot was discovered.
8. Just a _____impse of her face was enough to make them all afraid.
9. A _____ood of people poured out of the disease-ridden city.
10. The little girl still tended to _____urp her food, and the noise drove her father crazy.
11. She _____ung to the seat to keep her balance.
12. To pass the test, they had to fill in each and every _____ank.

The following teams can appear at the beginning, middle, and end of words. Even if they are at the end of a word, they are usually sounded as they are in the following sample word list:

Vowels and Consonant Sounds 471

Consonant teams	Sample words
st	first, steam, bust, stone
sh	fish, shoe, dish, ship
sk	skate, task, skip, mask
sp	wisp, spit, gasp, spot

PRACTICE 10 Read through the following word list. Note how the consonant teams are sounded when they appear at the beginning of words and at the end. Put an X next to any word that gives you trouble. Check to see if you have pronounced every word correctly. Pay special attention to the words you marked with an X.

stop	ship	skate	spot	span
fast	ash	ask	clasp	mash
stone	shell	skin	spill	skid
cast	trash	mask	grasp	still

PRACTICE 11 Read through the following list of words. They all begin and end with consonant teams, and the teams are sounded as they were in the sample word list.

Put an X next to any word that gives you trouble. Check to see if you have pronounced all the words correctly. Pay special attention to those marked with an X.

bask (bat)	mish (mit)	mast (mat)
husk (hug)	shag (bag)	spat (pat)
stale (whale)	cusp (cup)	stark (park)
skill (bill)	span (pan)	flask (flat)

PRACTICE 12 Some of the italicized words in the following sentences may be unfamiliar to you, but you should be able to pronounce them if you sound the consonant teams just as you have in the previous exercises.

Put an X next to any word that gives you trouble. Check to see that you have pronounced every word correctly. Pay special attention to those you have marked with an X.

1. He's just trying to *stall* for time; he doesn't really want to see the trial continue.   (all)

2. It was supposed to be a *jest,* but nobody took it as a joke. (jet)
3. The roof was made of *shale,* a clay-like rock. (sale)
4. Breakfast was a disgusting bowl of *mush.* (mud)
5. The play was a collection of short *skits,* and none of them was very good. (hits)
6. The children love to *bask* in the sun; they can lie there for hours. (bat)
7. It was a mistake to *spurn* the prince's love; he was a dangerous man to reject. (burn)
8. The queen killed herself with an *asp.* (gasp)

PRACTICE 13 Read each sentence aloud and think of a word that would fit the blank and make sense. Then see if you can find a consonant team that would, if added to the letters in the blank, form the word you thought of or another word that would also fit the rest of the sentence.

Consonant Teams: st, sh, sk, sp

1. The prisoner was given only a few mouthfuls of water and a piece of _____ale bread.
2. He liked to boa_____ about how easy it had been to become a millionaire.
3. Her lack of _____ills made it hard for her to get a good job.
4. Rather than parking under the _____ade of a tree, he chose to park in the sun.
5. Due to the oil _____ill, dead fish were lying all over the beach.
6. The speech teacher tried to help her get rid of her li_____.
7. After the accident she had a terrible ga_____ on her forehead.

8. At twelve o'clock everyone was allowed to take off his ma_____ .

Troublesome Consonant Teams

Like some of the single consonants, some consonant teams can be a bit difficult. Sometimes they are not sounded as you would expect, for example, *ph* in *phone, photo, photograph*. At other times you may have to choose between two possible sounds. For example, the consonant team *th* can be sounded like the *the* in the word *thank* or the *th* in the word *their*.

Just briefly, we want to go over some of the most troublesome consonant teams.

wr at the Beginning of Words: You already know what sound you usually give the consonant *w*, for example, *war*, *was*, and *always*. But think for a moment about the words *write* and *wrap*. In these words you don't give the *w* any sound at all. You pronounce the word as though the *w* were not there.

Whenever the consonant team *wr* appears at the beginning of a word, you should sound the word as if it began with *r* rather than *wr*.

PRACTICE 14 Pronounce all the words on the following list. Put an X next to any word that gives you trouble. Check to see if you have pronounced every word correctly. Pay special attention to those words you marked with an X.

wring (sing)	wrath (bath)	wroth (cloth)
writ (bit)	wren (hen)	wreck (neck)
wrench (bench)	wrest (best)	wrap (nap)
wrung (sung)	wrack (lack)	wry (why)

kn and gn at the Beginning of Words: When you see either one of these two consonant teams, *kn* or *gn*, at the beginnings of words, you should sound it as if only the *n* wre there, for example, *knee*.

PRACTICE 15 Pronounce every word on the following list. Put an X next to any word that gives you trouble. Check to see if you pronounced every word correctly. Pay special attention to those words you marked with an X.

gnome (home)	gnarl (Carl)	gnaw (saw)
knot	knead (need)	knife (life)
knew	knave (save)	kneel (wheel)
gnat (at)	gnash (ash)	knell (bell)

ch: The consonant team *ch* can be troublesome. Most of the time when you see it in a word, you will sound it like the *ch* in the word *chair*. Occasionally you will sound it like the *ch* in the word *chord*, and once in a while like the *ch* in the word *machine*.

PRACTICE 16 Read the following list and pronounce every word. Put an X next to any word that gives you trouble. Check to see if you have pronounced every word correctly. Pay special attention to the words you marked with an X.

child	chide (hide)	church
chime (time)	chit (hit)	chore
chock (sock)	punch	chorus
choral (oral)	chef (deaf)	chump (dump)

Vowels

Most consonants represent only one sound. However, we cannot say the same for vowels. Each vowel represents three* or more sounds.

Let's take the word *pate* for example. The word is probably unfamiliar, and you are therefore not sure how to pronounce it. But it is not the *p* or the *t* that is troublesome. It is the vowels that are confusing.

Since you've had a lot of experience with short words that end in *e* such as *hate*, *bone*, and *fine*, you're probably not ready to sound the *e* at all. In this case you are correct. The *e* is not sounded. But you're still left with the letter *a*. How are you going to sound it? Should the *a* be sounded as it is in the word *date*, or the way it is sounded in the word *hat*?

*The third vowel sound, represented by the symbol called the *schwa* (ə) is not discussed until page 495.

Actually, you were correct if you sounded the *a* in *pate* as it is sounded in the word *date*. We just wanted to go through some of the possible sounds *a* can represent so that you can see why it is sometimes difficult to give vowels the correct sounds.

Since vowels can give you some difficulty, you should make sure that you have a clear idea of the sounds they represent.

It is easier for us to talk about the sounds of the vowels if we divide them first into two groups and call them *long* and *short* vowel sounds. We'll begin with the long vowel sounds.

Vowels	Sample words
ā	dāte, lāte, māte
ē	wē, mē, bē
ī	hī, tīe, līe
ō	gō, nō, hōpe
ū	mūsic, ūse, fūse *or* prūne, dūne, trūe

The following list contains several examples of words containing what we call the *short* vowel sounds:

Vowels	Sample words
ă	băt, măt, făt
ĕ	bĕt, mĕt, lĕt
ĭ	bĭt, mĭt, sĭt
ŏ	cŏt, pŏt, mŏp
ŭ	cŭp, mŭd, sŭn

Note: Rather than writing out "long *a* vowel sound" and "short *a* vowel sound" every time, we will use these two marks to tell you what sound to give a vowel: ā and ĭ.

PRACTICE 17

Have someone read the following list aloud to you. Next to the number of the word write what vowel you think appears in the word—*a, e, i, o, u*—and what vowel sound you think it represents, for example, ā or ă, ē or ĕ. For example, if you heard the word *shape*, you would write ā.

1. sup
2. cope
3. bleat
4. fan
5. bid
6. kite
7. knack
8. coat
9. fetch
10. wheat
11. pun
12. tune
13. wine
14. June
15. muse
16. sin
17. fate
18. pat
19. flute
20. hack

Appendix

Note: Before you go on to the next exercise, there is one thing you should notice about the one you just finished: there may be two vowels in a word, but you hear only one vowel sound, for example, *wheat*. When you see two vowels in a word, you do not always sound both vowels.

PRACTICE 18 Go through the following list of words and say each word aloud. Mark the vowels according to the sound you hear. If you don't know a word, have someone pronounce the word for you and then mark the letter depending on what vowel sound you heard. If there are two vowels in the word and both are sounded, mark both vowels. The first one is done for you.

at	lit	cup	tip	dip	pen
bud	bite	top	accept	refuse	let
white	hope	prune	clock	lot	rule
whip	wipe	traffic	face	drip	hatch

PRACTICE 19 The following is a list of words containing long and short vowel sounds. Next to each one write another word from your own vocabulary that contains the same vowel sound. Note that we said *sound*, not vowel or vowel letter. You may use other words that have the same vowel sound although the sound is represented by two vowels instead of one, for example, he, *bee*; late, *laid*. The first one is done for you.

bat ___mat___   find _____

rate _____   mop _____

rope _____   flip _____

hip _____   kind _____

set _____   sun _____

me _____   hope _____

gum _____   sip _____

fuse _____   hat _____

Vowels and Consonant Sounds 477

rude _____   get _____

late _____   brush _____

y: You already know that *y* is counted as a consonant whenever it is the first letter in a word. When it appears anywhere else in a word, it is almost always counted as a vowel.

Like the other vowels we have dealt with, *y* can represent a variety of sounds. Think for a moment about the words *gym*, *pretty*, and *shy*. All those words contain a *y*, but the sound you give the letter *y* is different for each word.

At this point it may sound as if deciding what sound to give *y* when it appears in an unfamiliar word is impossible. But actually there are some clues you can use.

For example, if a word ends in *y* and contains no other vowel, give the *y* the sound of the *y* in the word *shy*.

If the word has one or more vowels and ends in *y*, you will usually be correct if you try the sound of *y* in the word *city*.

If *y* comes in the middle of a word, try first the sound of *y* in the word *gym*. If that doesn't give you a word you know, switch to the sound of *y* in the word *shy*.

PRACTICE 20 You probably know most of the words on the following list. Read them aloud just to give yourself some practice with the sounds of the letter *y*. Put an X next to any word that gives you trouble. Check to see that you have pronounced every word correctly. Pay special attention to those marked with an X.

rye	try	honey	sunny	rusty
pretty	dry	crusty	funny	by
cry	fry	fly	city	gym
misty	rhyme	pry	myth	happy

PRACTICE 21 Every word on the following list contains the letter *y*. See if you can figure out what sound you should give the *y*, and try to pronounce every word on the list. Some of the words will be unfamiliar to you, but try to pronounce them anyway. Put an X next to any word that gives you trouble. Check to see if you have pronounced every word correctly. Pay special attention to those you marked with an X.

pity	ply	witty	yeasty
gritty	middy	gyp	ditty
wry	tryst	giddy	rynd
rye	cyst	sly	lye

Vowels Followed by *r*: When a vowel is followed by an *r*, you will usually make a sound that is considered neither long nor short. The following list contains sample words that should give you an idea how the vowels are usually sounded when followed by *r*.

Vowels	Sample words
ar	star, smart, card
er	fern, serve, certain
or	horn, born, corn
ir	bird, dirt, skirt
ur	hurt, turn, burn

Note: Vowels followed by *r* will not always be sounded the way they are in the sample word list. For example, when the letters *or* come after the letter *w*, you will sound them quite differently, for example, *word, work, worst*. However, much of the time, sounding vowels followed by *r* as they are sounded in the sample word list will lead you to the correct pronunciation of an unfamiliar word.

PRACTICE 22 Some of these words will not be familiar. Still, you will be able to pronounce them fairly correctly if you keep in mind how vowels followed by *r* are usually sounded.

Put an X next to any word that gives you trouble. Check to see that you have pronounced every word correctly. Pay special attention to those you have marked with an X.

cur	kern	scorch	hark	nor	stir
burr	spar	torch	urn	shorn	curve
tort	tar	lark	perch	ark	swerve

a Followed by *l*, *ll*, *w*, or *u*: Like the vowels followed by *r*, the letter *a* followed by *l*, *ll*, *w*, or *u* does not receive either a long or short vowel sound. When you see an *a* followed by any one of these letters, you will usually have to make a different sound, one that is unlike the sound you make when *a* is followed by other letters. The following list will give you an idea of how to respond when an *a* is followed by any one of the previously mentioned letters.

al	always, salt, altar
all	ball, fall, tall
au	haul, cause, Paul
aw	paw, saw, law

PRACTICE 23 Some of these words may not be familiar to you. Still you should be able to pronounce them fairly correctly if you keep in mind how *a* is usually sounded when followed by *l*, *ll*, *w*, or *u*.

balk	caulk	prawn	mall
drawn	lawn	halt	taunt
brawn	pause	pall	maul
gall	haunt	dawn	spawn

Vowel Teams

Earlier in this section you learned that some consonants frequently appear together in words. Usually when they are together, you make a new sound, one that is different than the sounds you make for the consonants when they are separated.

This can also be true of vowels that appear together in words. Often when vowels come together in a word, you respond differently than you do when they are separated. You may, for example, not sound one of the vowels at all, for example, *coat, boat, beat, meat*. Or you may respond with a sound quite different than the sounds you make when the vowels are alone, for example, *boil, soil, mouth, south*.

The following chart shows nine common vowel teams on the left-hand side. On the right-hand side is a list of words containing the vowel teams. These sample words should give you a good idea of how the teams are usually sounded.

Vowel Teams	Sample Words
ee	seen, knee, see
oo	book, took, look *or* booth, tooth, moon
oa	coat, boat, float
oi	coil, boil, coin
oy	boy, toy, joy
ai	paid, laid, maid

ea	bead, lead, bean *or* head, dead, bread
ou	mouth, couch, south *or* ought, bought, fought
ay	pay, may, say

PRACTICE 24   Read through the following list of words. Some of the words may be unfamiliar, but you should be able to pronounce them fairly correctly if you keep in mind how the vowel teams are secured in the sample word list. Put an X next to any word that gives you trouble. Check to see that you have pronounced every word correctly. Pay special attention to those you marked with an X.

ploy	Troy	tread	drain	pray	meek
slain	pray	toil	teak	foul	couch
plain	crook	hook	booth	tooth	breed
feed	foy	beach	deed	ouch	seek
screed	preach	leek	sought	dray	bleak

PRACTICE 25   Some of the italicized words in the following sentences may be unfamiliar to you, but you should be able to pronounce them since the vowel teams are sounded as they were in the sample word list. Put an X next to any word that gives you trouble. Check to see that you have pronounced every word correctly. Pay special attention to those you marked with an X.

1. She tried to live by the following *creed:* Get them before they get you.
2. She wanted to build a small breakfast *nook* in the kitchen; she liked the idea of eating her meals in a quiet corner.
3. The gangster hired several big *goons* as his bodyguards.
4. I don't know why you wanted to *poach* that egg since you know I hate eggs cooked that way.
5. He had to *toil* in the fields about sixteen hours a day just to earn enough to eat.
6. For some reason, many people think it is better for a little girl to be *coy* rather than straightforward.

7. The moonstruck young *swain* walked around the block five times in the hopes of seeing his sweetheart.
8. To win the weight-lifting title, he had to perform a difficult *feat* with barbells.
9. Why do tall girls think they have to *slouch?*
10. She *sought* him out because he was so shy.
11. In many fairy tales the handsome young prince has to *slay* the dragon to win the beautiful princess.
12. The boy's face had an expression of *dread* as he looked at the enormous snake.

PRACTICE 26 Read each sentence aloud and think of a word that would fit the blank and make sense. Then see if you can find a vowel team that would if added to the letters in the blank, form the word that you thought of or another word that would also fit the rest of the sentence.

Vowel Teams: ee, oo, oa, oi, oy, ai, ea, ou, ay

1. He is famous for his gr_____d; he just can't seem to get enough money.
2. In the fairy tale the ugly t_____d turned into a prince.
3. He knew it was a rattler because it had a c_____l on the end of its tail.
4. The chef loaded the Chinese food with s_____ sauce.
5. They thought she was an old gr_____ch because she always yelled at them.
6. She was very g_____ after drinking three glasses of wine.
7. The th_____ght of having to leave home frightened him.
8. To disguise himself, he had to bl_____ch his hair.

9. Everyone knew he was a cr_____k even though he tried to act like a gentleman.

10. The t_____t of the tugboat echoed in the summer air.

11. The sn_____l moved slowly along the floor of the ocean.

12. She was a woman who was ah_____d of her time.

Vowel and Consonant Combinations

Up to this point we have talked mostly about how to respond to vowels or consonants appearing together. In this section we will concentrate on what we call *vowel and consonant combinations.* When the vowels and consonants appear together in words, they are almost always sounded in the same way.

Occasionally you may have to respond to them with a different sound, but, in general, the following vowel and consonant combinations are always sounded as they are in the sample word list.

The chart given below shows six common vowel and consonant combinations on the left-hand side. On the right-hand side are words that will give you a good idea of how the combinations are sounded.

eep	deep, sleep, creep
ick	stick, sick, lick
ill	pill, will, mill
ock	rock, lock, dock
est	best, west, nest
ent	went, sent, tent

PRACTICE 27 Read through the following list and pronounce every word. You probably know most of the words, but we want you to hear that the vowel and consonant combinations are sounded as they were in the sample word list. Put an X next to any word that gives you trouble. Check to see if you have pronounced every word correctly. Pay special attention to those you marked with an X.

fill	till	chest	keep
bent	pick	click	rest

Vowels and Consonant Sounds

enter   sock   lent   tricky

kick   illness   knock   refill

PRACTICE 28   The following words may not all be familiar to you, but you should be able to pronounce them fairly correctly if you keep in mind how the vowel and consonant combinations were sounded in the sample word list. Put an X next to any word that gives you trouble. Check to see if you have pronounced every word correctly. Pay special attention to those you marked with an X.

wrent	slick	hick	flick	shrill	dent
pent	crick	mock	hock	frill	dill
crock	sill	crest	quill	blest	gent
cheep	jest	seep	rent	vest	knick

The following vowel and consonant combinations are also almost always sounded as they are in the sample word list.

ist	wrist, list, dentist
ex	sex, expect, extra
ain	train, pain, explain
tion	motion, lotion, action
ing	ring, playing, singing
ight	light, might, night

PRACTICE 29   Read through the following list and pronounce every word. You probably know all the words, but we want you to hear that the vowel and consonant combinations are sounded as they were in the sample word list. Put an X next to any word that gives you trouble. Check to see if you have pronounced every word correctly. Pay special attention to those you marked with an X.

fist	station	assist	text
Texas	sing	tight	florist
mist	slight	friction	grain
pain	sexy	sight	wing

PRACTICE 30 The following words may not all be familiar to you, but you should be able to pronounce them fairly correctly if you keep in mind how the vowel and consonant combinations were sounded in the sample word list. Put an X next to any word that gives you trouble. Check to see if you have pronounced every word correctly. Pay special attention to those you marked with an X.

lighter	plight	hex	expand	saint	lex
faint	cist	ration	Ming	gist	knight
flight	notion	slain	wain	taint	ding
fling	mist	portion	cling	strain	grist

PRACTICE 31 Some of the italicized words in the following sentences may be unfamiliar, but you should be able to pronounce them if you review the lists of vowel and consonant combinations.

Put an X next to any word that gives you trouble. Check to see if you have pronounced every word correctly. Pay special attention to those marked with an X.

1. Because there was no *wick* in the candle, she brought it back.
2. He refused to sit in a bar all night and *swill* beer till he fell on the floor.
3. She always wore a *smock* over her clothes when she painted.
4. He was afraid to look up *lest* the strange face appear again in the window.
5. The air came through a small *vent* in the side of the car.
6. *Whist* is a card game no longer played by many people.
7. The weightlifter refused to *flex* his muscles for the photographers.
8. The *strain* of the funeral showed on her face.
9. There was a time when people believed that witches could invent a magic *potion* that could make people fall in love.

Vowels and Consonant Sounds 485

10. She had left the water running too long, and it began to *seep* beneath the door.

11. The *zing* of the arrow made him turn his head just in time to avoid being struck.

12. The crops had been destroyed by a terrible *blight*, and there was hardly a leaf left on the plants.

PRACTICE 32 Read the following sentences aloud and think of a word that would fit the blank and make sense. Then see if you can find a vowel and consonant combination that would, if added to the letters in the blank, form the word you thought of or another word that would also fit the rest of the space.

Vowel and Consonant Combinations: eep, ick, ill, ock, est, ent, ist, ain, tion, ing, ight

1. He was very v_____; he just couldn't resist looking at himself in the mirror.
2. The prisoner knew he was going to die and the t_____ t_____ of the clock was driving him crazy.
3. The region under the fish's right g_____ had been badly cut.
4. They had to force the p_____ down the dog's throat.
5. The bank had l_____ her a great deal of money.
6. With a slight tw_____, she managed to open the container.
7. After the accident she had her arm in a sl_____.
8. Because of his sl_____ build, he could not play football.
9. The doctor used a small hammer to test his refl_____es.
10. He had been told to sw_____ out the store, but he refused to do it.
11. After the accident they had to put his leg in trac_____.

WORDS INTO SYLLABLES

Can you answer the question: What is a syllable? For example, could the letters *mnpl* possibly make up a syllable in a word? The answer is no. There is no vowel in the group of letters. If there is no vowel, then there is no vowel sound, and every syllable must have a vowel sound. Without a vowel sound, groups of consonant sounds are hard to pronounce. For example, you can read off the letters *mnpl*, but it's rather difficult to blend together the sounds that go with those letters. You are not used to pronouncing a string of consonant sounds with no vowel sound coming in between.

If you put vowels between the consonants, it is at least possible to pronounce a nonsense word, for example, *monapul*. The addition of the vowels makes a difference. You are no longer with a strange-looking tongue twister. *Monapul* is a nonsense word. But it looks familiar, and it can be easily pronounced.

A syllable can be made up of one letter or several. The number of letters is not important; the number of vowel sounds is important. You may have three vowels in a word, but if when the word is pronounced, you hear only one vowel sound, then the word has only one syllable.

A *syllable* then is a letter or group of letters that can be easily pronounced because there is a vowel sound present.

PRACTICE 33 Remember that you can count the number of syllables by counting the number of vowel sounds. Have somebody read the following list to you. When you hear the word, write down the number of syllables in the word. Check to see if you have given every word the correct syllable count.

1. history
2. glamour
3. shyster
4. motion
5. battering
6. flattering
7. plush
8. disagreeable
9. mystery
10. crunch
11. nomadic
12. blissful
13. preparation
14. vividly
15. screechingly
16. beseechingly

Obviously, hearing the number of syllables in an unfamiliar word will not be of much concern to you when you are trying to decide how to pronounce it. In order to count the syllables, you have to be able to pronounce the word.

Words into Syllables

Usually the first step in figuring out how to pronounce a word you have never seen before in print is to divide the word into syllables. In the following section we will introduce some of the basic rules of syllabication. We'll begin by dividing only two-syllable words.

Rule 1
When two consonants come between two vowels, divide the word between the two consonants (VC/CV).

The pattern VCCV appears quite frequently in words of more than one syllable. When you see an unfamiliar word containing this pattern, you should usually divide it between the two consonants. The word *confuse*, for example, would be divided *con/fuse*.

PRACTICE 34 Using Rule 1, divide the following words into syllables. Check to see if you have divided all the words correctly. Don't worry about trying to pronounce any of the words on the list; just apply the rule you learned.

percent	trumpet	subject	distant
mental	invent	object	dental
tablet	formal	butter	admit
conduct	batter	normal	transfer

PRACTICE 35 The following words may not all be familiar, but you will be able to divide them into syllables anyway. Check to see if you have divided every word correctly. The first one is done for you.

toc/sin	frantic	index	whimper
context	bedlam	goblet	random
gasket	hectic	dragnet	tonsil
gambit	lentil	cantor	lorry

Rule 2
When a consonant team appears in a word, divide the word so that the consonants in the team stay together (V/CCV).

When you see a word containing one of the consonant teams you learned about in the previous section, you should usually

488   Appendix

divide the word so that the letters in the team remain together. For example, the word *hatred* would be divided *ha/tred*.

PRACTICE 36   Divide the following words into syllables. Check to see if you have divided every word correctly.

reply	refract	asleep	matrix
respect	decline	defrost	duplex
hatred	reflect	matron	refresh
aglow	ablaze	retract	recline

PRACTICE 37   Divide the following words into syllables. You will have to decide whether to use Rule 1 or Rule 2 for each word. Check to see if you have divided all the words correctly. The first two are done for you.

som/ber	urban	supreme	regress
pro/gram	morsel	petrol	Tampa
siphon	tansy	unrest	canvas
vibrate	gremlin	mascot	morbid
neglect	progress	deflect	agley

Rule 3
If there are three consonants between two vowels, divide the word so that the first consonant goes with the first vowel and the other two consonants with the second (VC/CCV).

The pattern *VCCCV* also appears frequently in words of more than one syllable. When you see an unfamiliar word containing this pattern, you should usually divide the word so that the first consonant goes with the first vowel and the next two consonants go with the second vowel. The word *surprise*, for example, would be divided *sur/prise*.

PRACTICE 38   Using Rule 3, divide the following words into syllables. Don't worry about pronouncing them. Just divide them into syllables. Check to see if you have divided every one correctly.

| children | complete | contract | surplus |
| mattress | pilgrim | entrance | perspire |

fortress   simply   pimply   district

PRACTICE 39 Divide the following words into syllables. You will have to use the three rules you have learned. Check to see if you have divided every word correctly. The first one is done for you.

dis/tress	tumbril	pennant	anvil	homburg
limber	extreme	timber	mistress	Atrek
dorsal	patron	ascot	weskit	defray
distract	fitful	minted	vintage	portal

Rule 4
If one consonant comes between two vowels, divide the word after the first vowel (V/CV).

VCV is another common spelling pattern. When you see this pattern in an unfamiliar word, you should usually divide the word after the first vowel. The word *awake*, for example, would be divided *a/wake*.

PRACTICE 40 Divide the following words into syllables. Check to see if you have divided them all correctly. The first one is done for you.

to/ken	radar	report	human	bridal
recess	music	moment	Mabel	motive
motor	final	tulip	bison	global
reduce	pilot	navel	vital	focal

PRACTICE 41 Review all the rules you have learned so far. Then divide the following list of words into syllables. Check to see if you have divided them all correctly. The first two are done for you.

su/ture	digress	deride	turgid	surcease
ac/tress	crocus	scuba	asphalt	proton
tendril	exclude	fecal	abscess	somber
linger	warden	tango	recluse	tonal
profess	fervid	convex	hombre	annals

Until now we have worked only with one- or two-syllable words. That seemed to be the easiest way to introduce you to the basic rules for breaking unfamiliar words into syllables. However, now that you have learned to use those rules with two-syllable words, it's time to start working with words that have more than two syllables. In this section you'll have to apply some old rules and learn some new ones.

Rule 5
When you see a word that contains prefixes and/or suffixes, divide the word after the prefix and before the suffix.

A *prefix* is a letter or group of letters that appears at the beginning of many words, for example, *re*play, *re*ject, *ex*pect, *ex*plain. A *suffix* is a letter or group of letters that appears at the end of words, for example, runn*ing*, see*ing*, dai*ly*, ful*ly*.

When you see an unfamiliar word containing prefixes of suffixes, divide it after the prefix and before the suffix. The word *unjustly*, for example, would be divided *un/just/ly*.

The following list of prefixes and suffixes contains several with which you are already familiar (see Vowel and Consonant Combinations).

Prefixes	Suffixes	Prefixes	Suffixes
im	tion	de	sion
in	ly	en	y
ex	or, er	re	ism
pre	ence, ance	per	ize
dis	ness	trans	ship
sub	ent, ant	mis	ate
con	ish	ad	ment
com	ful	un	less
pro	ous	ob	ture

PRACTICE 42 Using the rule you have just learned, divide the following words into syllables. Check to see if you have divided every word correctly. In some cases you may have a choice between the rule you just learned and one of the others. For example, the word *misspelling* could be divided *mis/spell/ing* according to Rule 5 or *mis/spel/ling* according to Rule 2 (when two consonants come between two vowels, divide between the two consonants). When you do have a choice between Rule 5 and one of the other rules, we ask you to choose Rule 5.

Check to see if you have divided all the words correctly. The first one is done for you.

flut/ter/ing   inaction   permission   displacement

extension	formally	demotion	adventure
rejection	protection	relationship	conduction
repulsion	revision	constitution	modernize
provoking	pervading	remission	detector

Note: Sometimes a word will contain more than one prefix or suffix, for example, *relationship*. When you run across a word like that, separate the prefixes or suffixes one by one, for example, *re/lation/ship, re/la/tion/ship.*

Rule 6
When a vowel team appears in a word, divide the word so that the vowels in the team stay together (C/VVC).

When you see a vowel team in a word, you should usually divide the word so that the vowels remain together. The word *preach*, for example, would not be divided at all because the vowels *e* and *a* usually form one of the teams you learned about previously.

PRACTICE 43 Using Rule 6, divide the following words into syllables. Check to see if you have divided every word correctly. The first one is done for you.

em/broid/er	deploying	cookery	defeatist
pronouncing	loitering	employer	lampooner
reappointing	prevailing	deadliness	defaulter
entertainer	misdemeanor	daintiness	nattering
defection	dismaying	uncoiling	meaningful

Rule 7
If a word ends in the letters *l* and *e*, divide the word just before the consonant preceding the *l*.

Many words end with a consonant followed by the letters *l* and *e*. When you see a word that ends with that spelling pattern, you should usually divide the word so that the last syllable begins with the consonant preceding the *l*. The word *restaple*, for example, would be divided *re/sta/ple*.

PRACTICE 44 Using Rule 7, divide the following words into syllables. Check to see if you have divided all the words correctly. The first one is done for you.

kis/sa/ble	syllable	visible	belittle
mandible	treatable	principle	dismantle
tentacle	endorsable	resemble	bespangle
indispensable	terminable	multiple	spectacle
perceptible	interminable	terrible	portable

Before we go any further, we want to make an important point about the rules for breaking words into syllables. We are explaining how to break words into syllables so that you can pronounce the words, not write them. If you were to look up in the dictionary every word introduced in this section, you would discover that the dictionary does not always divide the word the way we have.

Therefore, if you want to use a word in a term paper, you should always divide it the way the dictionary does. However, you can continue to divide words according to the rules we present if you are mainly concerned with figuring out how to pronounce words you have never seen before in print.

SOUNDING THE VOWELS

Dividing an unfamiliar word into syllables is the first step to take when you are trying to decide whether or not the word is part of your listening vocabulary. But dividing the word into syllables is only the first step. The second step is what we call sounding the vowels.

For example, let's say you saw the word *dictate* in print and were not sure if you knew it. You would first divide the word into syllables, *dic/tate*, but that would not automatically tell you how to pronounce it. After all, you could sound the *i* as it is sounded in the word *ice* or as it is sounded in the word *it*. Similarly, you could sound the *a* as it is sounded in the word *pat* or as it is sounded in the word *pasta*.

Of course, you could use trial and error until you hit upon the correct pronunciation and recognized the word *dictate*, or were sure that the word was unfamiliar. But there is an easier way. There are rules that can frequently tell you right away what sounds to give the vowels in an unfamiliar word. These

Sounding the Vowels 493

rules don't work all the time, but they work often enough for us to suggest that you try them first.

Rule 1
When a syllable ends in a consonant and there is only one vowel in the syllable, try the short vowel sound first (CV̆C, V̆C).

You already learned that the letters of the alphabet are called vowels or consonants depending on what kind of sounds they represent. Vowels represent open sounds and consonants represent ones. Perhaps that will help you remember that syllables ending in a consonant are called *closed syllables*.

If you divide a word into syllables and see that a syllable ends in a consonant, five the vowel in that syllable the short vowel sound; that will usually lead you to the correct pronunciation of an unfamiliar word.

PRACTICE 45 The following list contains only one-syllable words, and every word ends in a consonant. You probably know all the words. Just read through them to see how they fit Rule 1. All the syllables are closed, and the vowels receive the short vowel sounds when the words are pronounced.

met	cot	pup	trip	lot
wet	bit	sat	hat	hop
set	mitt	bless	mat	shop
clap	cup	miss	fit	clot

PRACTICE 46 Divide the following words into syllables; pronounce each syllable and then blend the syllables together to pronounce the word. Some of the words may be unfamiliar, but you can pronounce them fairly correctly if you make use of the rule you just learned.

Put an X next to any word that gives you trouble. Check to see if you have pronounced all the words correctly. Pay special attention to those you marked with an X.

rancid	flimflam	chitchat	limpid	bodkin
nitwit	wilted	lactic	wombat	octad
dictum	fatling	optic	welkin	entrust
hispid	fragment	flipflop	sextet	summit

Rule 2
When a syllable ends in a vowel and there is only one vowel in the syllable, try the long vowel sound first ($\bar{V}$, $C\bar{V}$).

As you may have already guessed, syllables that end in a vowel are called *open syllables*. When you have divided a word into syllables and see that one or more of the syllables ends in a vowel, try first giving the vowel the long vowel sound; that will usually lead you to the correct pronunciation of the word.

PRACTICE 47   Divide the following words into syllables. Some of the words will be unfamiliar, but you can pronounce them fairly correctly if you make use of the two rules you just learned.

Put an X next to any word that gives you trouble. Check to see if you have pronounced all the words correctly. Pay special attention to those you marked with an X.

hobo	nomad	combo	superb	osmic
gonad	matrix	coptic	pogo	duplex
tunic	humid	mogul	hapten	lotto
Punic	onus	veto	gopher	tripod

Important notes: Before going any further, we want to make several important points about breaking words into syllables and sounding the vowels. First of all, *none of these rules is foolproof.* Try them first, but if they do not lead you to a word you recognize, feel free to break them.

For example, you learned that you should divide an unfamiliar word so that vowel teams stay together. But suppose you ran across the word *oasis* in your reading and were not sure if it was part of your listening vocabulary. Your first attempt to divide the word would be *oa/sis*. When you pronounced the word that way, however, you would not recognize it since you would probably sound the *oa* as it sounds in the word *boat*. Rather than giving up, though, you would try another method of dividing the word such as *o/a/sis*. Then since the first two syllables end in vowels, you would try the long sounds of the vowels *o* and *a*. This method of sounding the vowels would lead you to the correct pronunciation of the word, and you would recognize it as one you knew all along.

Similarly, you should not be afraid of breaking the rules for sounding the vowels. Let's say, for example, you saw the word *scolding* in print and did not recognize it. You would first divide the word *scolding* and then try the short *o* sound (the second syllable offers no difficulty since you know that *ing* is almost always sounded as it is in the word *playing*). The short *o* sound, however, would not give you a word you recognized. But before giving up, you would try the long *o* sound. This time the word would be familiar.

Try the rules you have been learning *first*. If they don't work, don't give up immediately. Use trial and error until you hit upon a word you know or are sure that the word is really unfamiliar.

The last point we'd like to make concerns the number of possible sounds you can make in response to the vowel letters. Up to this point we have talked mainly about long and short vowel sounds. However, if you have tried both without success, try, no matter what the letter, making the sound you make in response to the *a* in the word *above*. This sound, which closely resembles the short *u* sound, can frequently lead you to the correct pronunciation of a word.*

For example, take the simple word *ago*. If we sound the vowels according to the rules already given *(a/go)*, the word is not one that is readily familiar. Even if we give the *a* the short vowel sound, the word is still not one we recognize immediately. But as soon as we give the *a* the short *u* sound, the word is immediately familiar.

Rule 3
When a syllable ends in a vowel-consonant-e pattern, try the long vowel sound first.

The vowel-consonant-e pattern is a very common one. You will see it quite often at the end of words. When you see this pattern at the end of a word, try giving the vowel the long vowel sound. Don't give the *e* any sound at all.

PRACTICE 48   Read the following list of one-syllable words aloud. If you are not sure how to pronounce all the words, use the rules you have learned about syllables that end in a consonant or in the vowel-consonant-e pattern. Put an X next to any word that gives you trouble. Check to see if you have pronounced all the words correctly. Pay special attention to those you have marked with an X.

*The sound is usually represented by a symbol called the schwa (ə).

grip	gap	snip	pan
gripe	gape	snipe	pane
trip	tap	sat	rap
tripe	tape	safe	rape
lop	nap	wan	dam
lope	nape	wane	dame

PRACTICE 49   Divide the following words into syllables. Decide what sounds to give the vowels. Then pronounce all the words on the list. Put an X next to any word that gives you trouble. Check to see that you have pronounced every word correctly. Pay special attention to those words you have marked with an X.

inflame	define	disrobe	microbe	precede
delete	replete	reptile	console	defame
disgrace	ornate	displace	obtund	protrude
placate	behave	defuse	deflate	ingrate

PRACTICE 50   The following list will probably contain several words with which you are not familiar. But if you make use of everything you have learned up to this point, you should be able to pronounce all the words fairly correctly.

    For example, let's say the word *confidence* appeared on the list and was unfamiliar. You would first of all divide the word into syllables, *con/fi/dence*. Since you already know how the suffix *ence* is sounded, you would concentrate on the first two syllables. They are both closed so you would try the short vowel sounds first. Once you blended the syllables together, you would recognize the word *confidence*.

    Since you will need the list of prefixes and suffixes again, we present it here rather than ask you to turn back to it. This time we have added a few notes which should help you with those suffixes that are sometimes difficult to pronounce.

Prefixes	Suffixes
im	tion
in	ly
ex	or, er
pre	ence, ance
dis	ness

sub	ent, ant	
con	ish	
com	ful	
pro	ous:	Usually sounded as it is in the word *famous* and *dangerous*. When *ous* is preceded by *t* and *i*, or *c* and *i*, it is usually pronounced as it is in the words *spacious* and *infectious*.
de		
en		
re		
per		
trans	y	
mis	ism:	Usually sounded as it is in the word *heroism*.
ad		
un	ize:	Usually sounded as it is in the words *legalize* and *modernize*.
ob		
	ship	
	ate	
	ment	
	less	
	ture:	Usually sounded as it is in the words *future* and *furniture*.
	sion:	Can be sounded as it is in *vision* or as it is in *mission*.

Again if you have a choice between Rule 5 (divide the word after the prefix and before the suffix) and any of the other rules, try Rule 5 first. It will usually lead you to the correct pronunciation of an unfamiliar word. Put an X next to any word that gives you trouble. Check to see if you have pronounced every word correctly. Pay special attention to those marked with an X.

1. replenish
2. advent
3. contortion
4. infraction
5. demeanor
6. germane
7. mesmerize
8. rebuke
9. confrontation
10. cursory
11. profoundly
12. rebound
13. organism
14. raven
15. memorize
35. strife
36. latent
37. crave
38. bout
39. concoction
40. flout
41. preclude
42. remote
43. kinship
44. terminate
45. confidant
46. inadvertent
47. culprit
48. concur
49. sordidly
68. confection
69. floundering
70. concise
71. ingrate
72. deletion
73. maiming
74. trenchantly
75. strobe
76. recanting
77. extraction
78. appeasement
79. promotion
80. plantation
81. sensation
82. prediction

16. fervidly
17. galvanize
18. gusto
19. indiscreet
20. transmission
21. obstruction
22. exploit
23. impede
24. cogent
25. debunk
26. senile
27. fluke
28. haven
29. torment
30. performance
31. extortion
32. delude
33. confirmation
34. incontinent
50. probe
51. joyousness
52. detest
53. strumpet
54. continent
55. drudgery
56. distaff
57. cretin
58. foment
59. solvent
60. redundant
61. adventure
62. obtrude
63. perfection
64. displacement
65. pogrom
66. rampage
67. distraction
83. devotion
84. impression
85. propulsion
86. hapless
87. inclusion
88. humanism
89. omission
90. convulsion
91. heedlessness
92. healthfulness
93. obtect
94. entrapment
95. entrancingly
96. denture
97. indenture
98. nursery
99. penalize
100. entrenchment

Index

Commonly confused words, 446–462
Connotation, 425–429
Consonant teams, 466–474
Context
  contrast clue, 4
  example clue, 3–4
  restatement clue, 4–5
  use of, 1–25
Critical reading
  connotation, 425–429
  denotation, 426
  fact and opinion, 414–420
  faulty reasoning, 420–424
  purpose of, 413
  review test, 437–441
  tone and mood, 429–436

Dictionary
  entries in, 27–32
  selections of, 26–27
  use of, 26–32

Essays
  analysis of, 333–334
  notes on, 334–356
  reading of, 325–369
  review test, 357–370
Etymology, def. of, 32

Foreign words and phrases, 443–446

General and Specific
  phrases, 68–73
  sentences, 69–73
  words, 57–68

Headings
  major and minor, 373
  purpose of, 373–374
  questions from, 373–374

Inference
  definition of, 124
  drawing of, 124–139

Main idea
  finding of, 106–123
  implied, 124–139
  paragraphs without, 139–144
  review test, 147–150
  supporting sentences suggest, 124–139
Major and minor
  headings, 373
  paragraphs, 334
  sentences, 171–188
Modifiers, 68–73
Mood, 430
Note taking
  essays, 334–336
  paragraphs, 221–231, 245–309
  textbooks, 390–395

Objective report, 429
Overview, need for, 382

Paragraphs
  causes and effects, 279–291
  classifications, 291–299
  comparisons, 268–278
  concluding, 332–333
  dates and events, 245–254
  introductory, 327–329

lists of characteristics, 262–268
mixed types, 300–309
note taking, 221–231, 245–309
review test, 311–323
sequence of steps, 255–262
supporting, 329–331
topic, 328–329
types of, 245–309
Prefixes
definition of, 2
lists of, 5–25

Review tests
critical reading, 437–441
essays, 357–370
general and specific, 92–96
sentence functions, 233–243
supporting sentences, 188–195
textbooks, 411–412
topic and main idea, 147–150
types of paragraphs, 311–323
vocabulary, 48–55
Reviewing
purpose of, 396
steps in, 395–396
Roots
definition of, 2
lists of, 5–25

Schwa, 474, 495
Sentences
concluding, 216–221
emphatic, 212–216
general and specific, 73–96
introductory, 206–212
kinds of, 151–243
review tests on, 188–195, 233–243
supporting, 151–195
topic, 106–123
transitional, 197–206
Specificity, levels of, 60–68
Speech sounds, 463–464
Subjective report, 429

Suffixes, 2
definition of, 2
lists of, 5–25
Surveying
purpose of, 371
steps in, 371–377
Syllabication, 486–498

Textbooks
note taking, 390–395
reading, 382–386
review test, 411–412
reviewing, 395–396
surveying, 371–381
vocabulary in, 41–47
writing in, 386–390
Tone, 428–429
Topic, finding of, 97–106
Topic paragraph, 328–329
Topic sentence, 108–111
Transitions, 197–206

Underlining, 388–389

Vocabulary
improving, 1–55
in textbooks, 41–47
review test, 48–55
Vowels, 474–479
Vowel teams, 479–482

Word analysis, 1–25
Word history, 32–41
Word recognition, 463–498
consonants, 464–466
consonant teams, 466–474
syllabication, 486–498
vowels, 474–482
vowel teams, 479–482
Words
commonly confused, 446–462
foreign, 443–446
general and specific, 57–68
recognition of unfamiliar, 463–498

To the Student:

Clearly you are the final judge of any reading textbook, and we are very interested in your reactions to **Reading for Results,** Second Edition. Your answers to the following questions will help us in further revisions of the text, so please be as honest and specific as possible. Naturally we want to know what you think we did right, but we are just as interested in knowing what you think we did wrong.

After you have completed the questionnaire, please send it to:

Laraine Flemming
c/o English Editor
College Division
Houghton Mifflin Company
One Beacon Street
Boston, Massachusetts 02108

1. Which chapters of *Reading for Results* did you find especially helpful?
   - ☐ Chapter 1. Building Your Vocabulary
   - ☐ Chapter 2. Defining the Terms General and Specific
   - ☐ Chapter 3. Finding the Topic and Main Idea
   - ☐ Chapter 4. Understanding How Sentences Provide Support
   - ☐ Chapter 5. Learning More About Sentence Functions
   - ☐ Chapter 6. Identifying Types of Paragraphs
   - ☐ Chapter 7. Reading an Essay
   - ☐ Chapter 8. Reading a Textbook
   - ☐ Chapter 9. Critical Reading

2. What did you find most useful to you in the chapters that you checked?

   _____

   _____

   _____

3. Which chapters did you find least helpful and why?

   _____

   _____

   _____

4. Were the explanations of key terms and concepts clear? Would additional examples of key terms be useful?

_____
_____

5. Were the directions for the exercises clear? If not, can you explain what made them confusing to you?

_____
_____

6. We made every effort to provide interesting reading material. Did you find most of the exercises interesting or stimulating? Which were your favorite selections?

_____
_____

7. Can you suggest other topics you would be interested in reading about?

_____
_____

8. Did you find that your reading improved after using this text?

_____
_____

9. How would you rate *Reading for Results*?
   ☐ excellent   ☐ good   ☐ fair   ☐ poor

10. Please make any additional comments you think might be useful.

_____
_____
_____